aRKHAM aSYLUM

BATMAN: ARKHAM ASYLUM 15TH
ANNIVERSARY EDITION. Published by
DC Comics. Cover, introduction and compilation copyright
© 2004 DC Comics. All Rights Reserved. Original
publication copyright © 1989 DC Comics. All rights
reserved. Arkham Asylum, Batman and all related characters
and elements are trademarks of DC Comics. The stories,
characters and incidents featured in this publication are
entirely fictional. DC Comics does not read or accept
unsolicited submissions of ideas, stories or artwork.

DC Comics
1700 Broadway
New York, NY 10019

A Warner Bros. Entertainment Company
Printed in the USA.
Seventh Printing.

ISBN: 978-1-4012-0425-9.

Cover art and original publication design by Dave McKean.

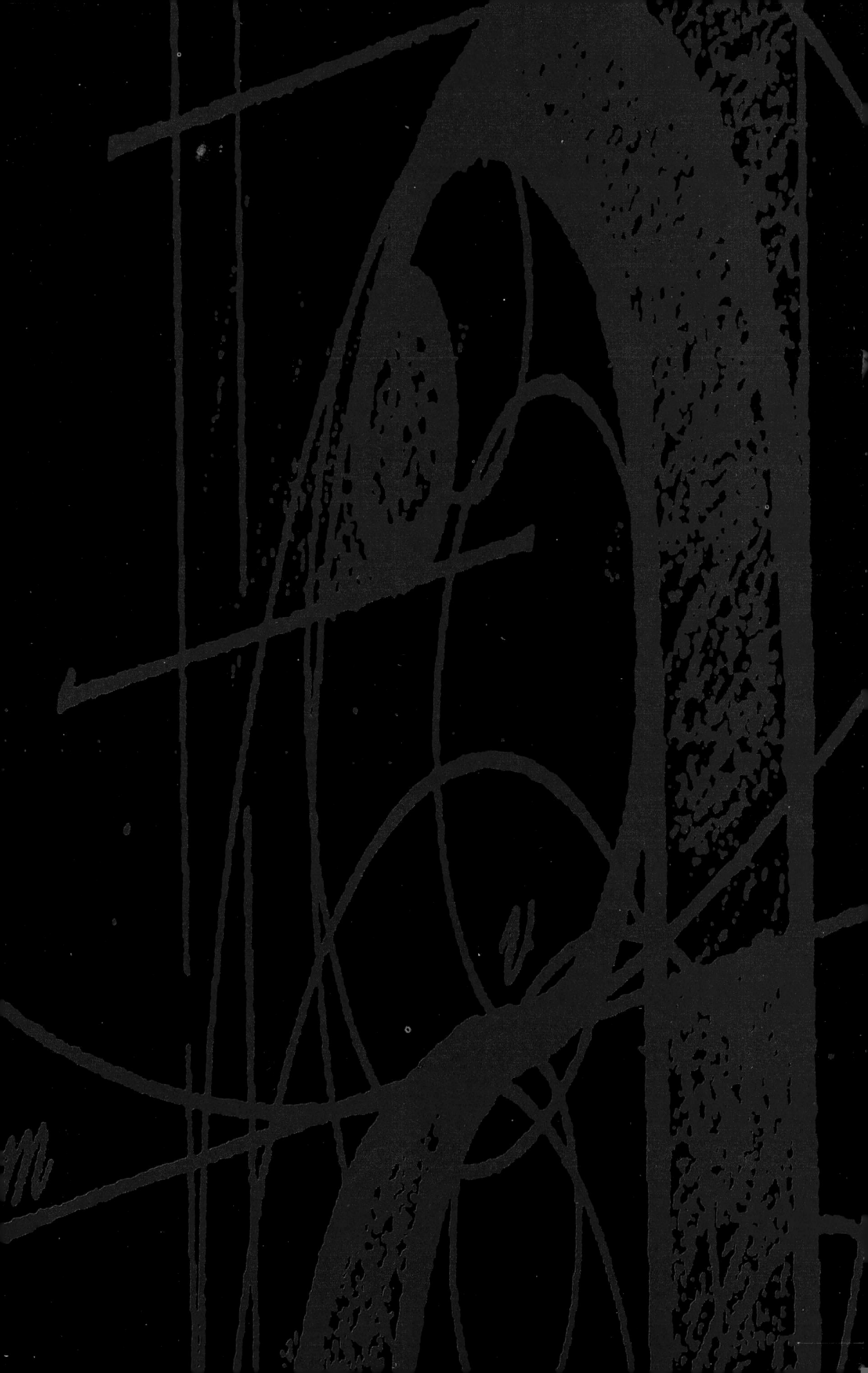

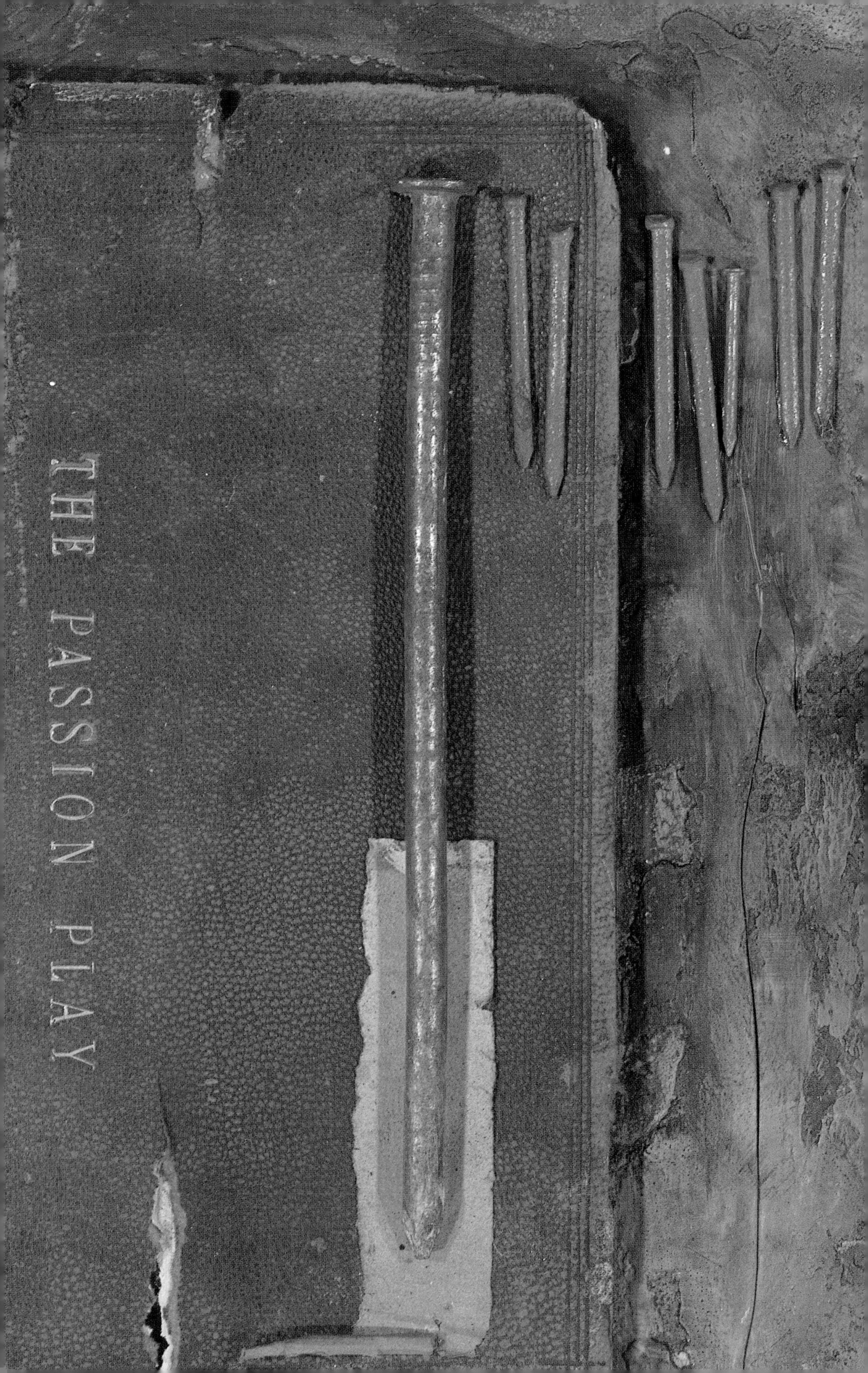
THE PASSION PLAY

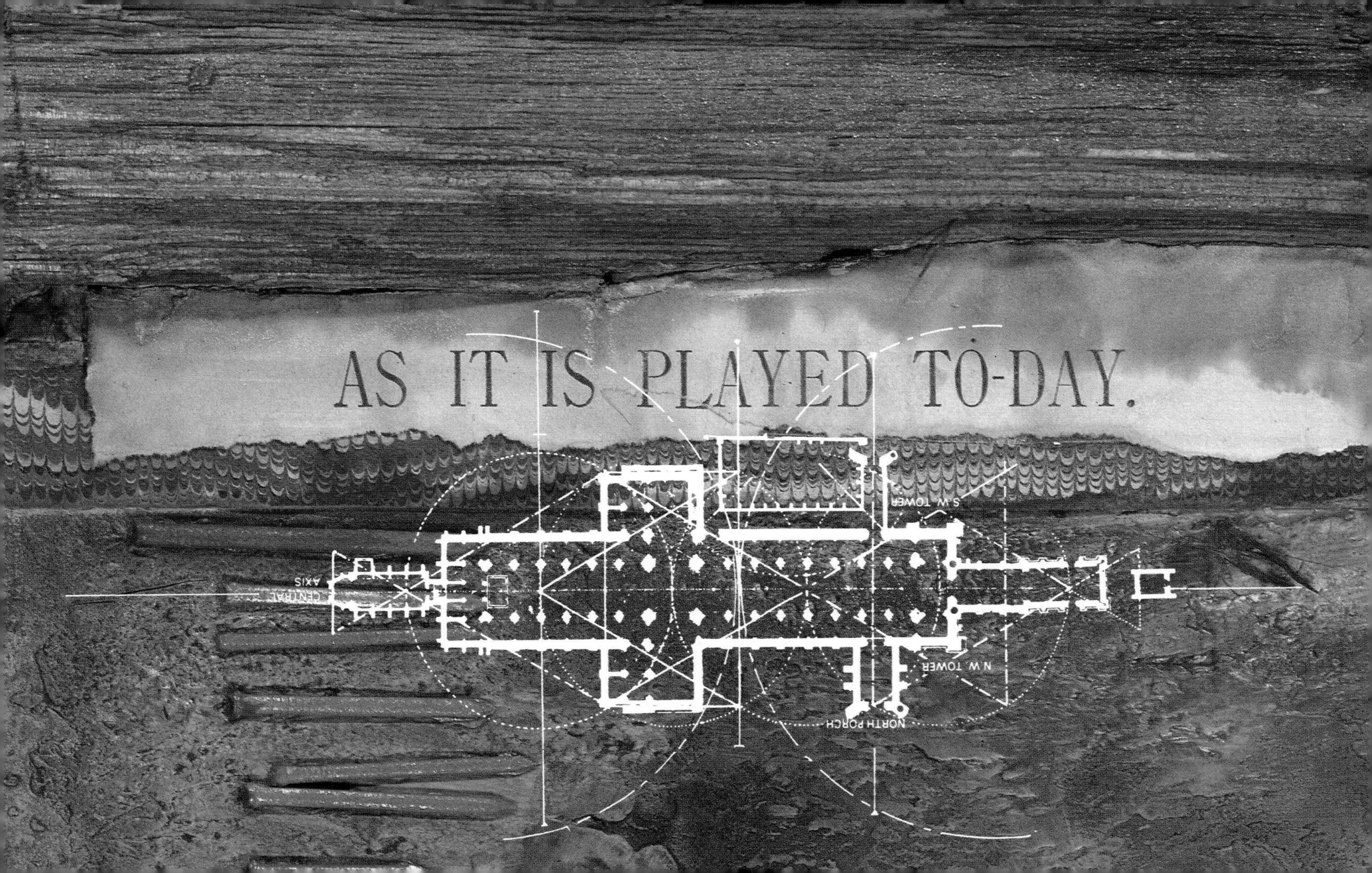
AS IT IS PLAYED TO-DAY.
CENTRAL AXIS
S.W. TOWER
N.W. TOWER
NORTH PORCH

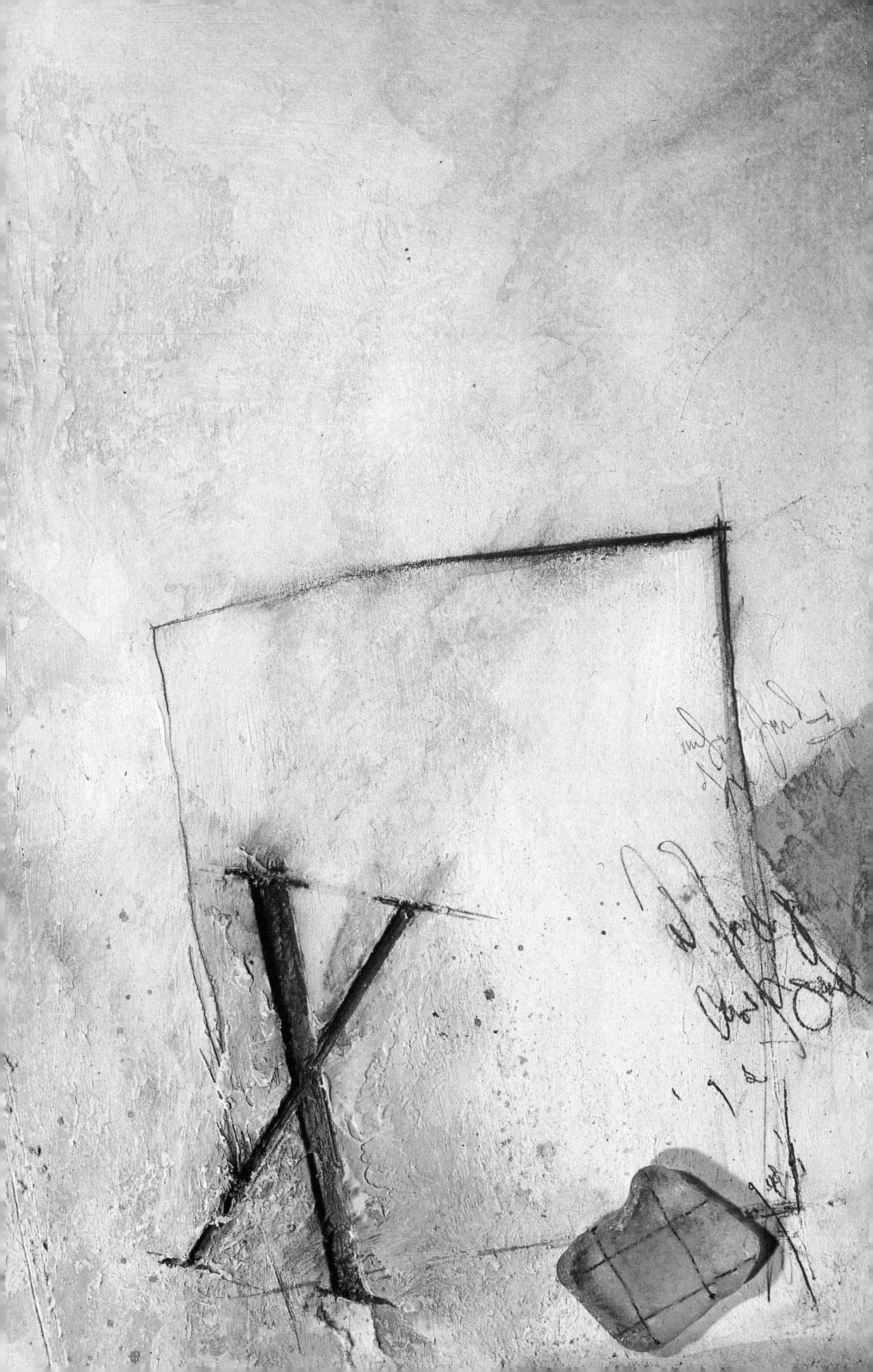

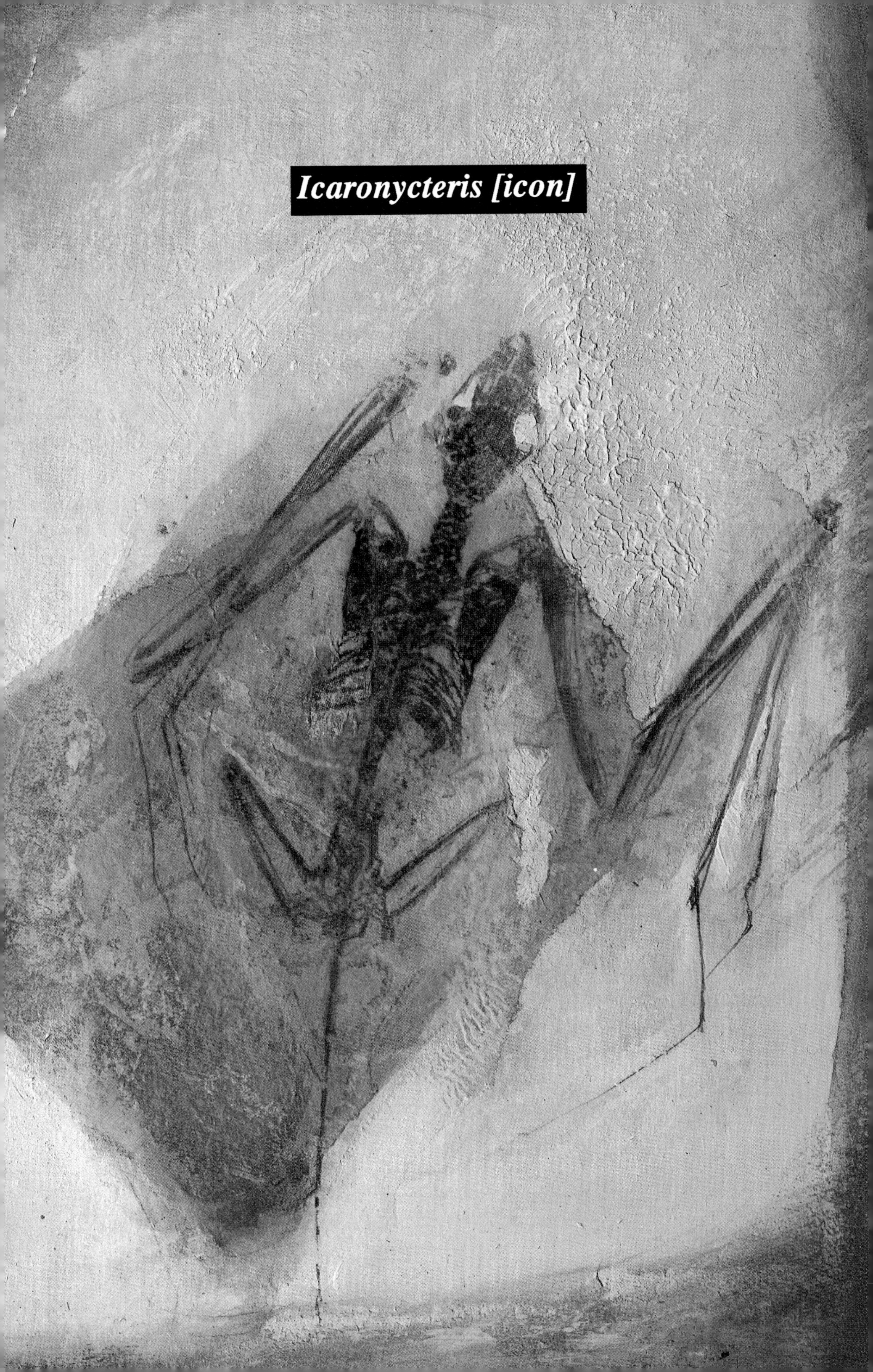
Icaronycteris [icon]

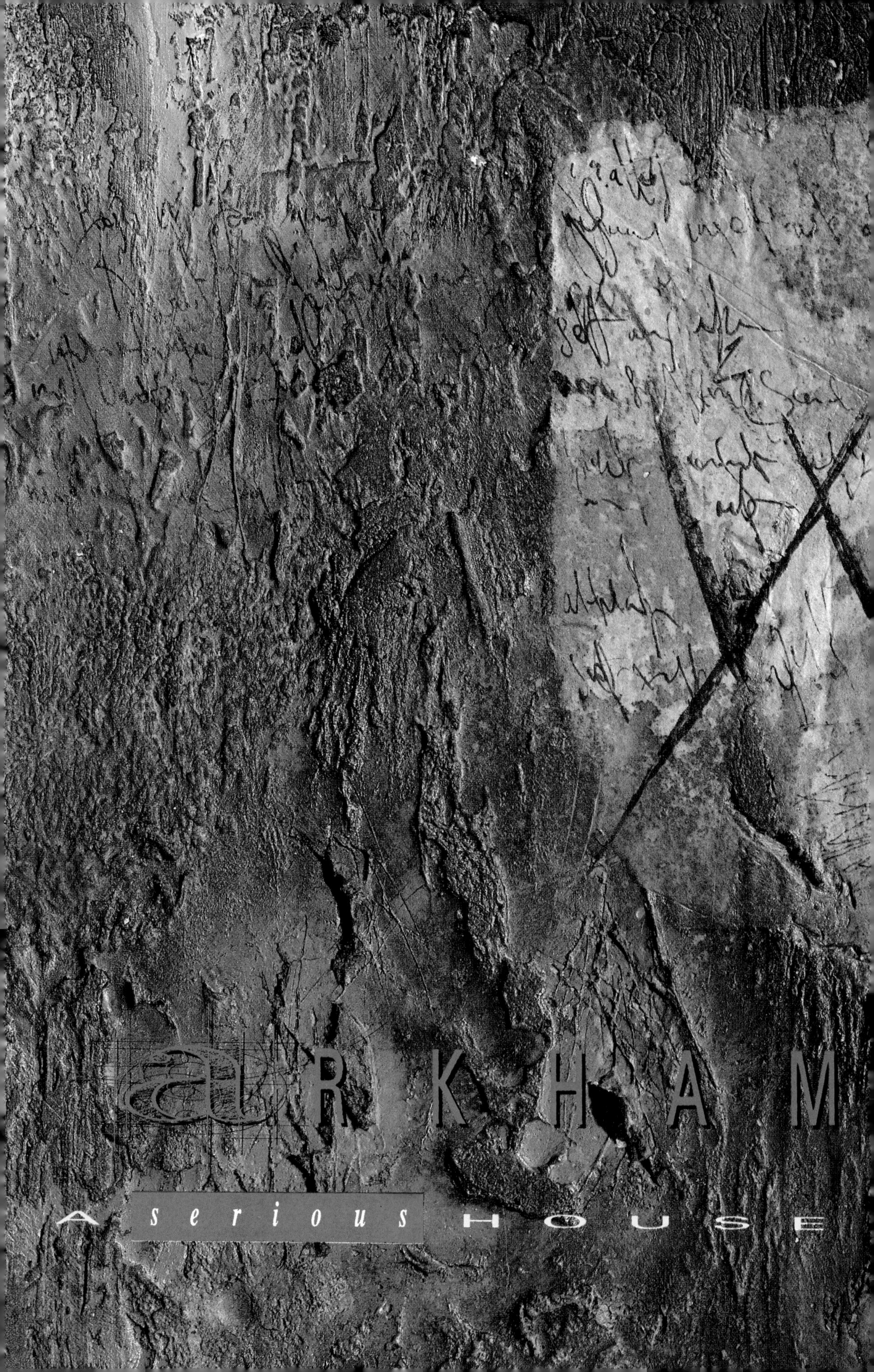
ARKHAM
A serious HOUSE

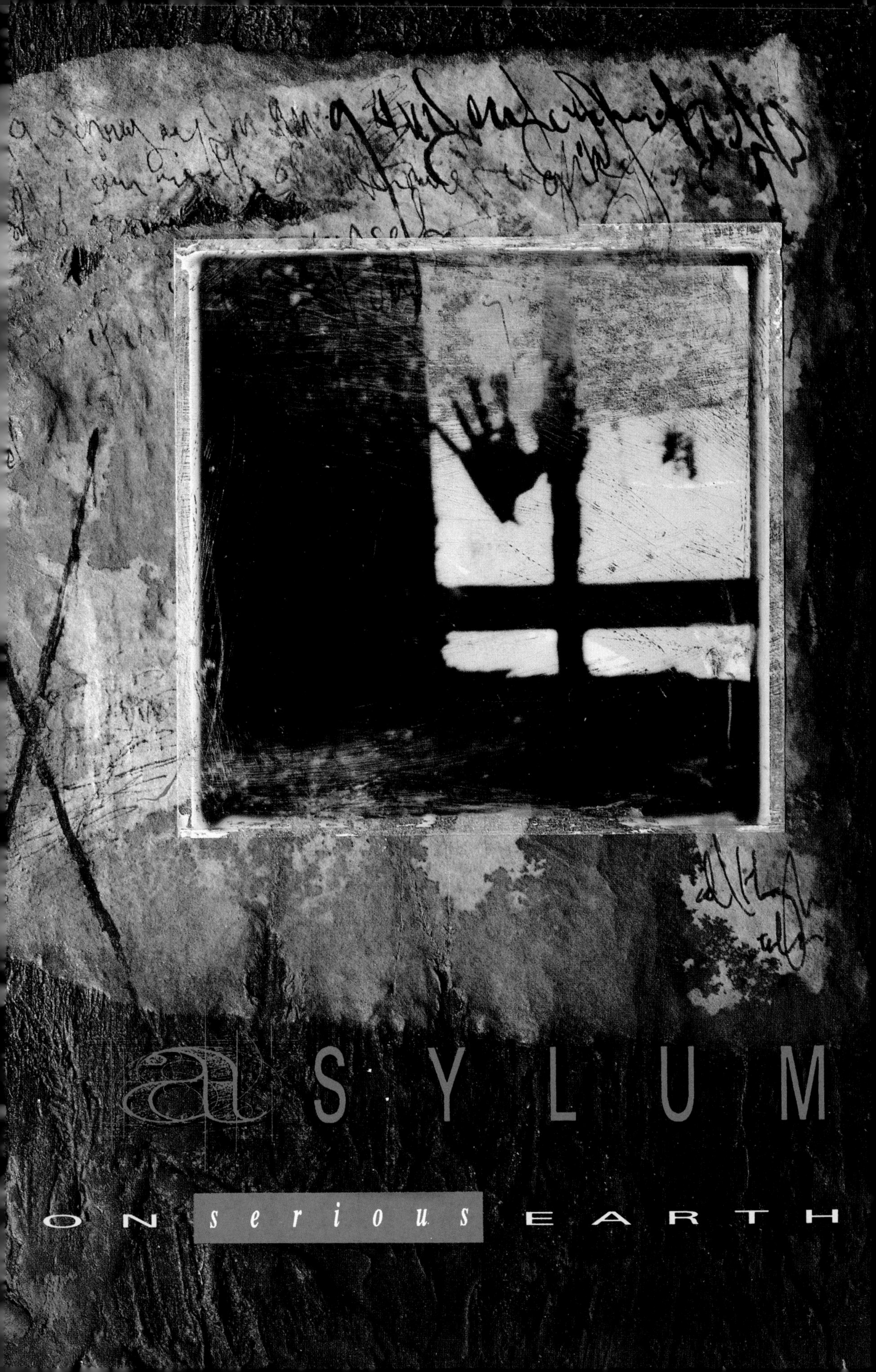
aSYLUM
ON serious EARTH

WRITTEN by

GRANT MORRISON

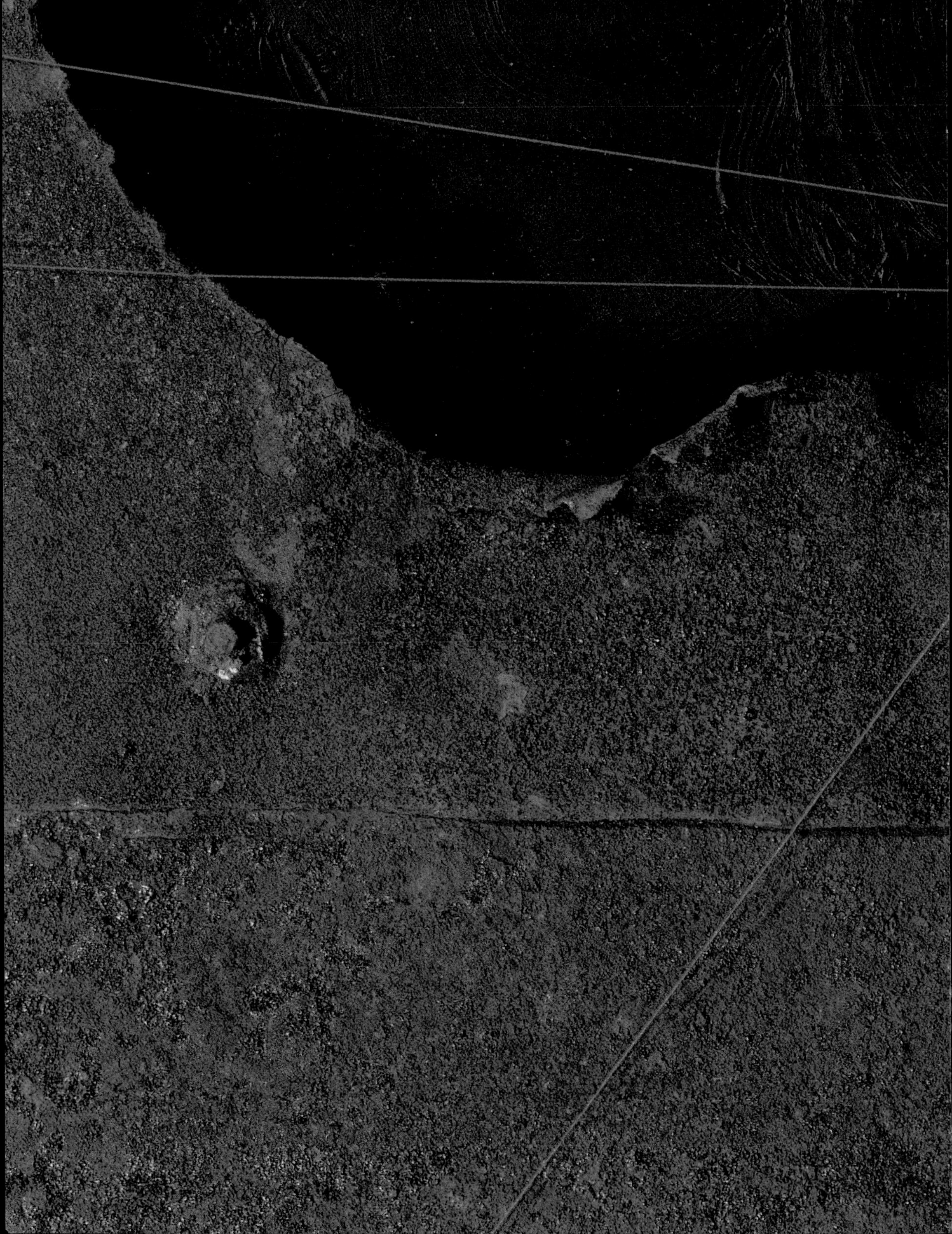

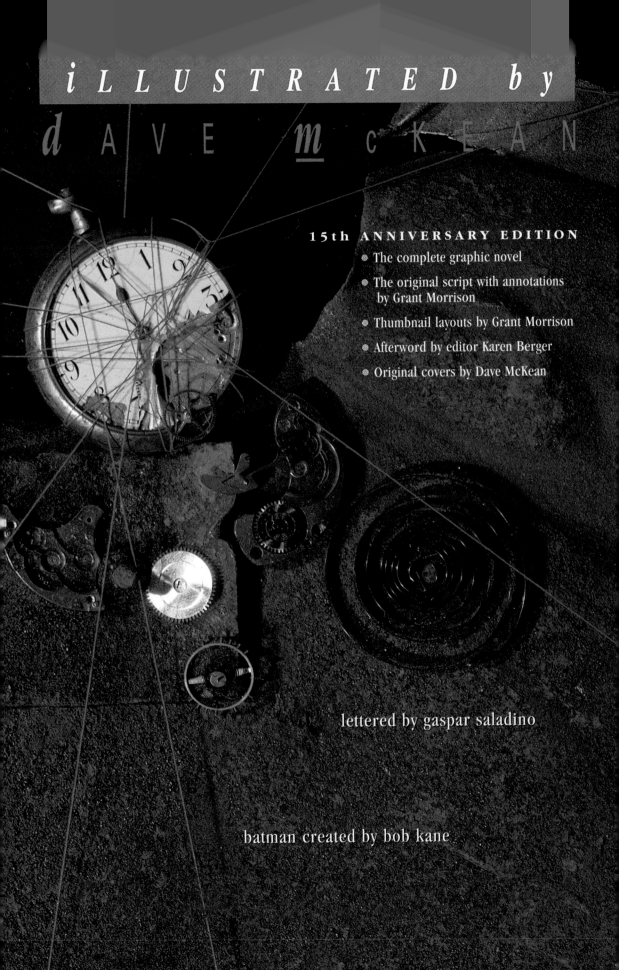

iLLUSTRATED by

_d_ A V E _m_ cK E A N

15th ANNIVERSARY EDITION

* The complete graphic novel
* The original script with annotations
  by Grant Morrison
* Thumbnail layouts by Grant Morrison
* Afterword by editor Karen Berger
* Original covers by Dave McKean

lettered by gaspar saladino

batman created by bob kane

*B*ut i don't want to go among mad people,' Alice remarked.

'Oh, you can't help that,' said the Cat: 'We're all mad here.

I'm mad,you're mad.'

'How do you know i'm mad?' said Alice.

'You must be,' said the Cat, 'or you wouldn't have come here.'

LEWIS CARROLL

'Alice's Adventures in Wonderland'

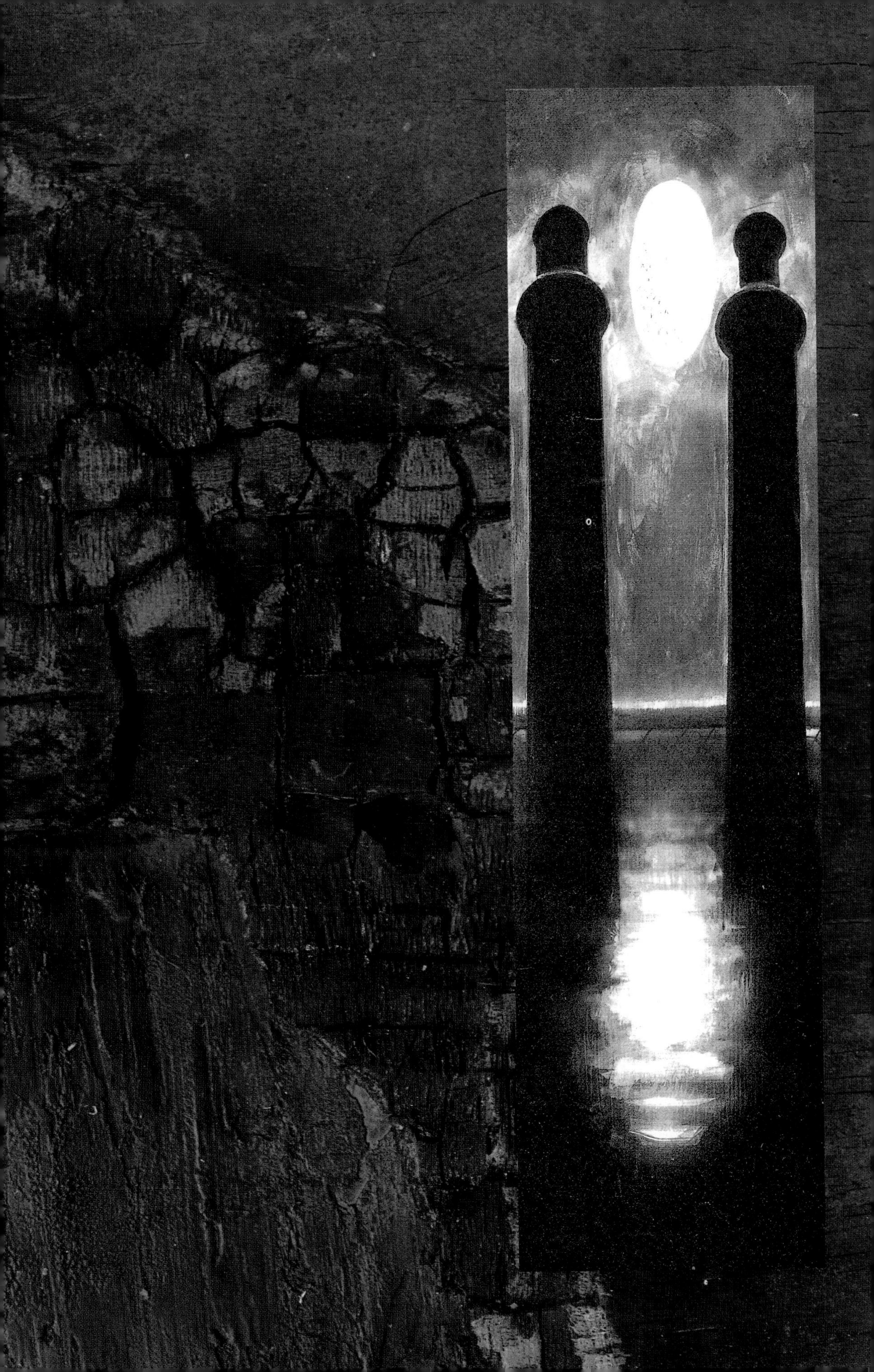

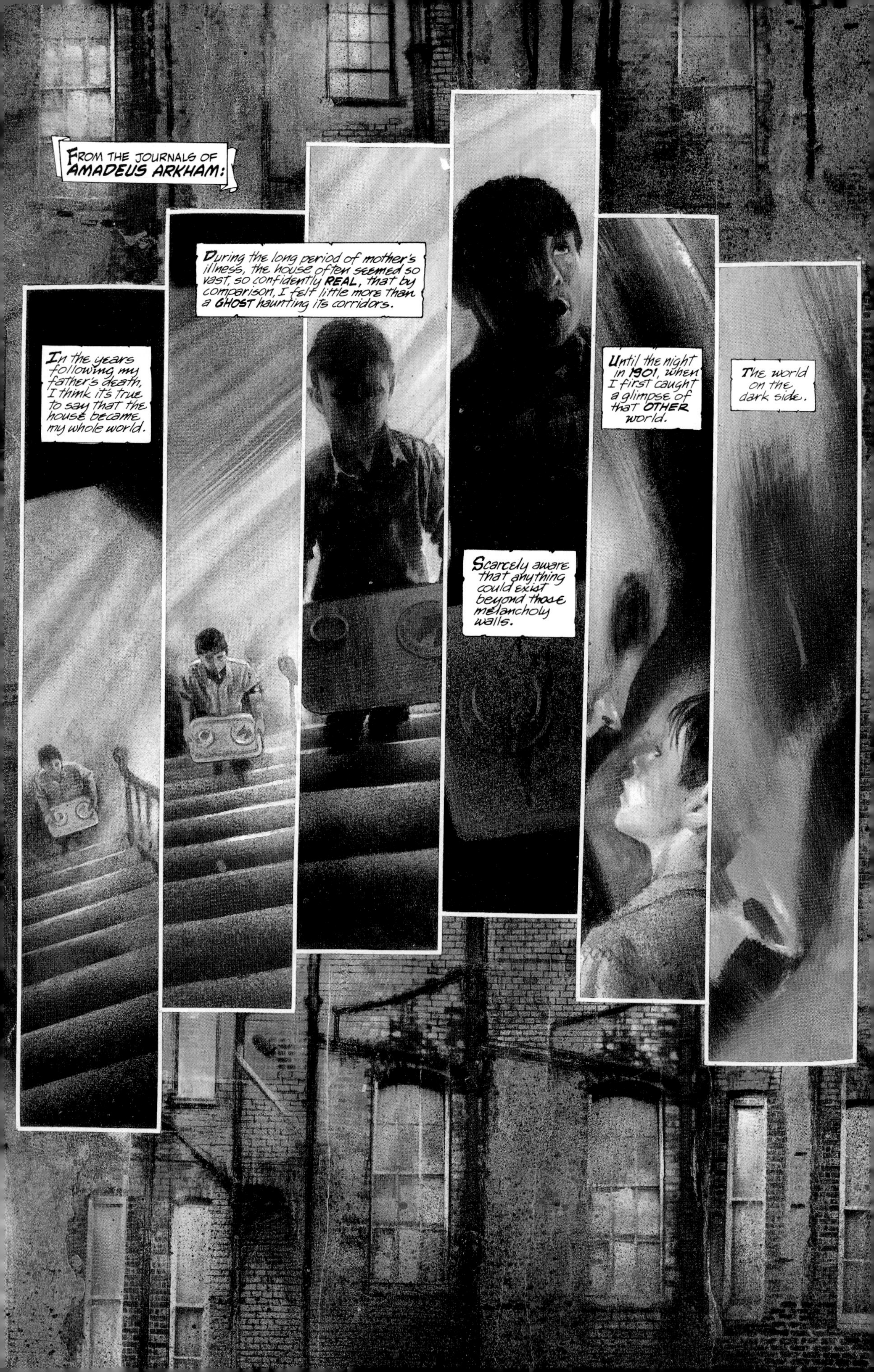
From the journals of Amadeus Arkham:
In the years following my father's death, I think it's true to say that the house became my whole world.
During the long period of mother's illness, the house often seemed so vast, so confidently REAL, that by comparison, I felt little more than a GHOST haunting its corridors.
Scarcely aware that anything could exist beyond those melancholy walls.
Until the night in 1901, when I first caught a glimpse of that OTHER world.
The world on the dark side.

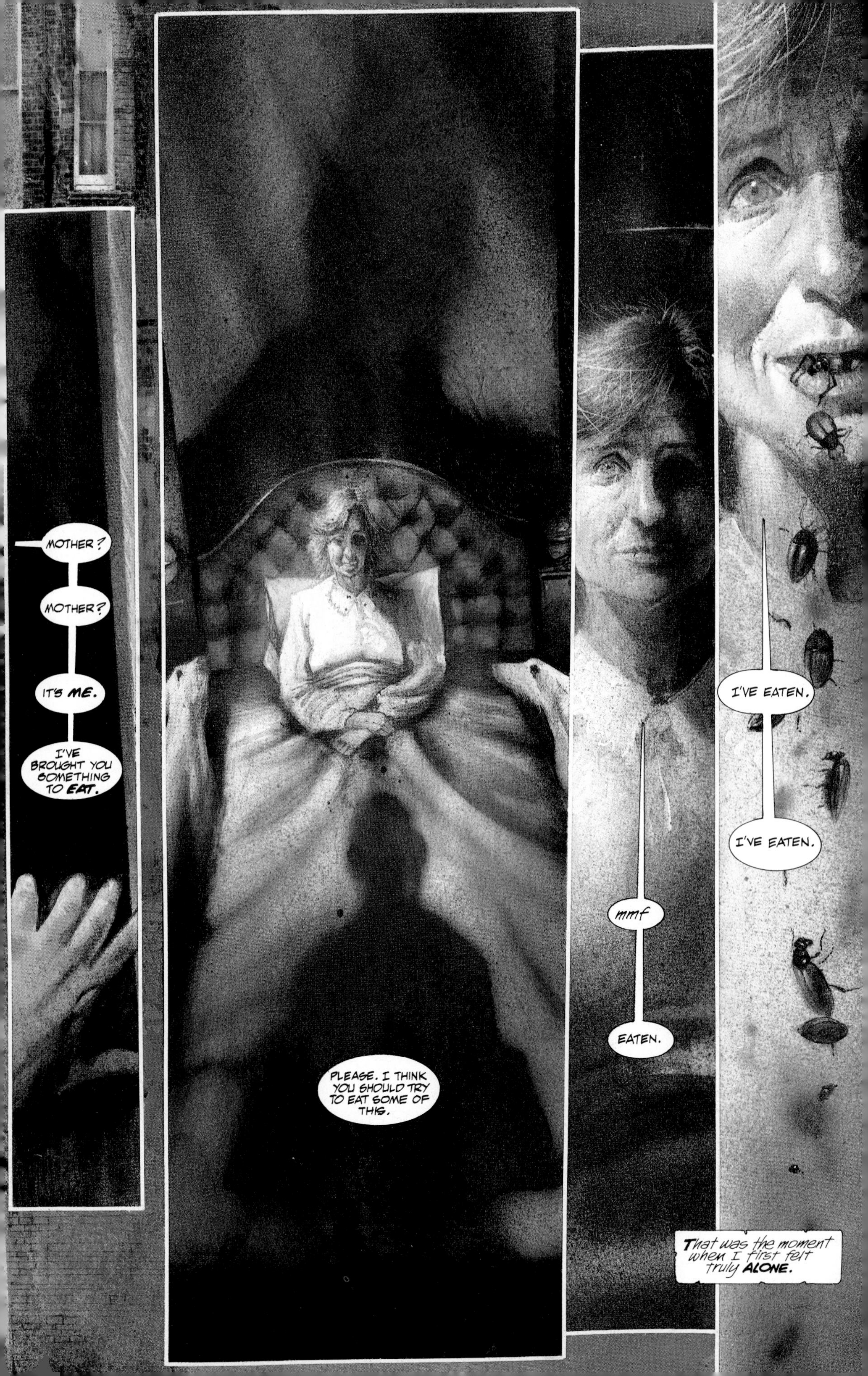
MOTHER?
MOTHER?
IT'S ME.
I'VE BROUGHT YOU SOMETHING TO EAT.
PLEASE. I THINK YOU SHOULD TRY TO EAT SOME OF THIS.
mmf
EATEN.
I'VE EATEN.
I'VE EATEN.
That was the moment when I first felt truly ALONE.

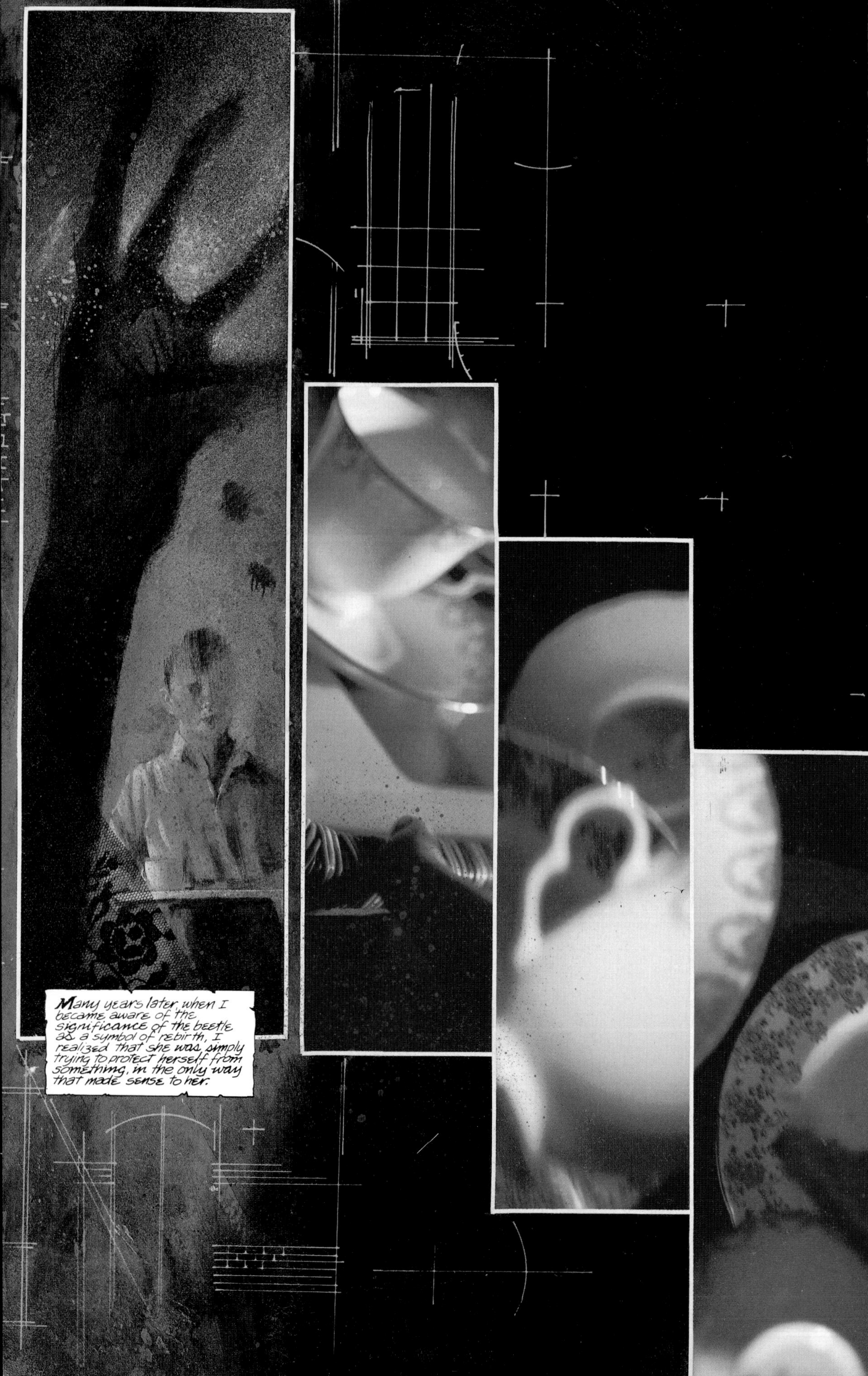
Many years later, when I became aware of the significance of the beetle as a symbol of rebirth, I realized that she was simply trying to protect herself from something, in the only way that made sense to her.

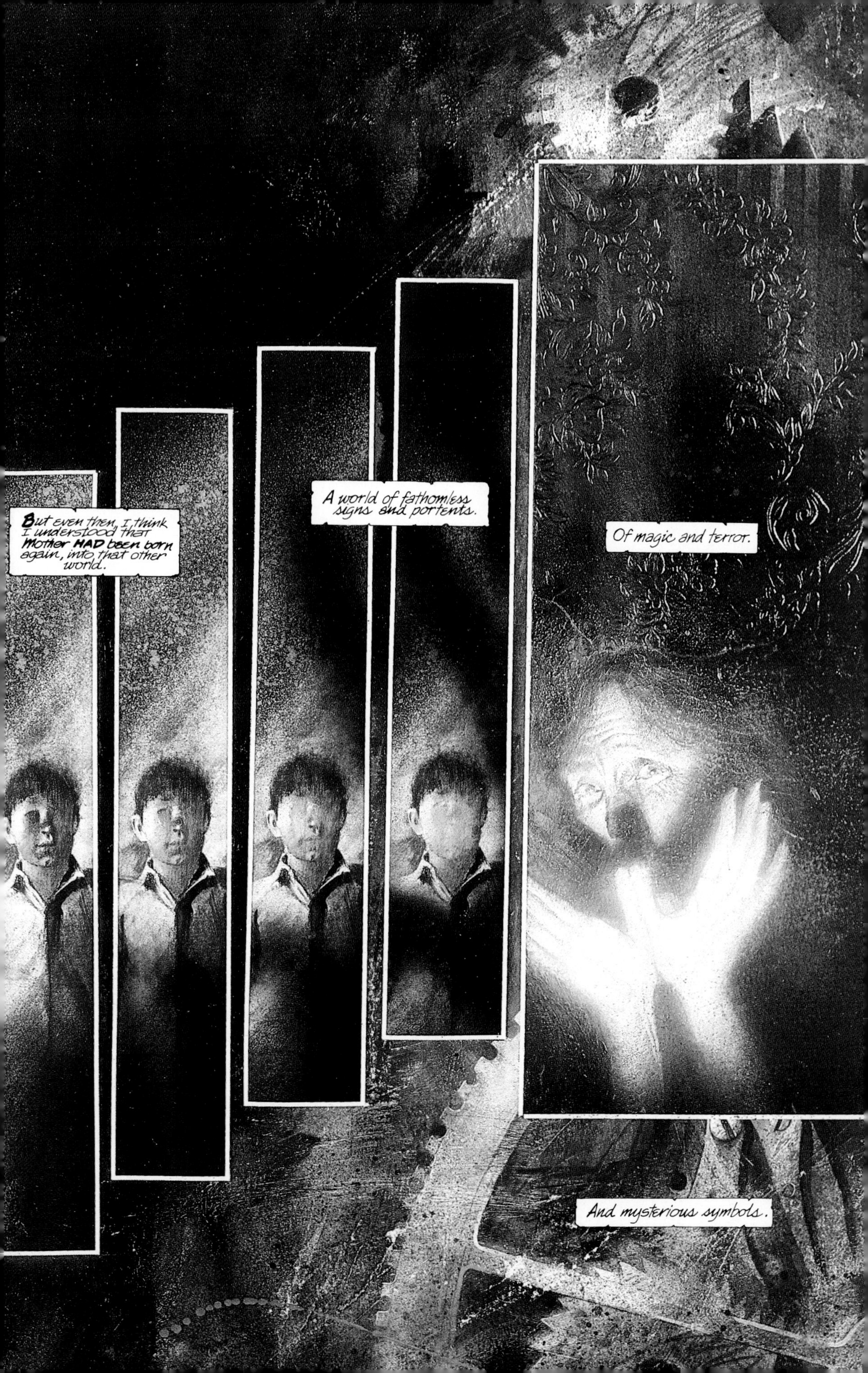
But even then, I think I understood that Mother HAD been born again, into that other world.
A world of fathomless signs and portents.
Of magic and terror.
And mysterious symbols.

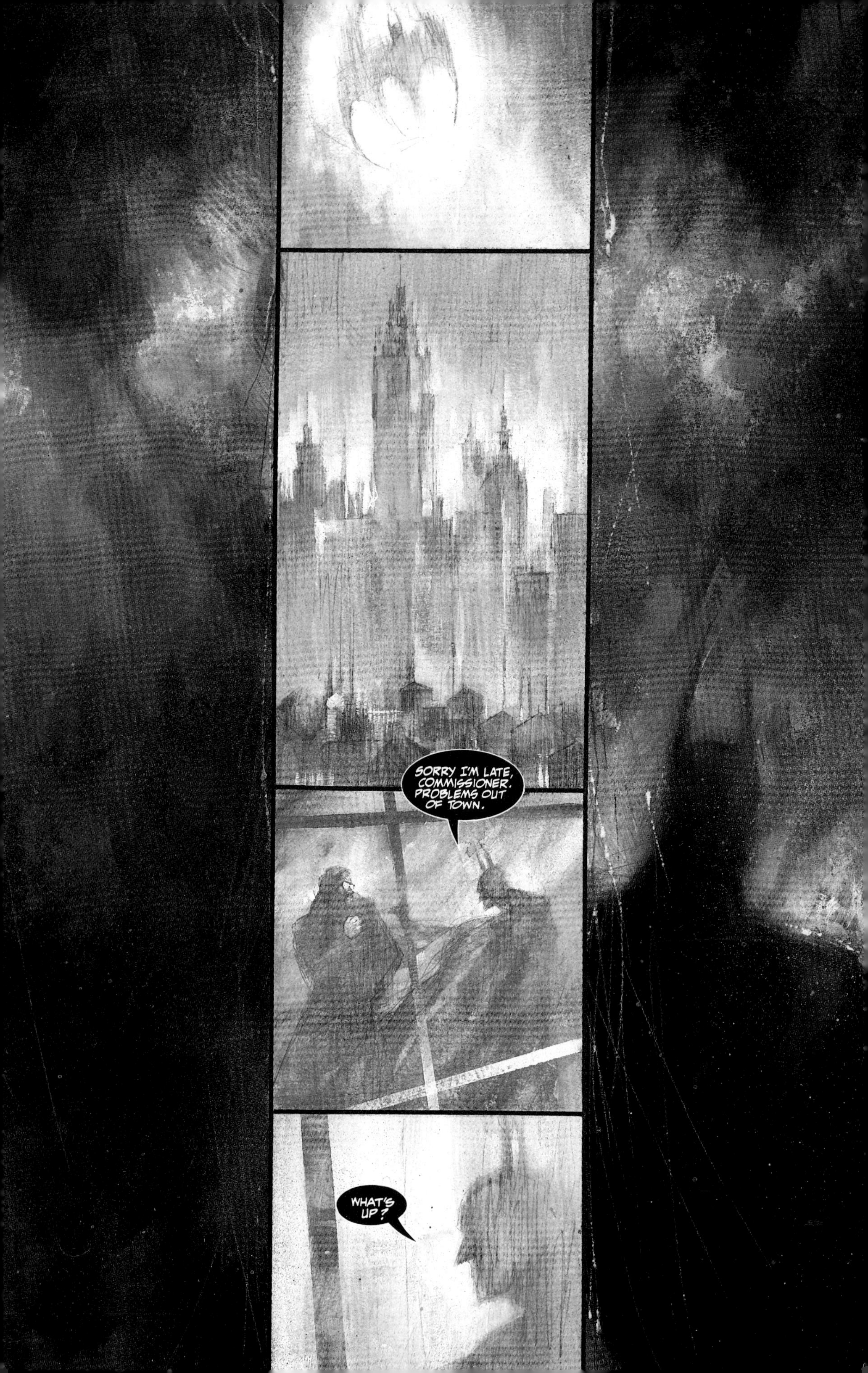
SORRY I'M LATE, COMMISSIONER. PROBLEMS OUT OF TOWN.
WHAT'S UP?

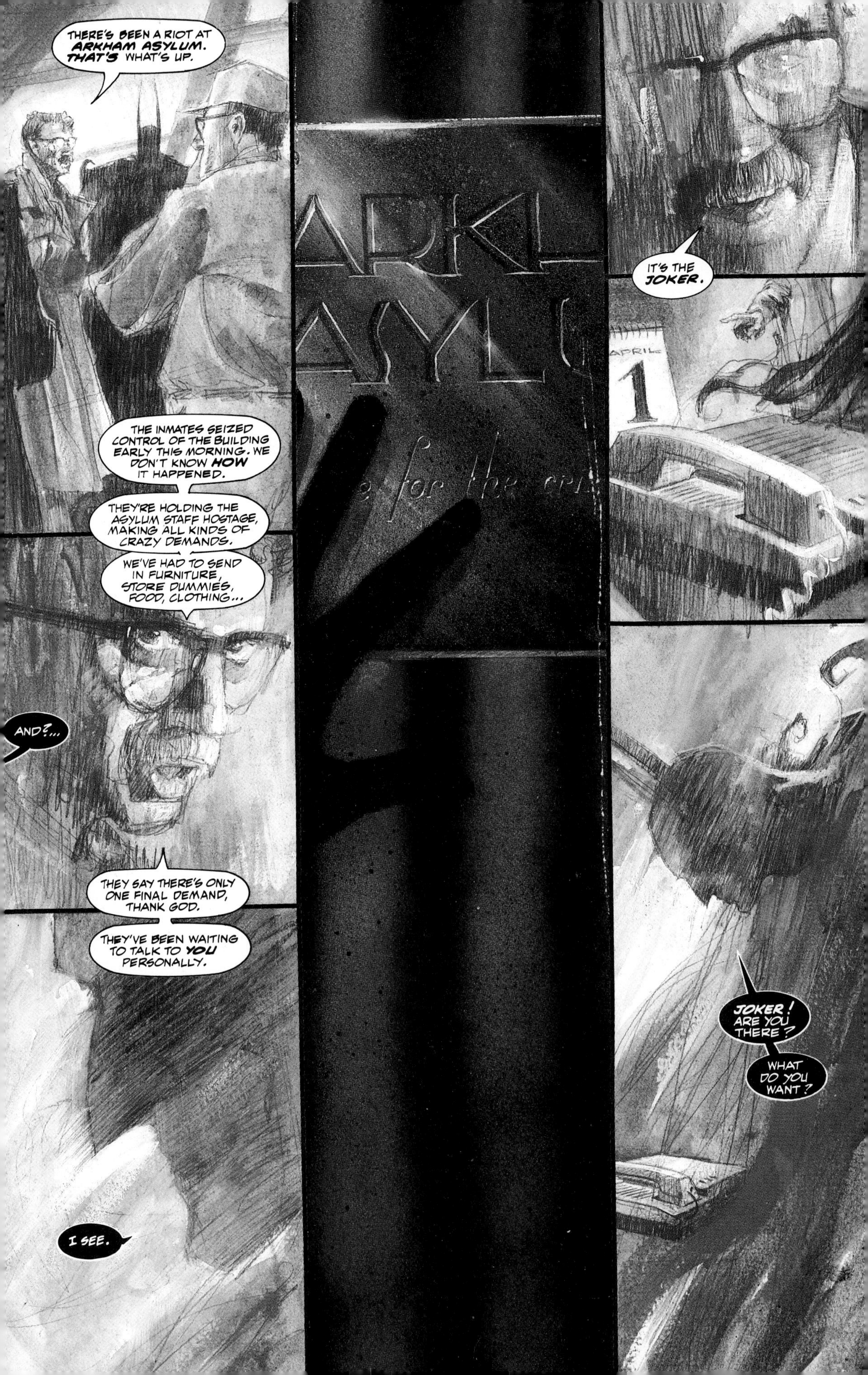

THERE'S BEEN A RIOT AT ARKHAM ASYLUM. THAT'S WHAT'S UP.
THE INMATES SEIZED CONTROL OF THE BUILDING EARLY THIS MORNING. WE DON'T KNOW HOW IT HAPPENED.
THEY'RE HOLDING THE ASYLUM STAFF HOSTAGE, MAKING ALL KINDS OF CRAZY DEMANDS.
WE'VE HAD TO SEND IN FURNITURE, STORE DUMMIES, FOOD, CLOTHING...
AND?...
THEY SAY THERE'S ONLY ONE FINAL DEMAND, THANK GOD.
THEY'VE BEEN WAITING TO TALK TO YOU PERSONALLY.
I SEE.
ARKH
ASYLU
IT'S THE JOKER.
APRIL
1
JOKER! ARE YOU THERE?
WHAT DO YOU WANT?

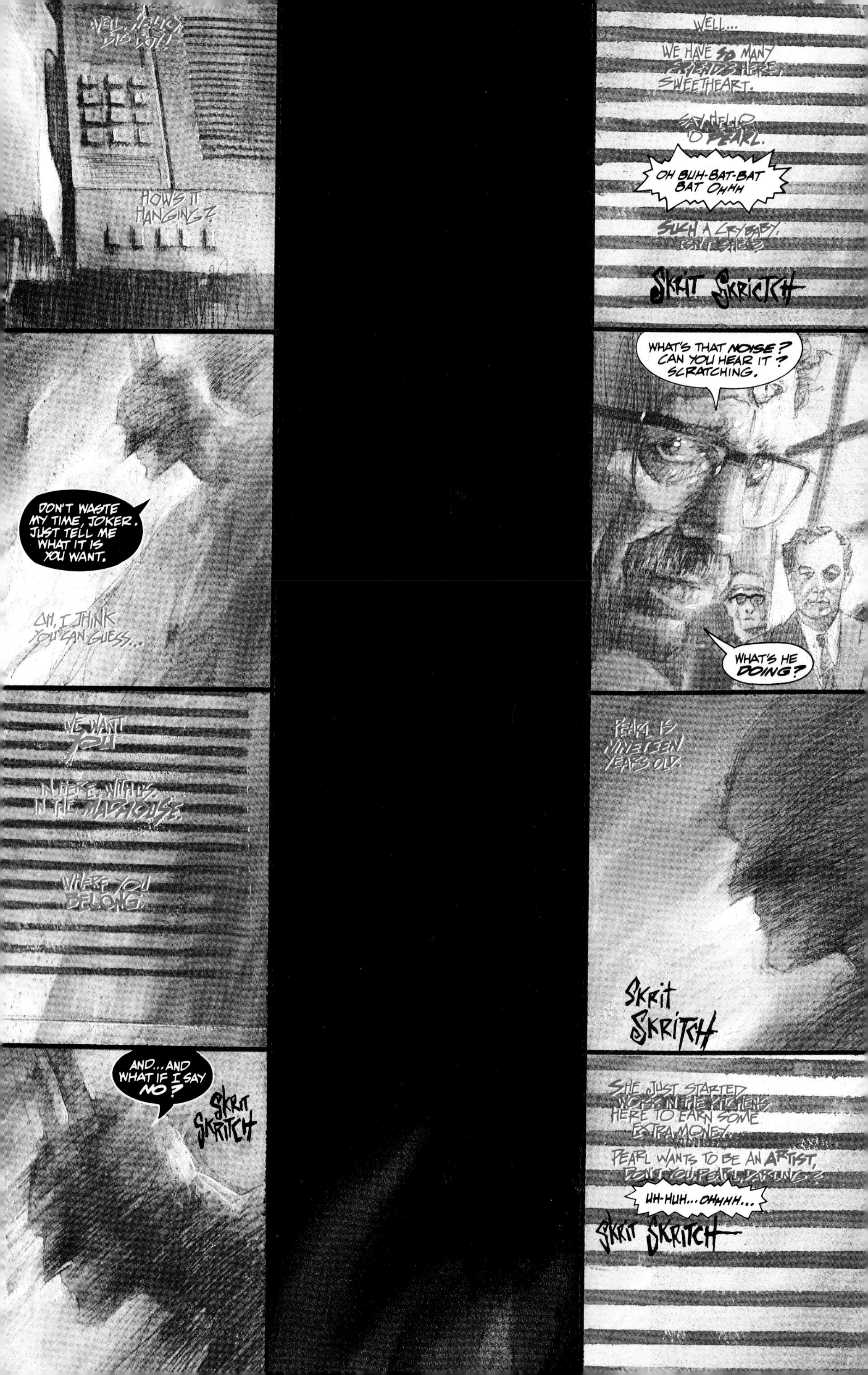
WELL, HELLO, BIG BOY!
HOW'S IT HANGING?
DON'T WASTE MY TIME, JOKER. JUST TELL ME WHAT IT IS YOU WANT.
OH, I THINK YOU CAN GUESS...
WE WANT YOU
IN HERE, WITH US. IN THE MADHOUSE.
WHERE YOU BELONG.
AND... AND WHAT IF I SAY NO?
SKRIT SKRITCH
WELL...
WE HAVE SO MANY FRIENDS HERE, SWEETHEART.
SAY HELLO TO PEARL.
OH BUH-BAT-BAT BAT OHHH
SUCH A CRYBABY, ISN'T SHE?
SKRIT SKRITCH
WHAT'S THAT NOISE? CAN YOU HEAR IT? SCRATCHING.
WHAT'S HE DOING?
PEARL IS NINETEEN YEARS OLD.
SKRIT SKRITCH
SHE JUST STARTED WORK IN THE KITCHENS HERE TO EARN SOME EXTRA MONEY.
PEARL WANTS TO BE AN ARTIST, DON'T YOU, PEARL, DARLING?
UH-HUH... OHHHH...
SKRIT SKRITCH

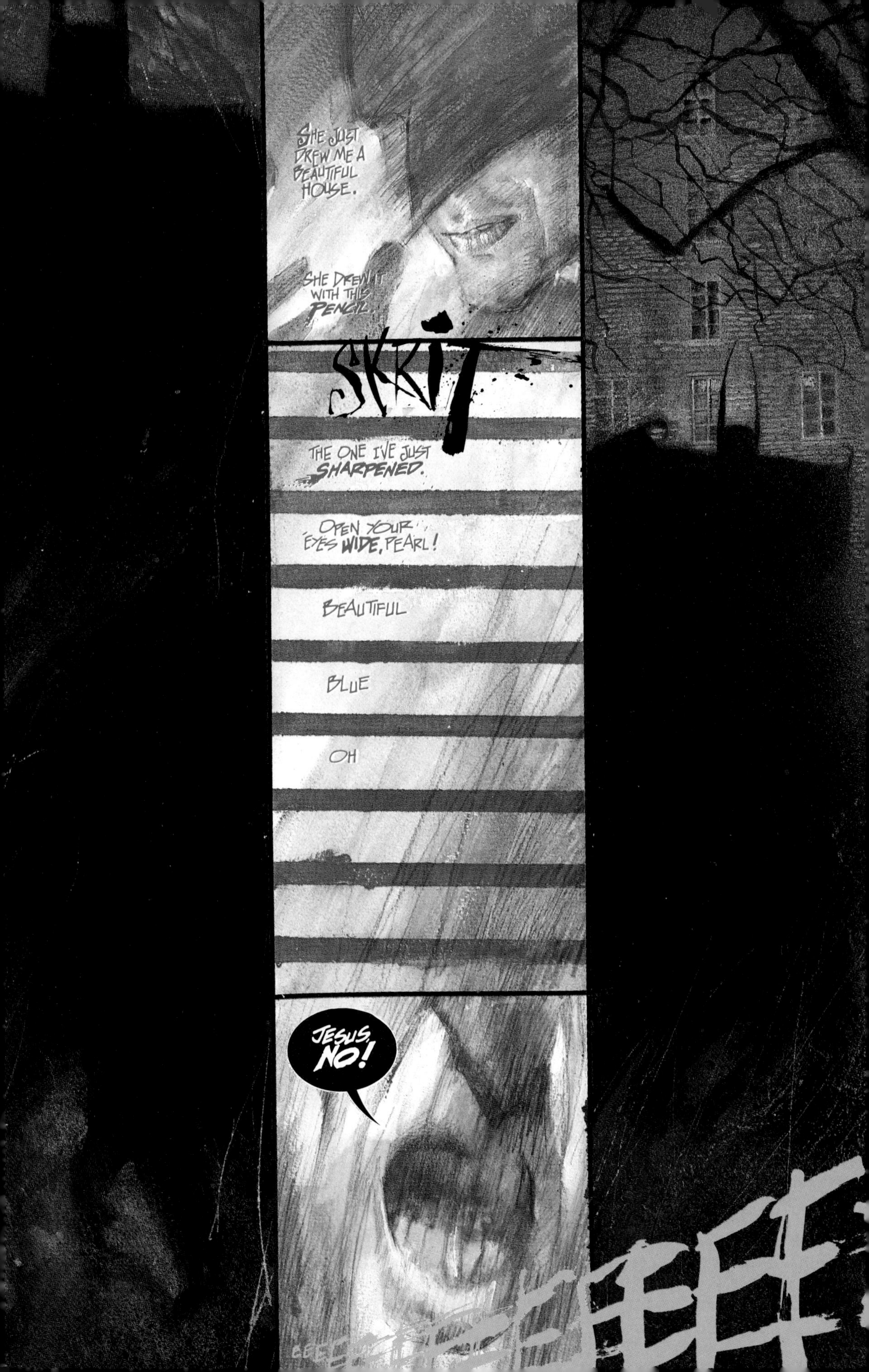

SHE JUST DREW ME A BEAUTIFUL HOUSE.
SHE DREW IT WITH THIS PENCIL.
SKRIT
THE ONE I'VE JUST SHARPENED.
OPEN YOUR EYES WIDE, PEARL!
BEAUTIFUL
BLUE
OH
JESUS, NO!

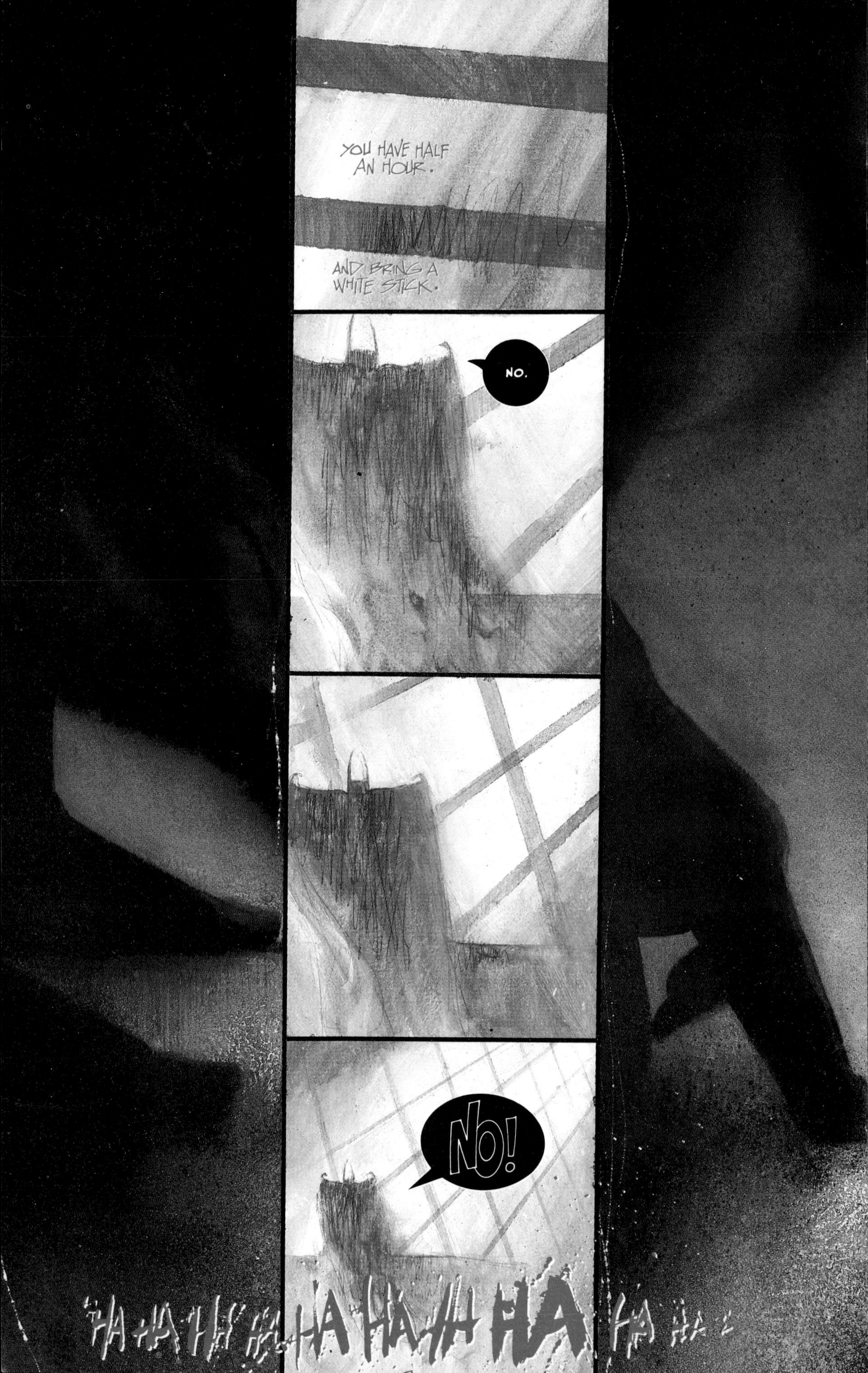
YOU HAVE HALF AN HOUR.
AND BRING A WHITE STICK.
NO.
NO!
HA HA HA HA HA HA HA HA HA HA

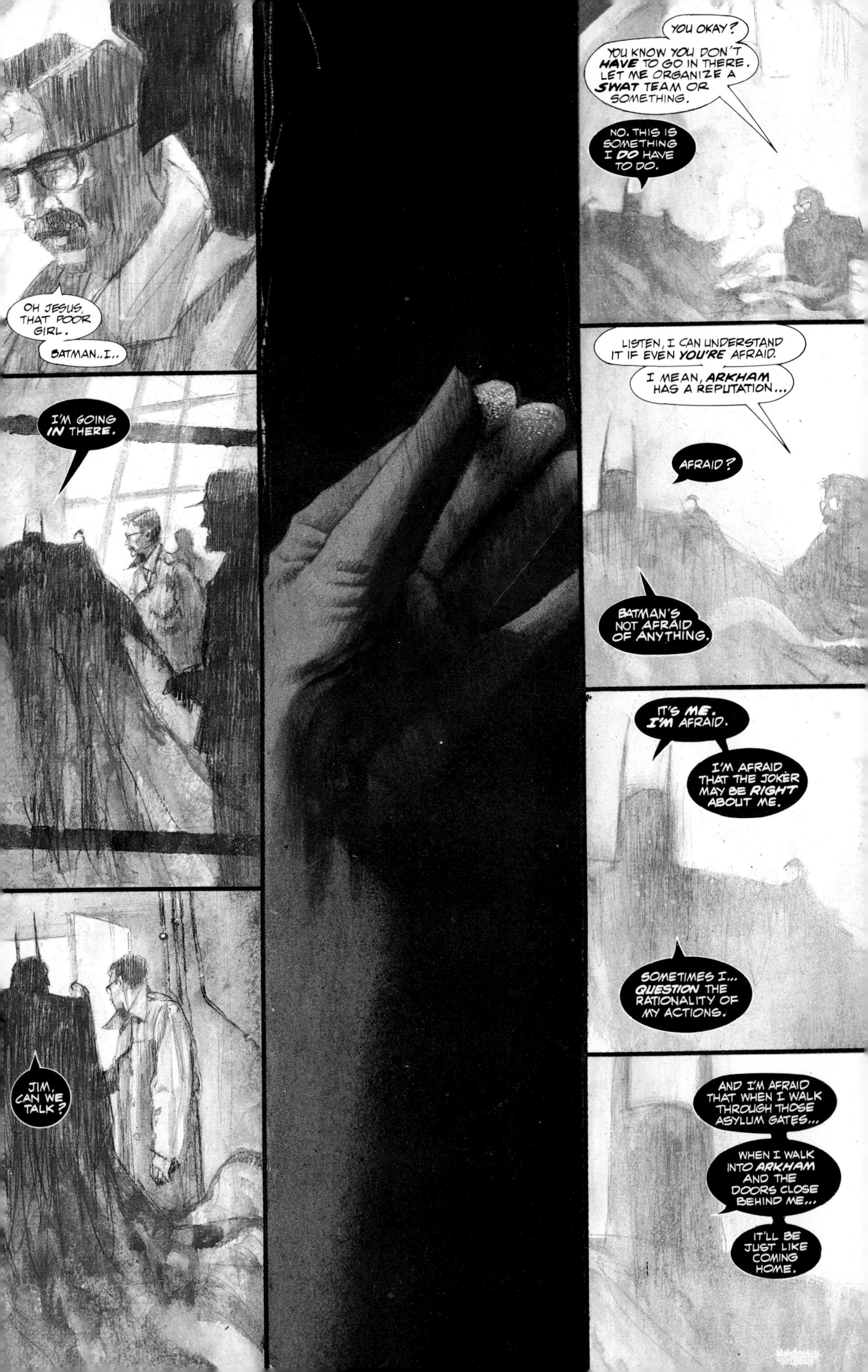
OH JESUS, THAT POOR GIRL.
BATMAN..I..
I'M GOING IN THERE.
JIM, CAN WE TALK?
YOU OKAY?
YOU KNOW YOU DON'T HAVE TO GO IN THERE. LET ME ORGANIZE A SWAT TEAM OR SOMETHING.
NO. THIS IS SOMETHING I DO HAVE TO DO.
LISTEN, I CAN UNDERSTAND IT IF EVEN YOU'RE AFRAID.
I MEAN, ARKHAM HAS A REPUTATION...
AFRAID?
BATMAN'S NOT AFRAID OF ANYTHING.
IT'S ME. I'M AFRAID.
I'M AFRAID THAT THE JOKER MAY BE RIGHT ABOUT ME.
SOMETIMES I... QUESTION THE RATIONALITY OF MY ACTIONS.
AND I'M AFRAID THAT WHEN I WALK THROUGH THOSE ASYLUM GATES...
WHEN I WALK INTO ARKHAM AND THE DOORS CLOSE BEHIND ME...
IT'LL BE JUST LIKE COMING HOME.

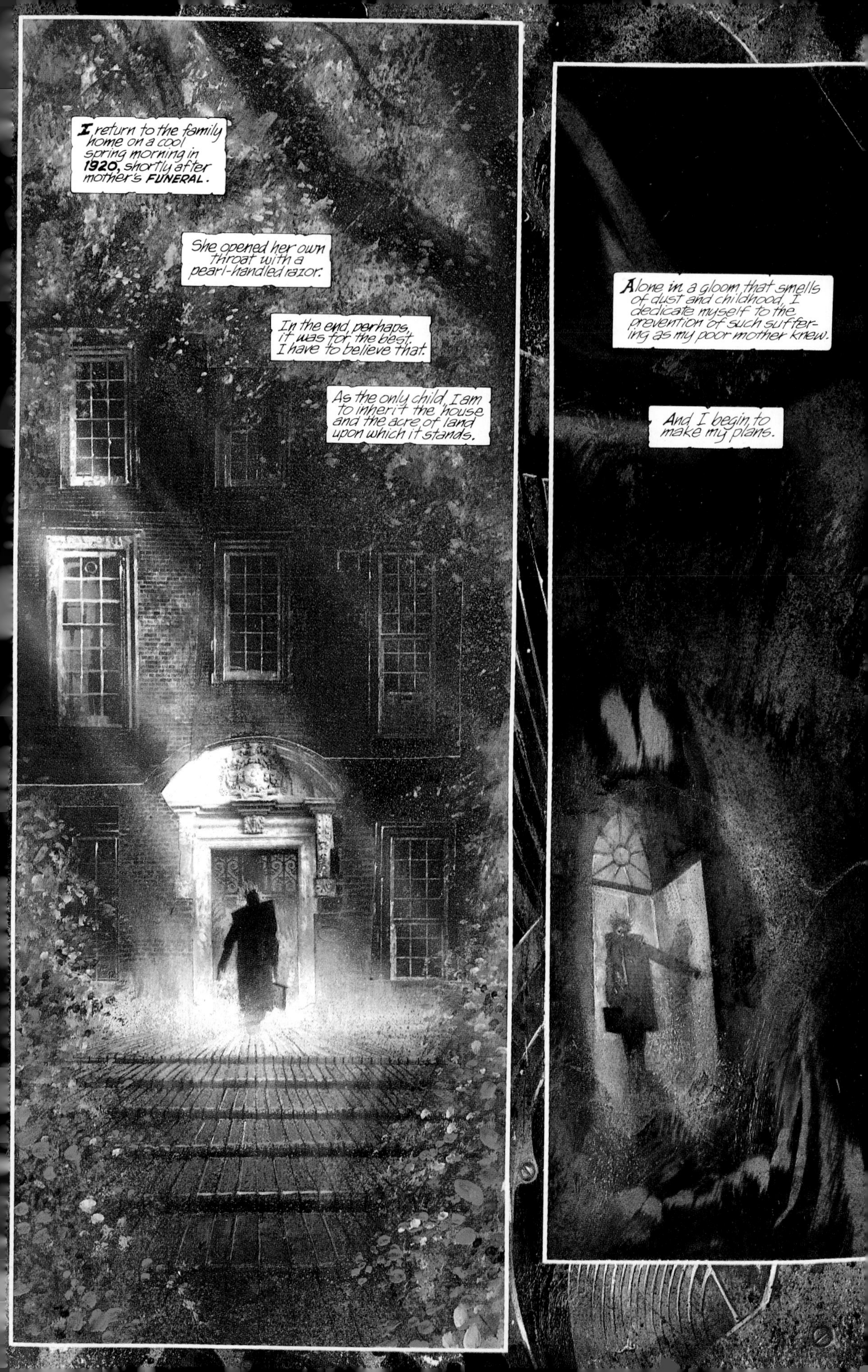
I return to the family home on a cool spring morning in 1920, shortly after mother's FUNERAL.
She opened her own throat with a pearl-handled razor.
In the end, perhaps, it was for the best. I have to believe that.
As the only child, I am to inherit the house and the acre of land upon which it stands.
Alone in a gloom that smells of dust and childhood, I dedicate myself to the prevention of such suffering as my poor mother knew.
And I begin to make my plans.

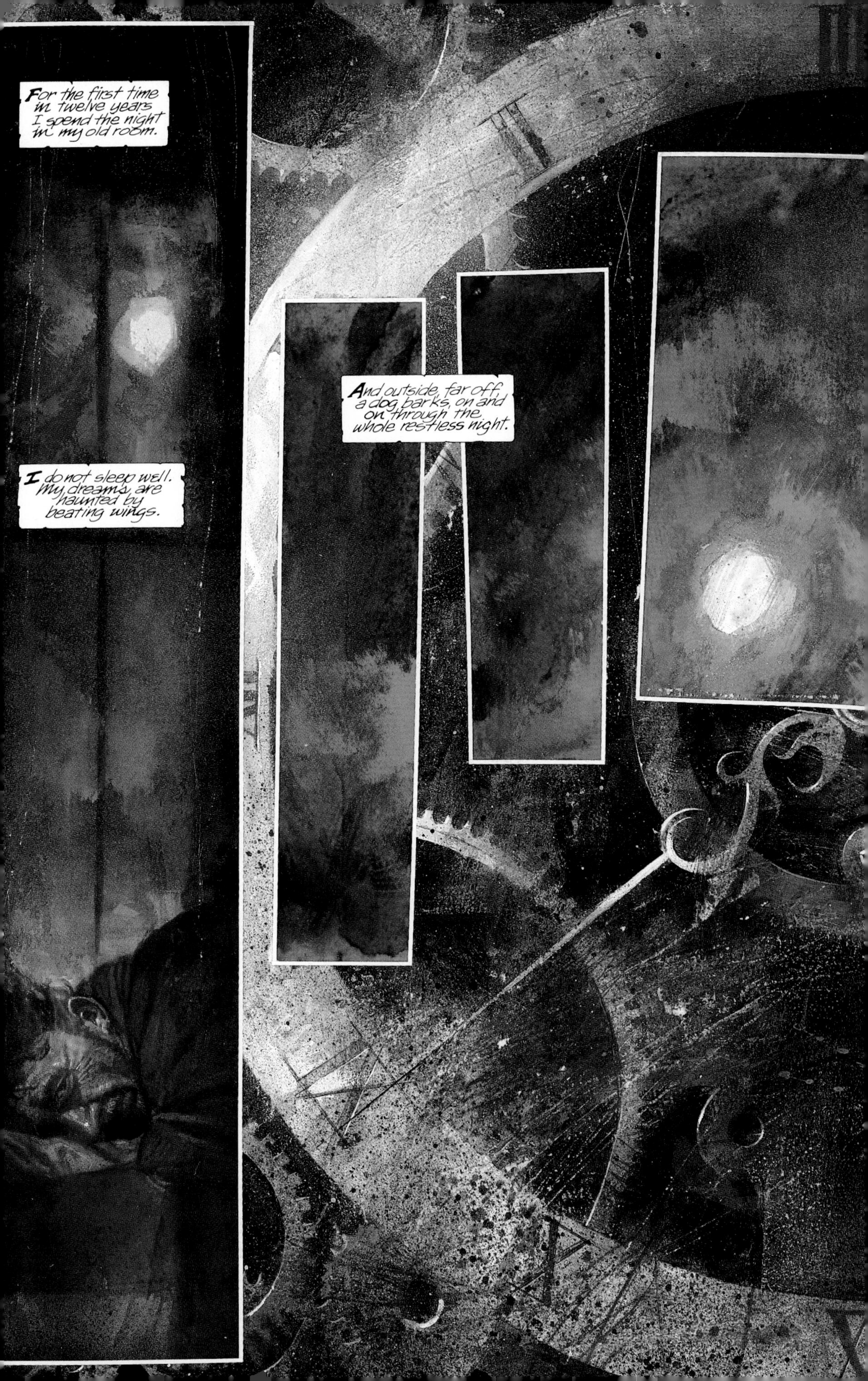
For the first time in twelve years I spend the night in my old room.
I do not sleep well. My dreams are haunted by beating wings.
And outside, far off, a dog barks, on and on through the whole restless night.

Next day, I return to **METROPOLIS**, where my family and I have been living for some time.

I'm working at the State Psychiatric Hospital and one of my patients today has been referred to me from Metropolis Penitentiary.

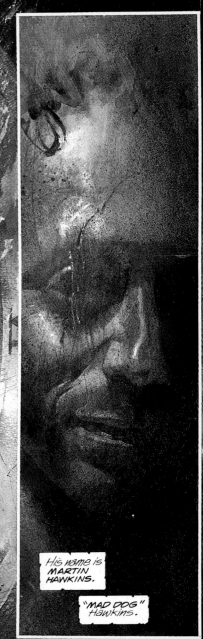

His name is **MARTIN HAWKINS**.

"MAD DOG" Hawkins.

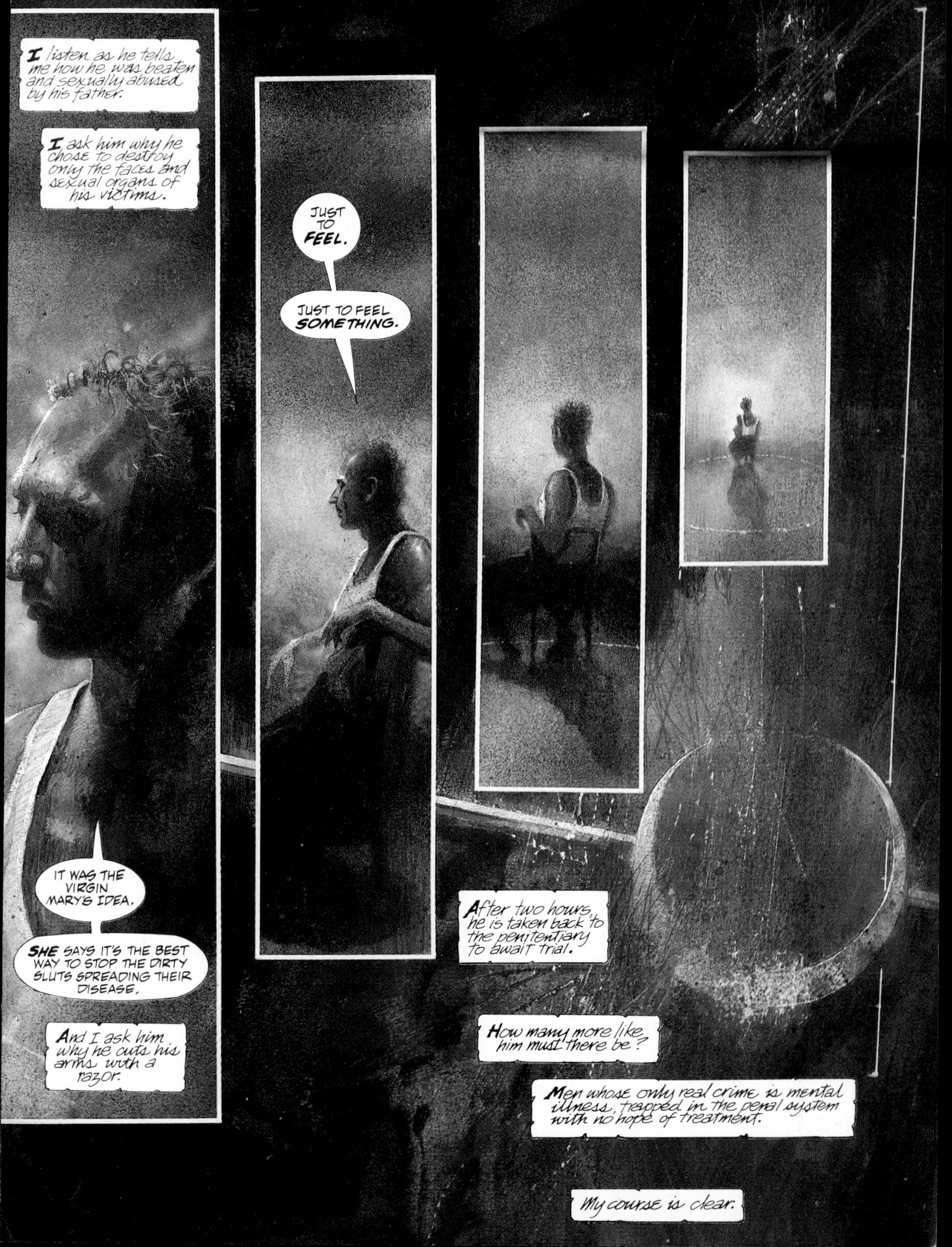

I listen as he tells me how he was beaten and sexually abused by his father.
I ask him why he chose to destroy only the faces and sexual organs of his victims.
IT WAS THE VIRGIN MARY'S IDEA.
SHE SAYS IT'S THE BEST WAY TO STOP THE DIRTY SLUTS SPREADING THEIR DISEASE.
And I ask him why he cuts his arms with a razor.
JUST TO FEEL.
JUST TO FEEL SOMETHING.
After two hours, he is taken back to the penitentiary to await trial.
How many more like him must there be?
Men whose only real crime is mental illness, trapped in the penal system with no hope of treatment.
My course is clear.

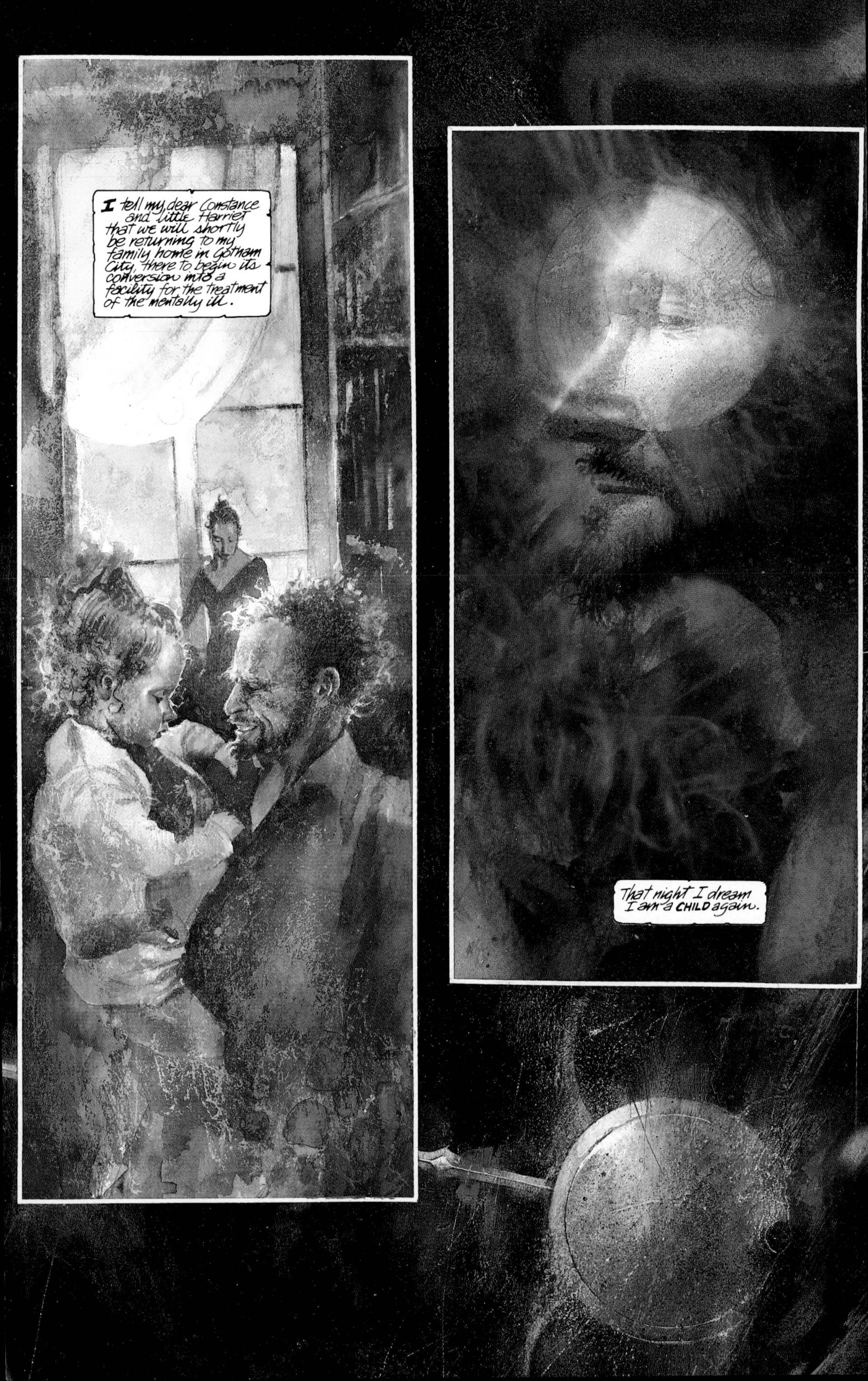
I tell my dear Constance and little Harriet that we will shortly be returning to my family home in Gotham City, there to begin its conversion into a facility for the treatment of the mentally ill.
That night I dream I am a CHILD again.

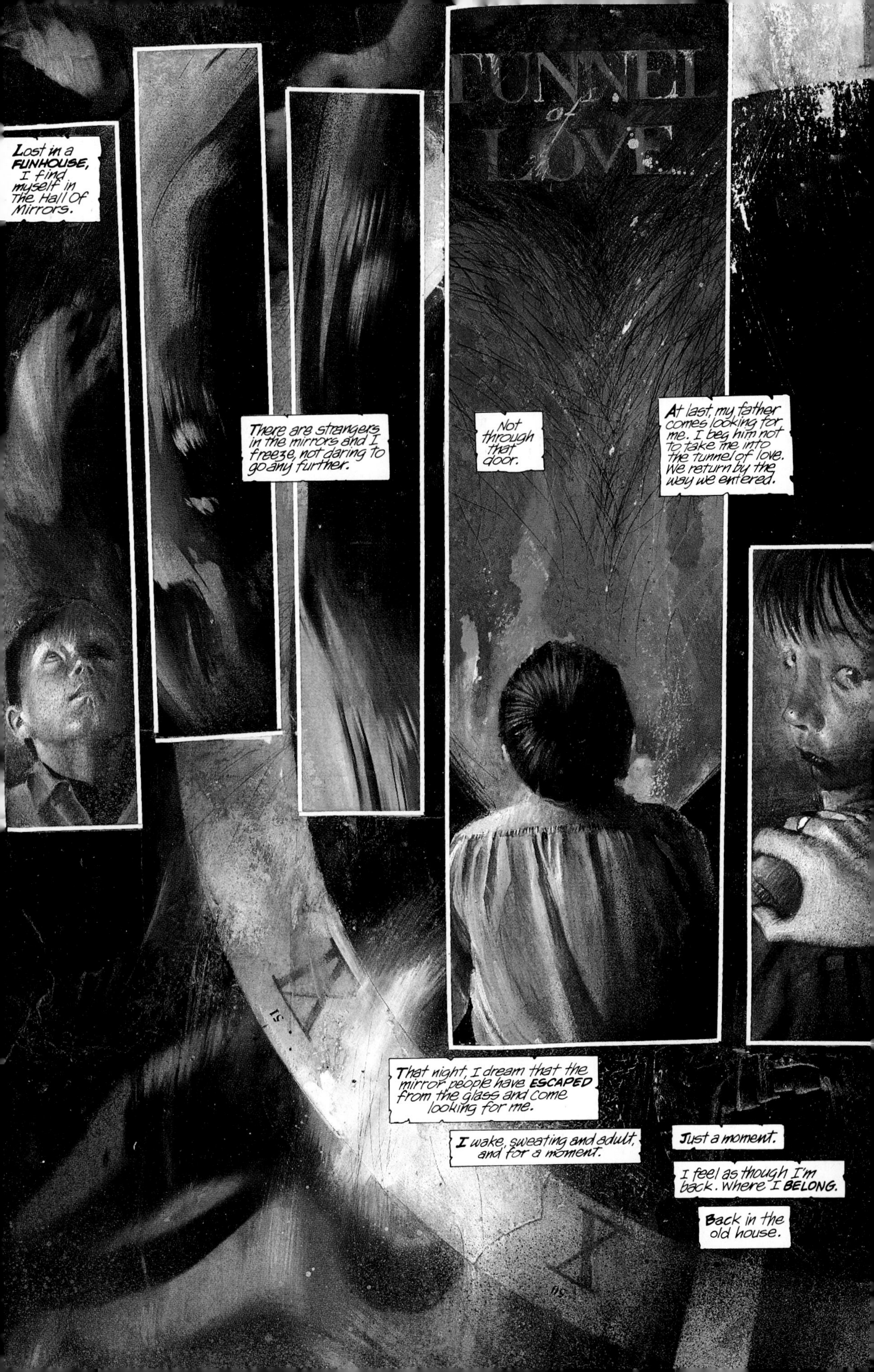
Lost in a FUNHOUSE, I find myself in The Hall Of Mirrors.
There are strangers in the mirrors and I freeze, not daring to go any further.
TUNNEL of LOVE
Not through that door.
At last, my father comes looking for me. I beg him not to take me into the tunnel of love. We return by the way we entered.
That night, I dream that the mirror people have ESCAPED from the glass and come looking for me.
I wake, sweating and adult, and for a moment.
Just a moment.
I feel as though I'm back. Where I BELONG.
Back in the old house.

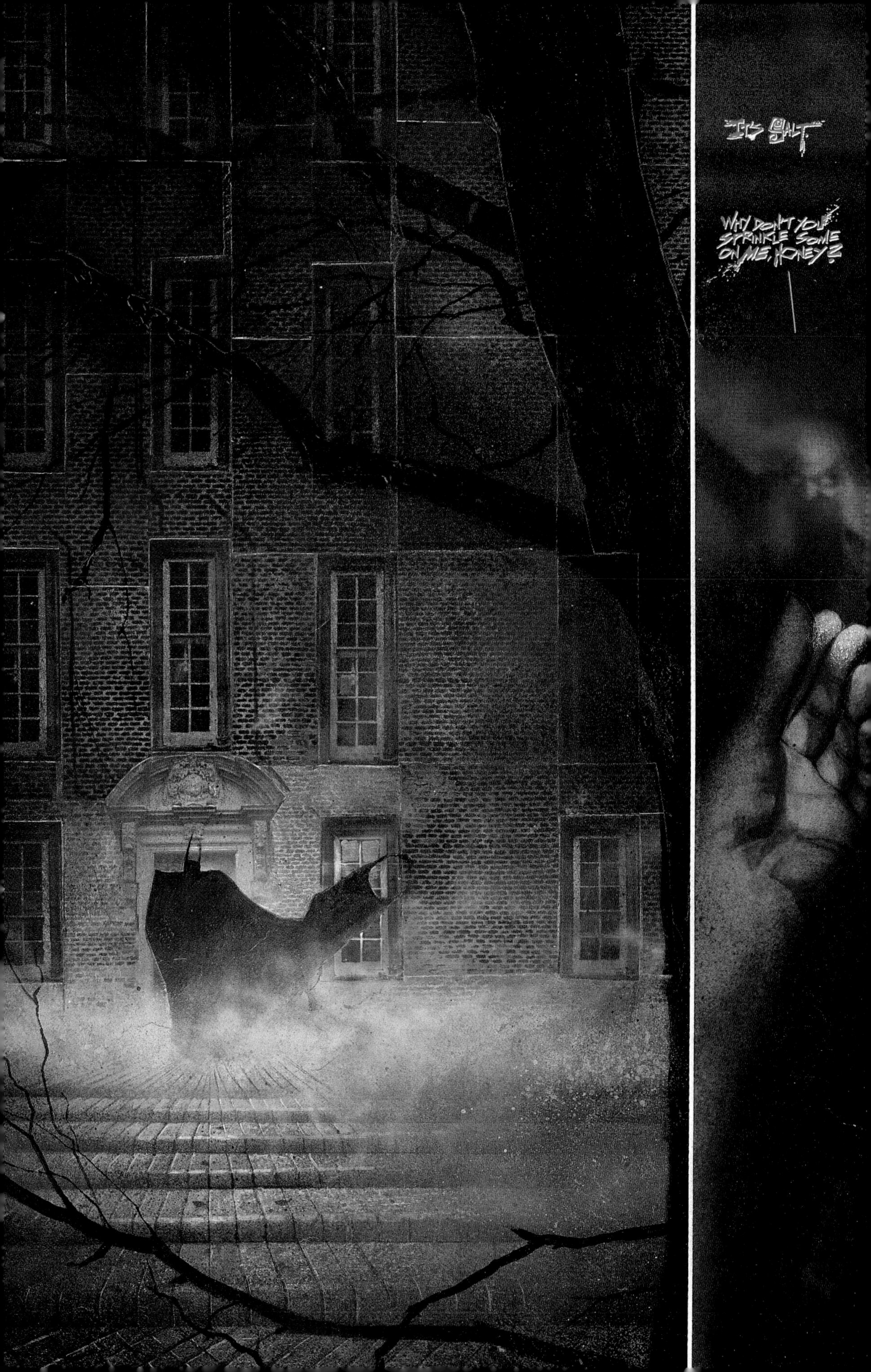
IT'S SALT.
WHY DON'T YOU SPRINKLE SOME ON ME, HONEY?

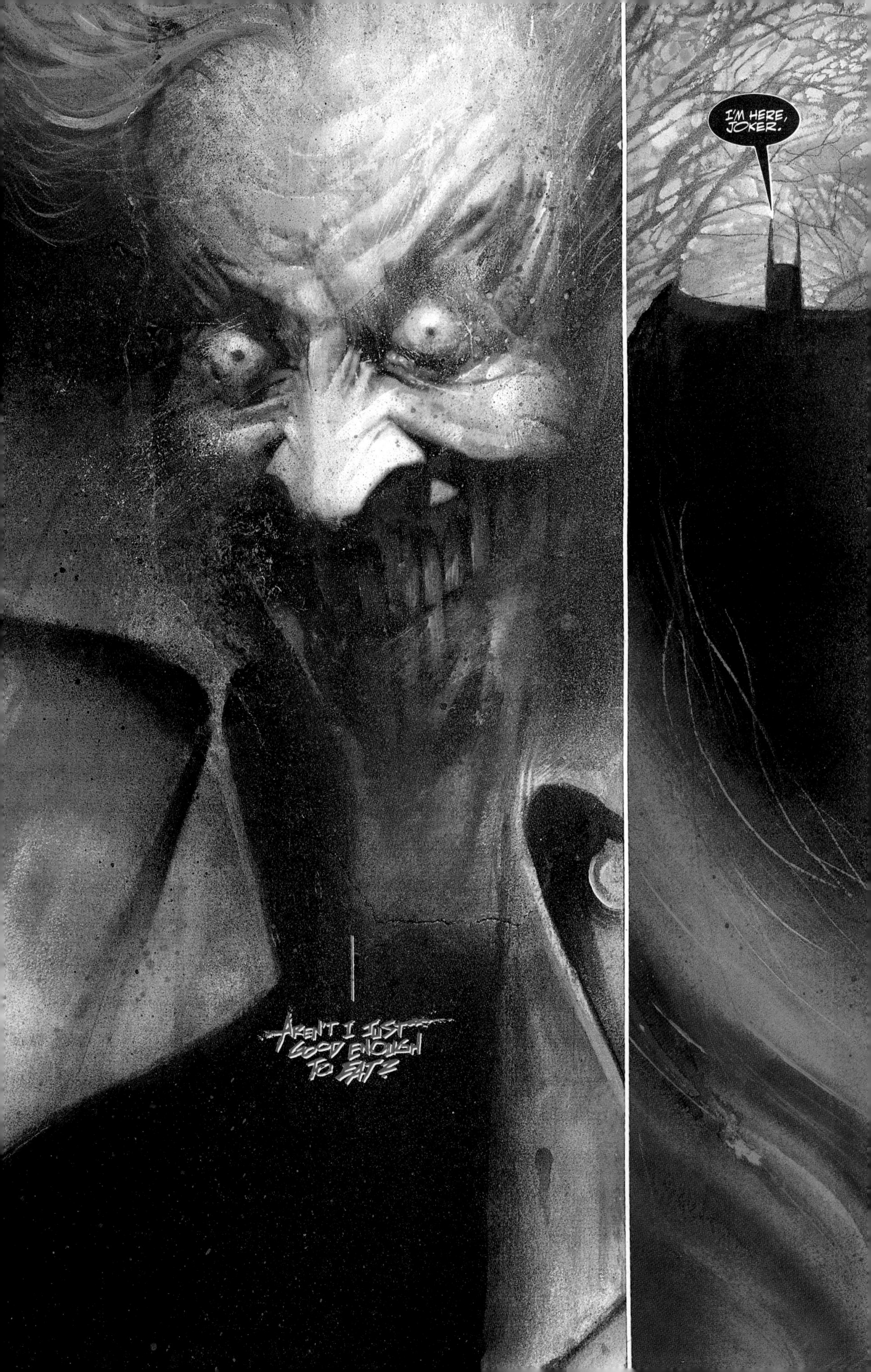
AREN'T I JUST GOOD ENOUGH TO EAT?
I'M HERE, JOKER.

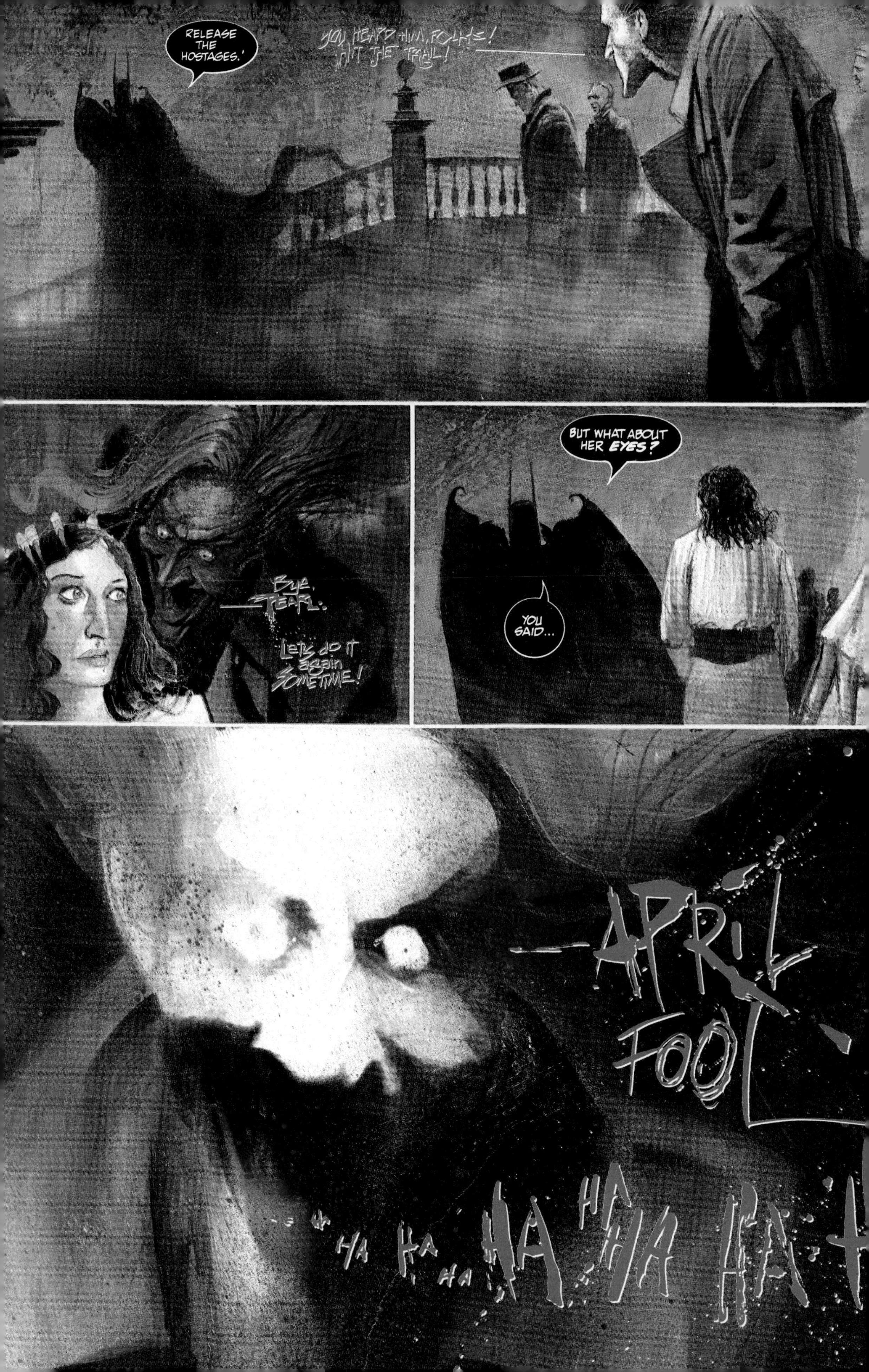
RELEASE THE HOSTAGES.'
YOU HEARD HIM, FOLKS! HIT THE TRAIL!
BYE, PEARL.
LET'S DO IT AGAIN SOMETIME!
BUT WHAT ABOUT HER EYES?
YOU SAID...
APRIL FOOL
HA HA HA HA HA HA HA HA

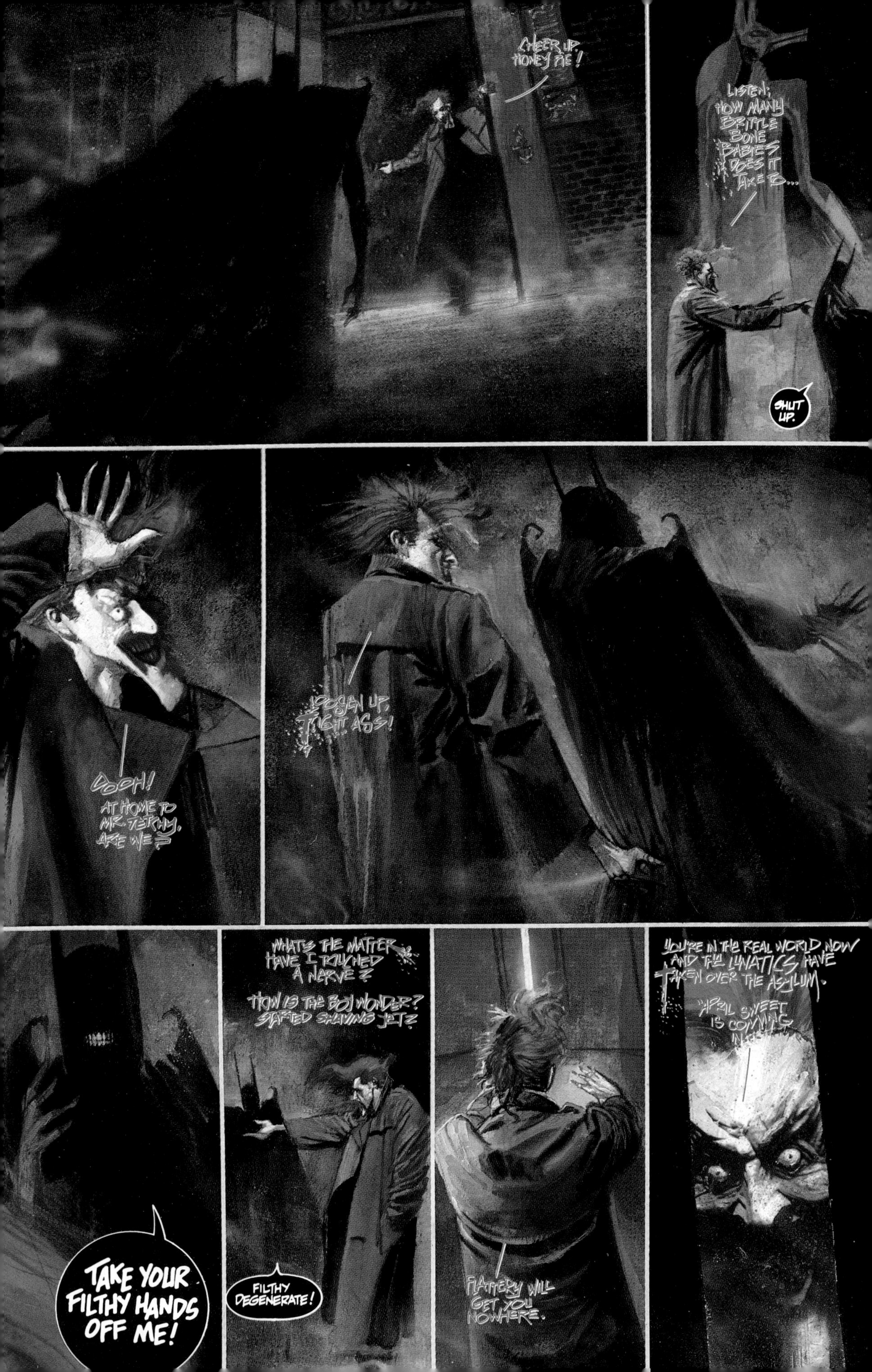
CHEER UP, HONEY PIE!
LISTEN; HOW MANY BRITTLE BONE BABIES DOES IT TAKE TO...
SHUT UP.
OOOH! AT HOME TO MR. TETCHY, ARE WE?
LOOSEN UP, TIGHT ASS!
TAKE YOUR FILTHY HANDS OFF ME!
WHAT'S THE MATTER HAVE I TOUCHED A NERVE?
HOW IS THE BOY WONDER? STARTED SHAVING YET?
FILTHY DEGENERATE!
FLATTERY WILL GET YOU NOWHERE.
YOU'RE IN THE REAL WORLD NOW AND THE LUNATICS HAVE TAKEN OVER THE ASYLUM.
"APRIL SWEET IS COMING IN..."

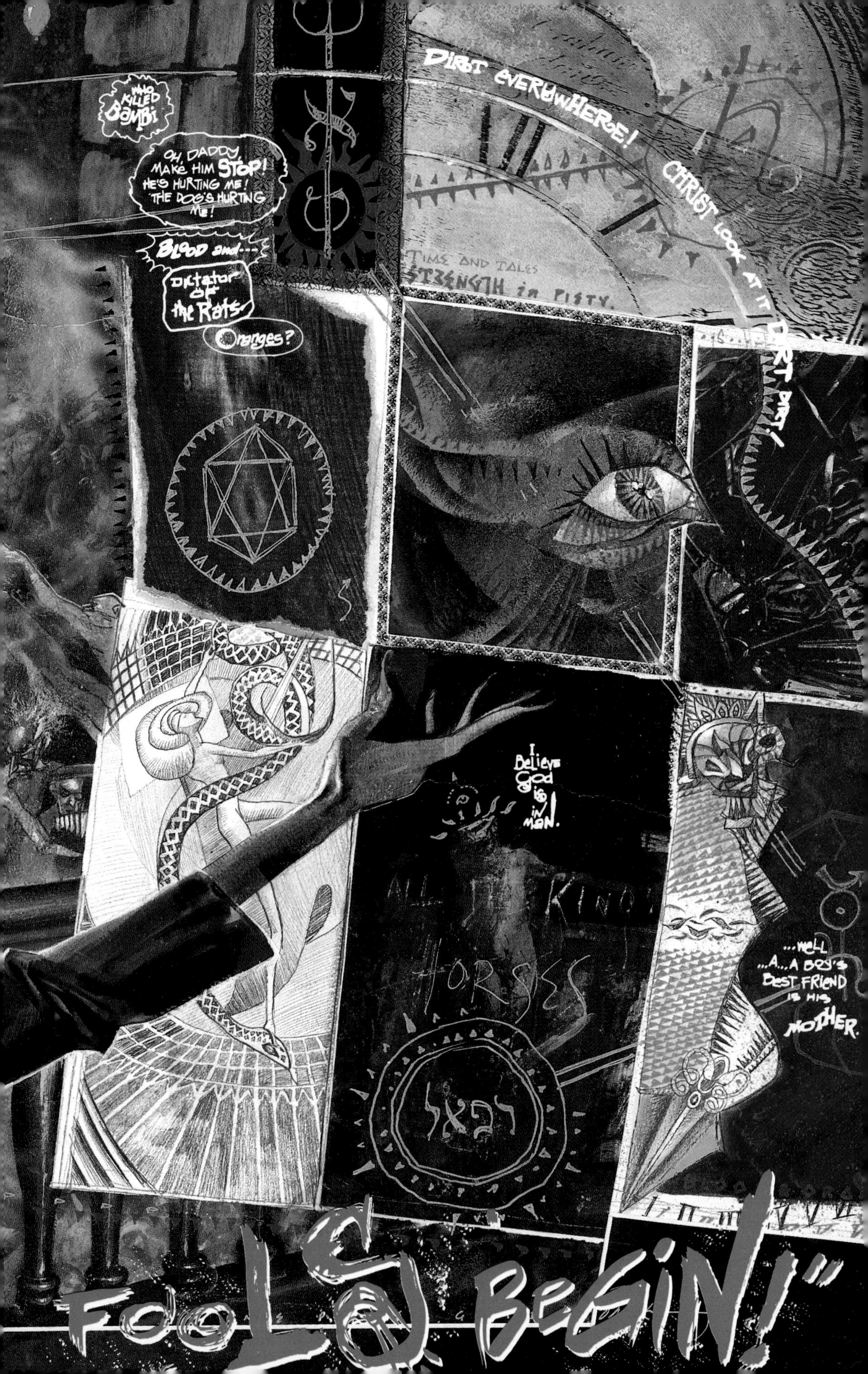
WHO KILLED BAMBI
OH, DADDY, MAKE HIM STOP! HE'S HURTING ME! THE DOG'S HURTING ME!
BLOOD AND---
DICTATOR OF THE RATS.
ORANGES?
DIRT EVERYWHERE!
CHRIST LOOK AT IT DIRT DIRT DIRT!
TIME AND TALES
STRENGTH IN PIETY.
I BELIEVE GOD IS IN MAN.
ALL THE KING'S
HORSES
...WELL ...A...A BOY'S BEST FRIEND IS HIS MOTHER.
FOOLS BEGIN!"

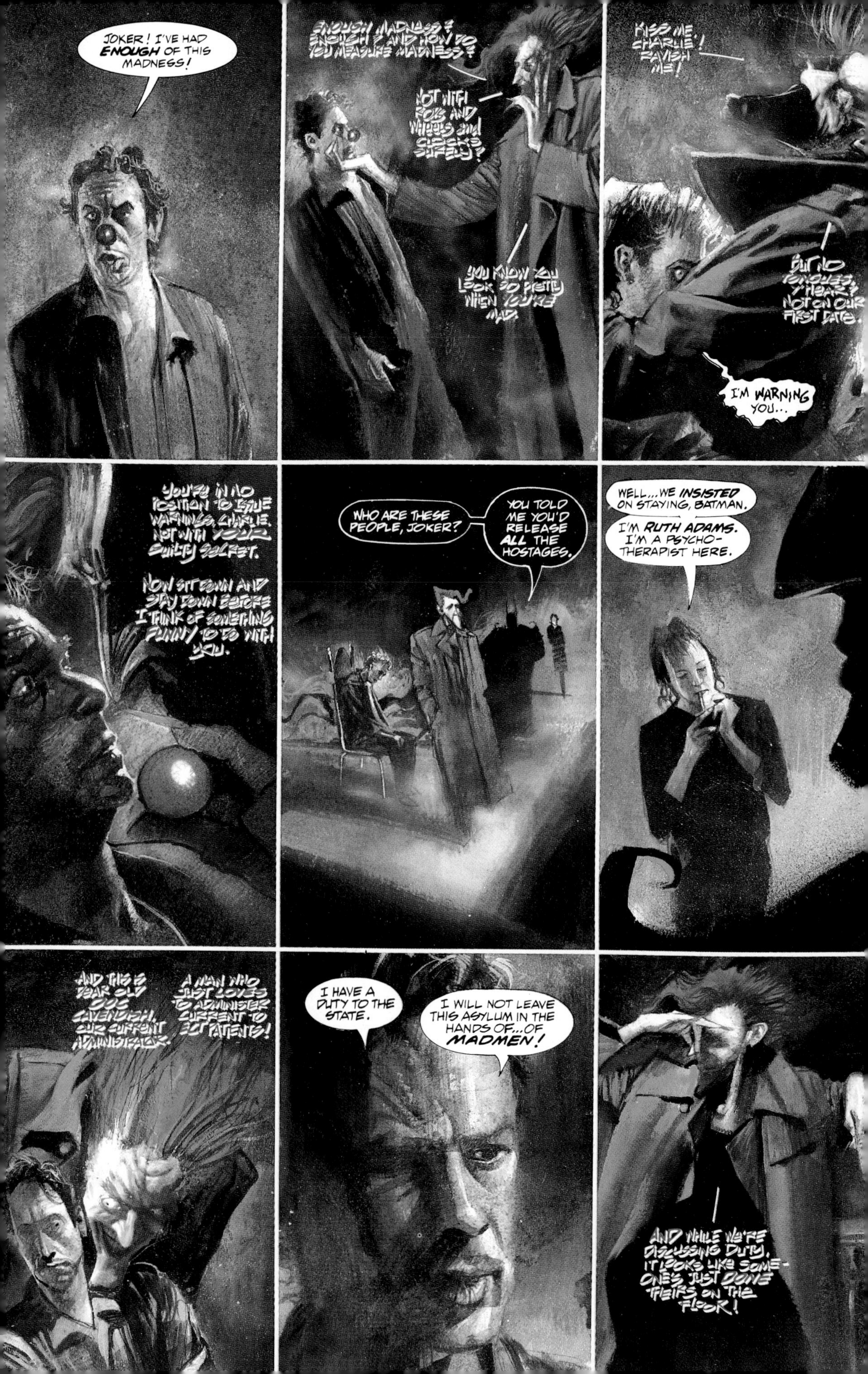
JOKER! I'VE HAD ENOUGH OF THIS MADNESS!
ENOUGH MADNESS? ENOUGH? AND HOW DO YOU MEASURE MADNESS?
NOT WITH RODS AND WHEELS AND CLOCKS, SURELY?
YOU KNOW YOU LOOK SO PRETTY WHEN YOU'RE MAD.
KISS ME, CHARLIE! RAVISH ME!
BUT NO TONGUES, Y'HEAR? NOT ON OUR FIRST DATE.
I'M WARNING YOU...
YOU'RE IN NO POSITION TO ISSUE WARNINGS, CHARLIE. NOT WITH YOUR GUILTY SECRET.
NOW SIT DOWN AND STAY DOWN BEFORE I THINK OF SOMETHING FUNNY TO DO WITH YOU.
WHO ARE THESE PEOPLE, JOKER?
YOU TOLD ME YOU'D RELEASE ALL THE HOSTAGES.
WELL... WE INSISTED ON STAYING, BATMAN.
I'M RUTH ADAMS. I'M A PSYCHO-THERAPIST HERE.
AND THIS IS DEAR OLD DOC CAVENDISH, OUR CURRENT ADMINISTRATOR.
A MAN WHO JUST LOVES TO ADMINISTER CURRENT TO ECT PATIENTS!
I HAVE A DUTY TO THE STATE.
I WILL NOT LEAVE THIS ASYLUM IN THE HANDS OF... OF MADMEN!
AND WHILE WE'RE DISCUSSING DUTY, IT LOOKS LIKE SOME-ONE'S JUST DONE THEIRS ON THE FLOOR!

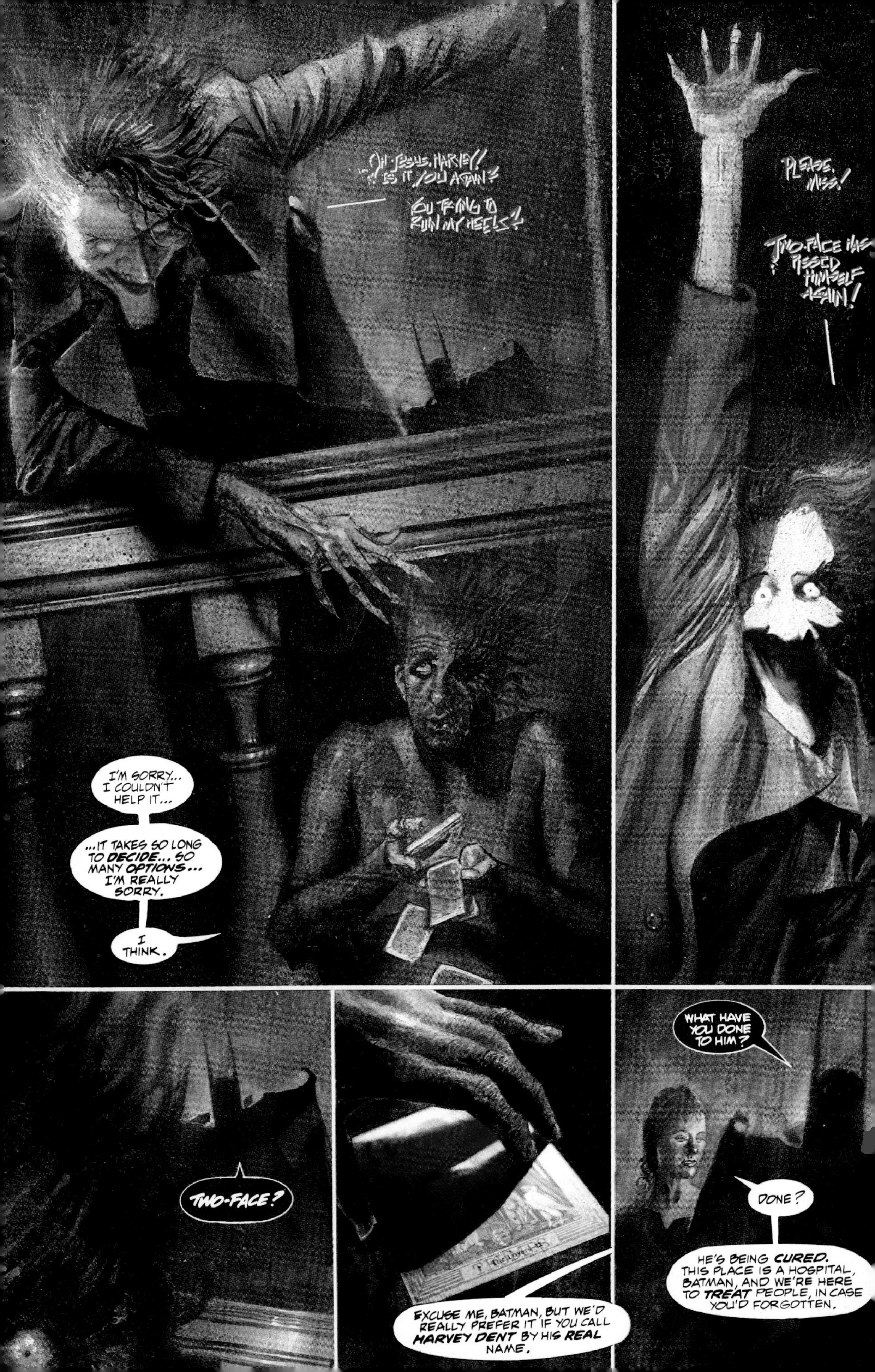
...OH JESUS, HARVEY! IS IT YOU AGAIN?
YOU TRYING TO RUIN MY HEELS?!
PLEASE, MISS!
TWO-FACE HAS PISSED HIMSELF AGAIN!
I'M SORRY... I COULDN'T HELP IT...
...IT TAKES SO LONG TO DECIDE... SO MANY OPTIONS... I'M REALLY SORRY.
I THINK.
TWO-FACE?
EXCUSE ME, BATMAN, BUT WE'D REALLY PREFER IT IF YOU CALL HARVEY DENT BY HIS REAL NAME.
WHAT HAVE YOU DONE TO HIM?
DONE?
HE'S BEING CURED. THIS PLACE IS A HOSPITAL, BATMAN, AND WE'RE HERE TO TREAT PEOPLE, IN CASE YOU'D FORGOTTEN.

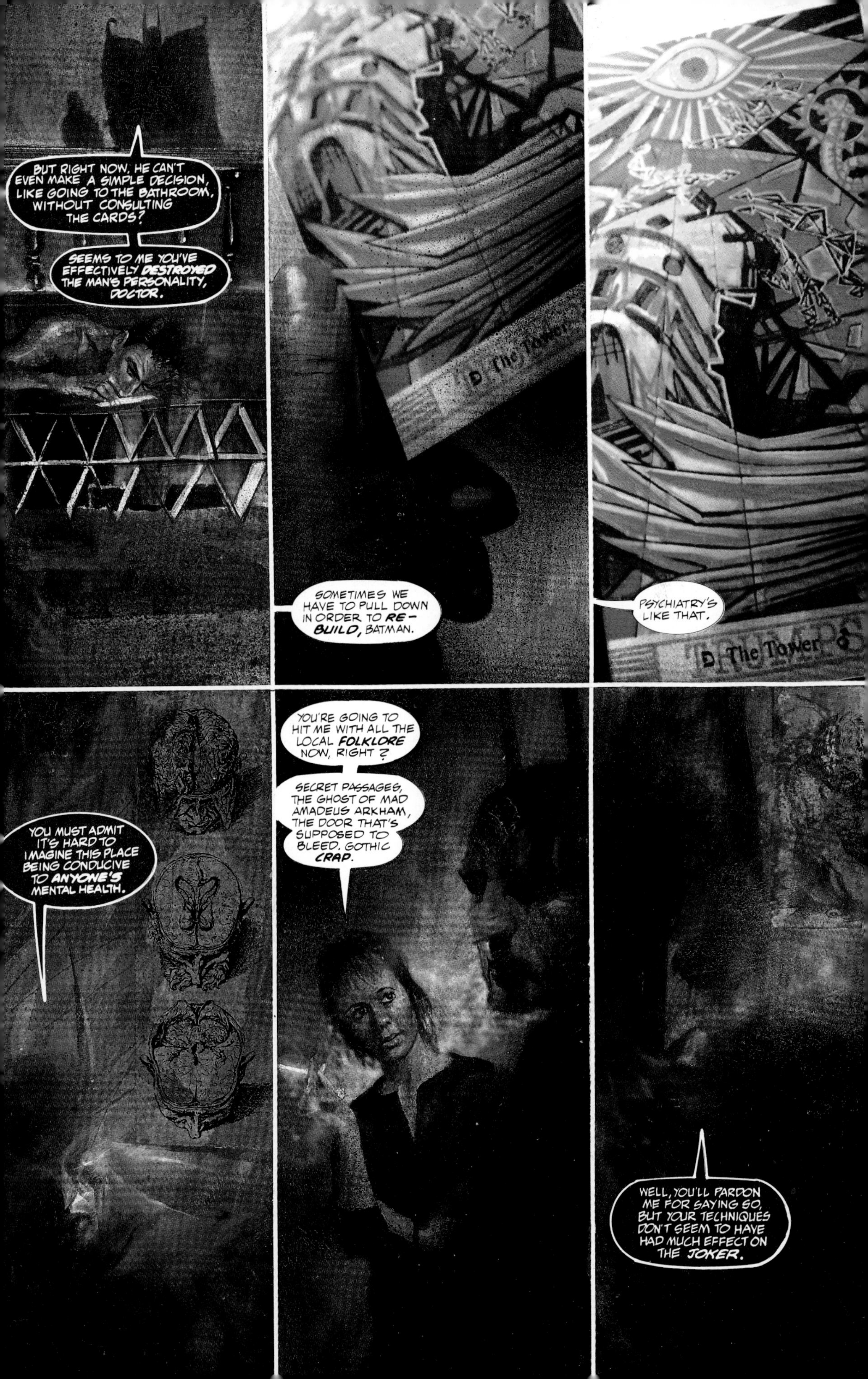
BUT RIGHT NOW, HE CAN'T EVEN MAKE A SIMPLE DECISION, LIKE GOING TO THE BATHROOM, WITHOUT CONSULTING THE CARDS?
SEEMS TO ME YOU'VE EFFECTIVELY DESTROYED THE MAN'S PERSONALITY, DOCTOR.
The Tower
SOMETIMES WE HAVE TO PULL DOWN IN ORDER TO RE-BUILD, BATMAN.
PSYCHIATRY'S LIKE THAT.
TRUMPS
The Tower
YOU MUST ADMIT IT'S HARD TO IMAGINE THIS PLACE BEING CONDUCIVE TO ANYONE'S MENTAL HEALTH.
YOU'RE GOING TO HIT ME WITH ALL THE LOCAL FOLKLORE NOW, RIGHT?
SECRET PASSAGES, THE GHOST OF MAD AMADEUS ARKHAM, THE DOOR THAT'S SUPPOSED TO BLEED. GOTHIC CRAP.
WELL, YOU'LL PARDON ME FOR SAYING SO, BUT YOUR TECHNIQUES DON'T SEEM TO HAVE HAD MUCH EFFECT ON THE JOKER.

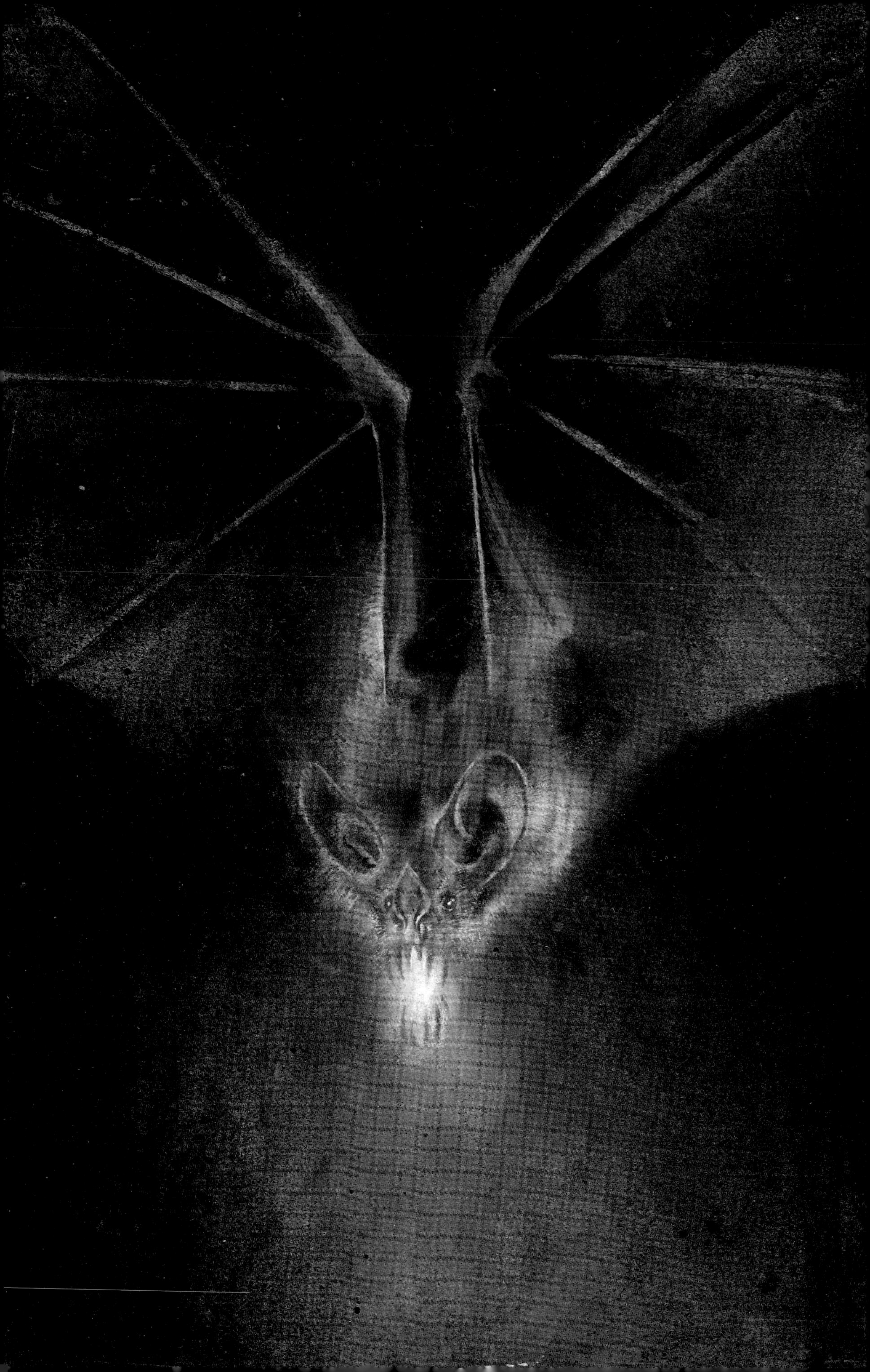

NOTHING. I DON'T SEE ANY-THING.

NOT EVEN A CUTE LITTLE LONG-LEGGED BOY IN SWIMMING TRUNKS?

STOP WASTING TIME, YOU UGLY, PRANCING BASTARD!

WELL, HE IS *OURS* TOO, YOU KNOW. THAT'S IF YOU DON'T MIND...

I SAY WE TAKE OFF HIS MASK.

I WANT TO SEE HIS *REAL* FACE.

OH, DON'T BE SO PREDICTABLE, FOR CHRIST'S SAKE!

THAT IS HIS REAL FACE.

AND I WANT TO GO MUCH DEEPER THAN THAT.

I WANT HIM TO KNOW WHAT IT'S LIKE TO HAVE STICKY FINGERS PICK THROUGH THE DIRTY CORNERS OF HIS MIND.

SO LET'S START WITH A WORD ASSOCIATION TEST, SHALL WE?

RUTHIE?

I DON'T REALLY WANT TO DO THIS...

GO AHEAD, DR. ADAMS. I'M NOT AFRAID.

IT'S JUST WORDS.

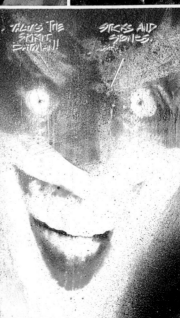

THAT'S THE SPIRIT, BATMAN!

STICKS AND STONES.

I LIKE A MAN WHO CAN TAKE THE PRESSURE.

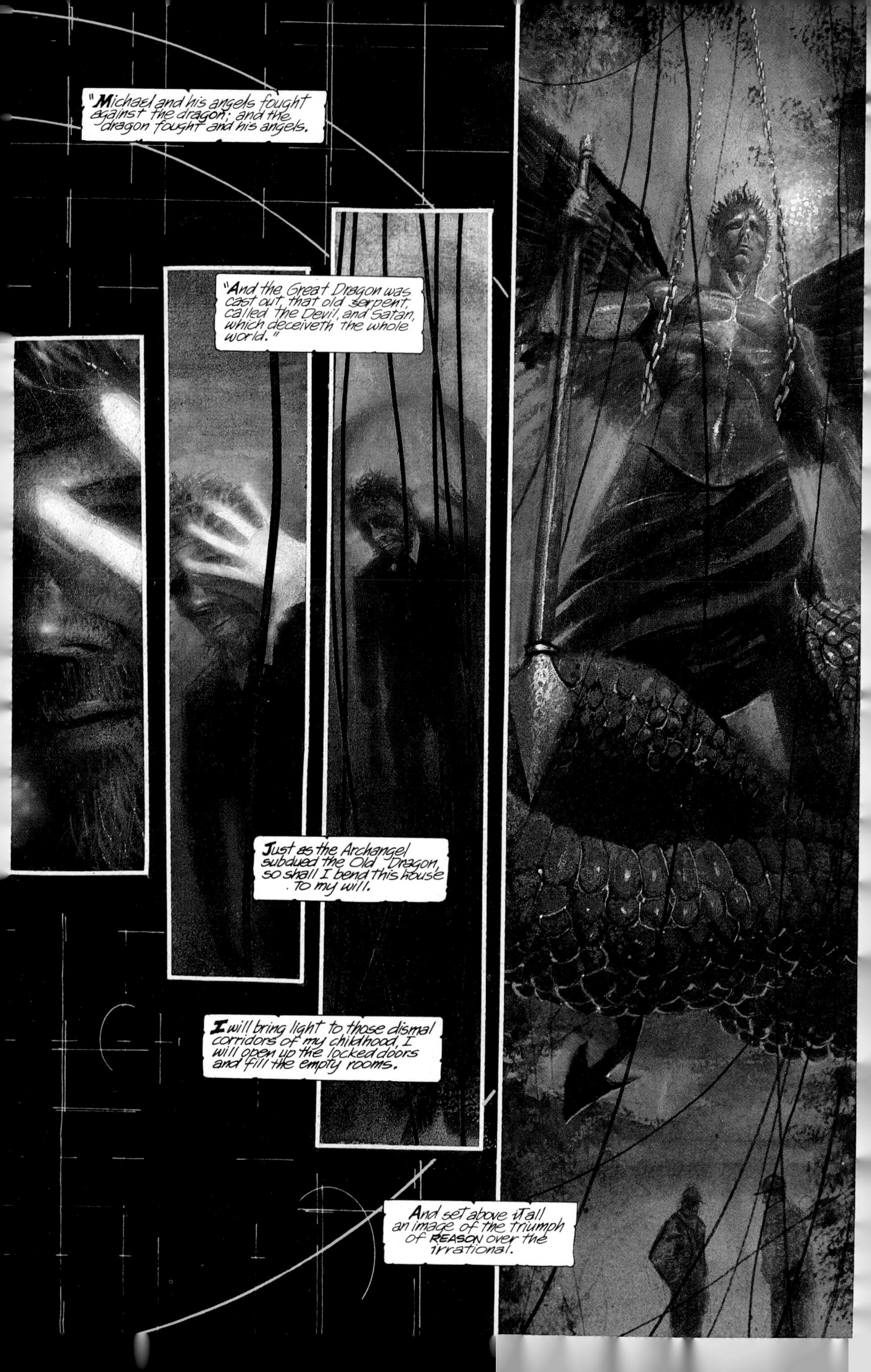
"Michael and his angels fought against the dragon; and the dragon fought and his angels.
"And the Great Dragon was cast out, that old serpent, called the Devil, and Satan, which deceiveth the whole world."
Just as the Archangel subdued the Old Dragon, so shall I bend this house to my will.
I will bring light to those dismal corridors of my childhood, I will open up the locked doors and fill the empty rooms.
And set above it all an image of the triumph of REASON over the irrational.

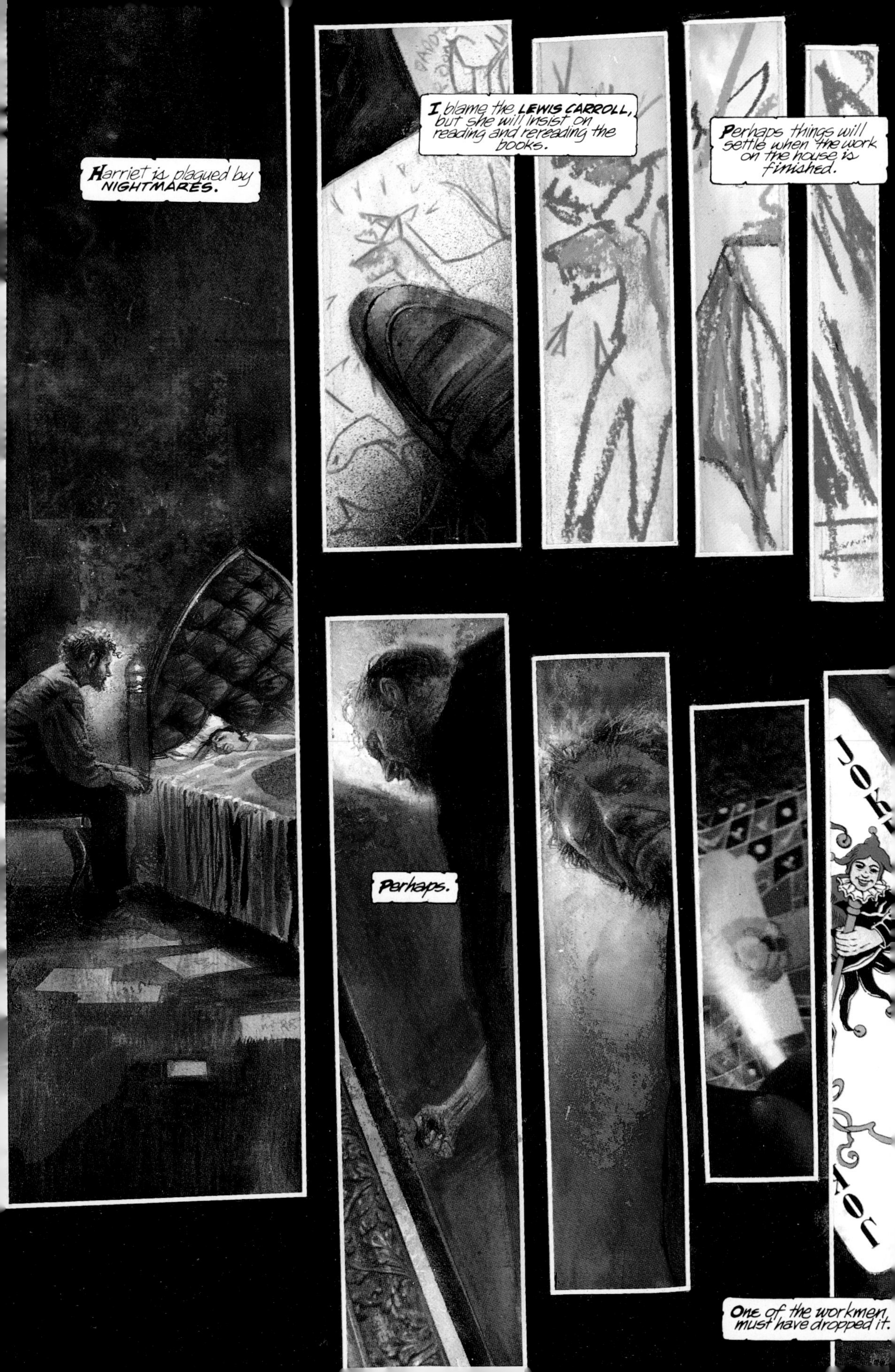
Harriet is plagued by NIGHTMARES.
I blame the LEWIS CARROLL, but she will insist on reading and rereading the books.
Perhaps things will settle when the work on the house is finished.
Perhaps.
One of the workmen must have dropped it.

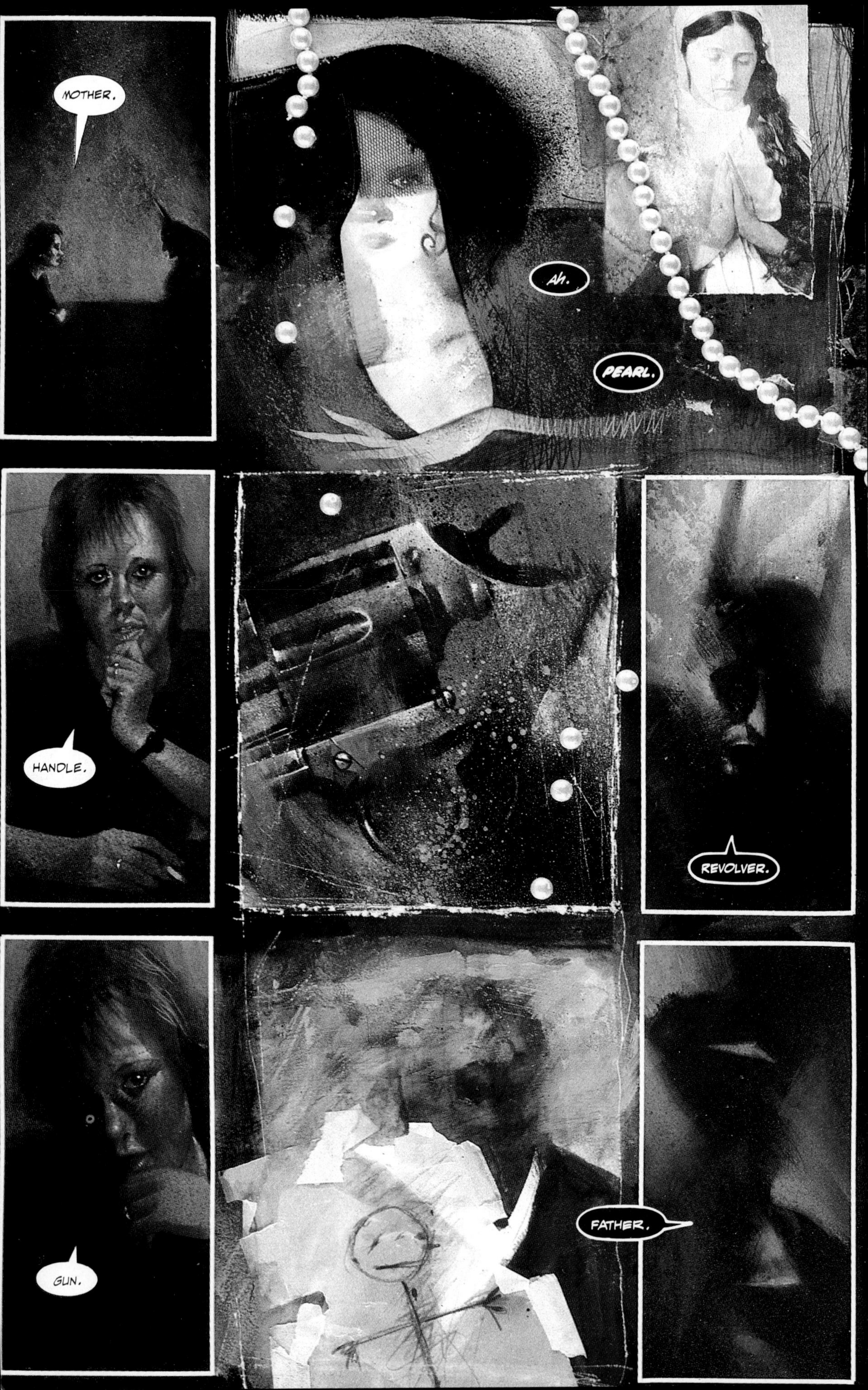
MOTHER.
Ah.
PEARL.
HANDLE.
REVOLVER.
GUN.
FATHER.

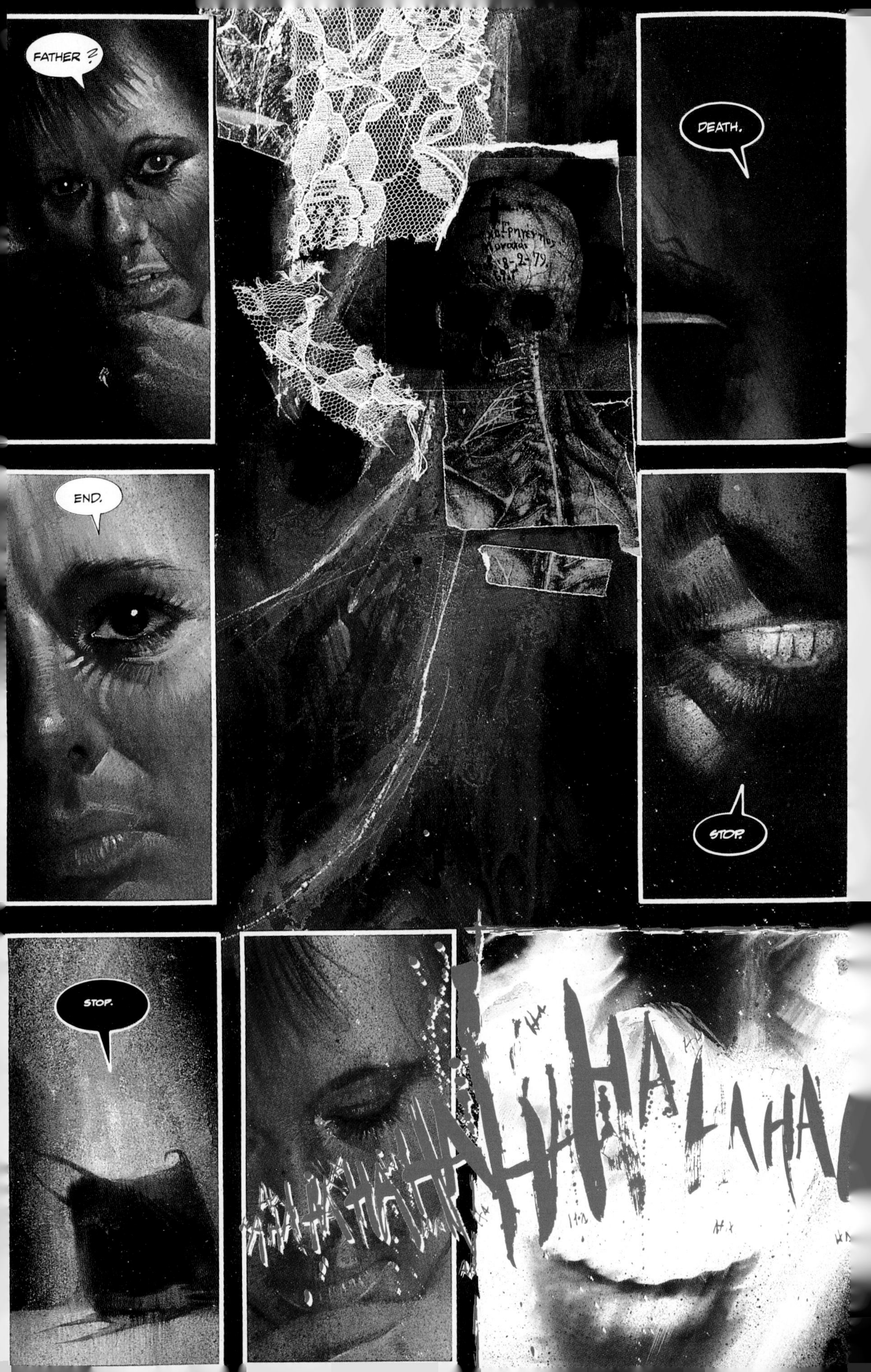
FATHER?
DEATH.
END.
STOP.
STOP.
HAHAHAHAHA HA HA HA

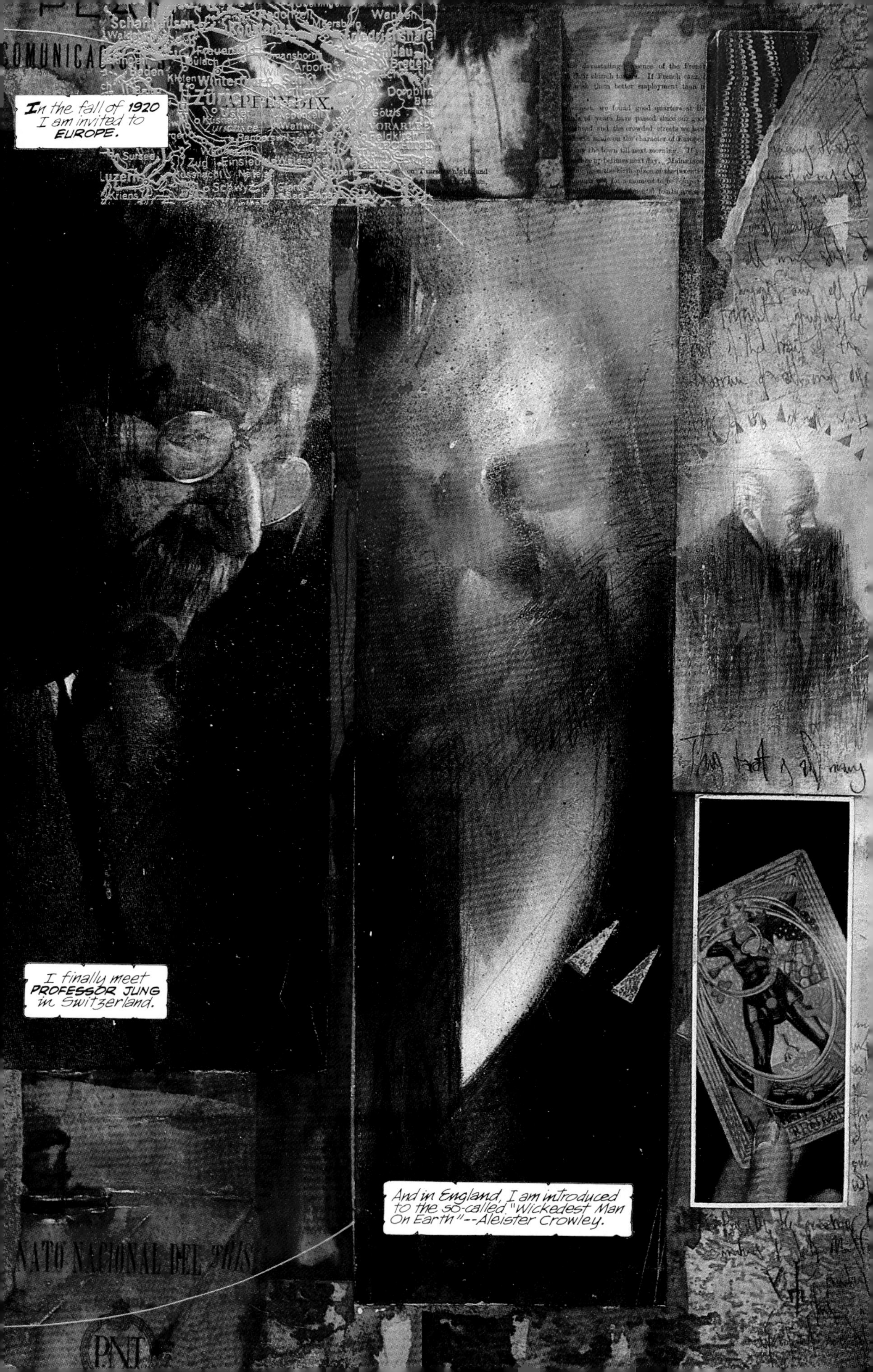
In the fall of 1920 I am invited to EUROPE.
I finally meet PROFESSOR JUNG in Switzerland.
And in England, I am introduced to the so-called "Wickedest Man On Earth"--Aleister Crowley.

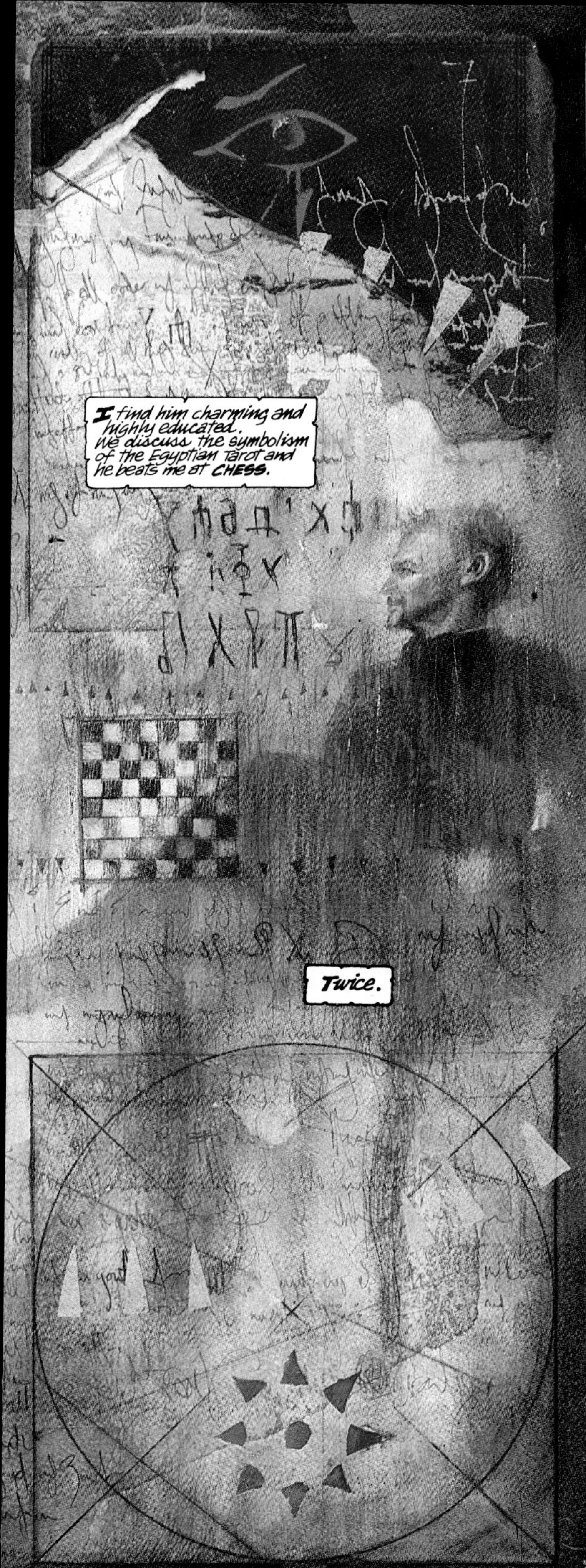
I find him charming and highly educated.
We discuss the symbolism of the Egyptian Tarot and he beats me at CHESS.
Twice.
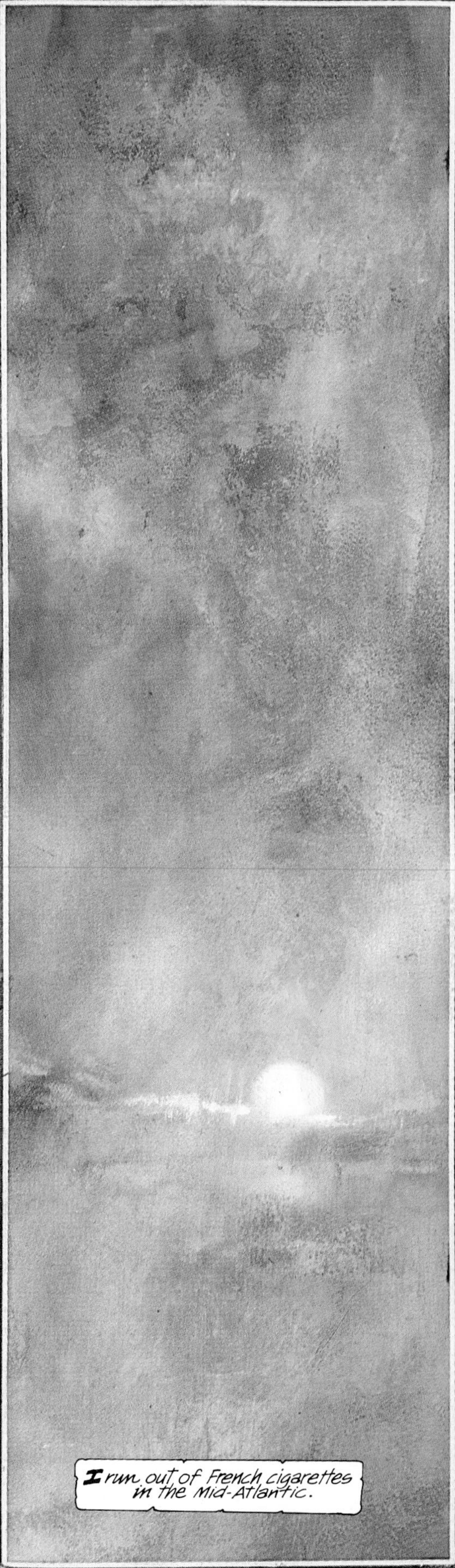
I run out of French cigarettes in the Mid-Atlantic.

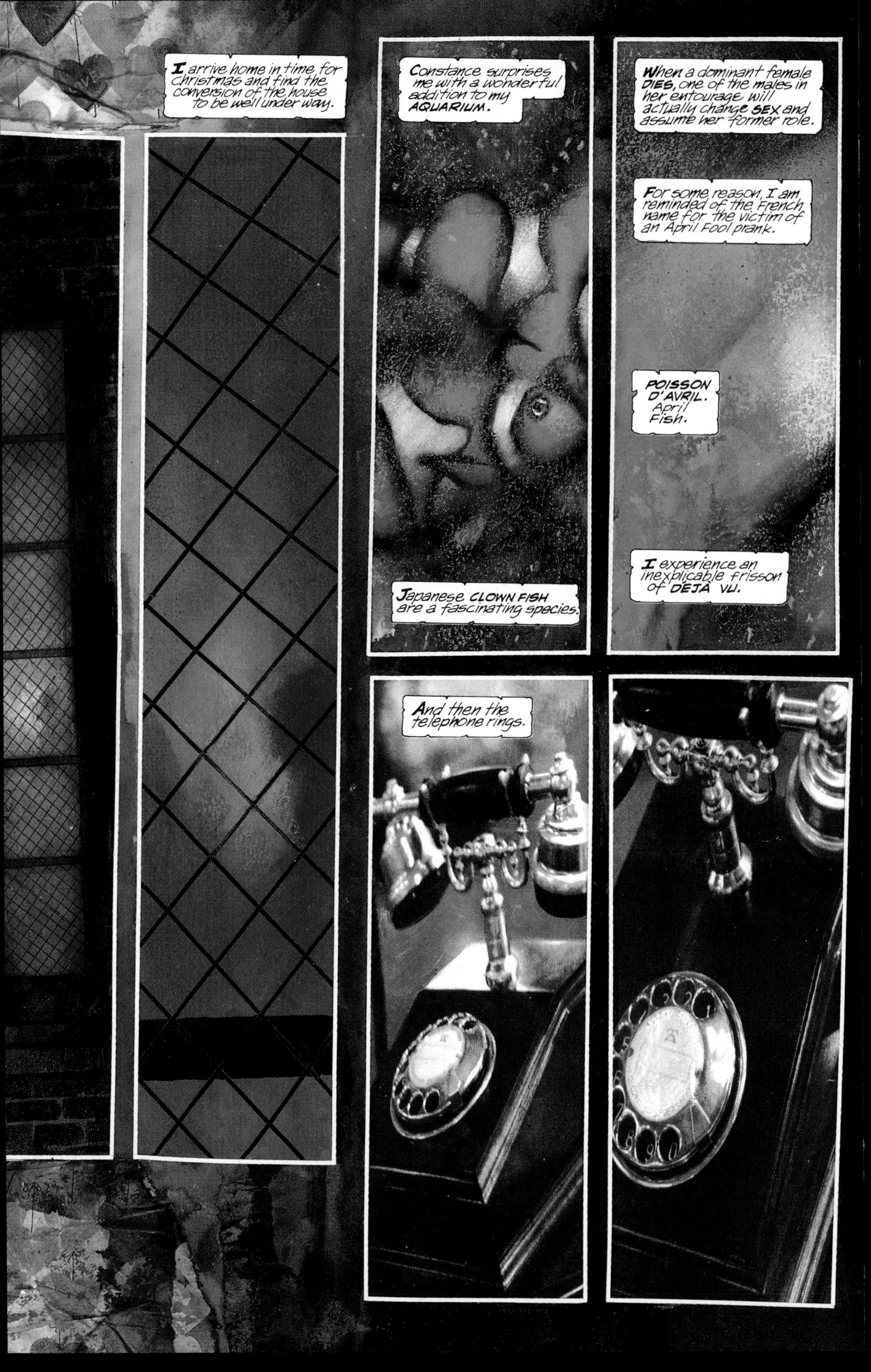
I arrive home in time for Christmas and find the conversion of the house to be well under way.
Constance surprises me with a wonderful addition to my AQUARIUM.
Japanese CLOWN FISH are a fascinating species.
When a dominant female DIES, one of the males in her entourage will actually change SEX and assume her former role.
For some reason, I am reminded of the French name for the victim of an April Fool prank.
POISSON D'AVRIL. April Fish.
I experience an inexplicable frisson of DÉJÀ VU.
And then the telephone rings.

It transpires that Martin Hawkins has escaped from the Penitentiary and the Police would like my considered opinion as to his state of mind.

I tell them he may be highly dangerous and I leave them to it.

It's not my problem.

Not tonight.

IS SOMETHING WRONG?

NO. IT'S **NOTHING**.

NOTHING AT ALL.

Harriet is enchanted by the Cuckoo Clock I have brought her from Switzerland.

I pray that it might take her mind from the bad dreams.

Then I remind myself that all intelligent children suffer bad dreams.

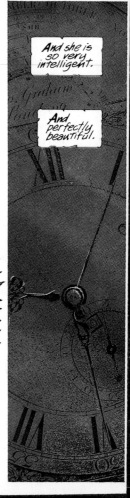

And she is so very intelligent.

And perfectly beautiful.

I almost wish she need never grow up.

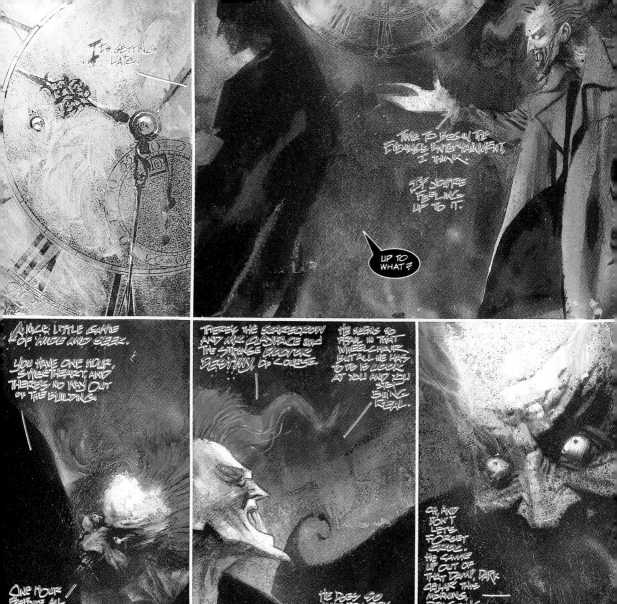

IT'S GETTING LATE.

TIME TO BEGIN THE EVENING'S ENTERTAINMENT, I THINK.

IF YOU'RE FEELING UP TO IT.

UP TO WHAT?

A NICE LITTLE GAME OF HIDE AND SEEK.

YOU HAVE ONE HOUR, SWEETHEART, AND THERE'S NO WAY OUT OF THE BUILDING.

ONE HOUR BEFORE ALL YOUR FRIENDS COME LOOKING FOR YOU.

THERE'S THE SCARECROW AND MR. CLAYFACE AND THE STRANGE DOCTOR DESTINY, OF COURSE.

HE DOES SO WANT TO LOOK AT YOU, DARLING.

HE SEEMS SO FRAIL IN THAT WHEELCHAIR, BUT ALL HE HAS TO DO IS LOOK AT YOU AND YOU'RE BEING REAL.

OH, AND DON'T LET'S FORGET ZELL. HE CAME UP OUT OF THAT DAMP, DARK CELLAR THIS MORNING, DRAGGING HIS CHAINS BEHIND HIM.

THEY'LL WANT TO SEE YOU, SO WHY DON'T YOU JUST RUN ALONG NOW!

I DON'T TAKE ORDERS FROM YOU.

WELL...

THIS GUY GOES INTO THE HOSPITAL, OKAY?...HIS WIFE'S JUST HAD A BABY AND HE CAN'T WAIT TO SEE THEM BOTH.

SO HE MEETS THE DOCTOR AND HE SAYS, "OH, GEE, I'VE BEEN SO WORRIED. HOW ARE THEY?"

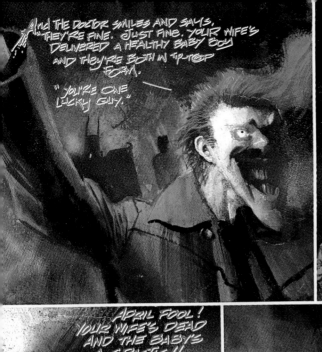

And the doctor smiles and says, "They're fine. Just fine. Your wife's delivered a healthy baby boy and they're both in tip-top form.

"You're one lucky guy."

So the guy rushes into the maternity ward with his flowers.

But it's empty.

His wife's bed is empty.

"Doc?" he says and turns around and the doctor and all the nurses wave their arms and scream in his face.

April fool! Your wife's dead and the baby's a spastic!!

Get it?

Oh, what a senseless waste of human life!

Now, Batman.

Run.

The game ends at midnight! Run!

RUN!

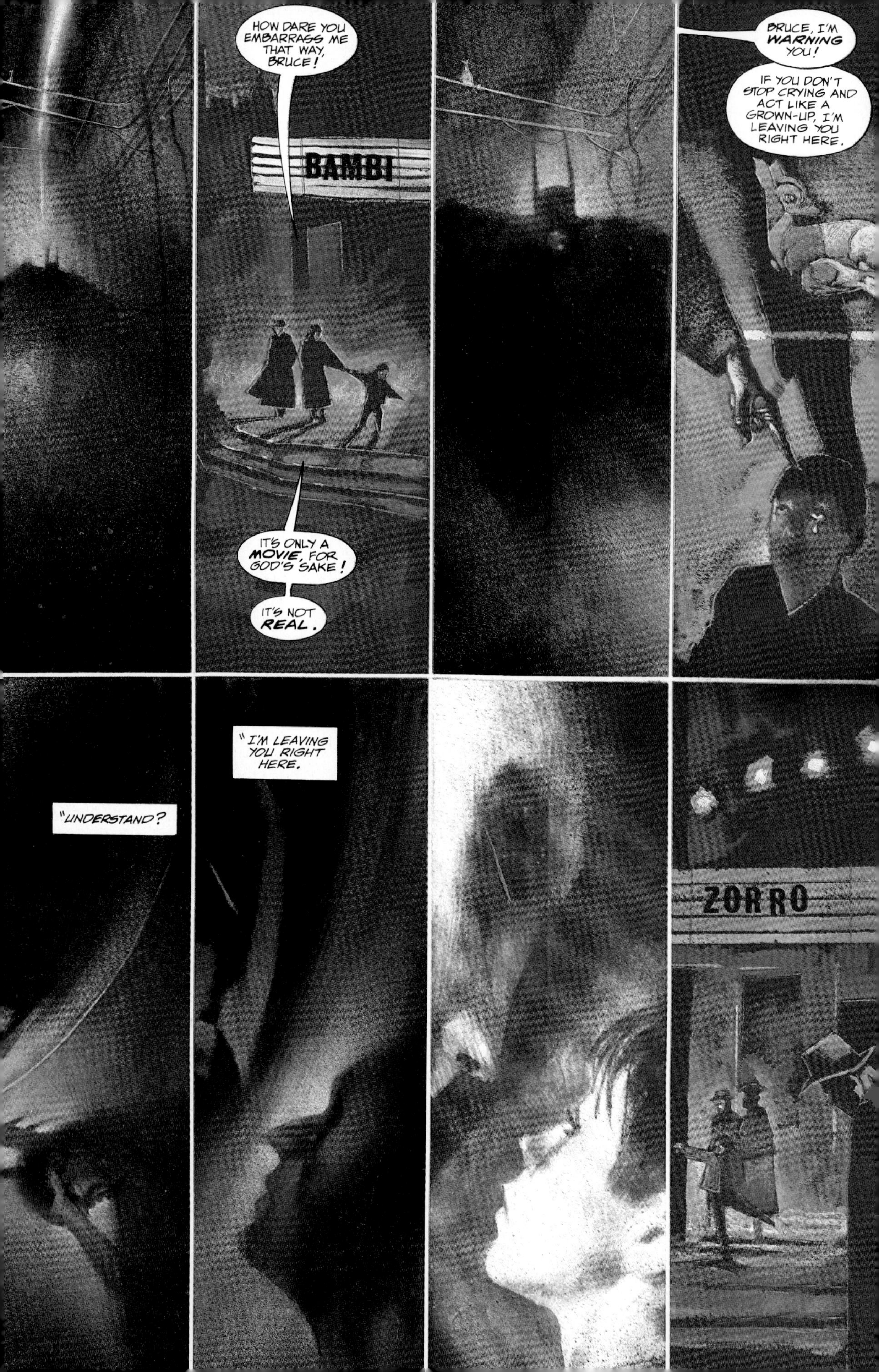
HOW DARE YOU EMBARRASS ME THAT WAY, BRUCE!
IT'S ONLY A MOVIE, FOR GOD'S SAKE!
IT'S NOT REAL.
BRUCE, I'M WARNING YOU!
IF YOU DON'T STOP CRYING AND ACT LIKE A GROWN-UP, I'M LEAVING YOU RIGHT HERE.
"UNDERSTAND?
"I'M LEAVING YOU RIGHT HERE.
ZORRO

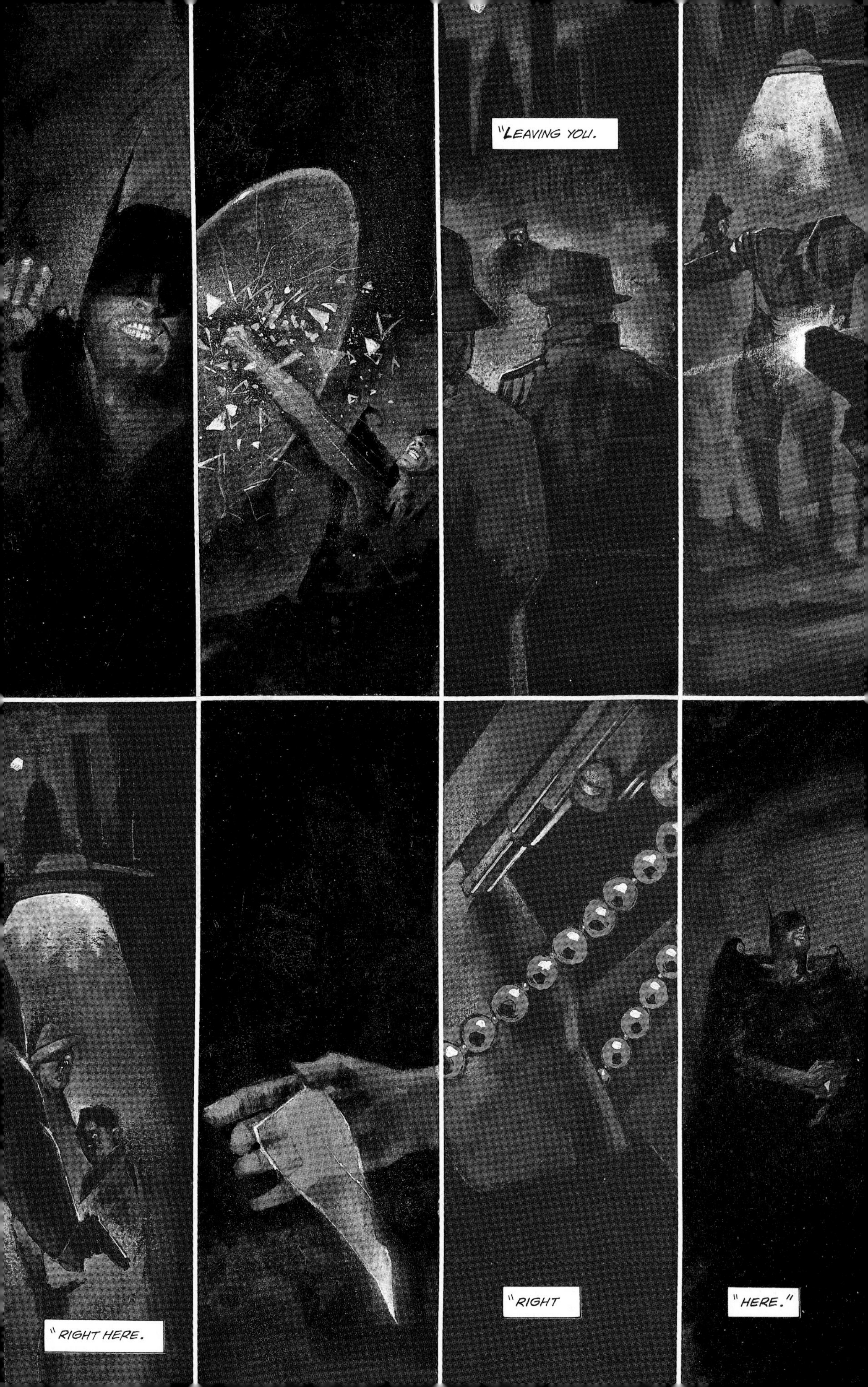
"LEAVING YOU.
"RIGHT HERE.
"RIGHT
"HERE."

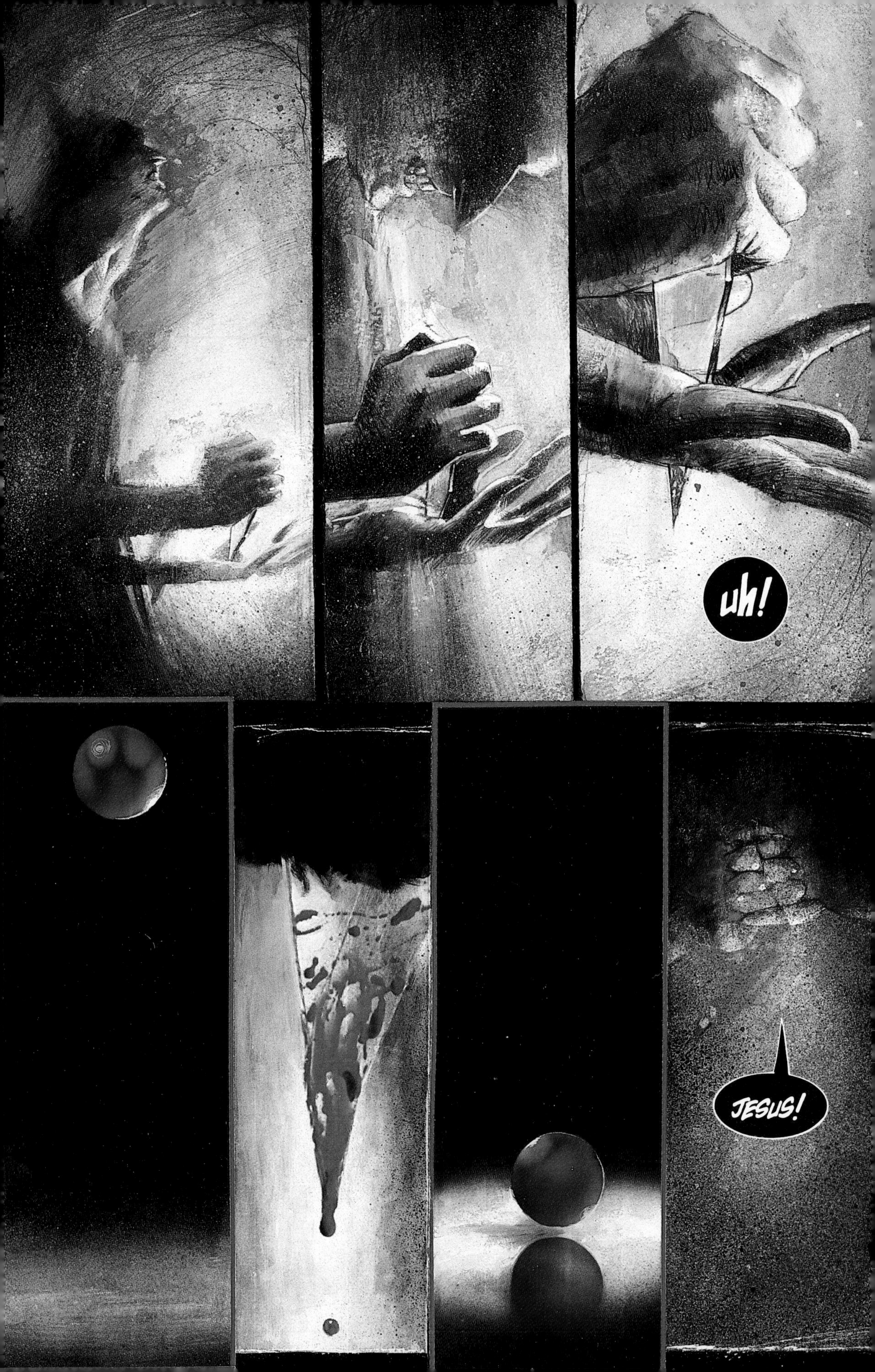
uh!
JESUS!

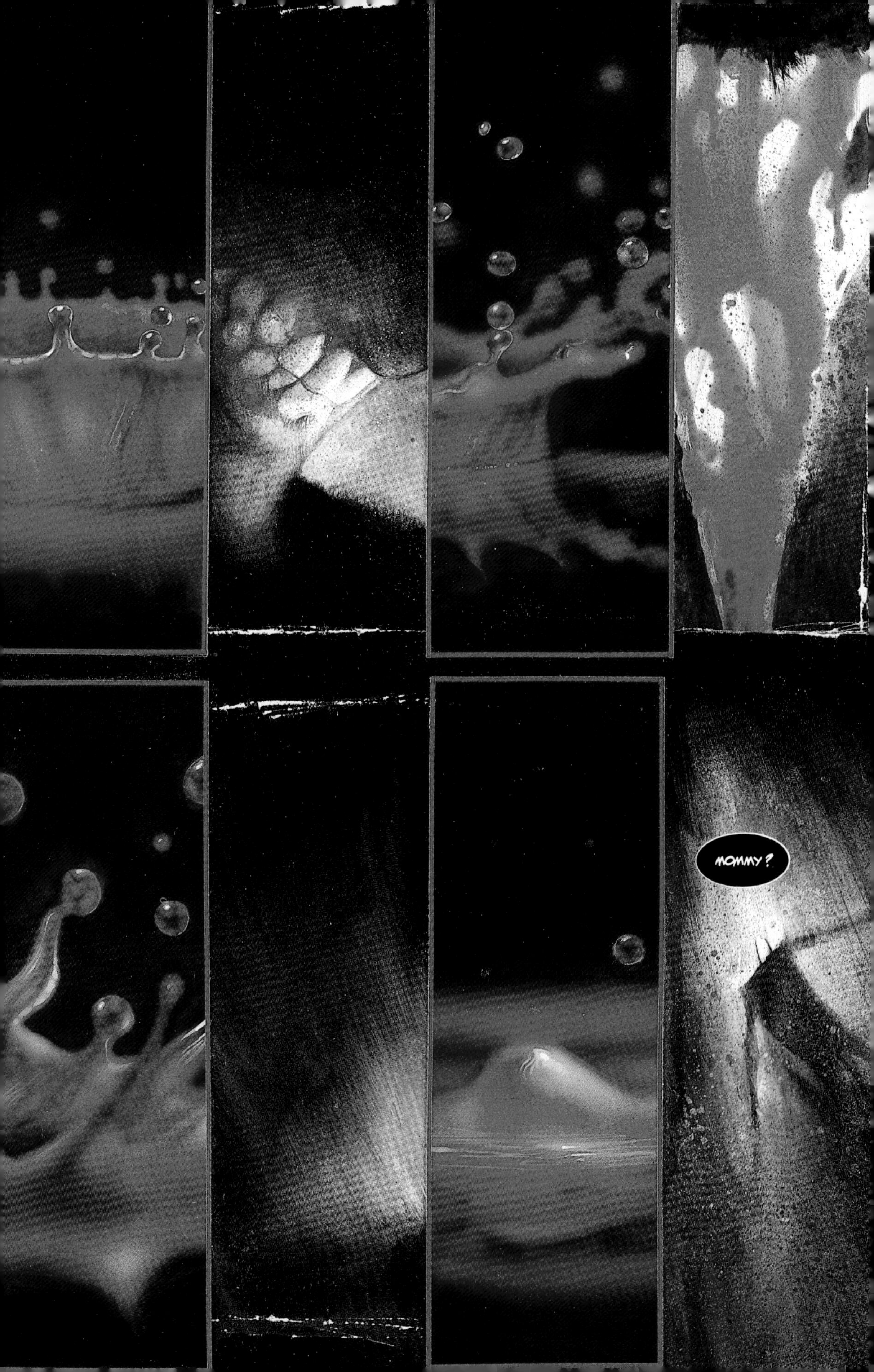
MOMMY?

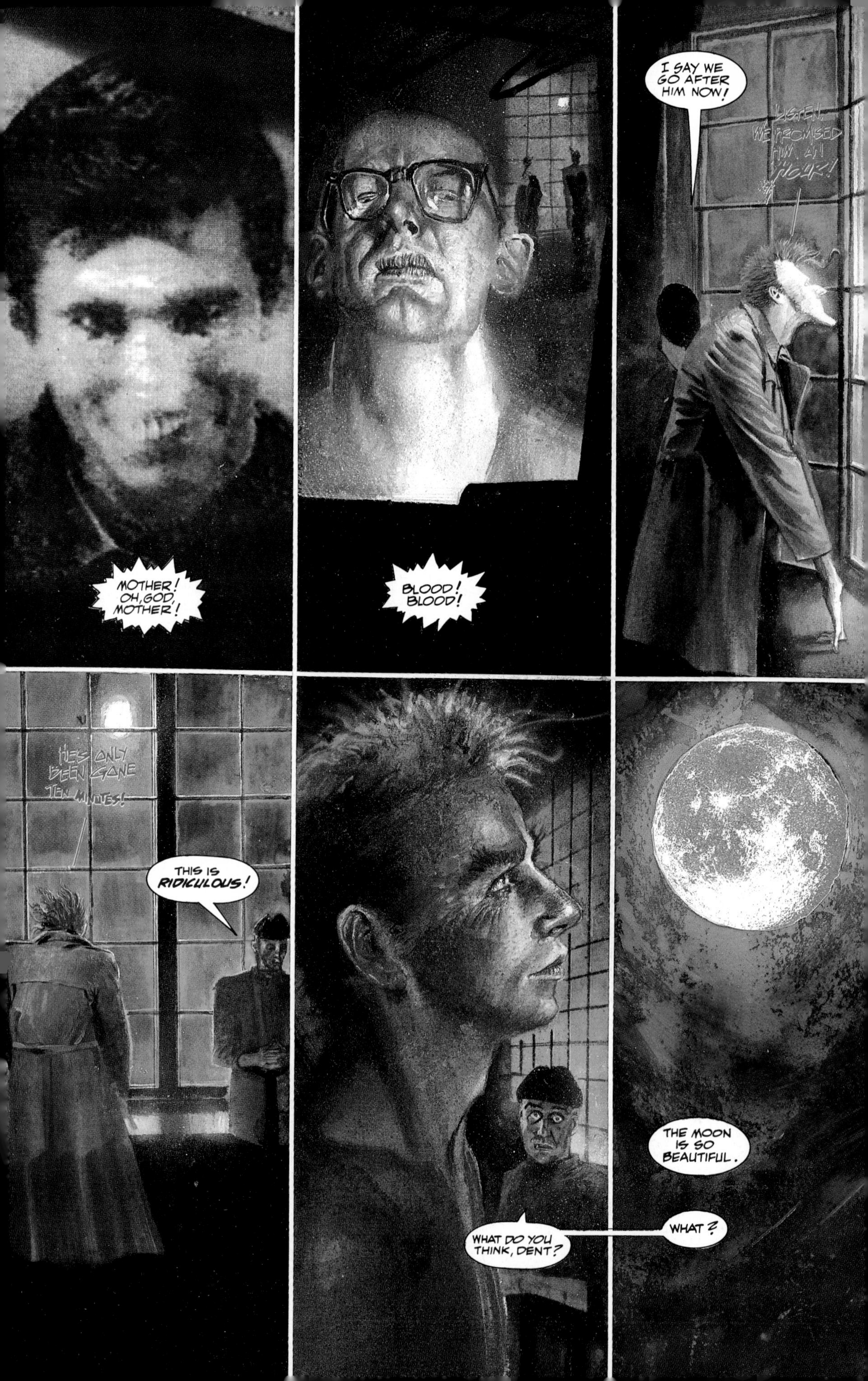
MOTHER! OH, GOD, MOTHER!
BLOOD! BLOOD!
I SAY WE GO AFTER HIM NOW!
LISTEN. WE PROMISED HIM AN HOUR!
HE'S ONLY BEEN GONE TEN MINUTES!
THIS IS RIDICULOUS!
WHAT DO YOU THINK, DENT?
WHAT?
THE MOON IS SO BEAUTIFUL.

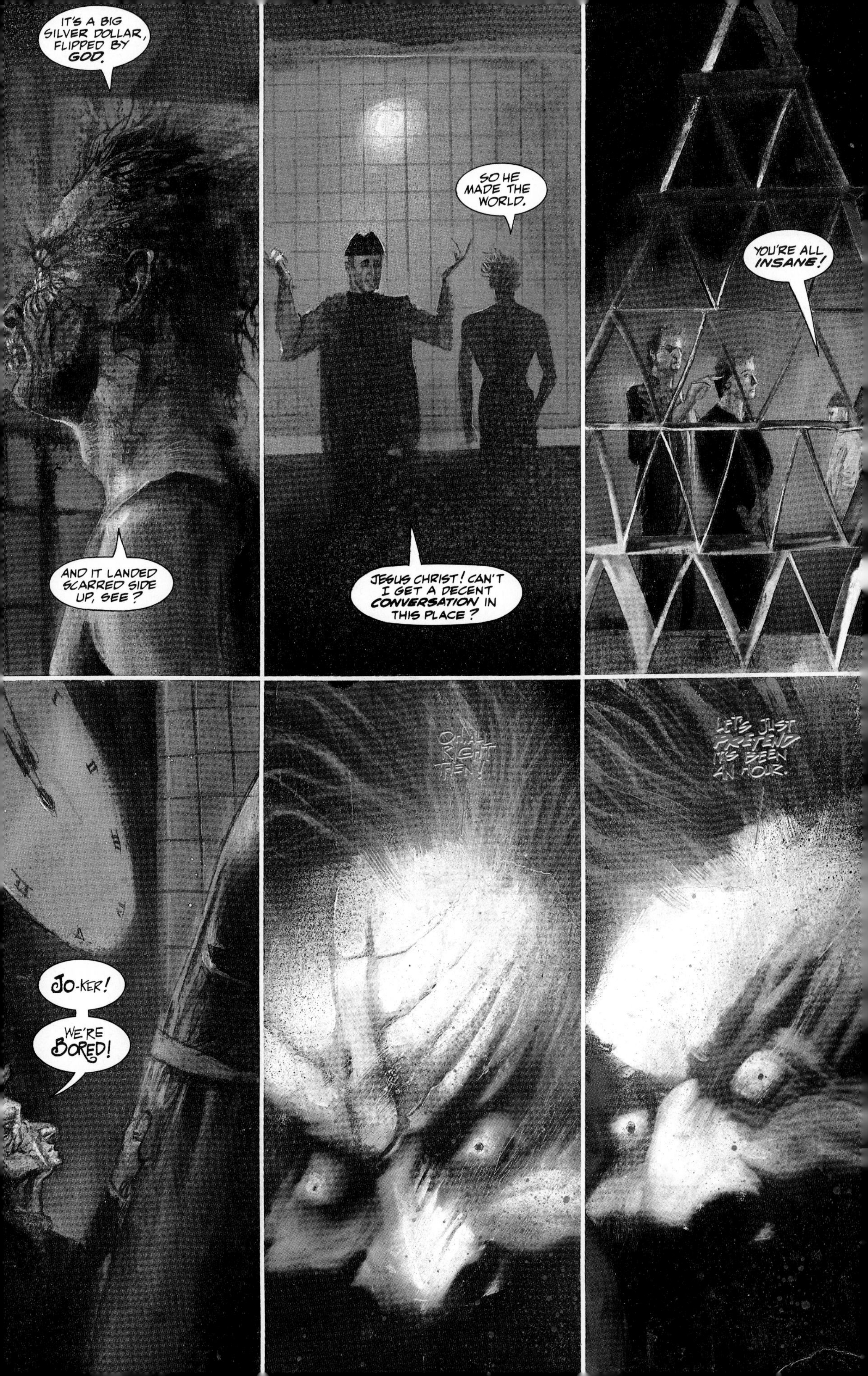
IT'S A BIG SILVER DOLLAR, FLIPPED BY GOD.
AND IT LANDED SCARRED SIDE UP, SEE?
SO HE MADE THE WORLD.
JESUS CHRIST! CAN'T I GET A DECENT CONVERSATION IN THIS PLACE?
YOU'RE ALL INSANE!
JO-KER!
WE'RE BORED!
OH ALL RIGHT THEN!
LET'S JUST PRETEND IT'S BEEN AN HOUR.

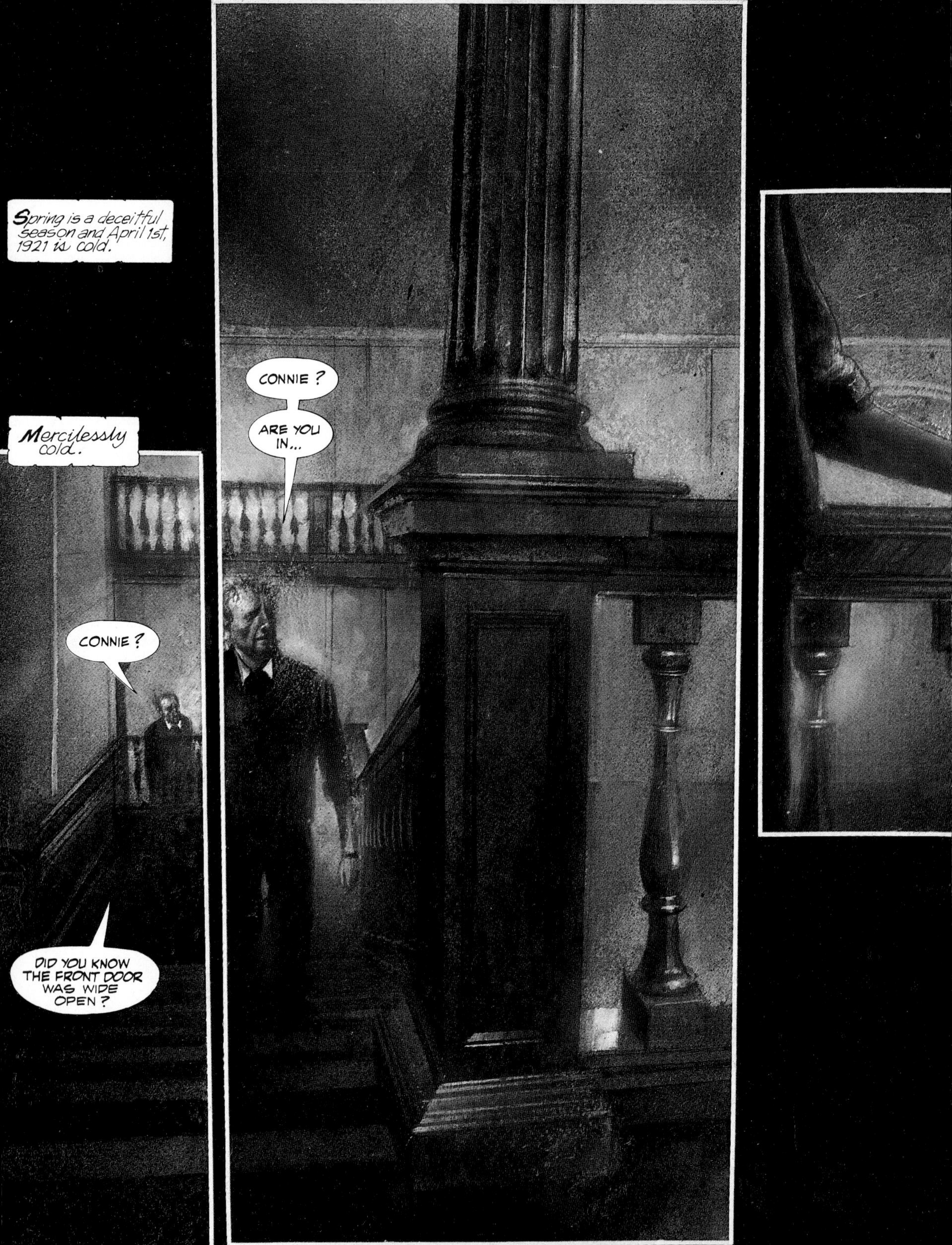
Spring is a deceitful season and April 1st, 1921 is cold.
Mercilessly cold.
CONNIE?
DID YOU KNOW THE FRONT DOOR WAS WIDE OPEN?
CONNIE?
ARE YOU IN...

I see my **WIFE** first, my do my **CONSTANCE**

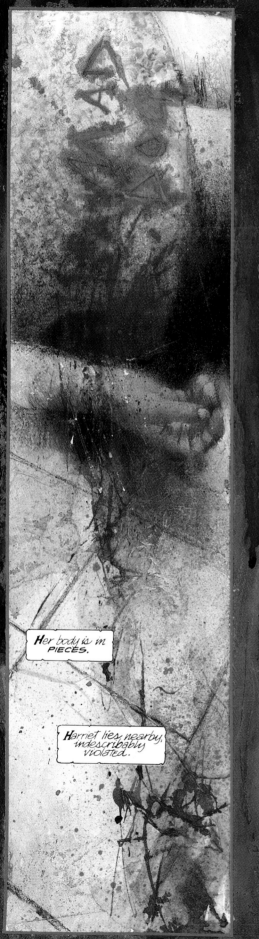

Her body is in **PIECES**.

Harriet lies nearby, indescribably violated.

Almost **IDLY**, I wonder where her **HEAD** is.

And then I look at the doll's house.

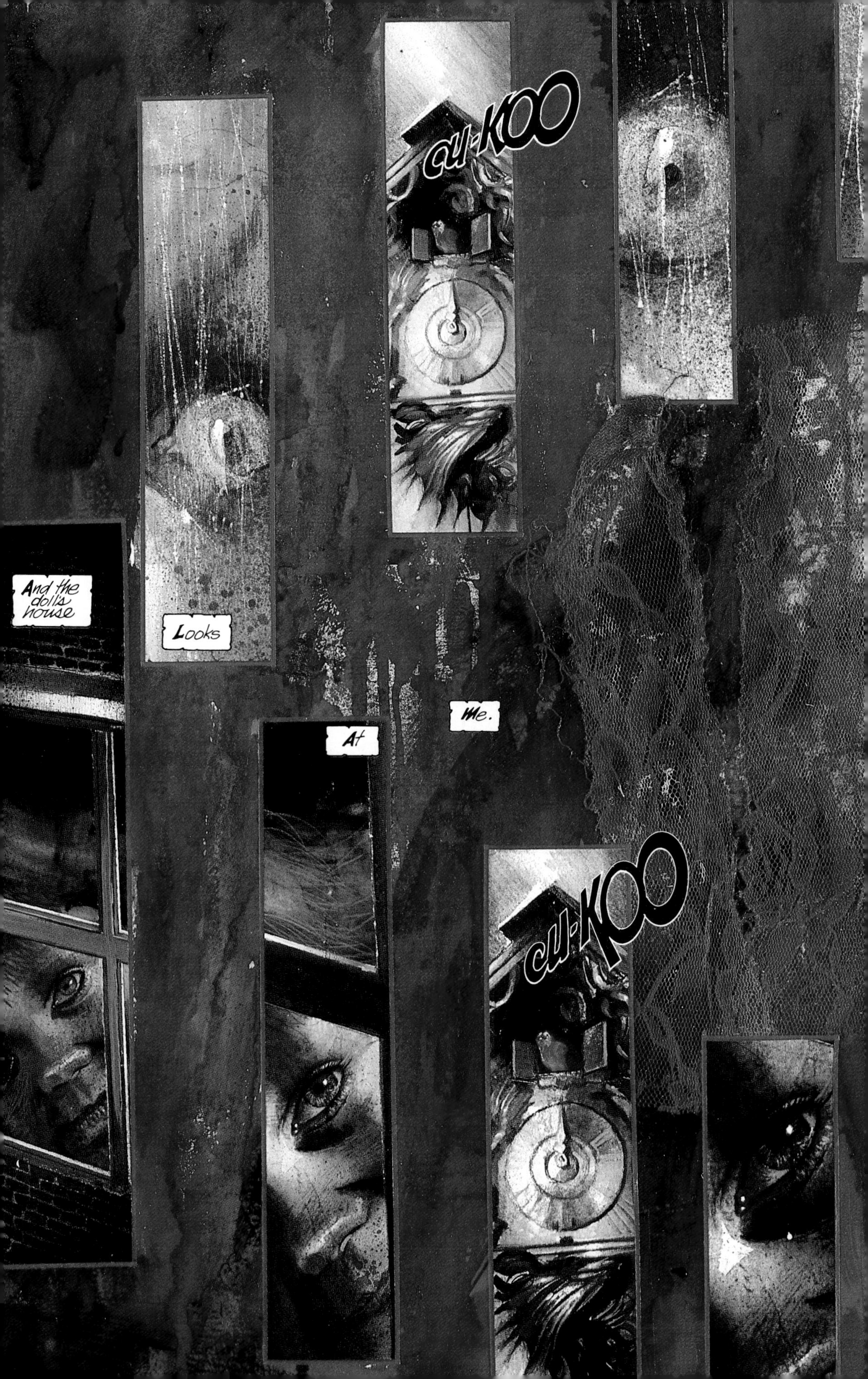
CU-KOO
And the doll's house
Looks
At
Me.
CU-KOO

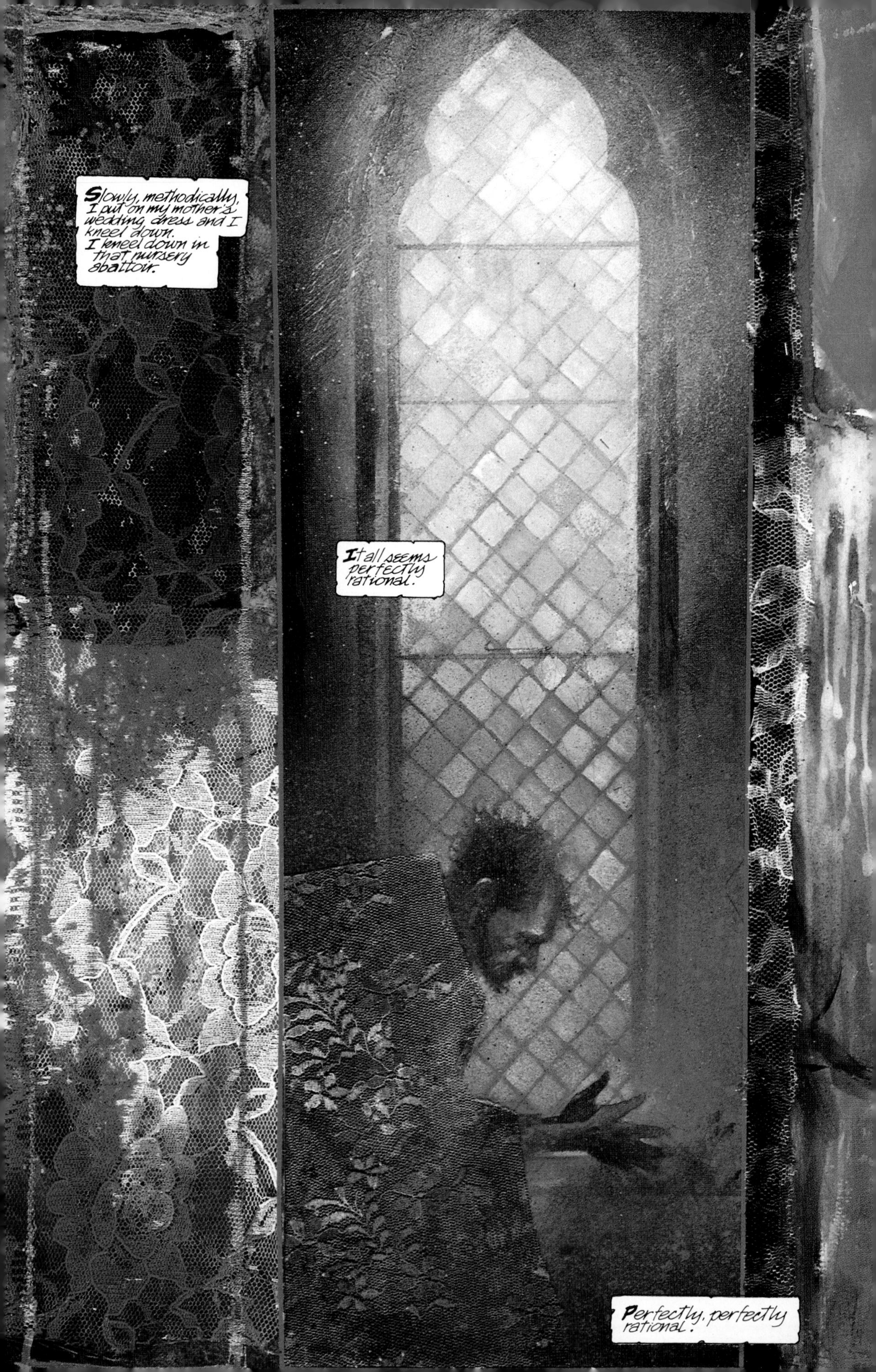
Slowly, methodically, I put on my mother's wedding dress and I kneel down. I kneel down in that nursery abattoir.
It all seems perfectly rational.
Perfectly, perfectly rational.

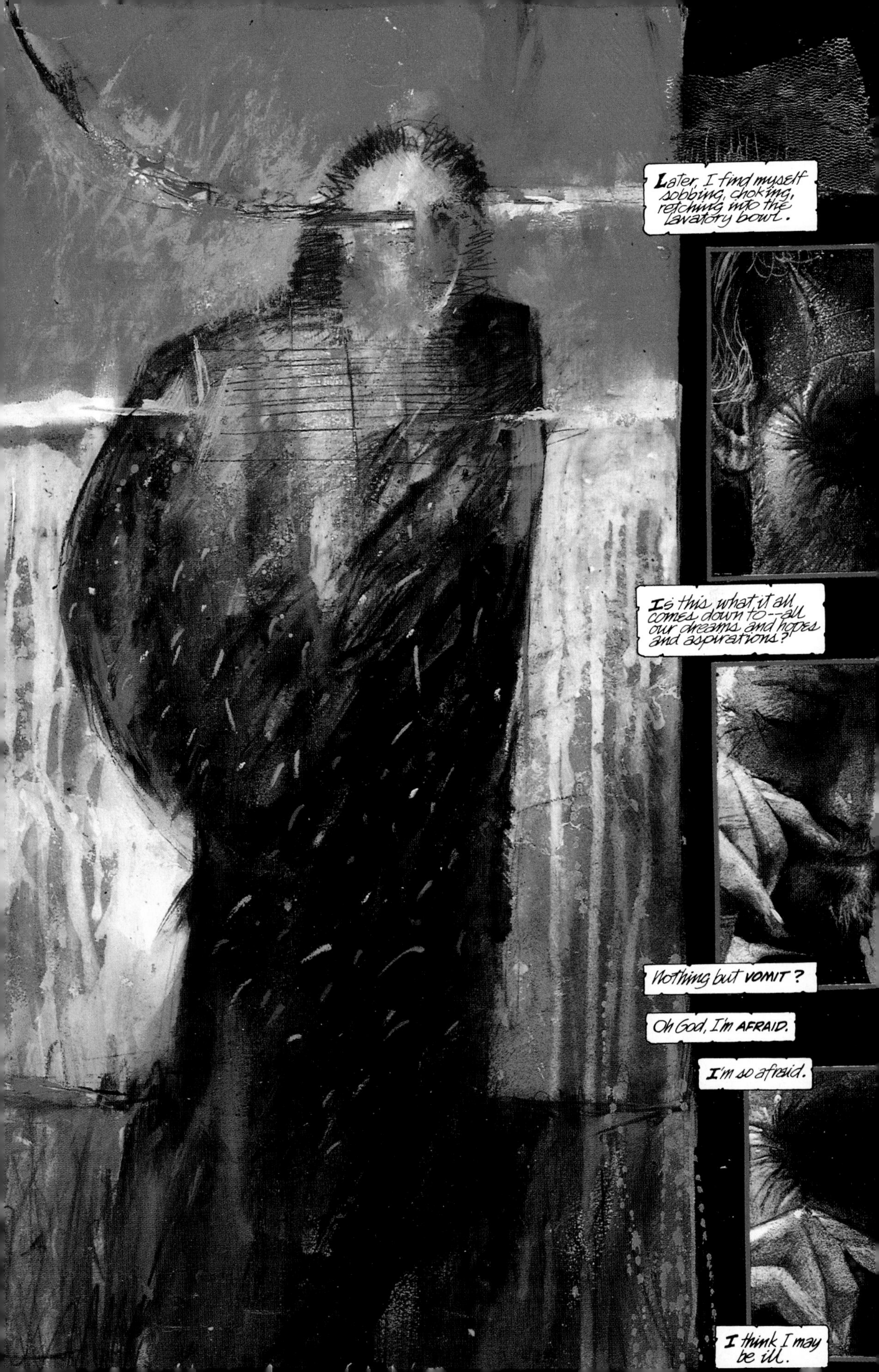
Later, I find myself sobbing, choking, retching into the lavatory bowl.
Is this what it all comes down to--all our dreams and hopes and aspirations?
Nothing but VOMIT?
Oh God, I'm AFRAID.
I'm so afraid.
I think I may be ill.

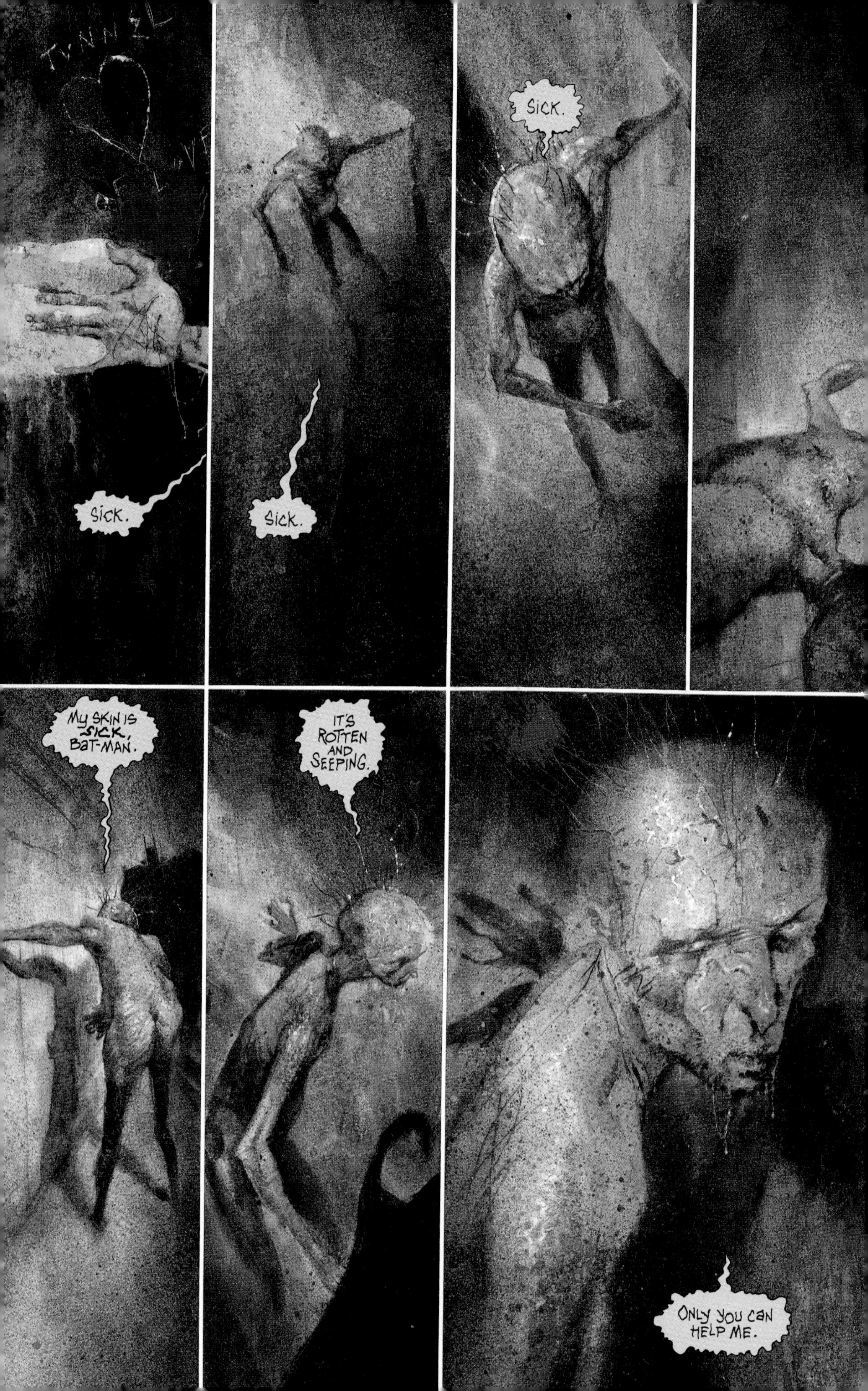
SICK.
SICK.
SICK.
MY SKIN IS SICK, BAT-MAN.
IT'S ROTTEN AND SEEPING.
ONLY YOU CAN HELP ME.

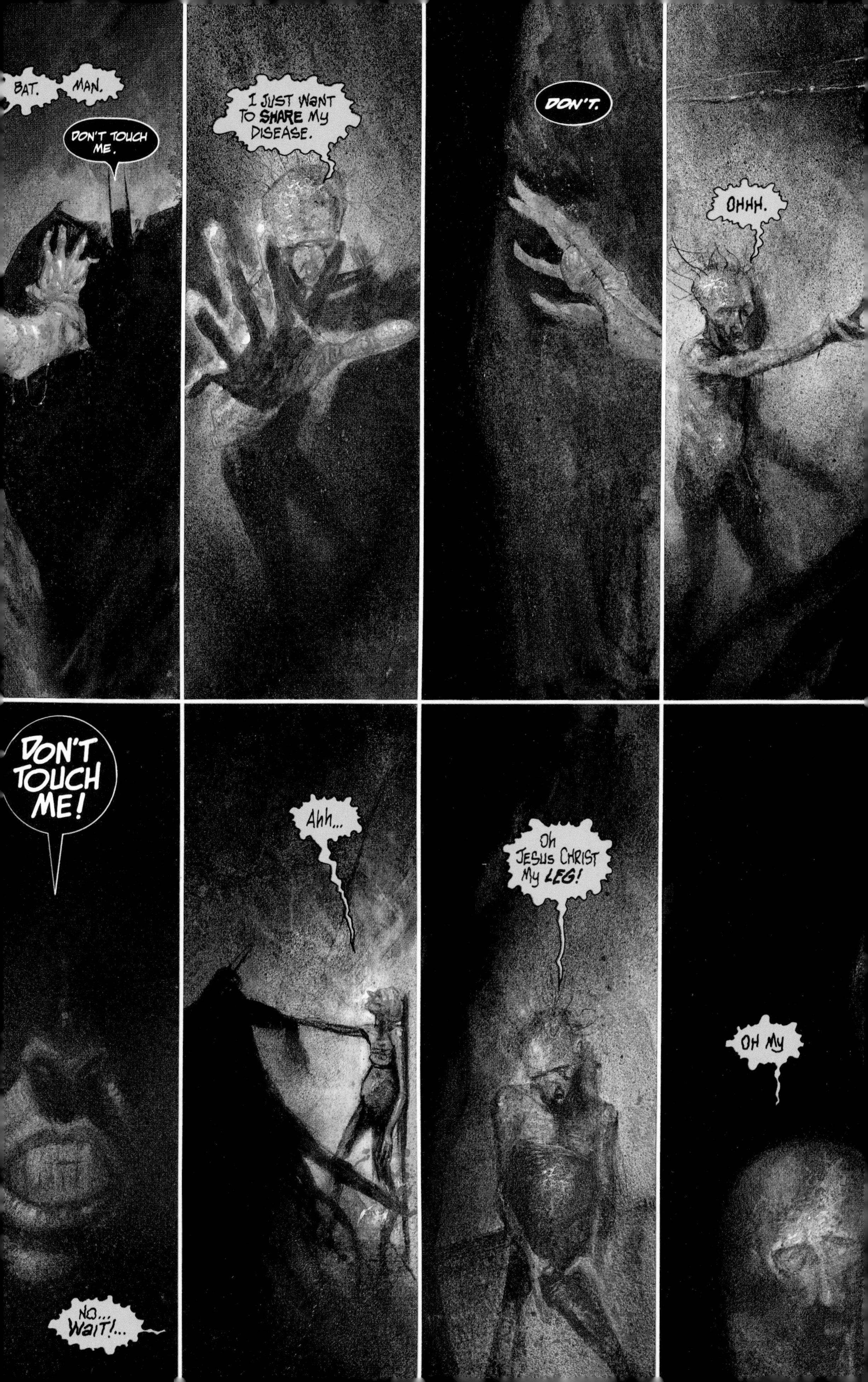
BAT.
MAN.
DON'T TOUCH ME.
I JUST WANT TO SHARE MY DISEASE.
DON'T.
OHHH.
DON'T TOUCH ME!
NO... WAIT!...
Ahh...
Oh JESUS CHRIST My LEG!
OH MY

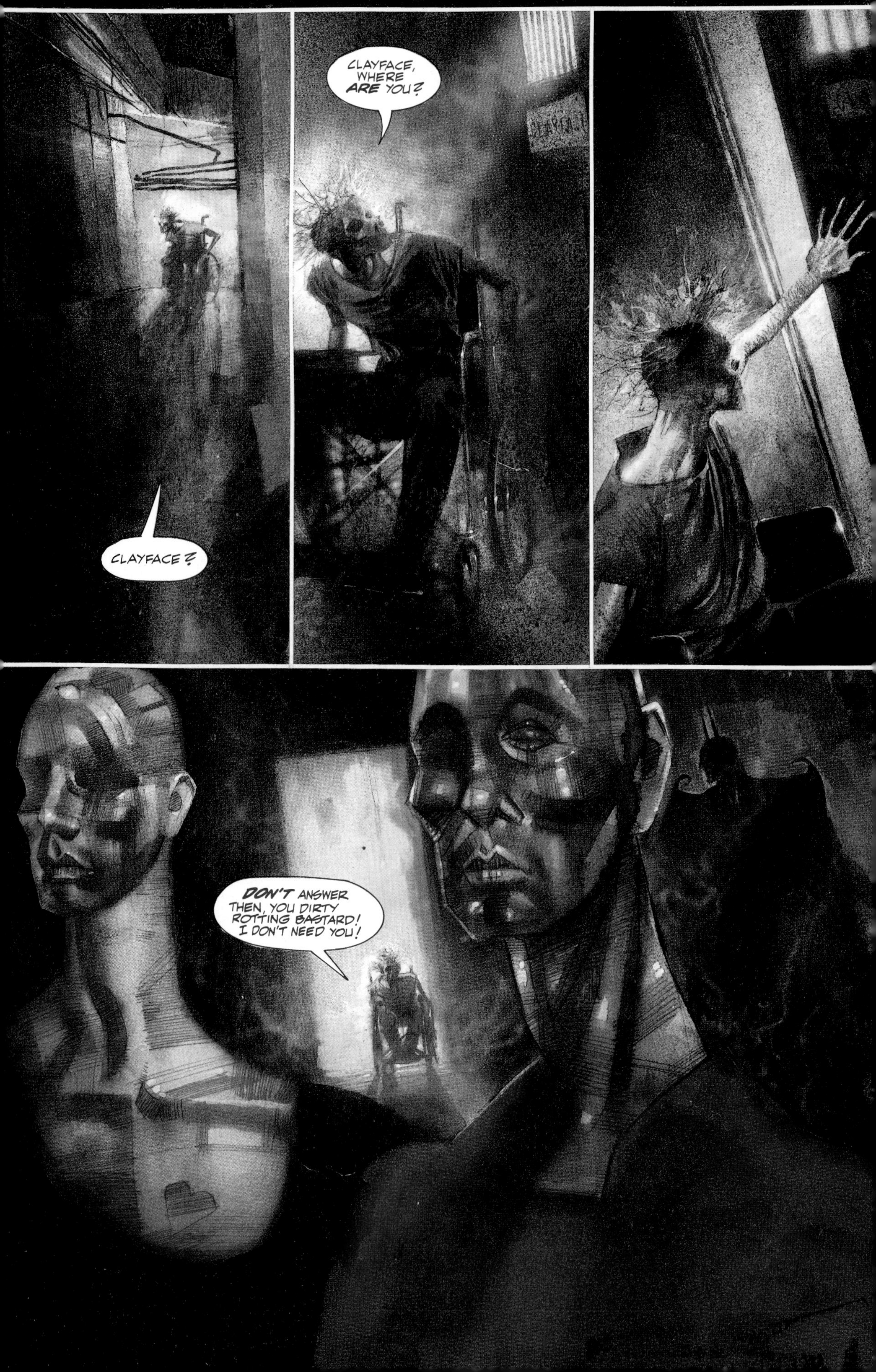
CLAYFACE?
CLAYFACE, WHERE ARE YOU?
DON'T ANSWER THEN, YOU DIRTY ROTTING BASTARD! I DON'T NEED YOU!

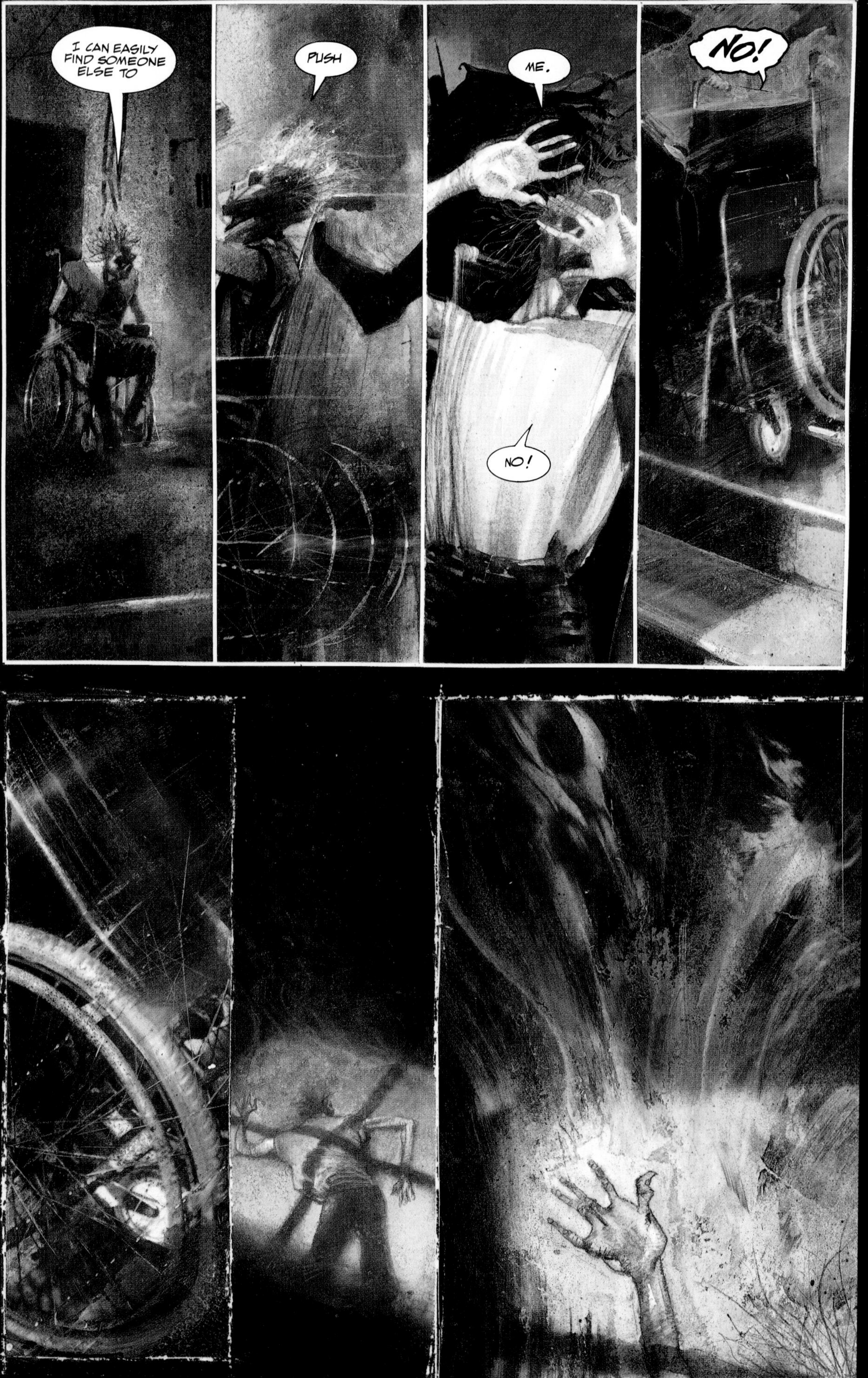
I CAN EASILY FIND SOMEONE ELSE TO
PUSH
ME.
NO!
NO!

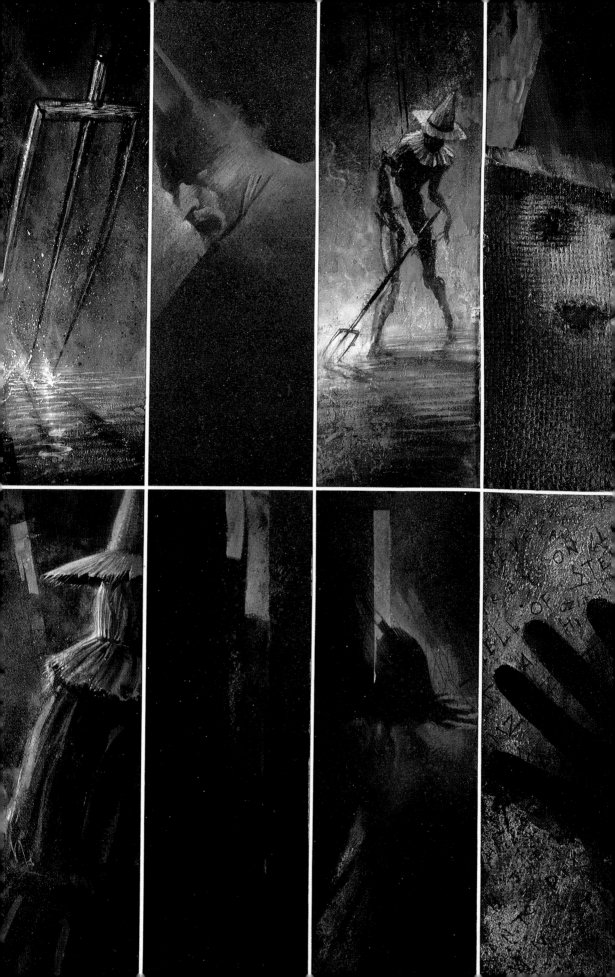

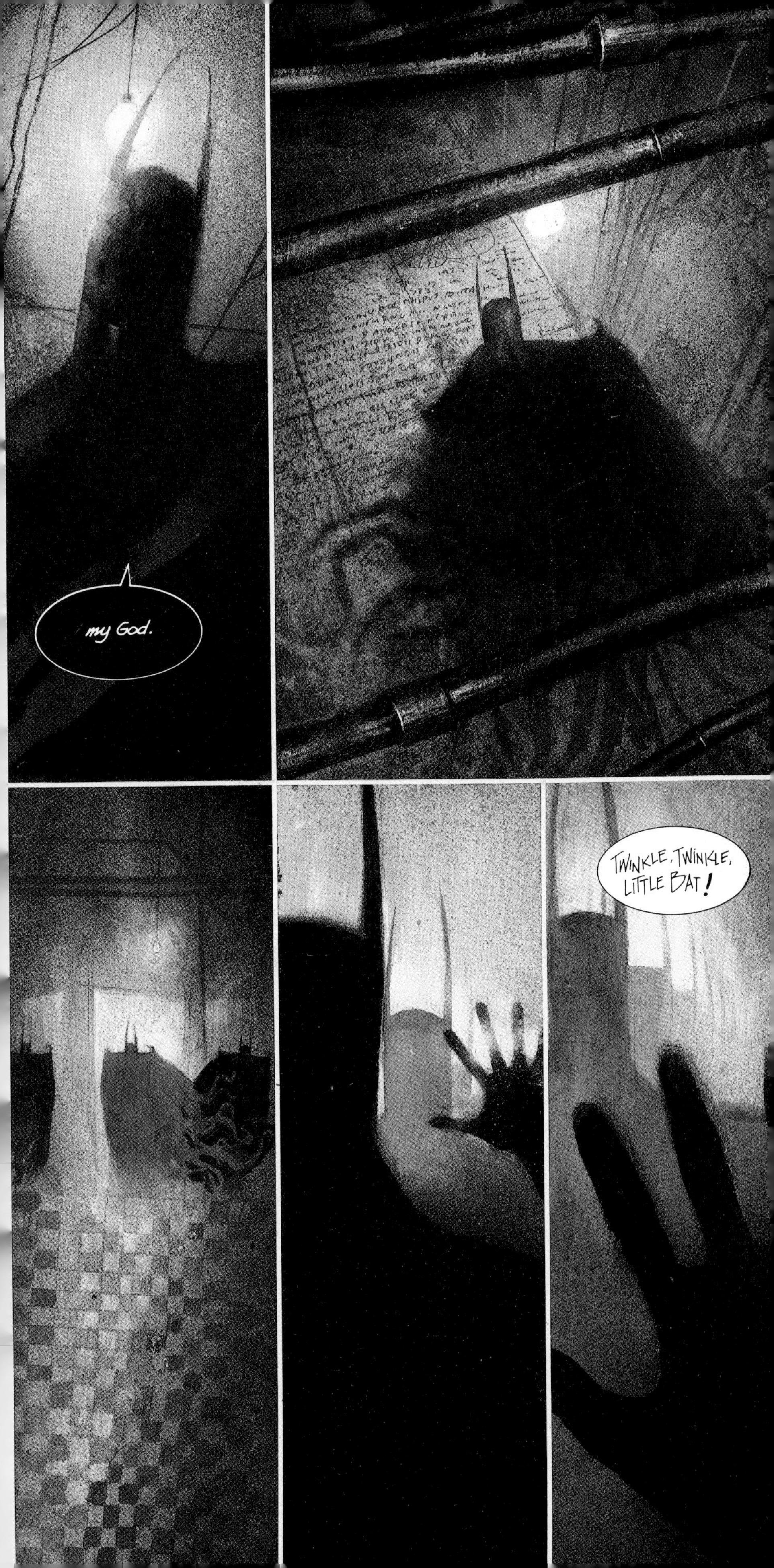
my God.
TWINKLE, TWINKLE, LITTLE BAT!

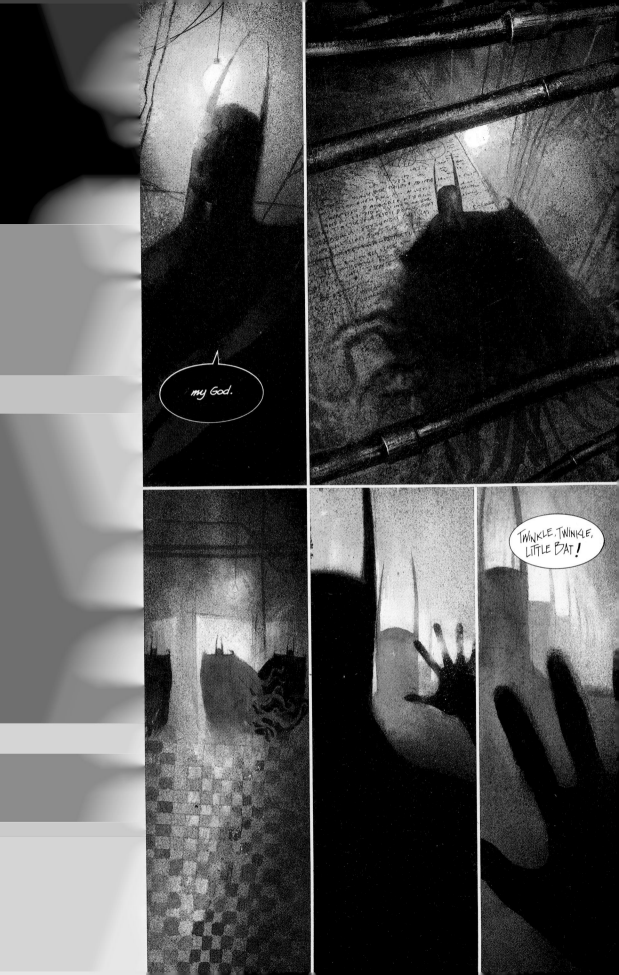

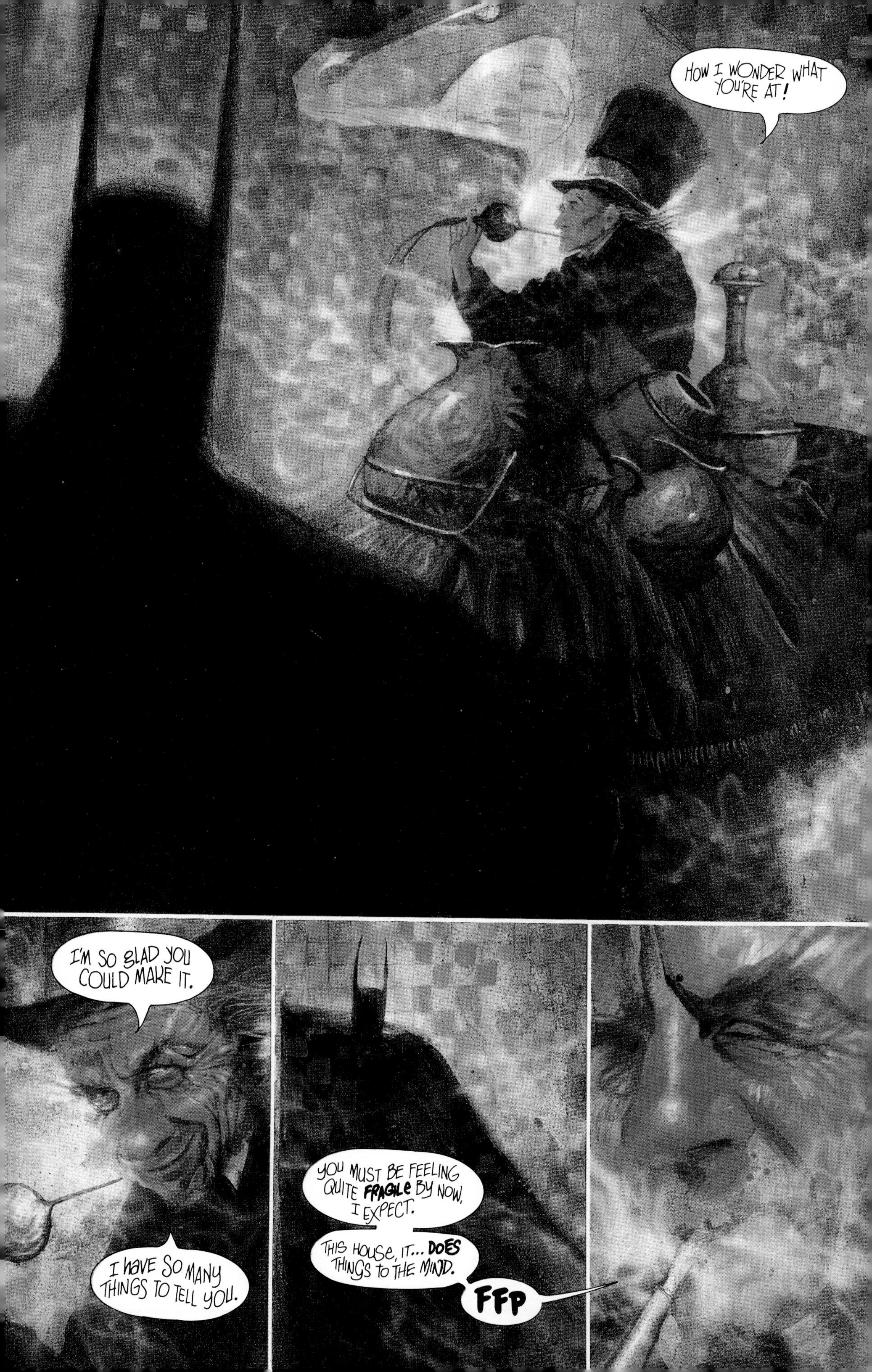
HOW I WONDER WHAT YOU'RE AT!
I'M SO GLAD YOU COULD MAKE IT.
I HAVE SO MANY THINGS TO TELL YOU.
YOU MUST BE FEELING QUITE FRAGILE BY NOW, I EXPECT.
THIS HOUSE, IT... DOES THINGS TO THE MIND.
FFP

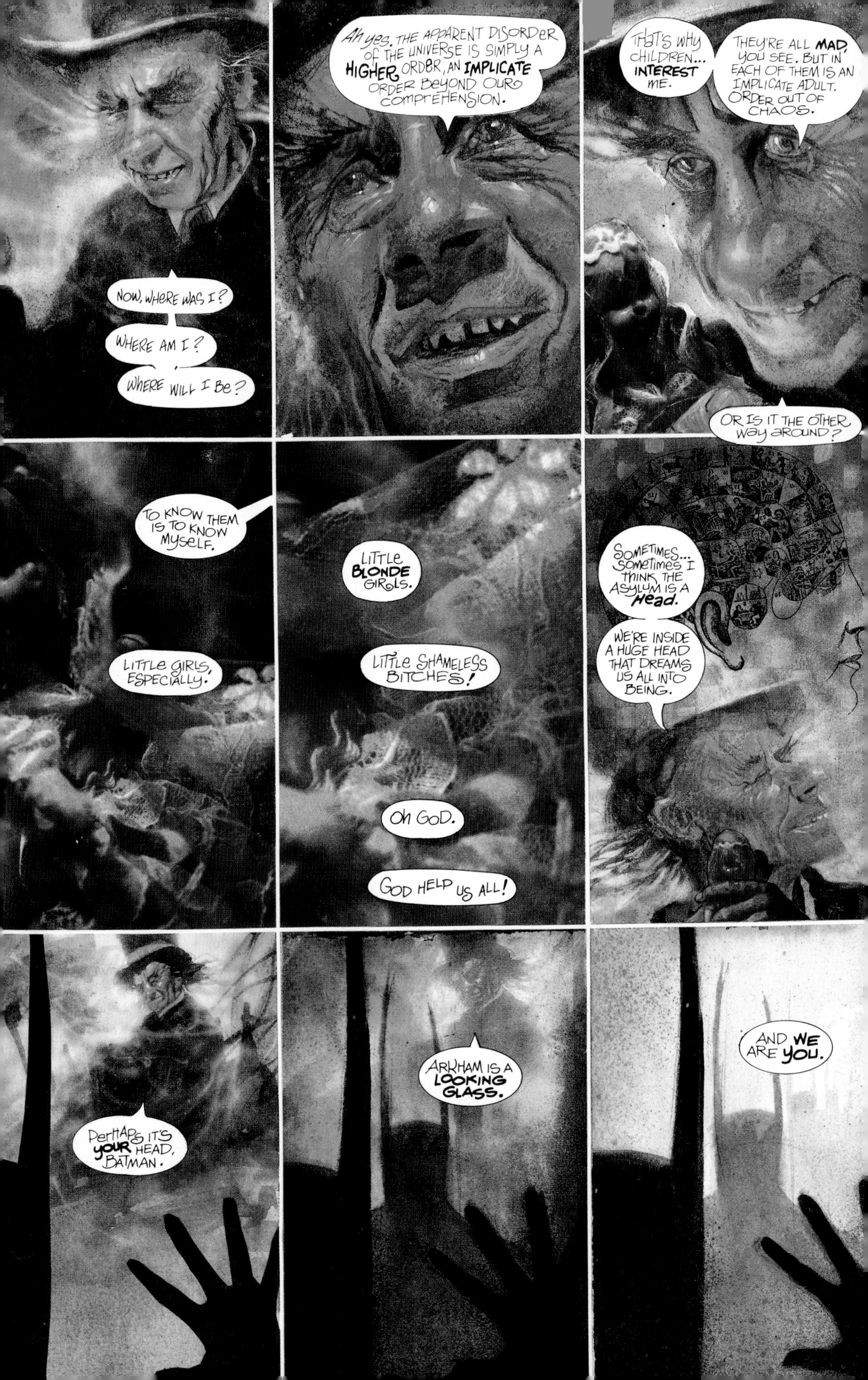
NOW, WHERE WAS I?
WHERE AM I?
WHERE WILL I BE?
Ah yes. THE APPARENT DISORDER OF THE UNIVERSE IS SIMPLY A HIGHER ORDER, AN IMPLICATE ORDER BEYOND OUR COMPREHENSION.
THAT'S WHY CHILDREN... INTEREST ME.
THEY'RE ALL MAD, YOU SEE. BUT IN EACH OF THEM IS AN IMPLICATE ADULT. ORDER OUT OF CHAOS.
OR IS IT THE OTHER WAY AROUND?
TO KNOW THEM IS TO KNOW MYSELF.
LITTLE GIRLS, ESPECIALLY.
LITTLE BLONDE GIRLS.
LITTLE SHAMELESS BITCHES!
OH GOD.
GOD HELP US ALL!
SOMETIMES... SOMETIMES I THINK THE ASYLUM IS A HEAD.
WE'RE INSIDE A HUGE HEAD THAT DREAMS US ALL INTO BEING.
PERHAPS IT'S YOUR HEAD, BATMAN.
ARKHAM IS A LOOKING GLASS.
AND WE ARE YOU.

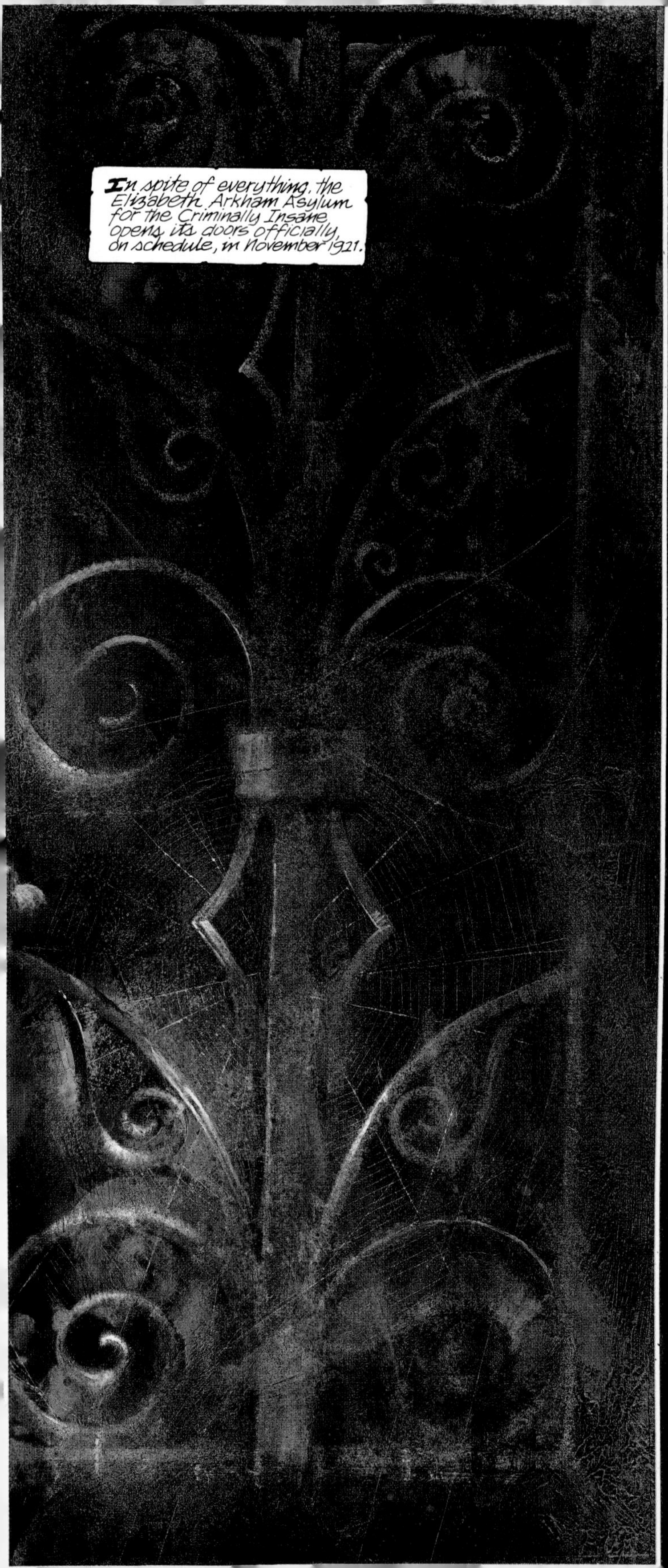
In spite of everything, the Elizabeth Arkham Asylum for the Criminally Insane opens its doors officially, on schedule, in November 1921.

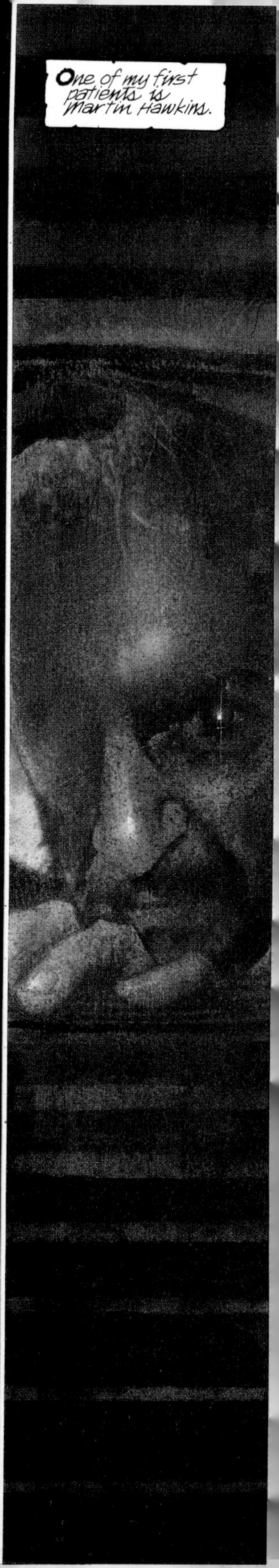
One of my first patients is Martin Hawkins.

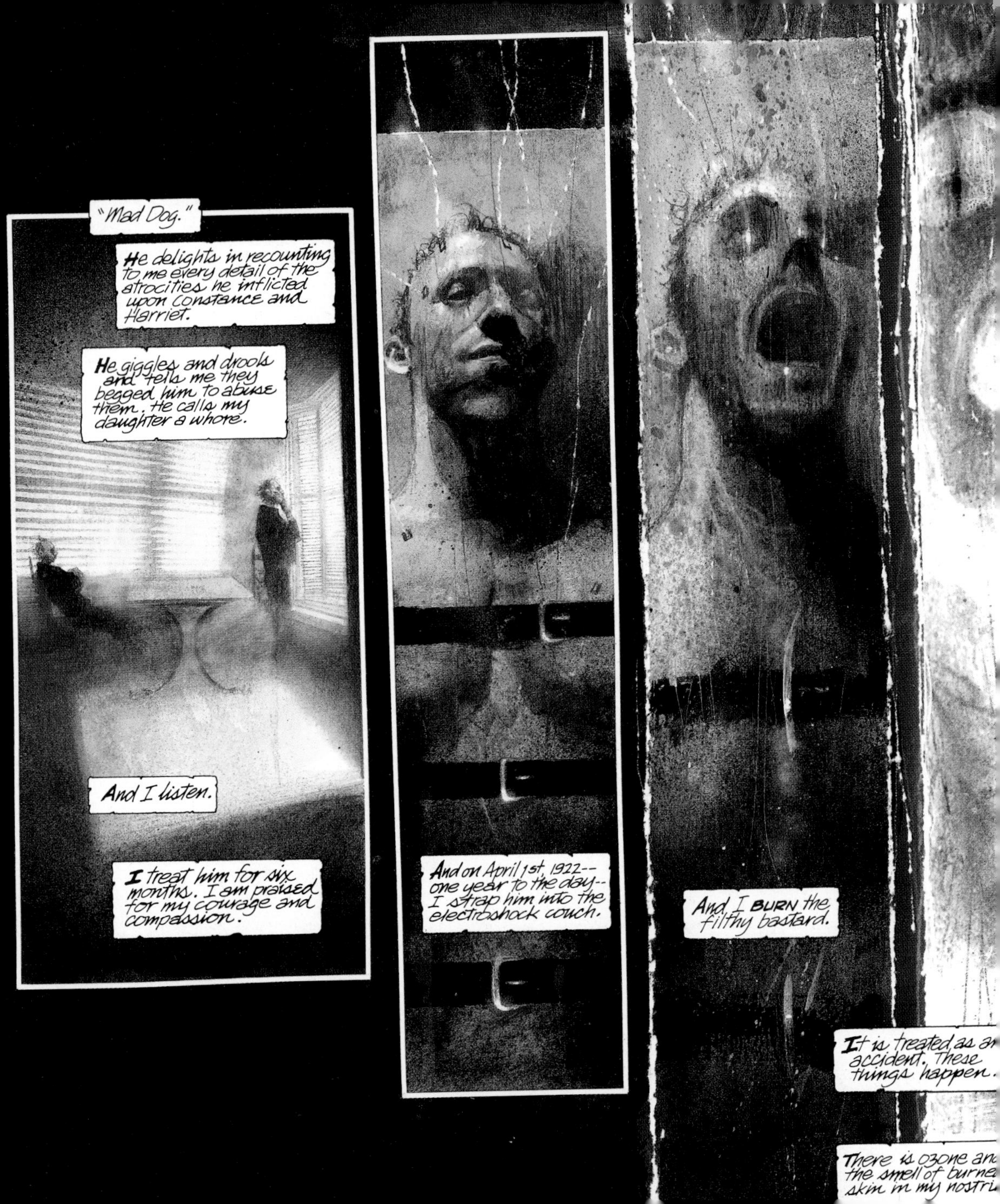
"Mad Dog."
He delights in recounting to me every detail of the atrocities he inflicted upon Constance and Harriet.
He giggles and drools and tells me they begged him to abuse them. He calls my daughter a whore.
And I listen.
I treat him for six months. I am praised for my courage and compassion.
And on April 1st, 1922--one year to the day--I strap him into the electroshock couch.
And I BURN the filthy bastard.
It is treated as an accident. These things happen.
There is ozone and the smell of burned skin in my nostrils

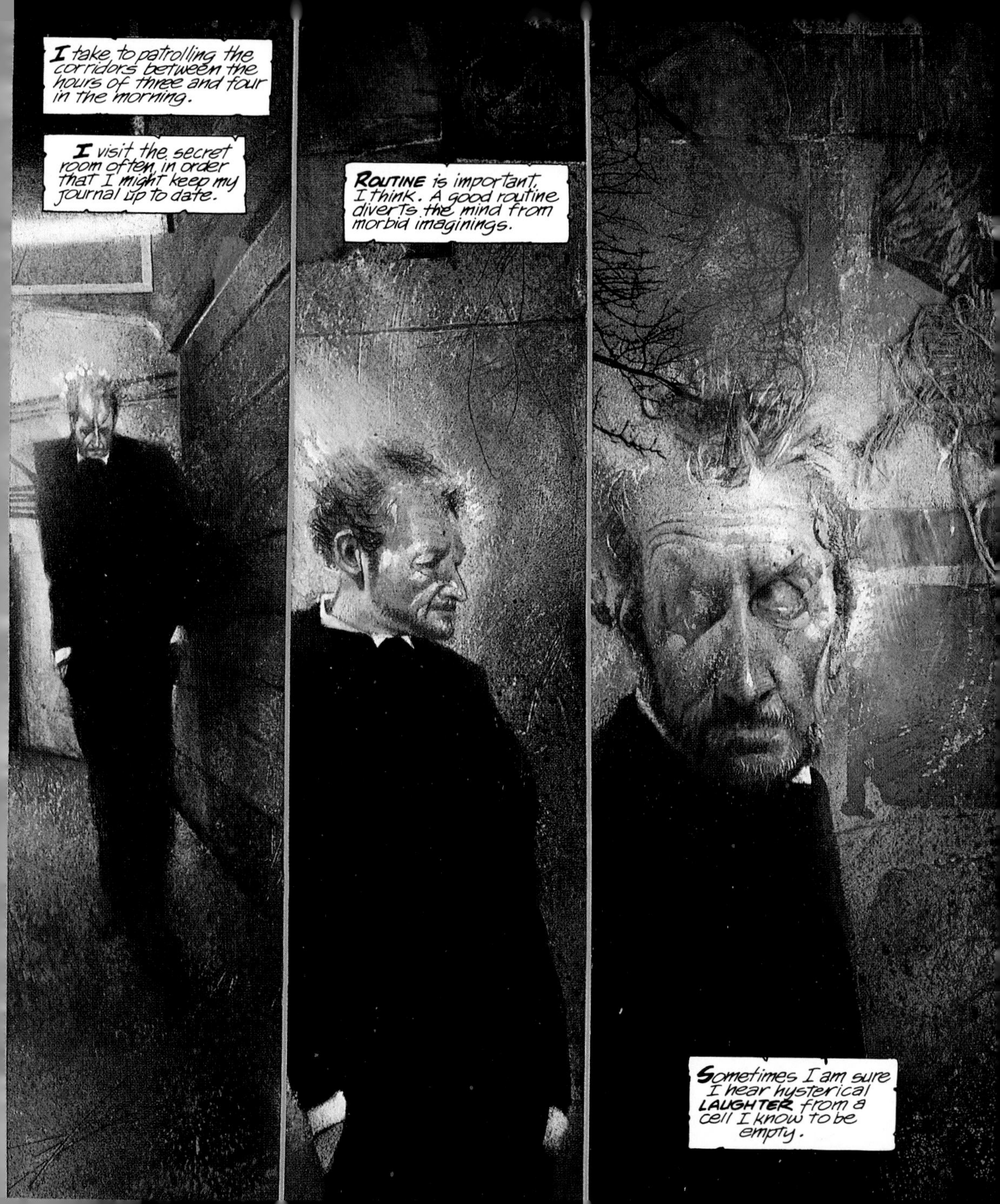
I take to patrolling the corridors between the hours of three and four in the morning.
I visit the secret room often, in order that I might keep my journal up to date.
ROUTINE is important, I think. A good routine diverts the mind from morbid imaginings.
Sometimes I am sure I hear hysterical LAUGHTER from a cell I know to be empty.

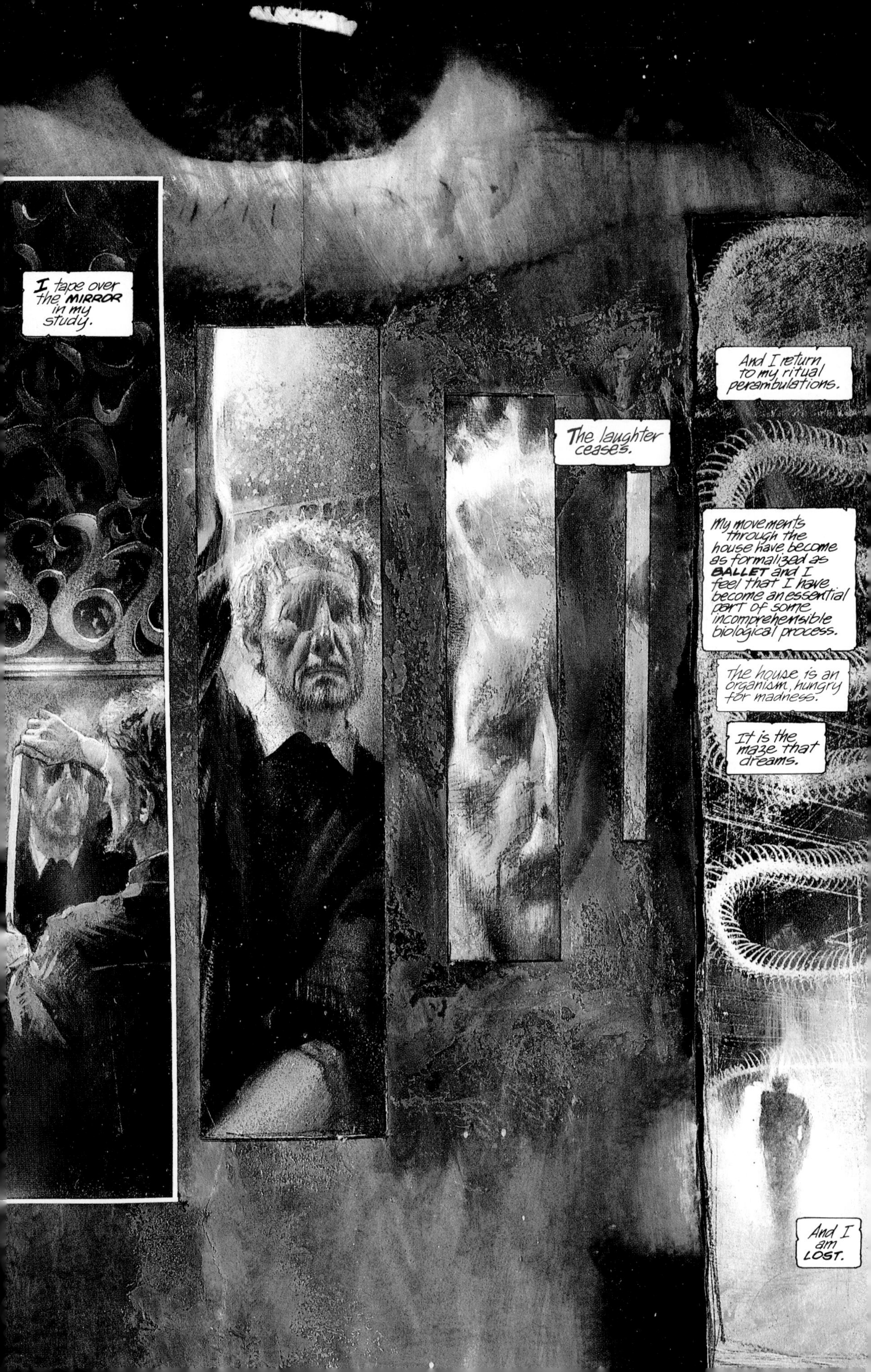

I tape over the MIRROR in my study.
The laughter ceases.
And I return to my ritual perambulations.
My movements through the house have become as formalized as BALLET and I feel that I have become an essential part of some incomprehensible biological process.
The house is an organism, hungry for madness.
It is the maze that dreams.
And I am LOST.

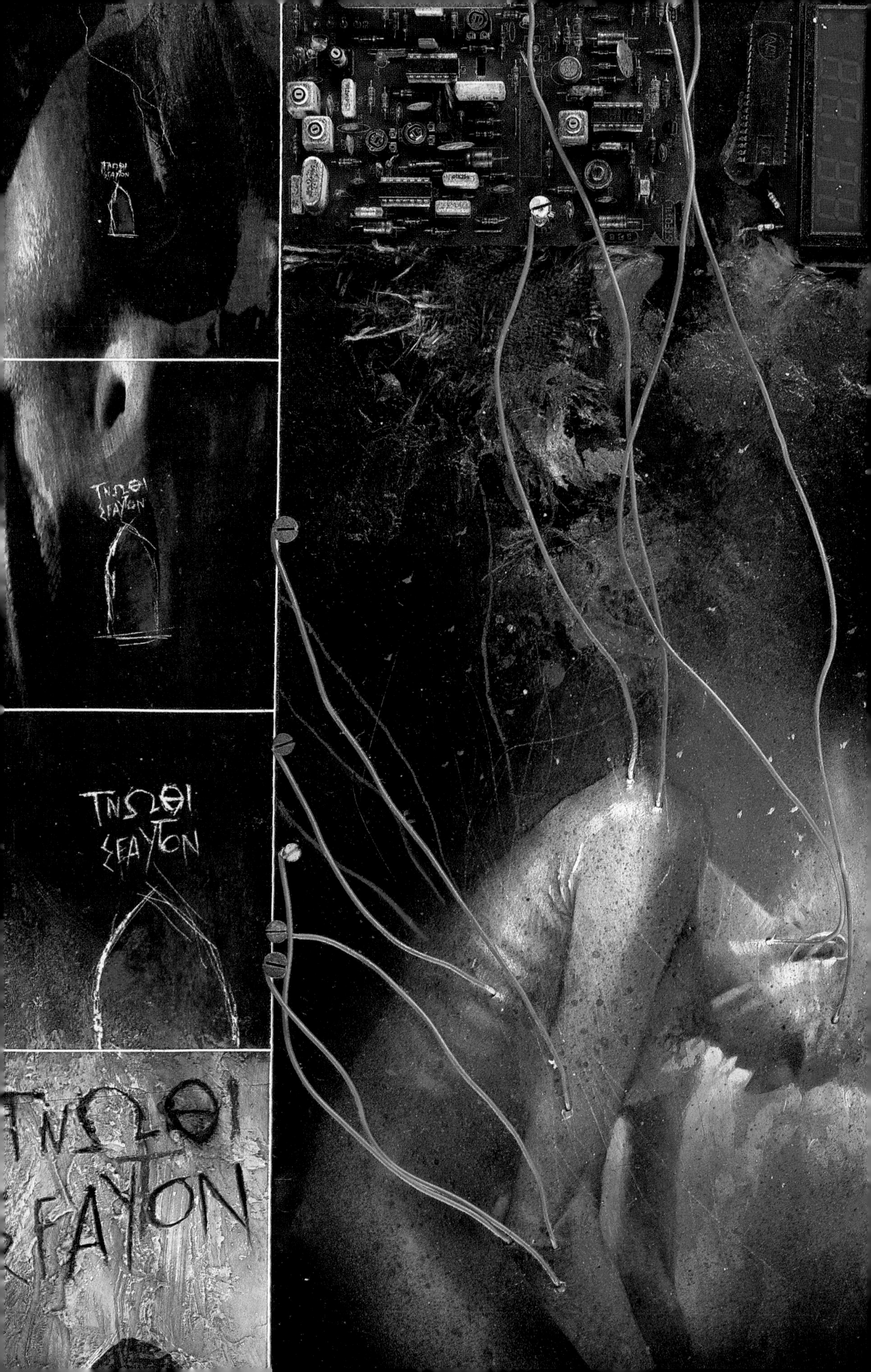
ΓΝΩΘΙ ΣΕΑΥΤΟΝ
ΓΝΩΘΙ ΣΕΑΥΤΟΝ
ΓΝΩΘΙ ΣΕΑΥΤΟΝ
ΓΝΩΘΙ ΣΕΑΥΤΟΝ

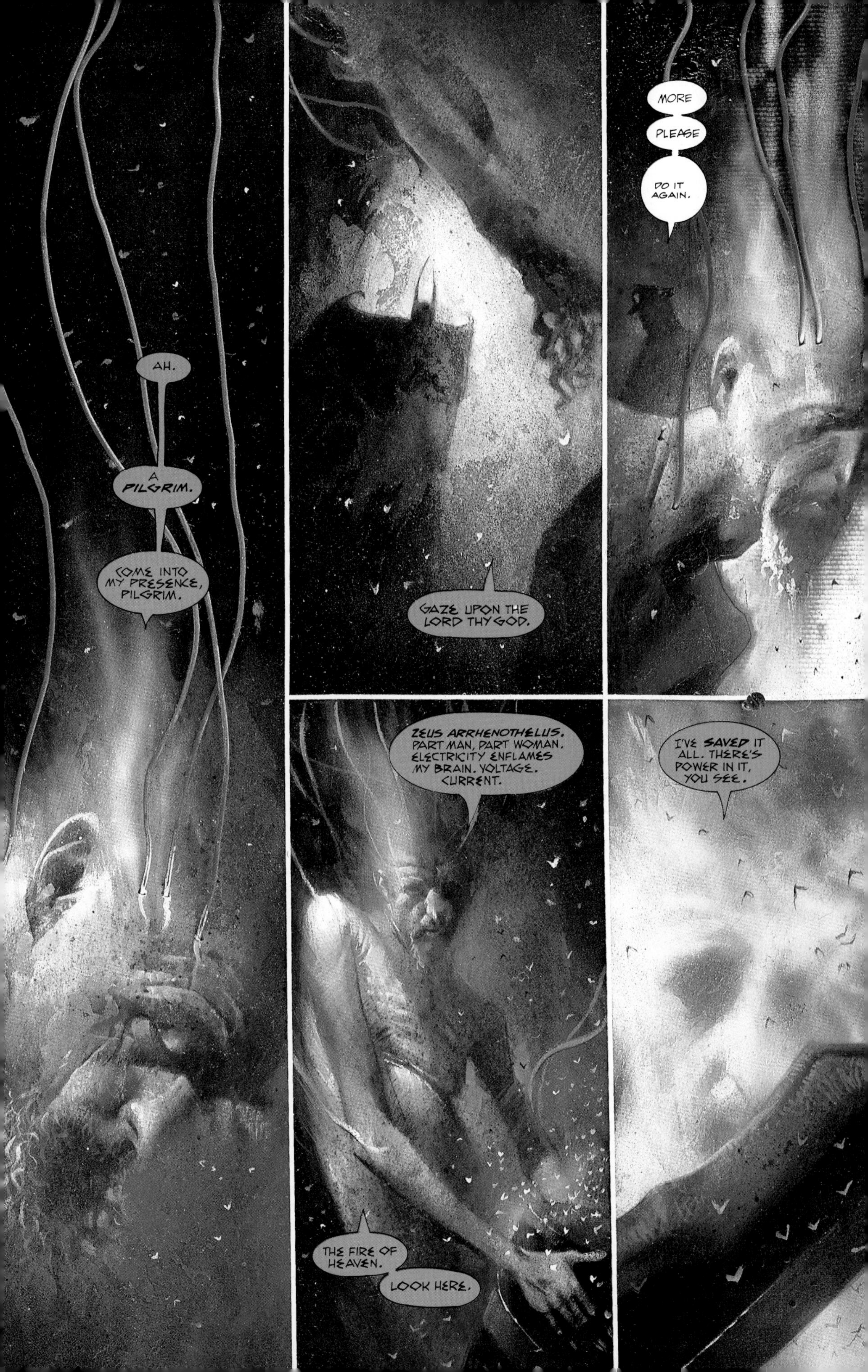
AH.
A PILGRIM.
COME INTO MY PRESENCE, PILGRIM.
GAZE UPON THE LORD THY GOD.
MORE
PLEASE
DO IT AGAIN.
ZEUS ARRHENOTHELUS. PART MAN, PART WOMAN. ELECTRICITY ENFLAMES MY BRAIN. VOLTAGE. CURRENT.
THE FIRE OF HEAVEN.
LOOK HERE.
I'VE SAVED IT ALL. THERE'S POWER IN IT, YOU SEE.

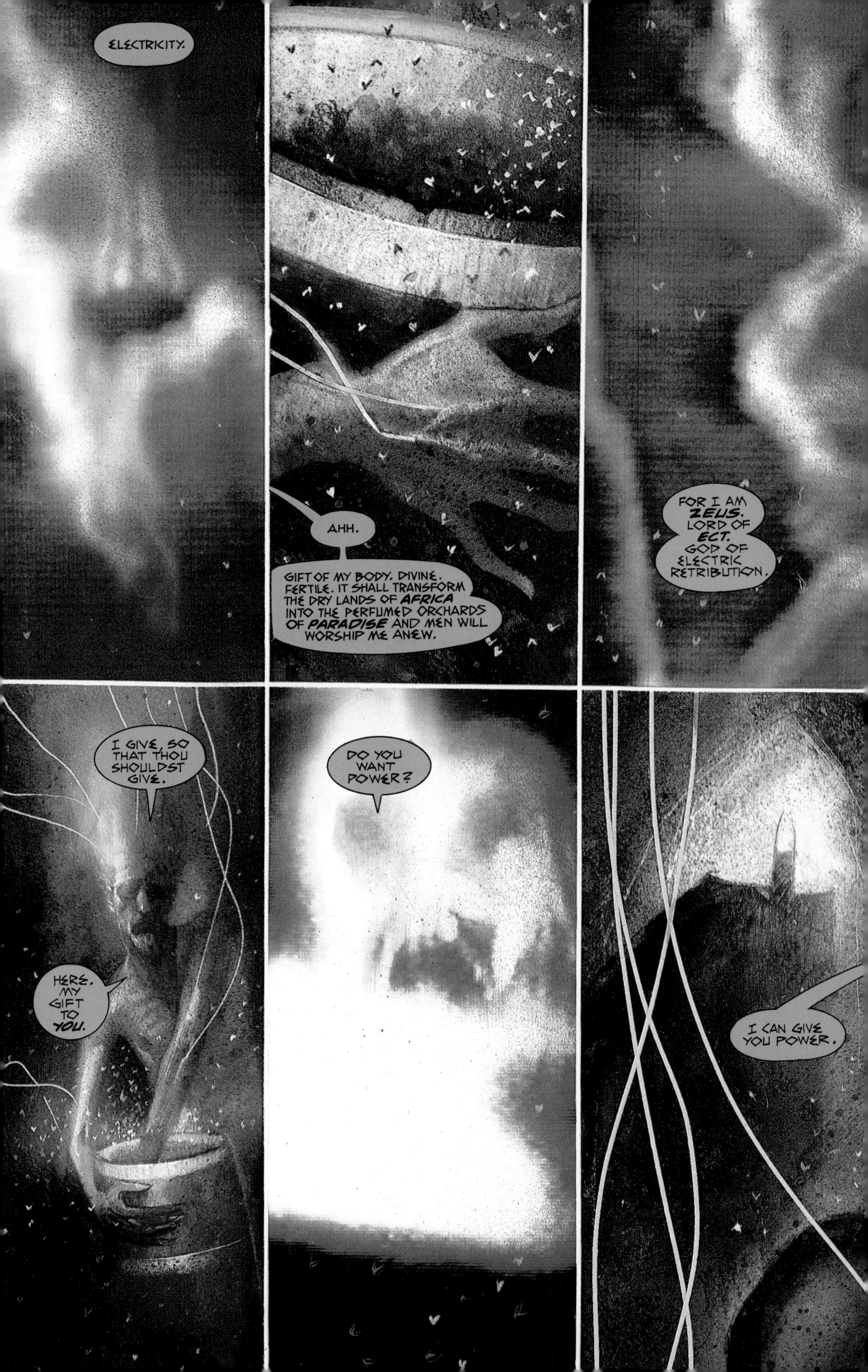
ELECTRICITY.
AHH.
GIFT OF MY BODY. DIVINE. FERTILE. IT SHALL TRANSFORM THE DRY LANDS OF AFRICA INTO THE PERFUMED ORCHARDS OF PARADISE AND MEN WILL WORSHIP ME ANEW.
FOR I AM ZEUS. LORD OF ECT.
GOD OF ELECTRIC RETRIBUTION.
I GIVE, SO THAT THOU SHOULDST GIVE.
HERE. MY GIFT TO YOU.
DO YOU WANT POWER?
I CAN GIVE YOU POWER.

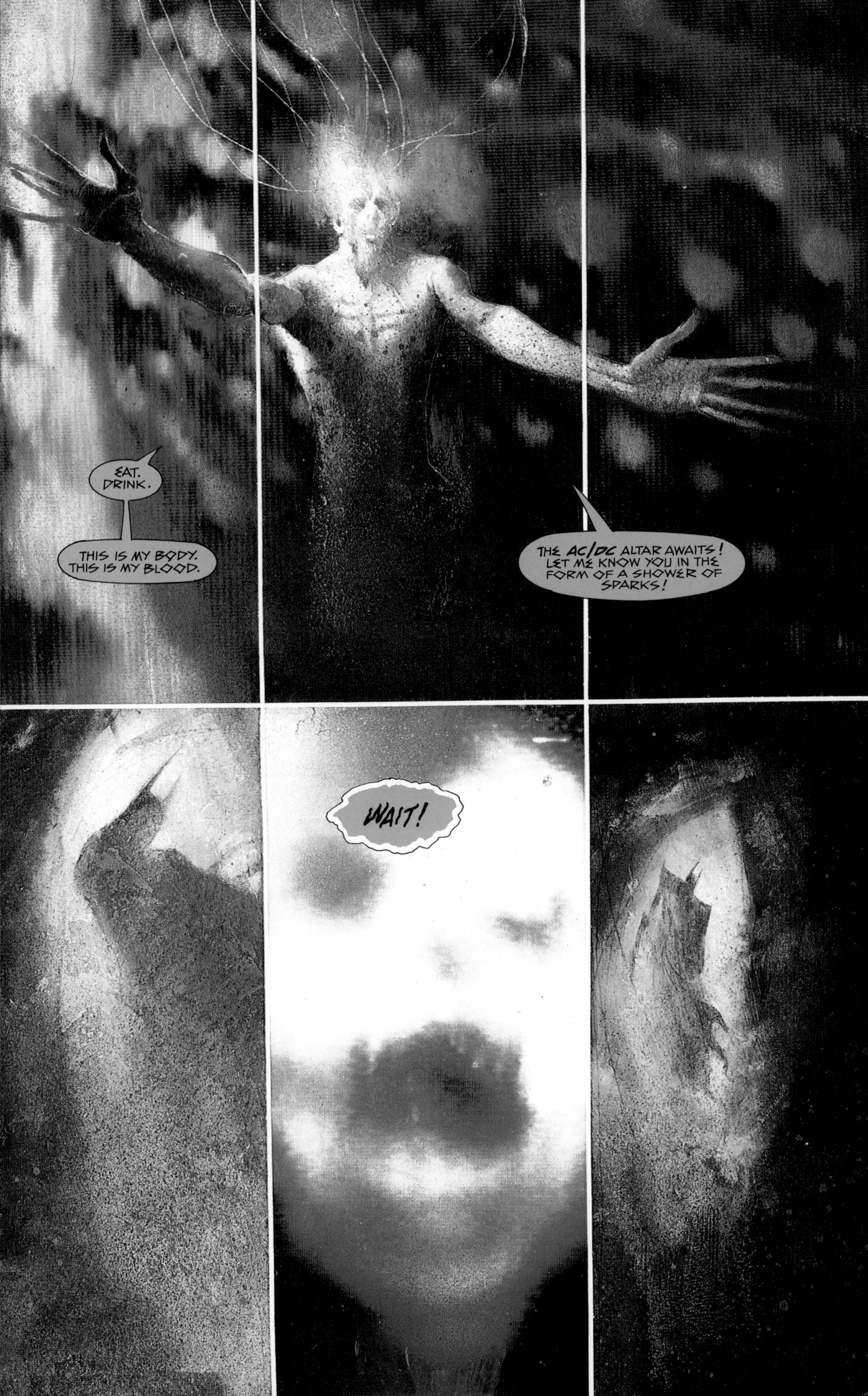
EAT. DRINK.
THIS IS MY BODY. THIS IS MY BLOOD.
THE AC/DC ALTAR AWAITS! LET ME KNOW YOU IN THE FORM OF A SHOWER OF SPARKS!
WAIT!

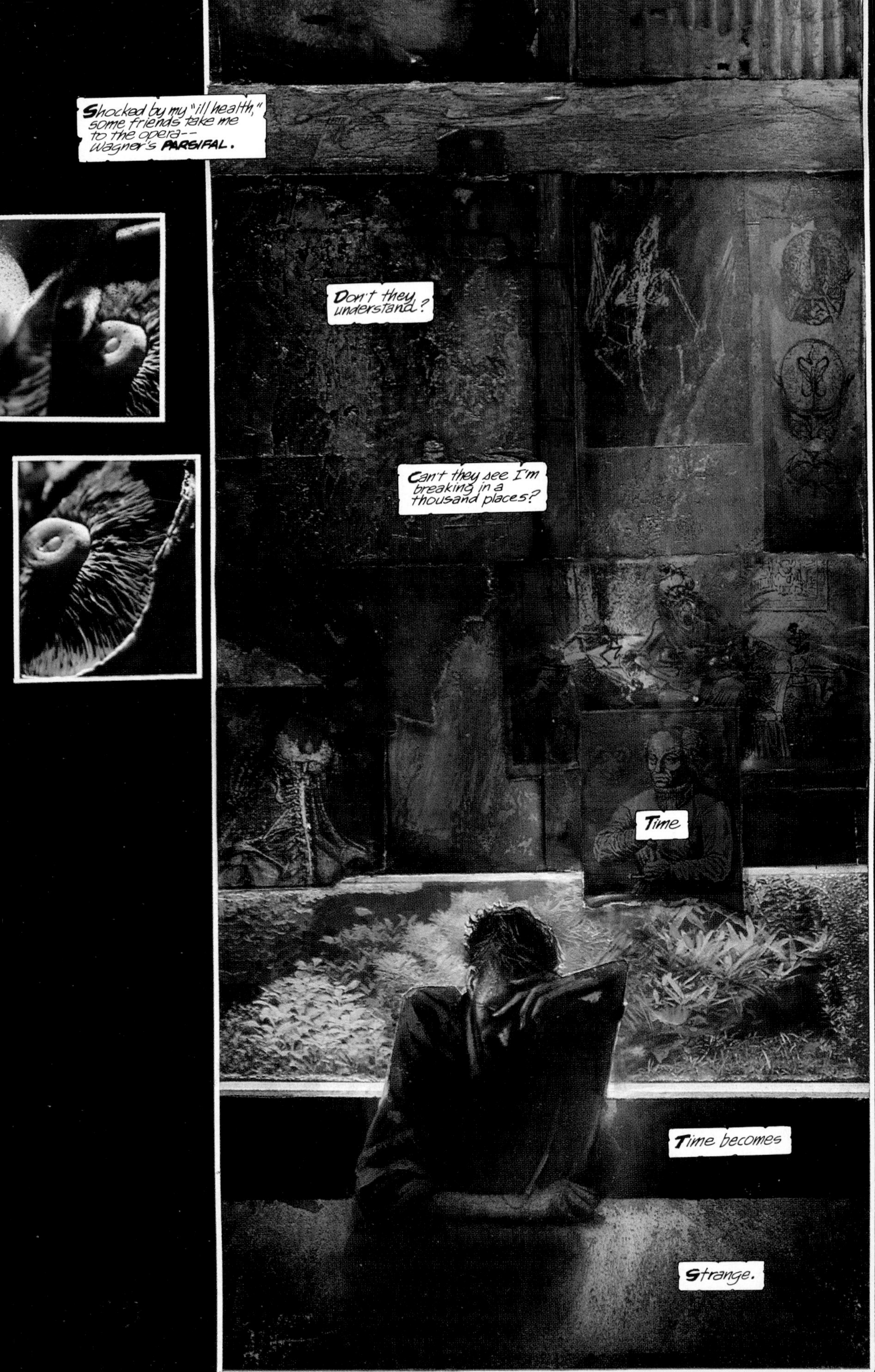
Shocked by my "ill health," some friends take me to the opera-- Wagner's PARSIFAL.
Don't they understand?
Can't they see I'm breaking in a thousand places?
Time
Time becomes
Strange.

portions of the **AMANITA** mush-room.

Abruptly, I become convinced that the house is alive, and trying to **COMMUNICATE** with me.

So far, no effect.

A **PRESSURE** at the back of my head makes me turn.

In their tiny, con-tained universe, two vast and shimmering clown fish glide toward one another.

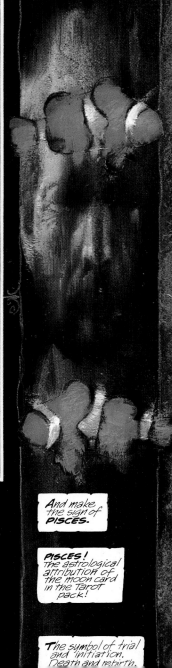

And make the sign of **PISCES**.

PISCES! The astrological attribution of the moon card in the Tarot pack!

The symbol of trial and initiation. Death and rebirth.

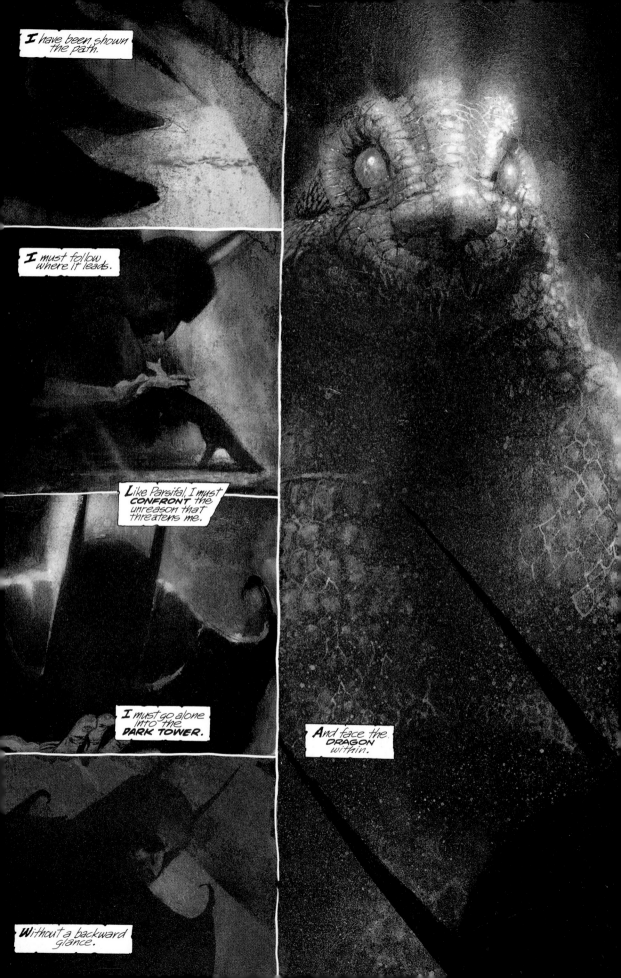

I have been shown the path.

I must follow where it leads.

Like Parsifal, I must **CONFRONT** the unreason that threatens me.

I must go alone into the **DARK TOWER**.

And face the **DRAGON** within.

Without a backward glance.

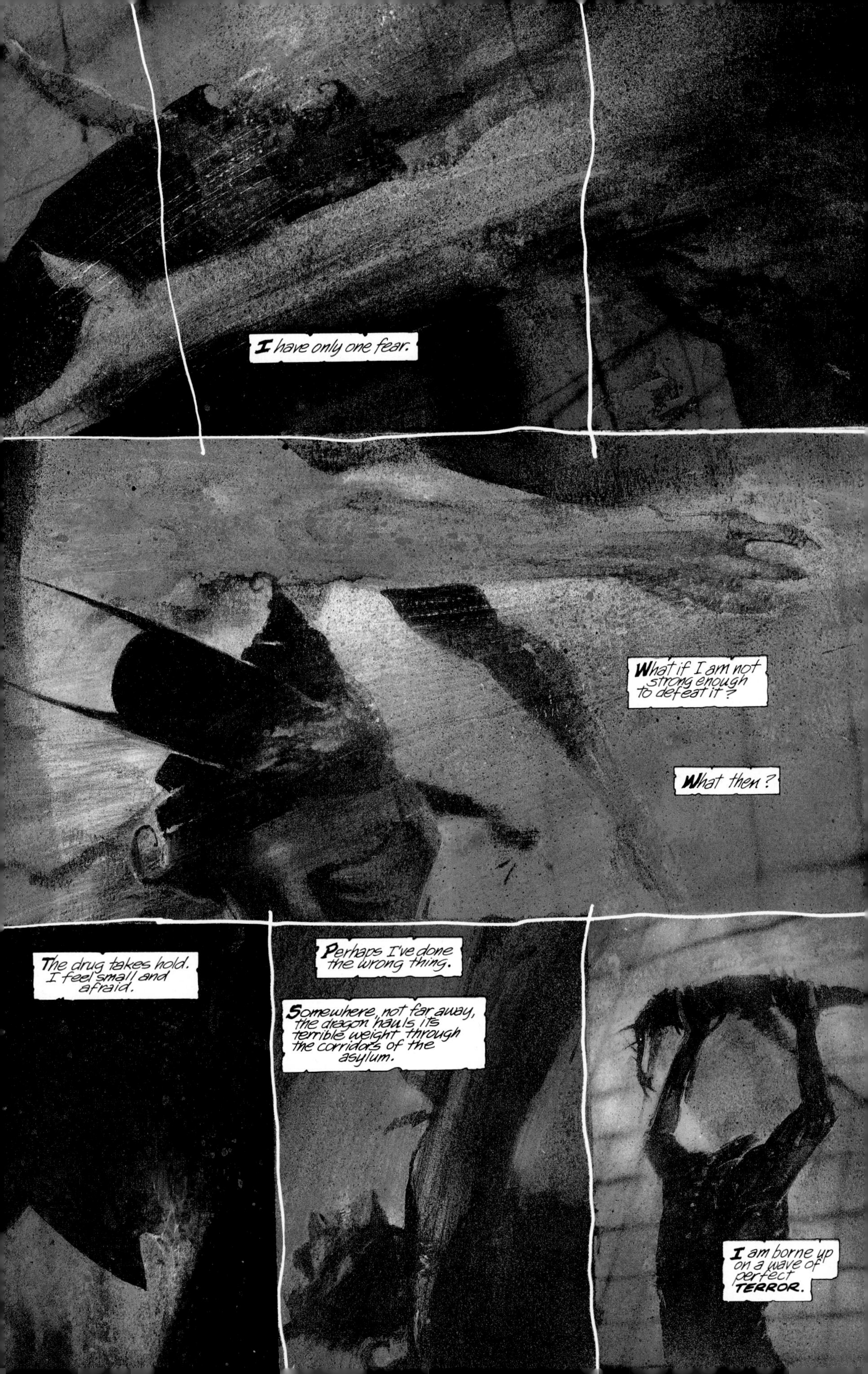
I have only one fear.
What if I am not strong enough to defeat it?
What then?
The drug takes hold. I feel small and afraid.
Perhaps I've done the wrong thing.
Somewhere, not far away, the dragon hauls its terrible weight through the corridors of the asylum.
I am borne up on a wave of perfect TERROR.

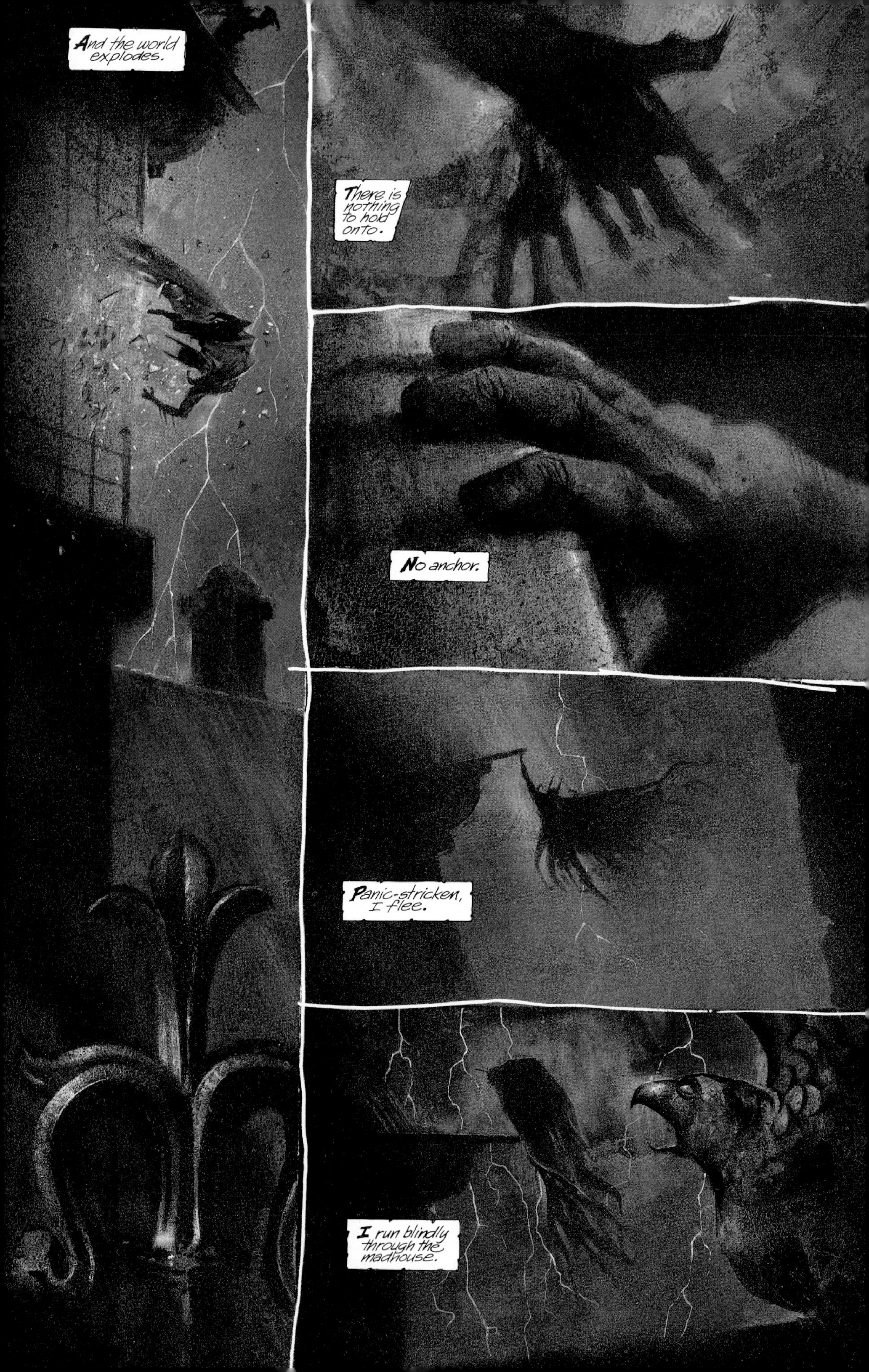
And the world explodes.
There is nothing to hold onto.
No anchor.
Panic-stricken, I flee.
I run blindly through the madhouse.

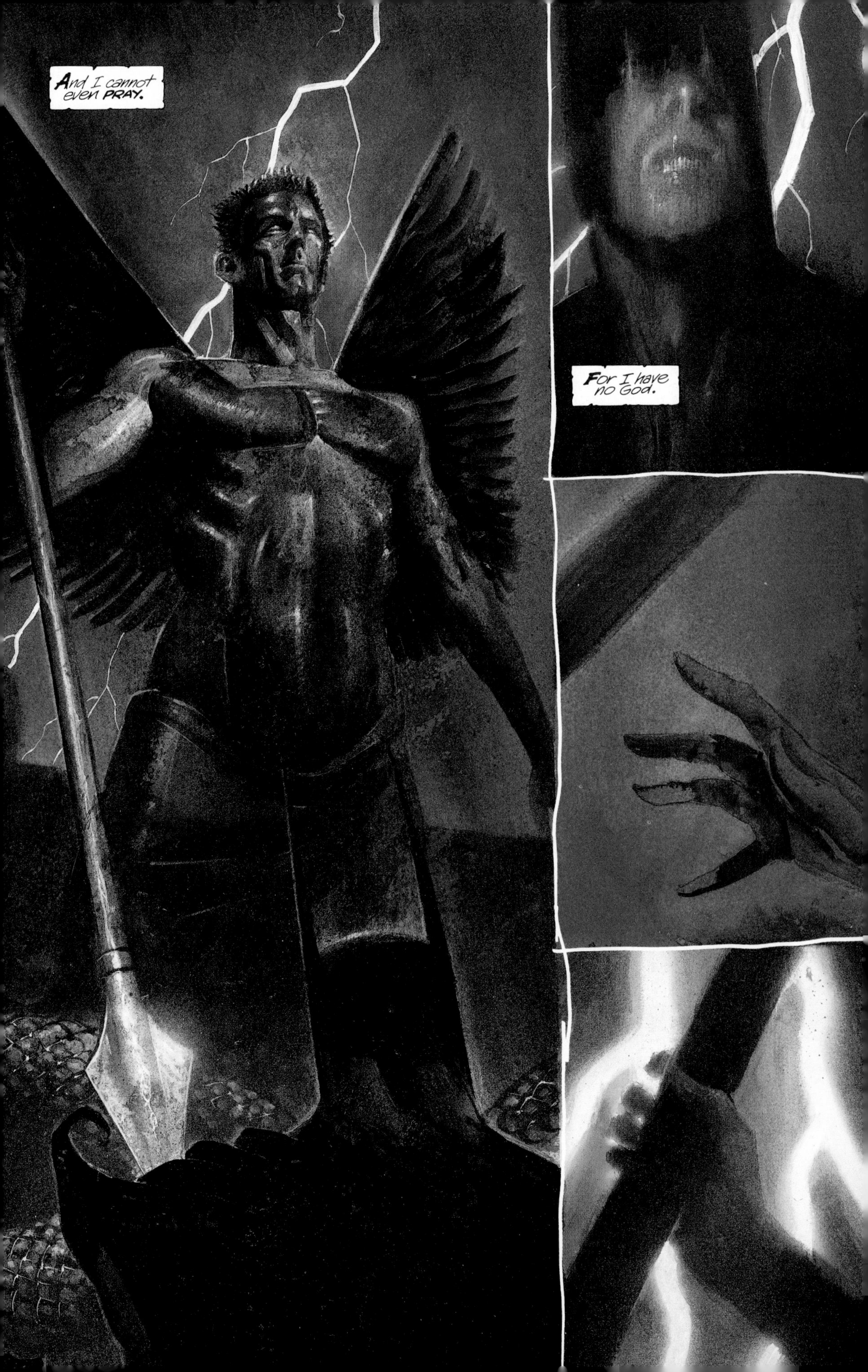
And I cannot even PRAY.
For I have no God.

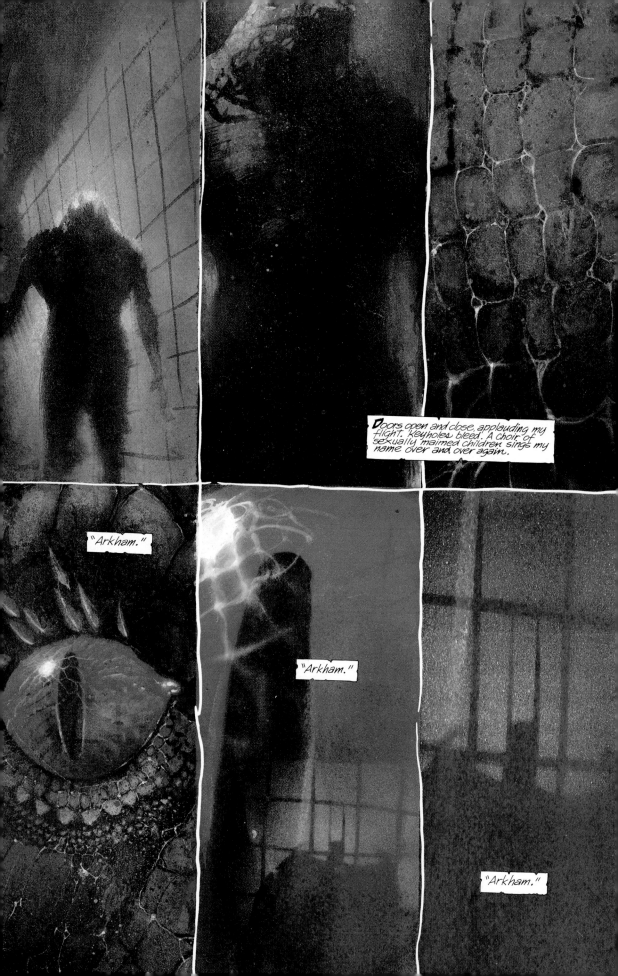

Doors open and close, applauding my flight. Keyholes bleed. A choir of sexually maimed children sings my name over and over again.

"Arkham."

"Arkham."

"Arkham."

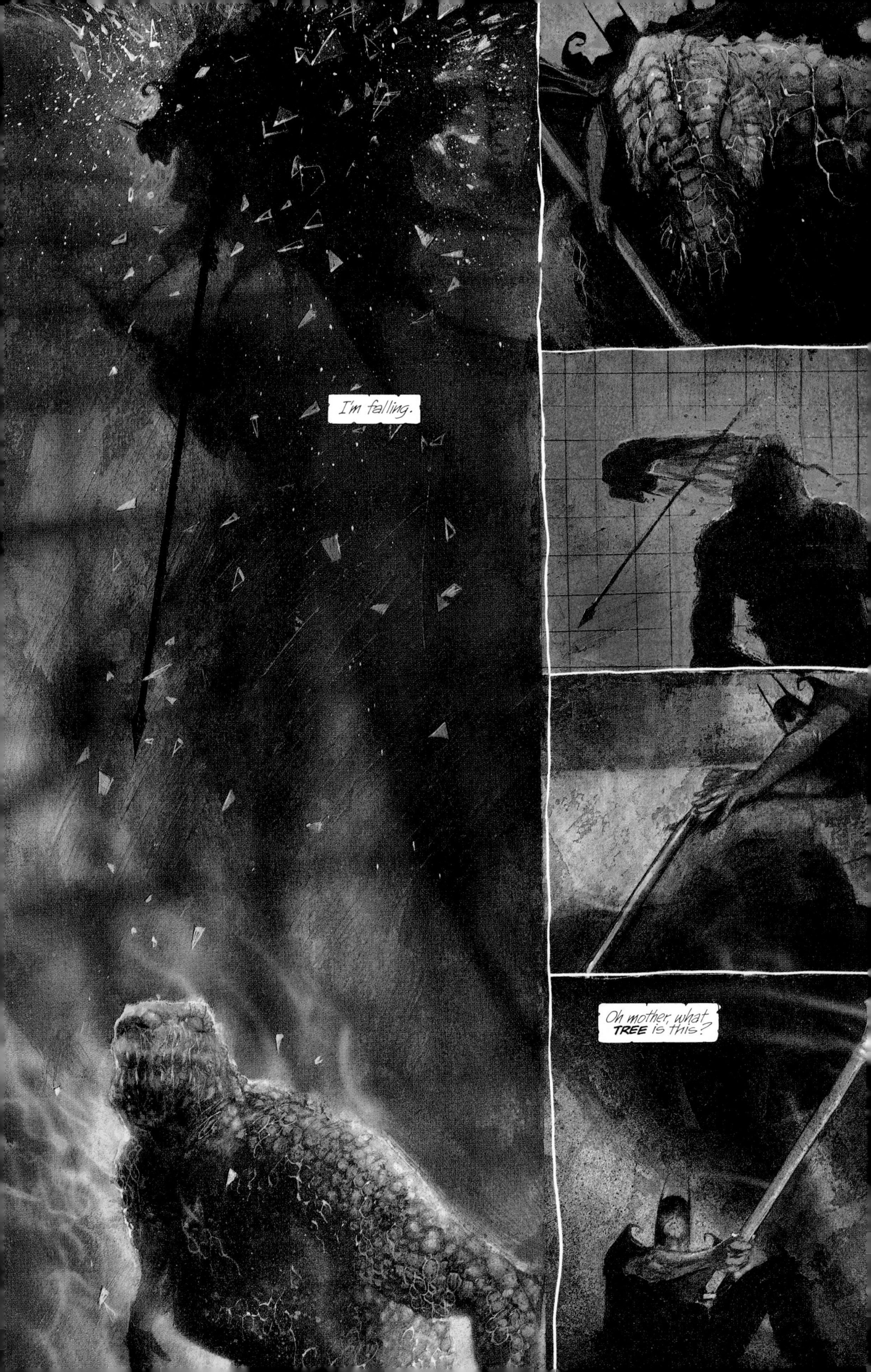
I'm falling.
Oh mother, what TREE is this?

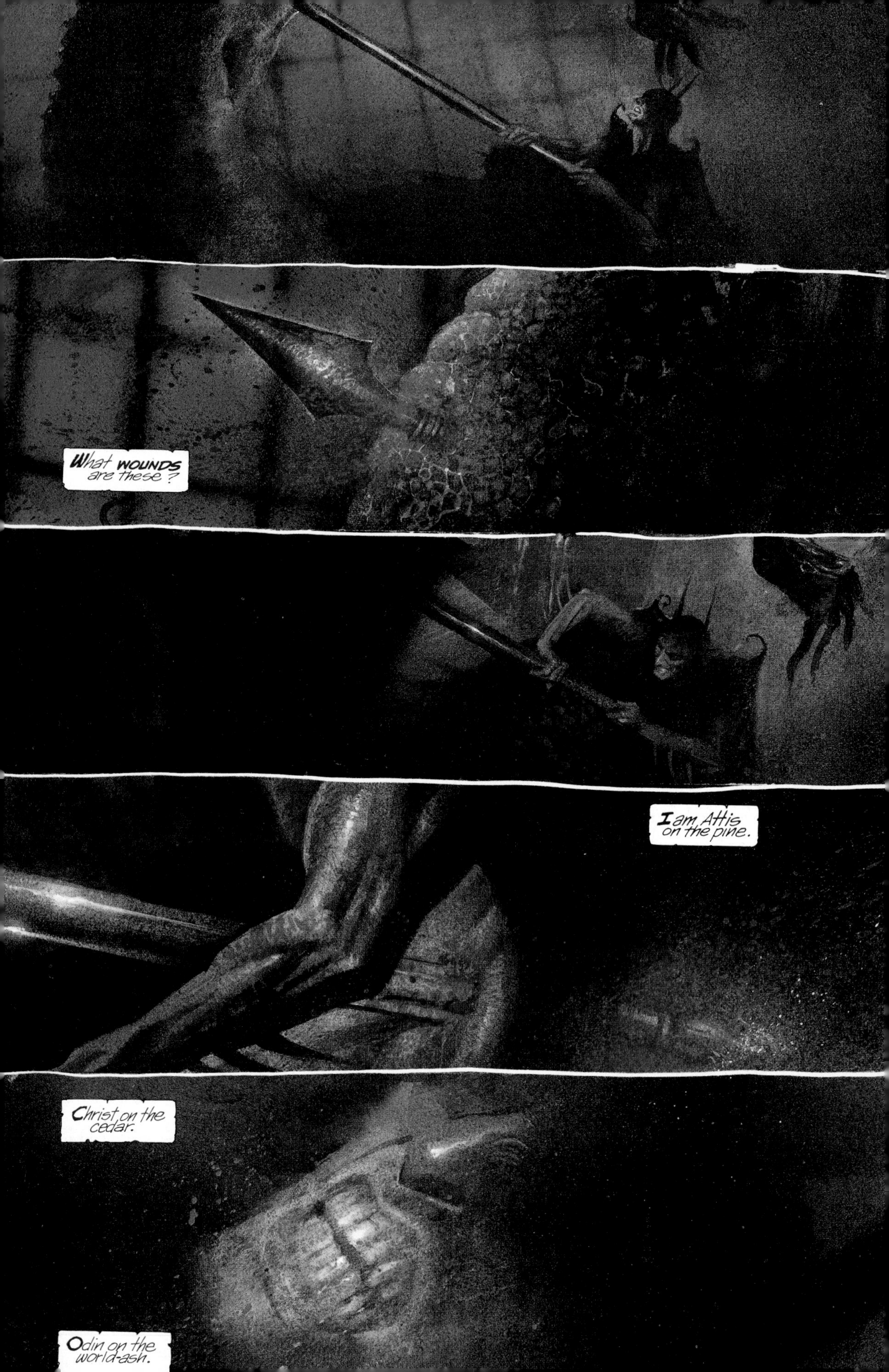
What WOUNDS are these?
I am Attis on the pine.
Christ on the cedar.
Odin on the world-ash.

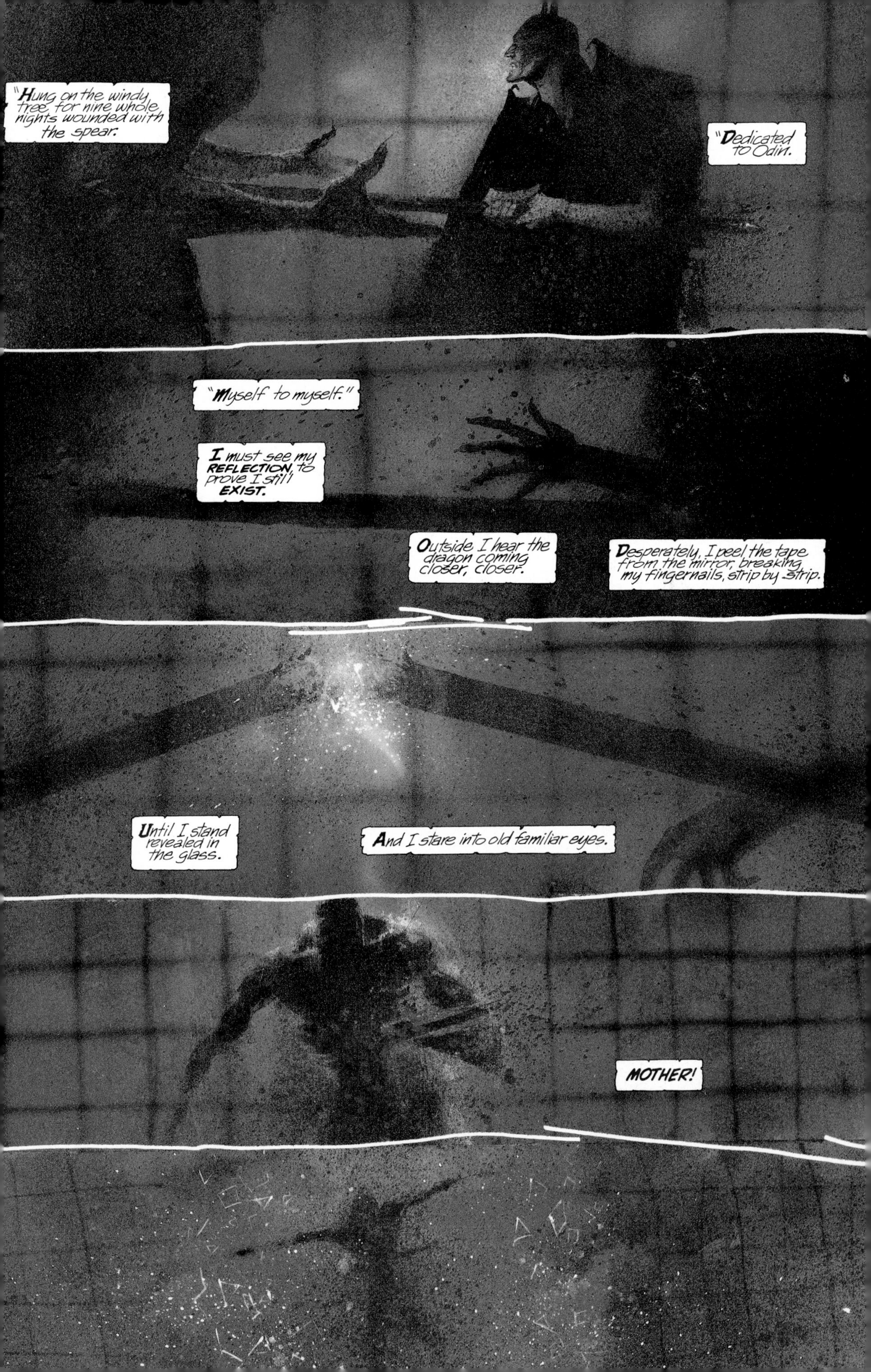
"Hung on the windy tree for nine whole nights wounded with the spear.
"Dedicated to Odin.
"Myself to myself."
I must see my REFLECTION, to prove I still EXIST.
Outside I hear the dragon coming closer, closer.
Desperately, I peel the tape from the mirror, breaking my fingernails, strip by strip.
Until I stand revealed in the glass.
And I stare into old familiar eyes.
MOTHER!

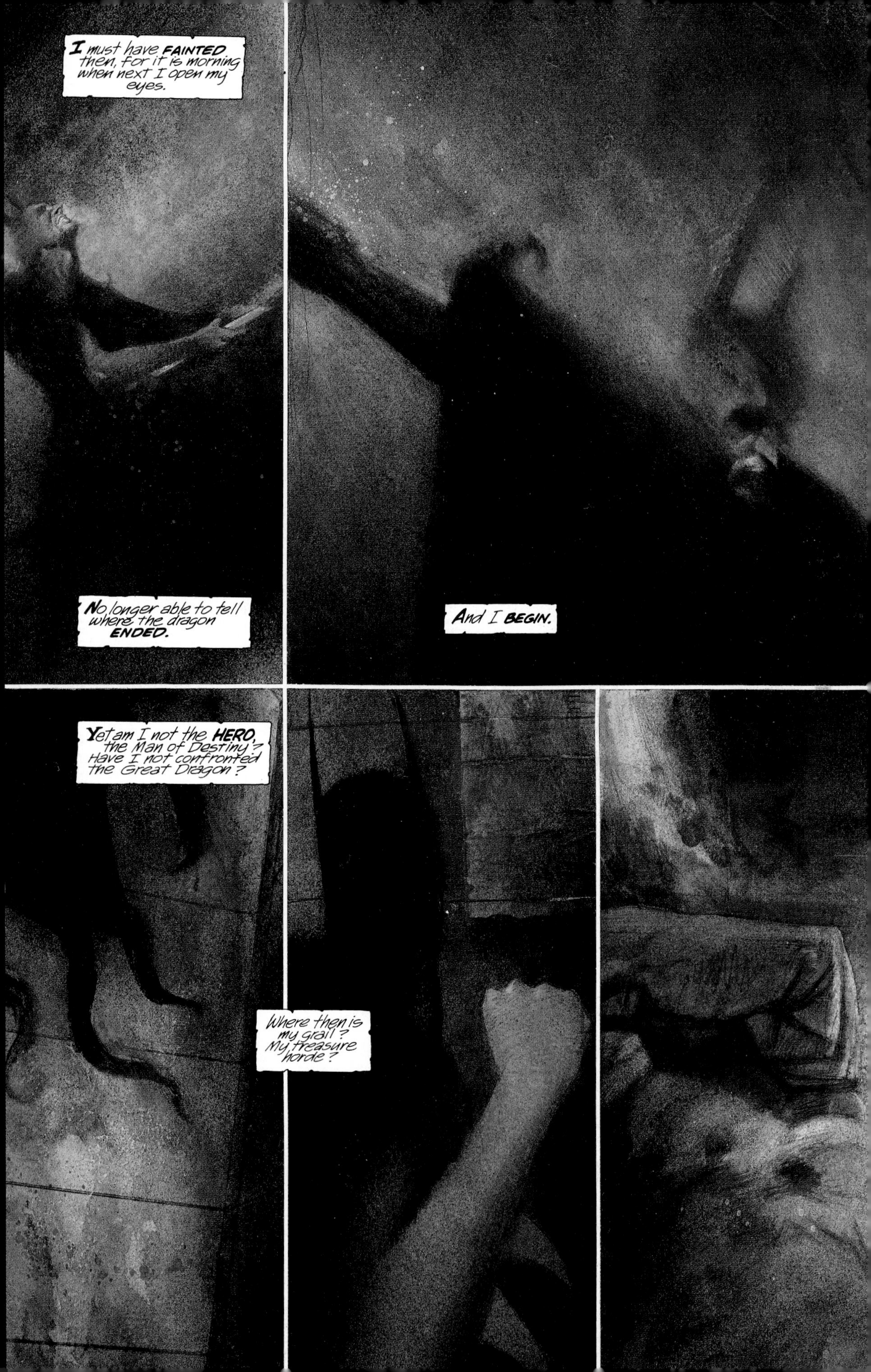
I must have FAINTED then, for it is morning when next I open my eyes.
No longer able to tell where the dragon ENDED.
And I BEGIN.
Yet am I not the HERO, the Man of Destiny? Have I not confronted the Great Dragon?
Where then is my grail? My treasure horde?

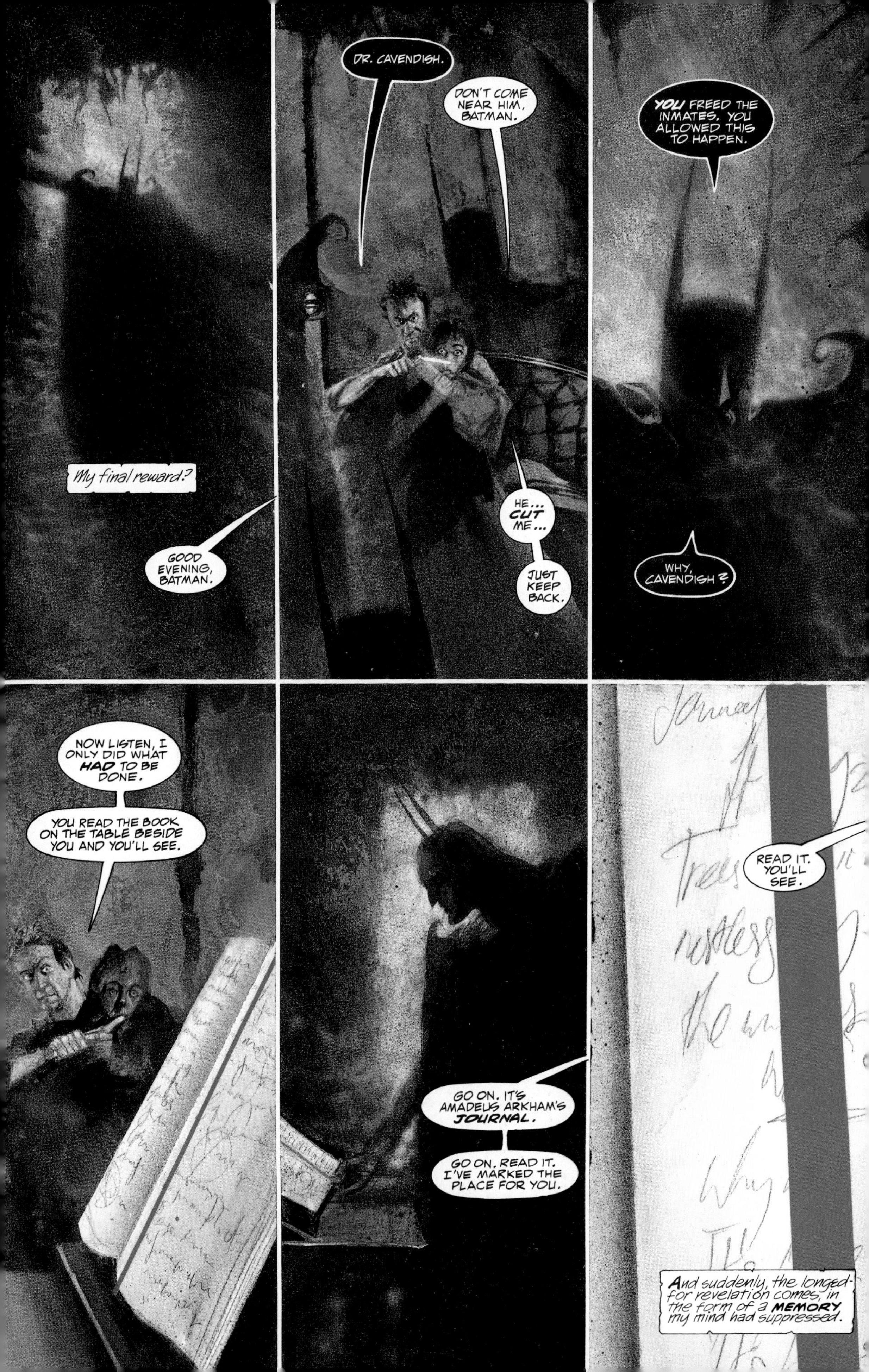

My final reward?
GOOD EVENING, BATMAN.
DR. CAVENDISH.
DON'T COME NEAR HIM, BATMAN.
HE... CUT ME...
JUST KEEP BACK.
YOU FREED THE INMATES. YOU ALLOWED THIS TO HAPPEN.
WHY, CAVENDISH?
NOW LISTEN, I ONLY DID WHAT HAD TO BE DONE.
YOU READ THE BOOK ON THE TABLE BESIDE YOU AND YOU'LL SEE.
GO ON. IT'S AMADEUS ARKHAM'S JOURNAL.
GO ON. READ IT. I'VE MARKED THE PLACE FOR YOU.
READ IT. YOU'LL SEE.
And suddenly, the longed-for revelation comes, in the form of a MEMORY my mind had suppressed.

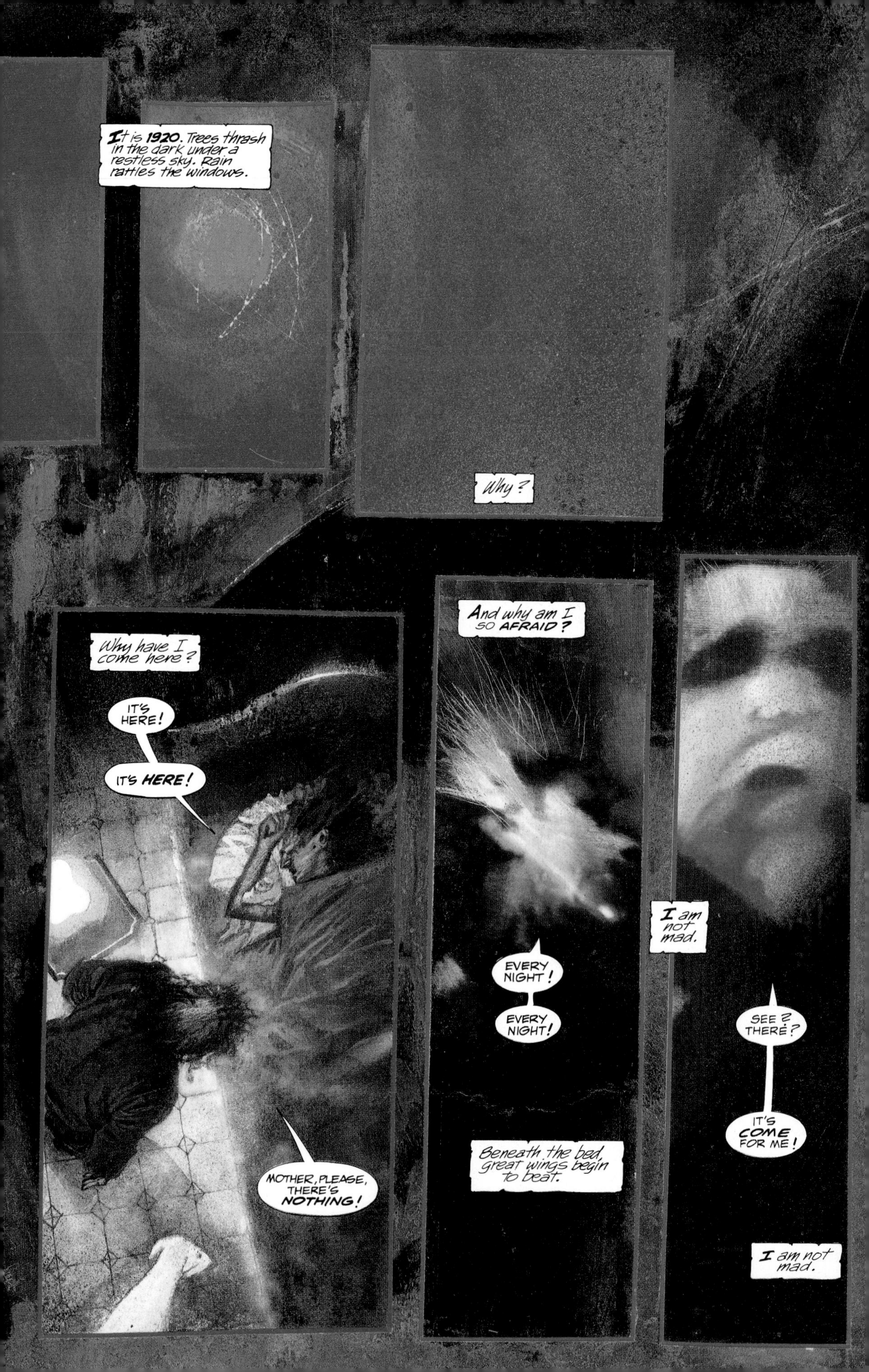
It is 1920. Trees thrash in the dark under a restless sky. Rain rattles the windows.
Why?
Why have I come here?
IT'S HERE!
IT'S HERE!
MOTHER, PLEASE, THERE'S NOTHING!
And why am I so AFRAID?
EVERY NIGHT!
EVERY NIGHT!
Beneath the bed, great wings begin to beat.
I am not mad.
SEE? THERE?
IT'S COME FOR ME!
I am not mad.

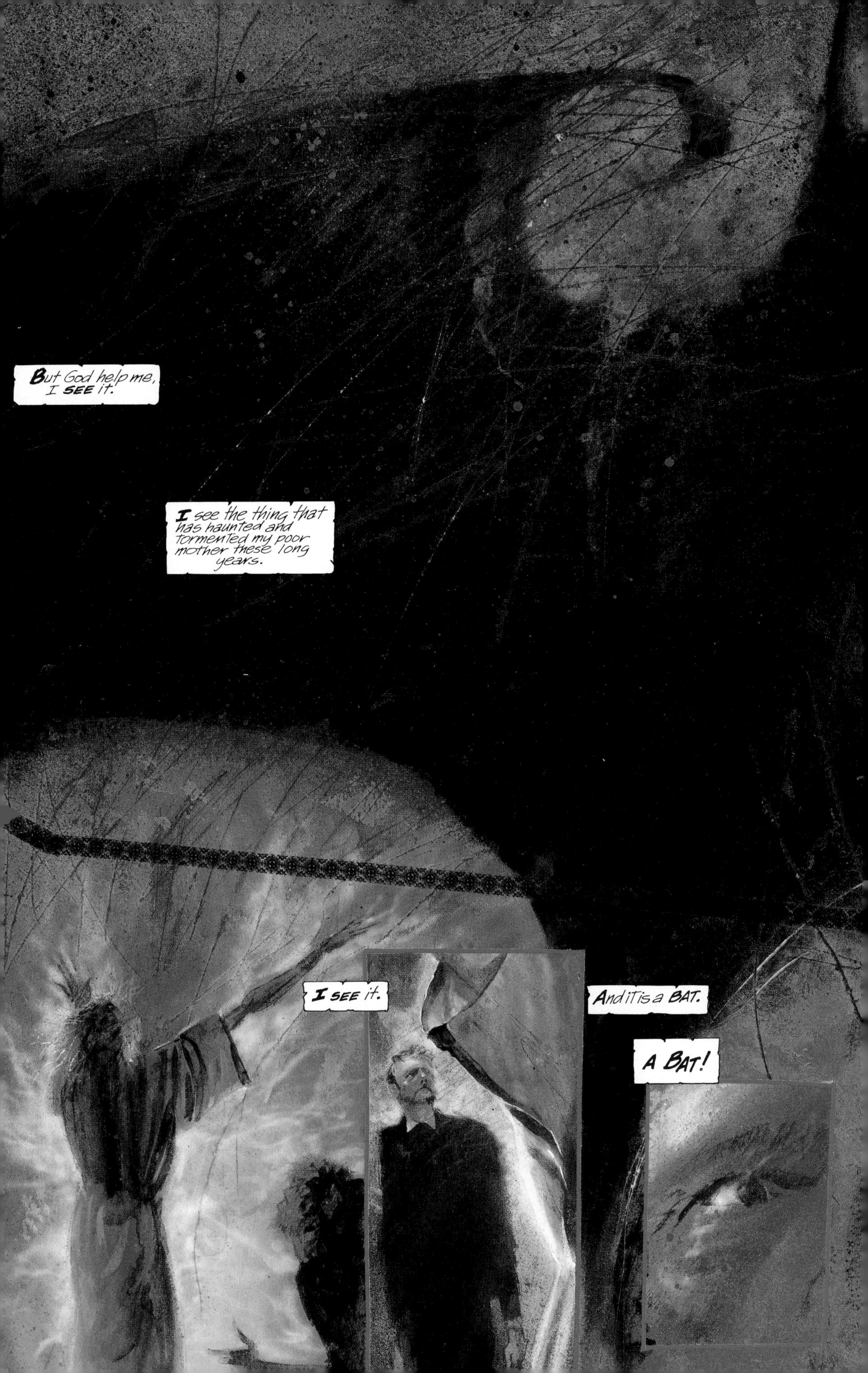
But God help me, I SEE it.
I see the thing that has haunted and tormented my poor mother these long years.
I SEE it.
And it is a BAT.
A BAT!

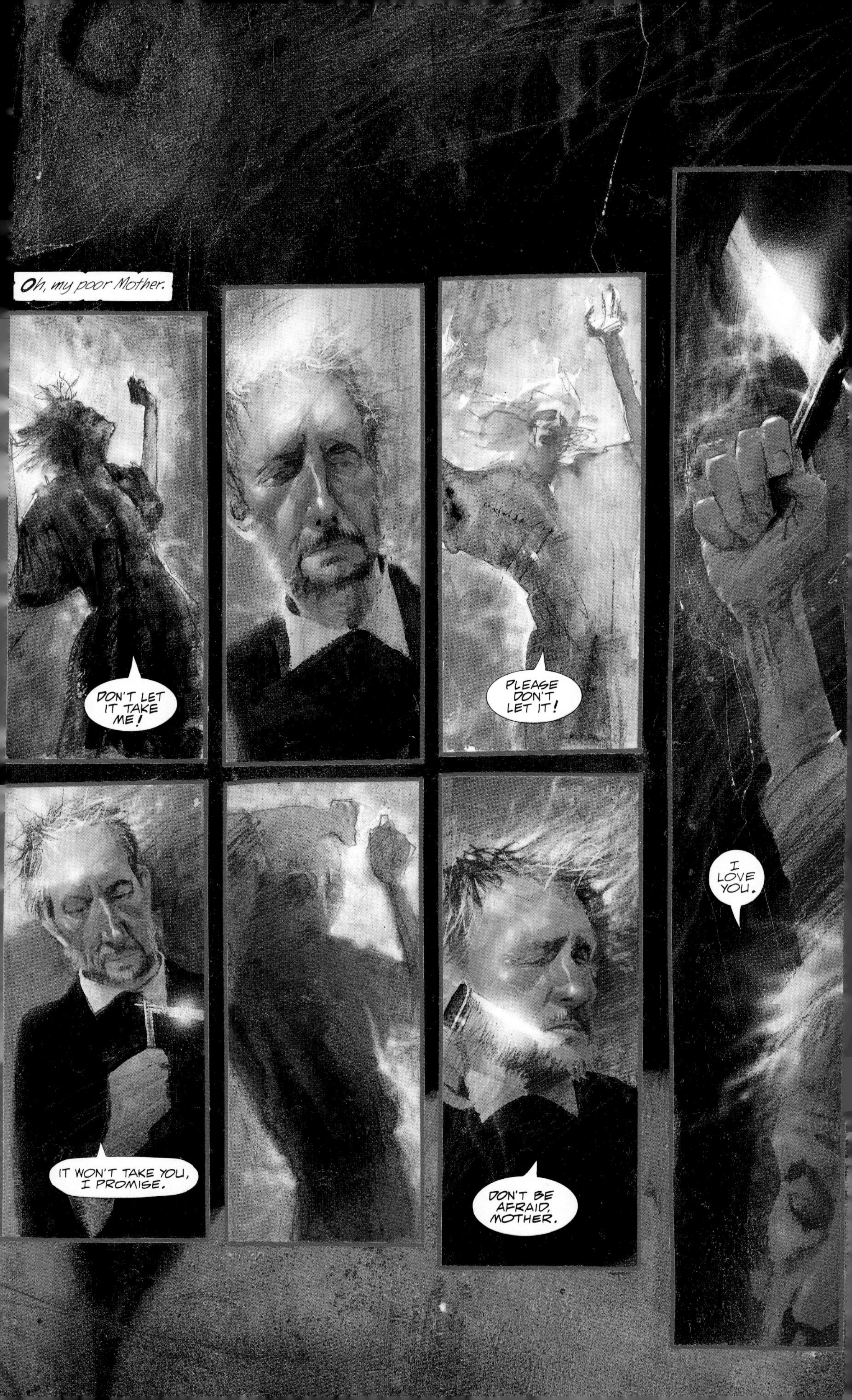
Oh, my poor Mother.
DON'T LET IT TAKE ME!
PLEASE DON'T LET IT!
I LOVE YOU.
IT WON'T TAKE YOU, I PROMISE.
DON'T BE AFRAID, MOTHER.

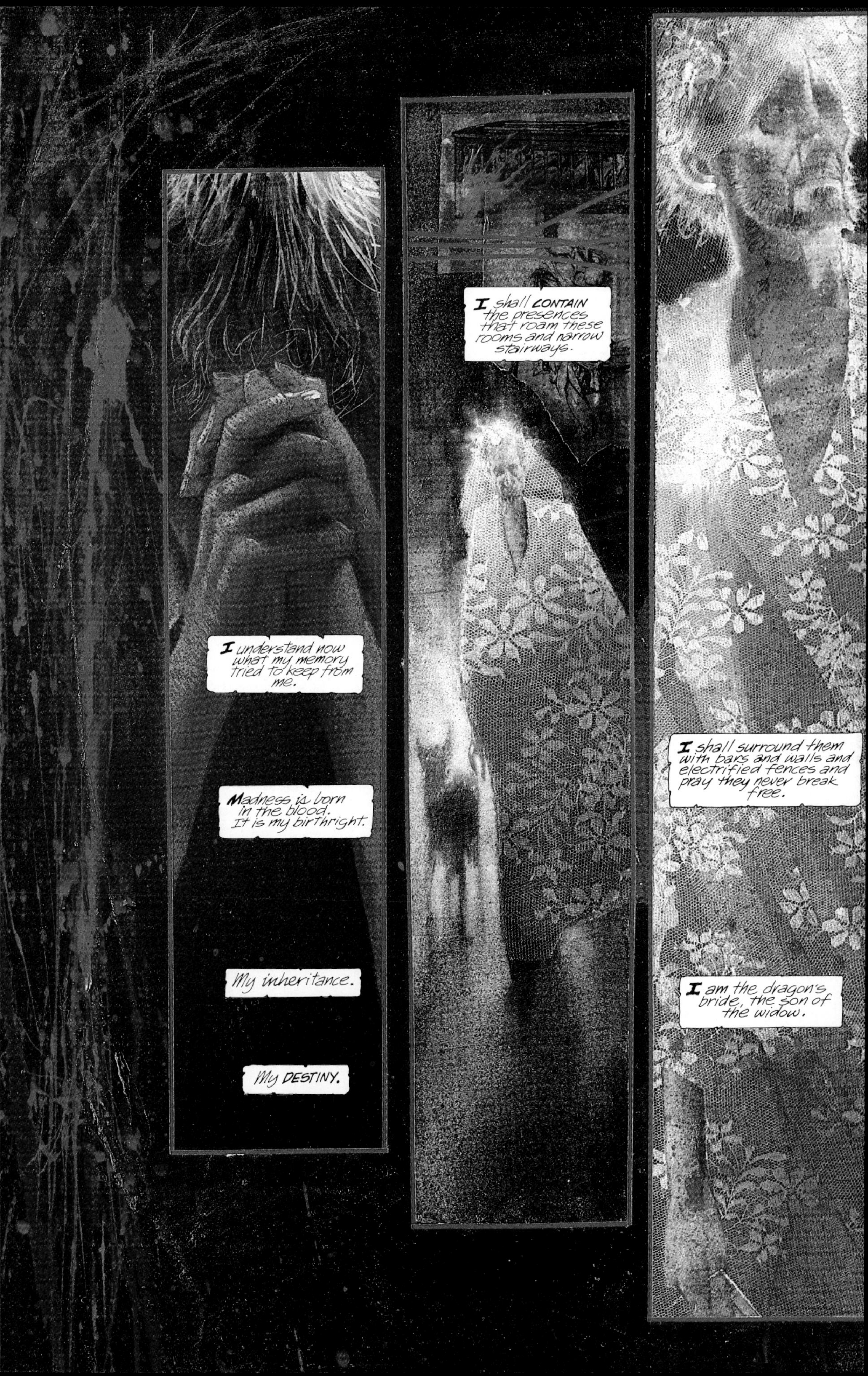
I understand now what my memory tried to keep from me.
Madness is born in the blood. It is my birthright.
My inheritance.
My DESTINY.
I shall CONTAIN the presences that roam these rooms and narrow stairways.
I shall surround them with bars and walls and electrified fences and pray they never break free.
I am the dragon's bride, the son of the widow.

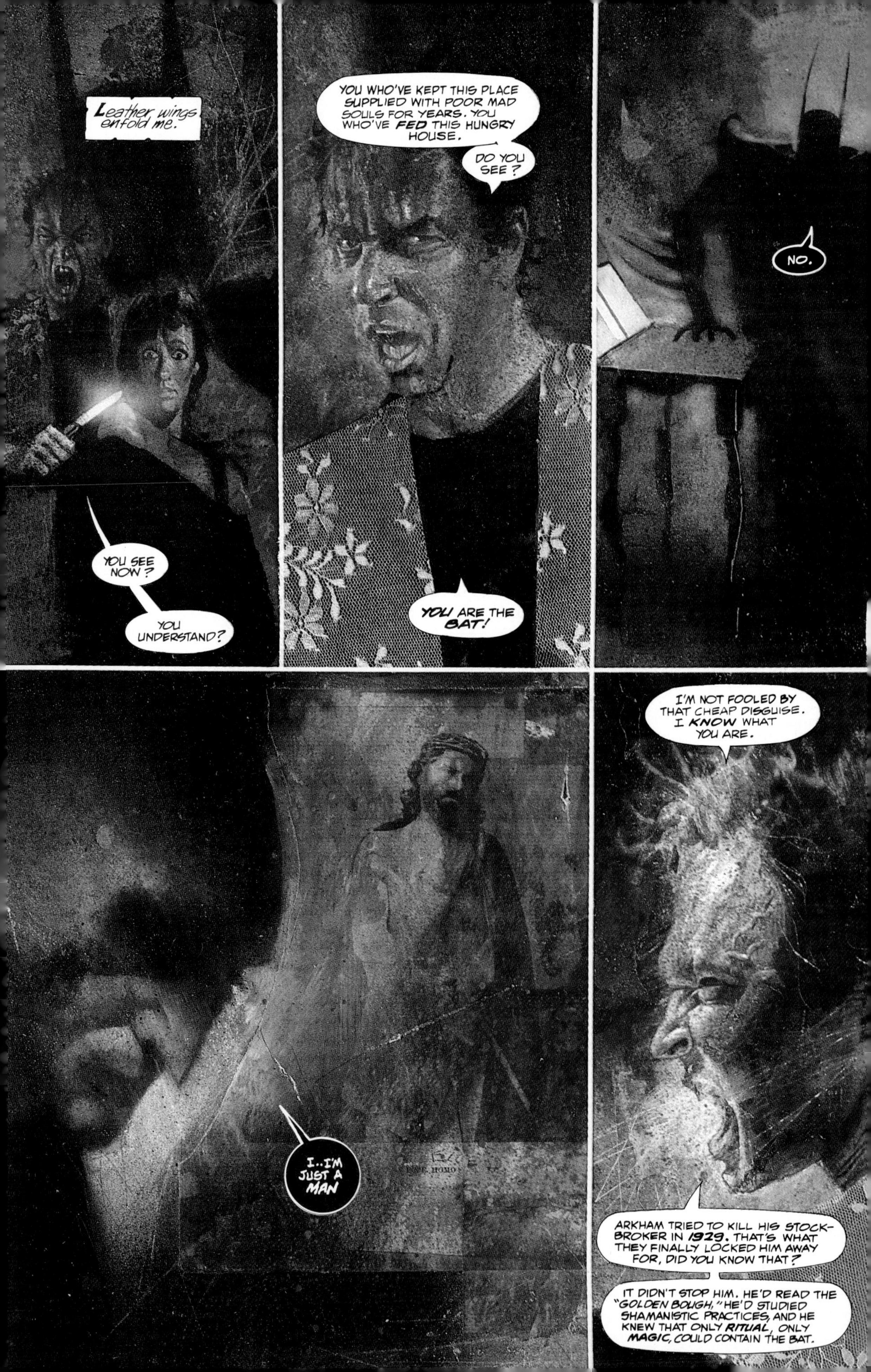
Leather wings enfold me.
YOU SEE NOW?
YOU UNDERSTAND?
YOU WHO'VE KEPT THIS PLACE SUPPLIED WITH POOR MAD SOULS FOR YEARS. YOU WHO'VE FED THIS HUNGRY HOUSE.
DO YOU SEE?
YOU ARE THE BAT!
NO.
I..I'M JUST A MAN
I'M NOT FOOLED BY THAT CHEAP DISGUISE. I KNOW WHAT YOU ARE.
ARKHAM TRIED TO KILL HIS STOCK-BROKER IN 1929. THAT'S WHAT THEY FINALLY LOCKED HIM AWAY FOR, DID YOU KNOW THAT?
IT DIDN'T STOP HIM. HE'D READ THE "GOLDEN BOUGH," HE'D STUDIED SHAMANISTIC PRACTICES, AND HE KNEW THAT ONLY RITUAL, ONLY MAGIC, COULD CONTAIN THE BAT.

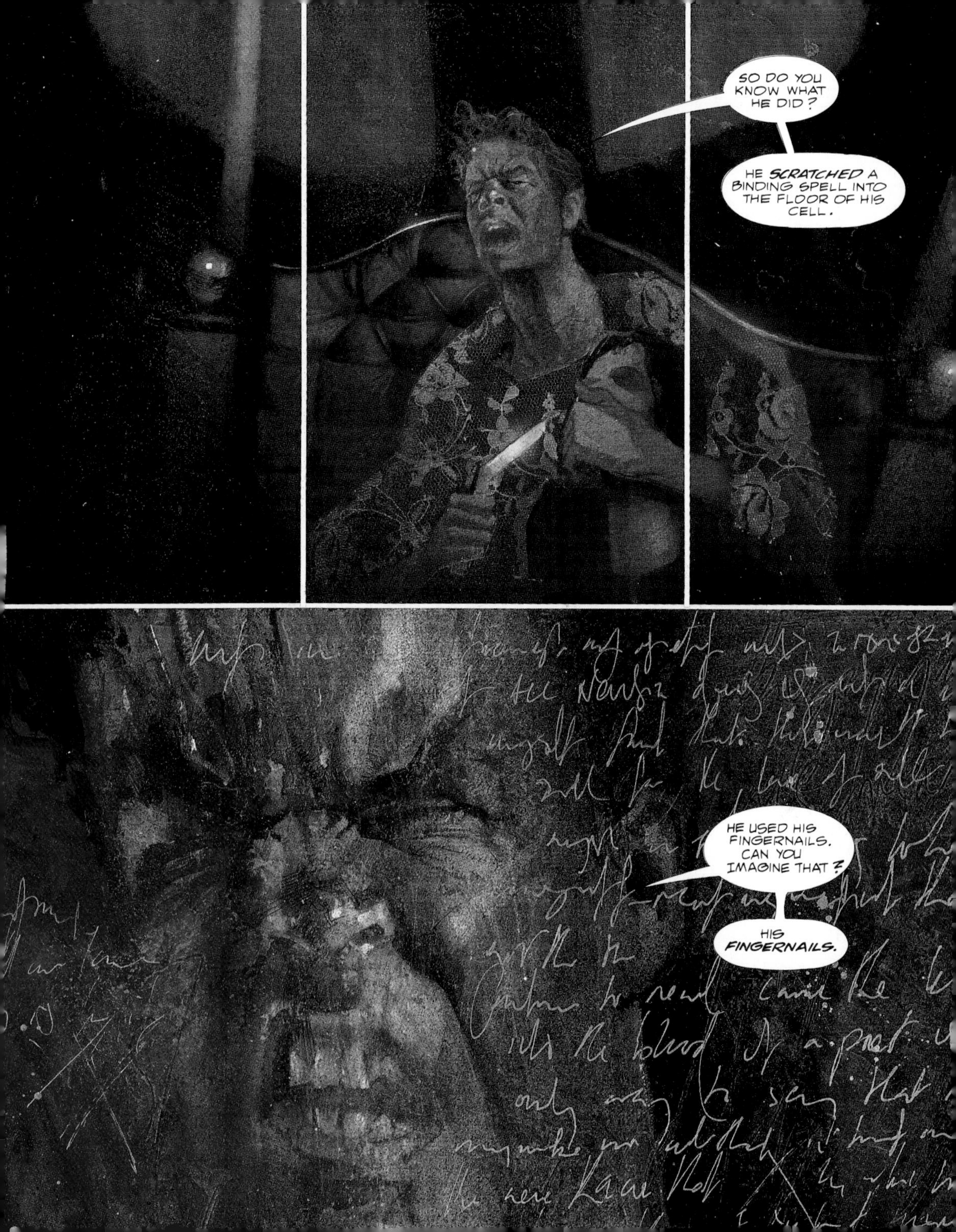
SO DO YOU KNOW WHAT HE DID?
HE SCRATCHED A BINDING SPELL INTO THE FLOOR OF HIS CELL.
HE USED HIS FINGERNAILS. CAN YOU IMAGINE THAT?
HIS FINGERNAILS.

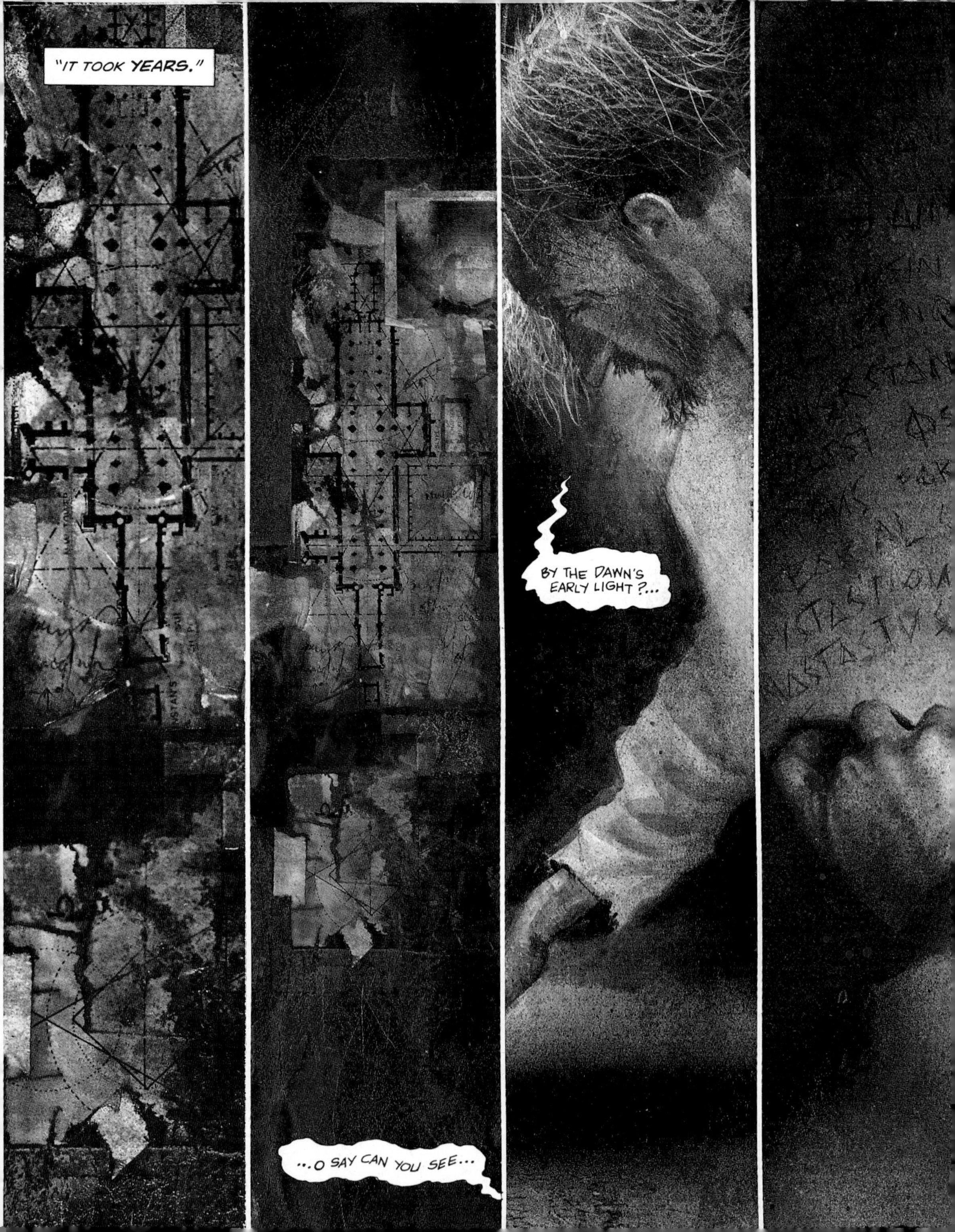
"IT TOOK YEARS."
...O SAY CAN YOU SEE...
BY THE DAWN'S EARLY LIGHT?...

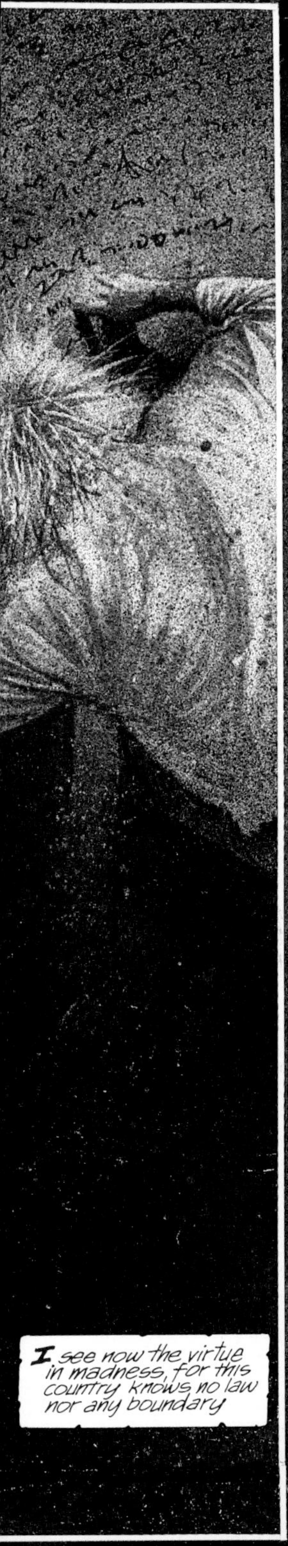
I see now the virtue in madness, for this country knows no law nor any boundary

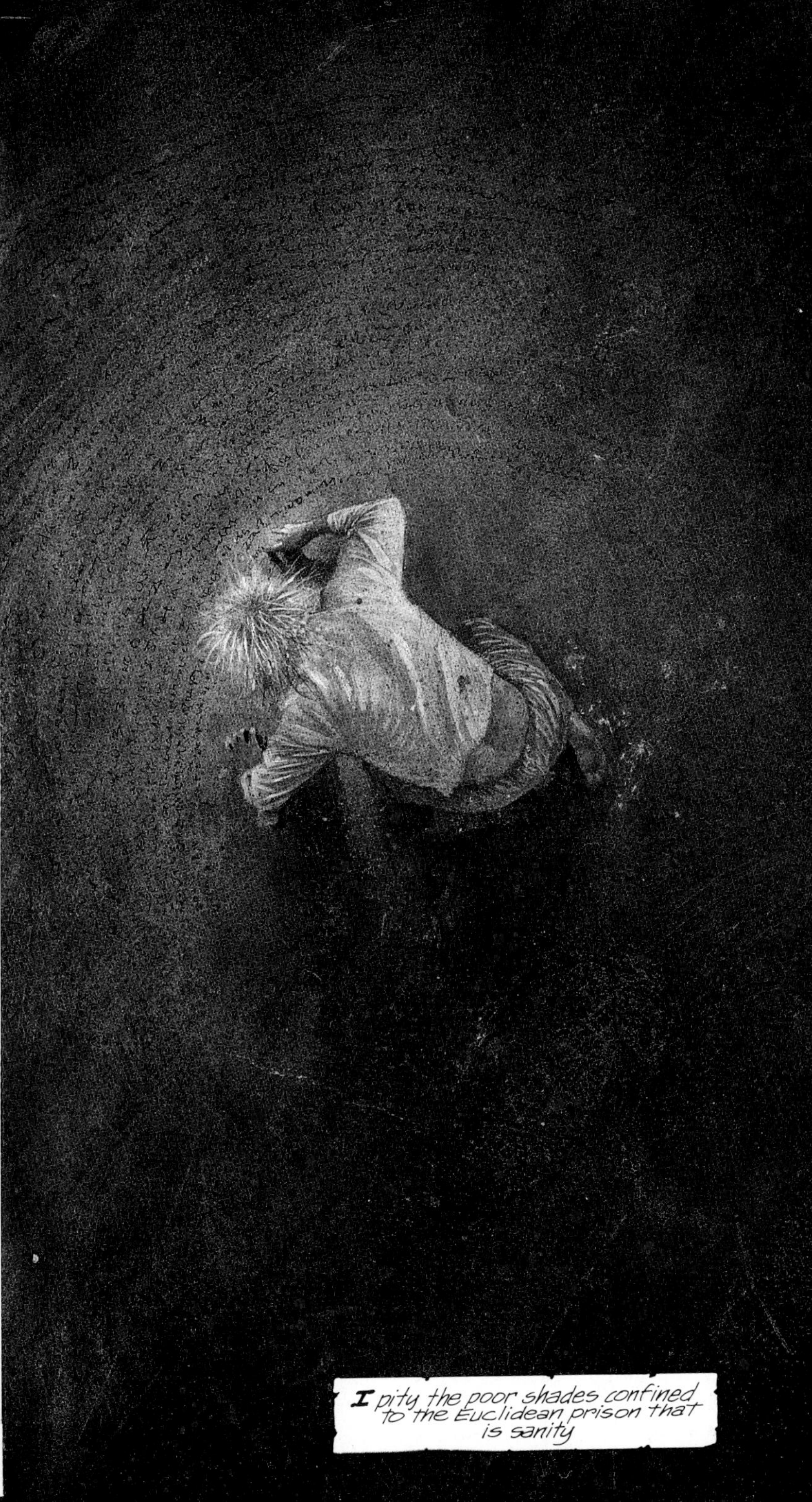
I pity the poor shades confined to the Euclidean prison that is sanity

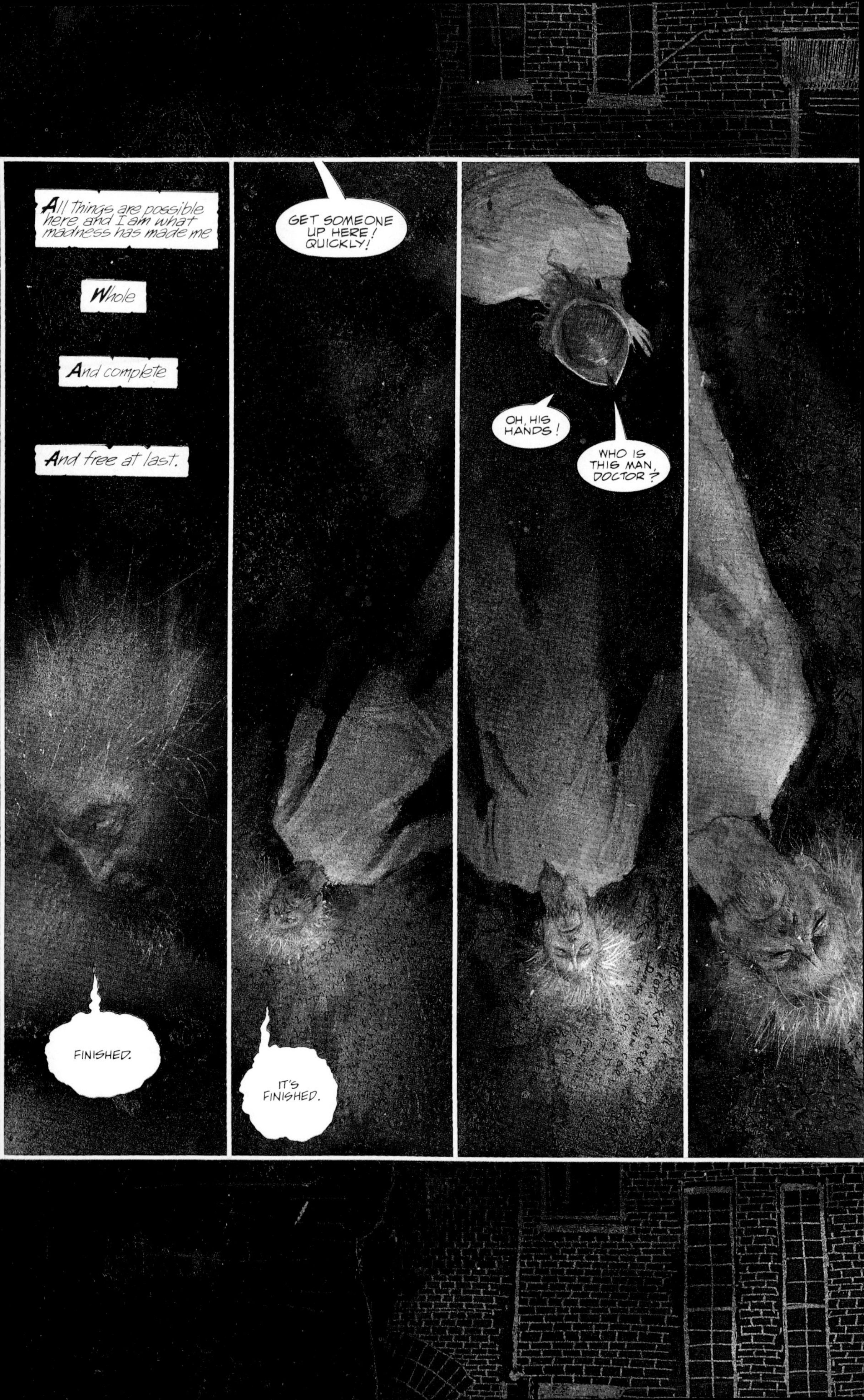
All things are possible here and I am what madness has made me
Whole
And complete
And free at last.
FINISHED.
GET SOMEONE UP HERE! QUICKLY!
IT'S FINISHED.
OH, HIS HANDS!
WHO IS THIS MAN, DOCTOR?

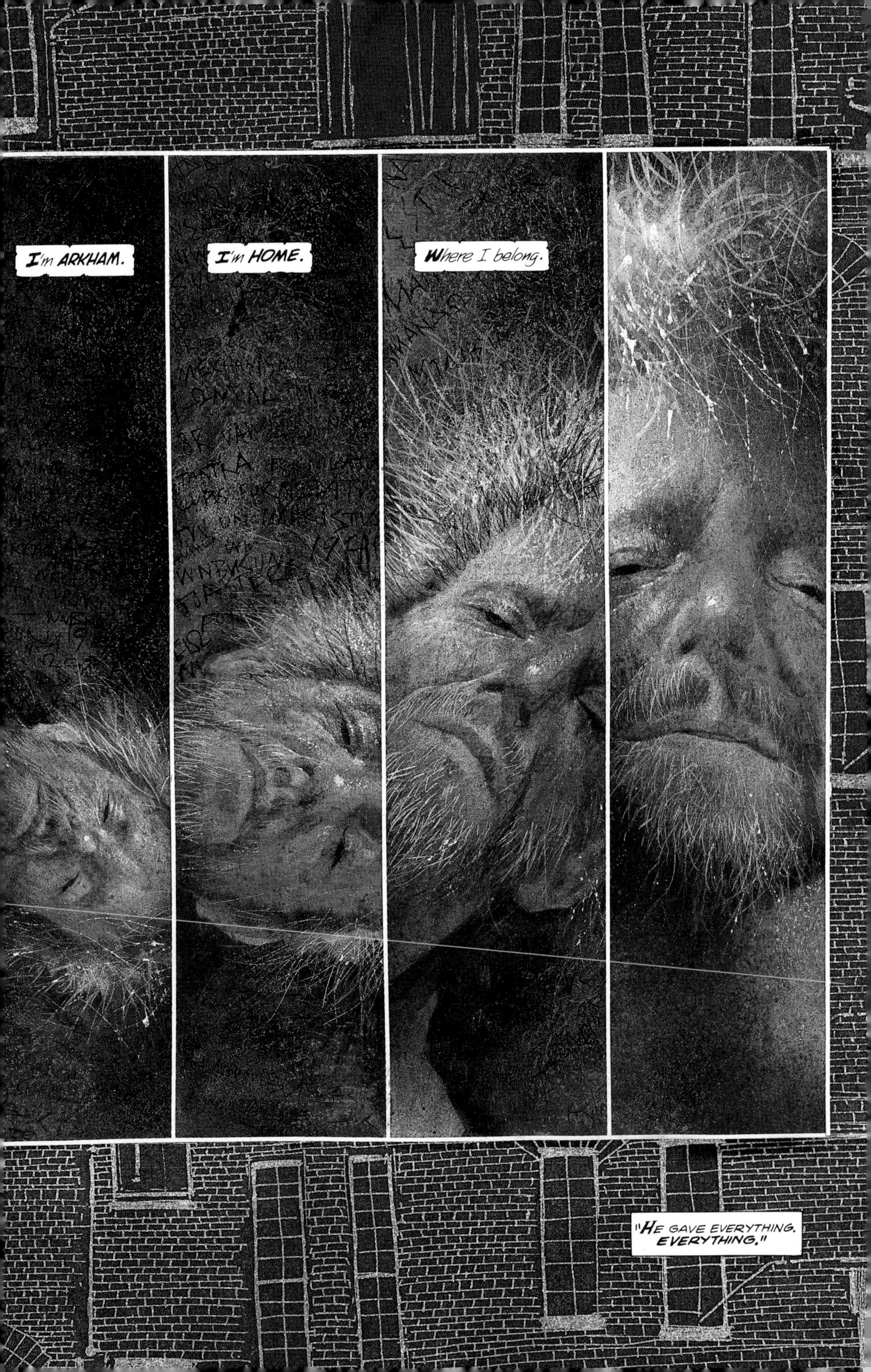
I'm ARKHAM.
I'm HOME.
Where I belong.
"HE GAVE EVERYTHING.
EVERYTHING."

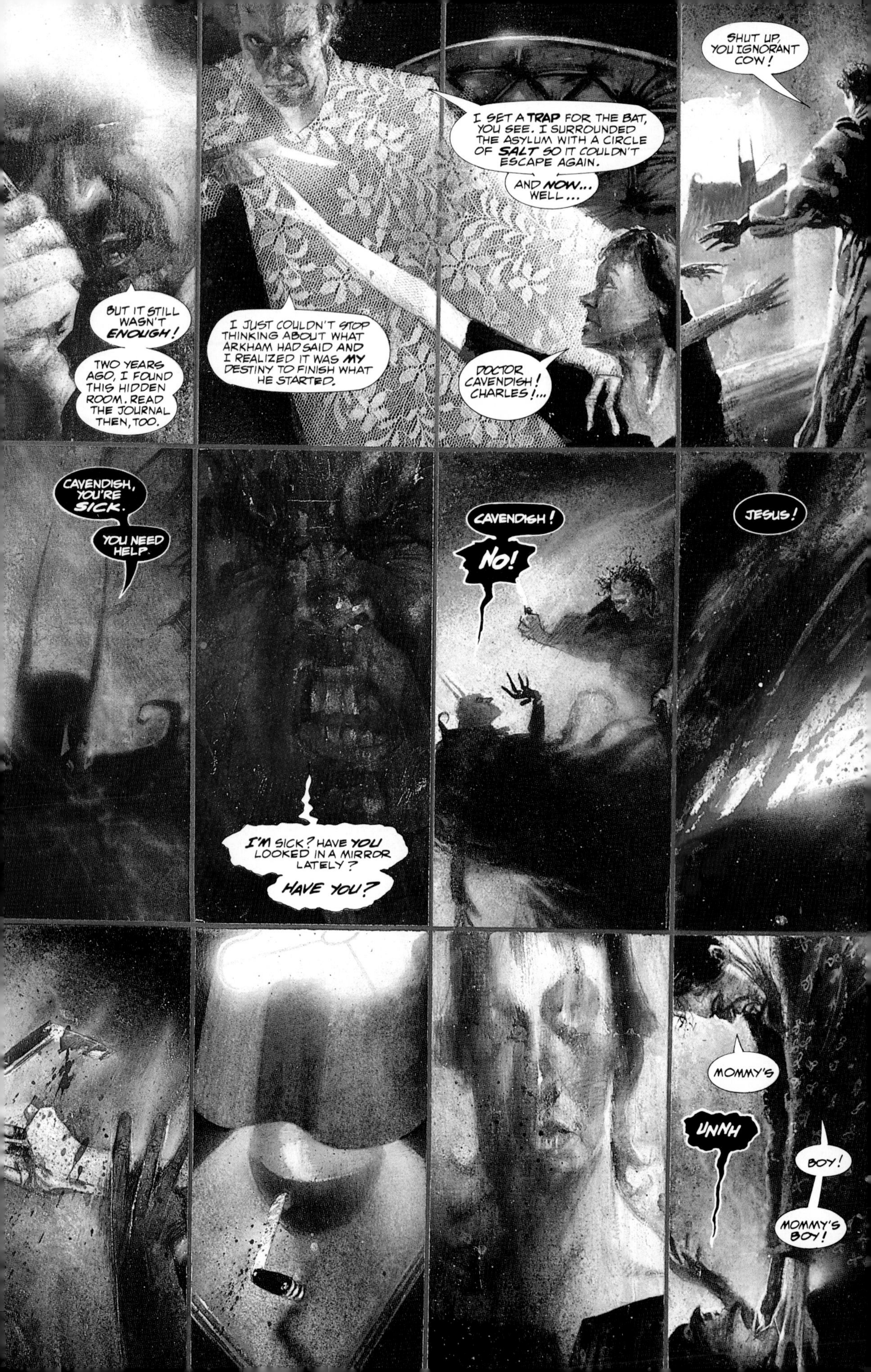
BUT IT STILL WASN'T ENOUGH!
TWO YEARS AGO, I FOUND THIS HIDDEN ROOM. READ THE JOURNAL THEN, TOO.
I JUST COULDN'T STOP THINKING ABOUT WHAT ARKHAM HAD SAID AND I REALIZED IT WAS MY DESTINY TO FINISH WHAT HE STARTED.
I SET A TRAP FOR THE BAT, YOU SEE. I SURROUNDED THE ASYLUM WITH A CIRCLE OF SALT SO IT COULDN'T ESCAPE AGAIN.
AND NOW... WELL...
DOCTOR CAVENDISH! CHARLES!...
SHUT UP, YOU IGNORANT COW!
CAVENDISH, YOU'RE SICK.
YOU NEED HELP.
I'M SICK? HAVE YOU LOOKED IN A MIRROR LATELY?
HAVE YOU?
CAVENDISH!
NO!
JESUS!
MOMMY'S
UNNH
BOY!
MOMMY'S BOY!

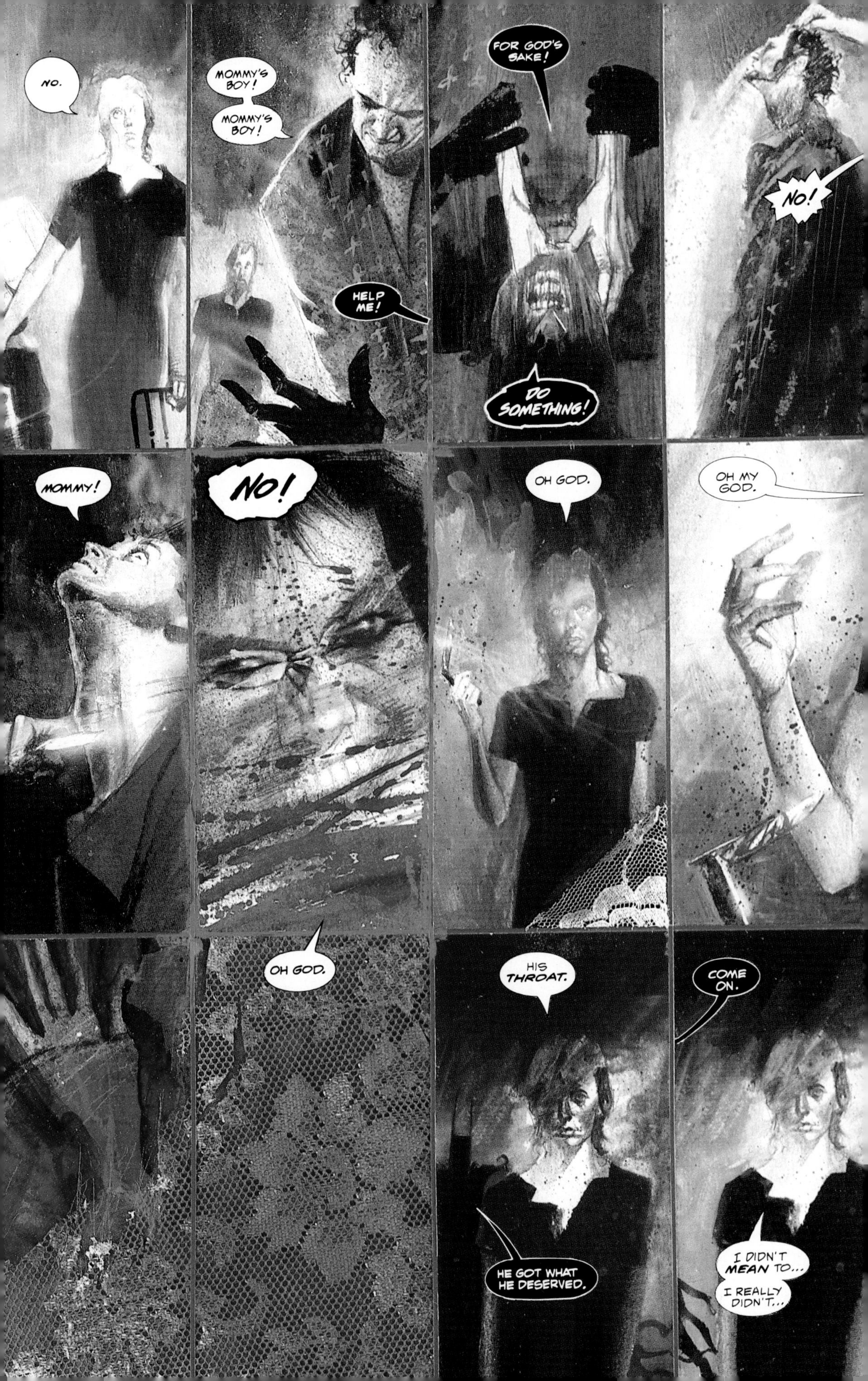
NO.
MOMMY'S BOY!
MOMMY'S BOY!
HELP ME!
FOR GOD'S SAKE!
DO SOMETHING!
NO!
MOMMY!
NO!
OH GOD.
OH MY GOD.
OH GOD.
HIS THROAT.
HE GOT WHAT HE DESERVED.
COME ON.
I DIDN'T MEAN TO...
I REALLY DIDN'T...

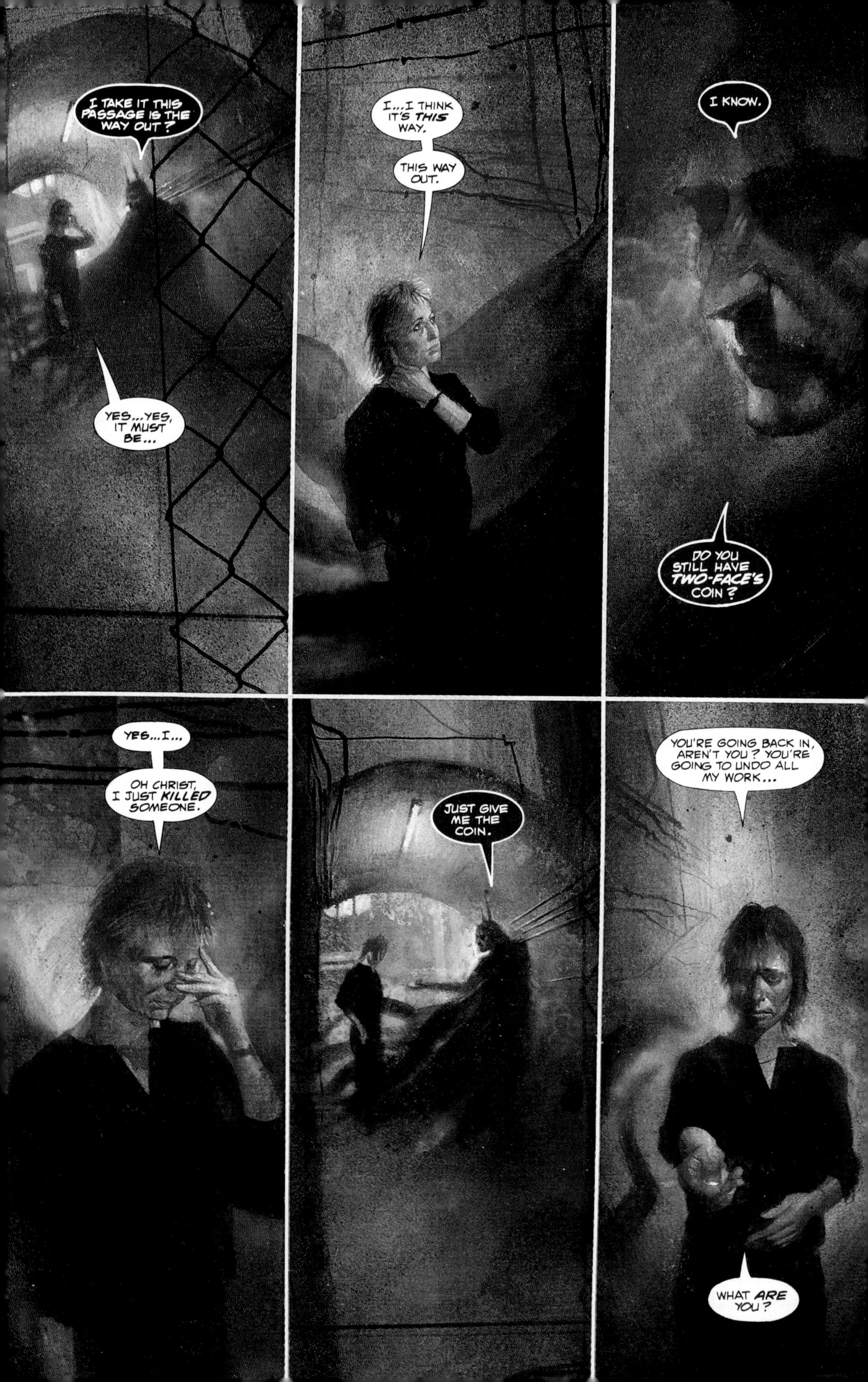
I TAKE IT THIS PASSAGE IS THE WAY OUT?
YES...YES, IT MUST BE...
I...I THINK IT'S THIS WAY.
THIS WAY OUT.
I KNOW.
DO YOU STILL HAVE TWO-FACE'S COIN?
YES...I...
OH CHRIST, I JUST KILLED SOMEONE.
JUST GIVE ME THE COIN.
YOU'RE GOING BACK IN, AREN'T YOU? YOU'RE GOING TO UNDO ALL MY WORK...
WHAT ARE YOU?

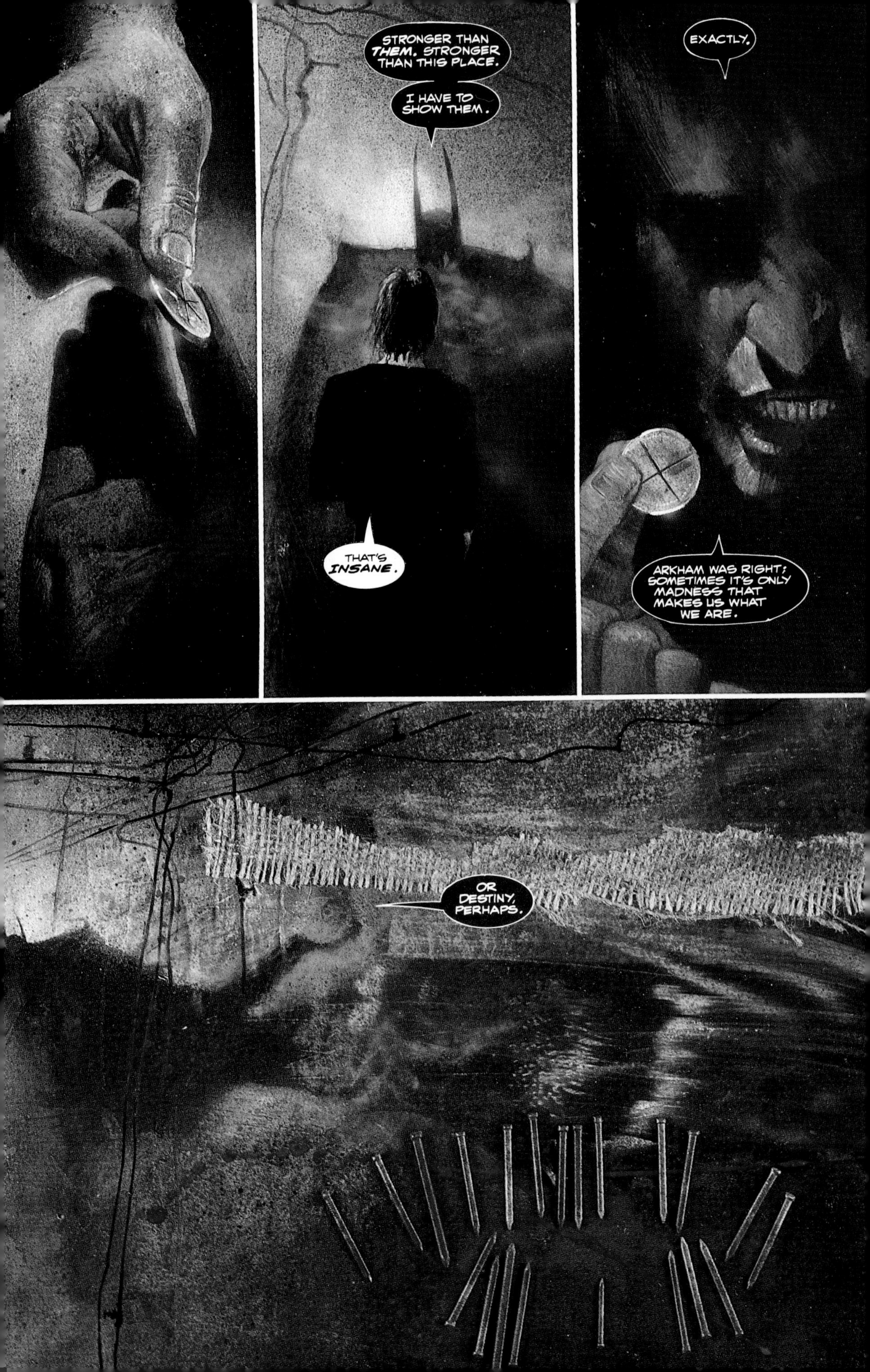

STRONGER THAN *THEM*. STRONGER THAN THIS PLACE.
I HAVE TO SHOW THEM.
THAT'S *INSANE*.
EXACTLY.
ARKHAM WAS RIGHT; SOMETIMES IT'S ONLY MADNESS THAT MAKES US WHAT WE ARE.
OR DESTINY, PERHAPS.

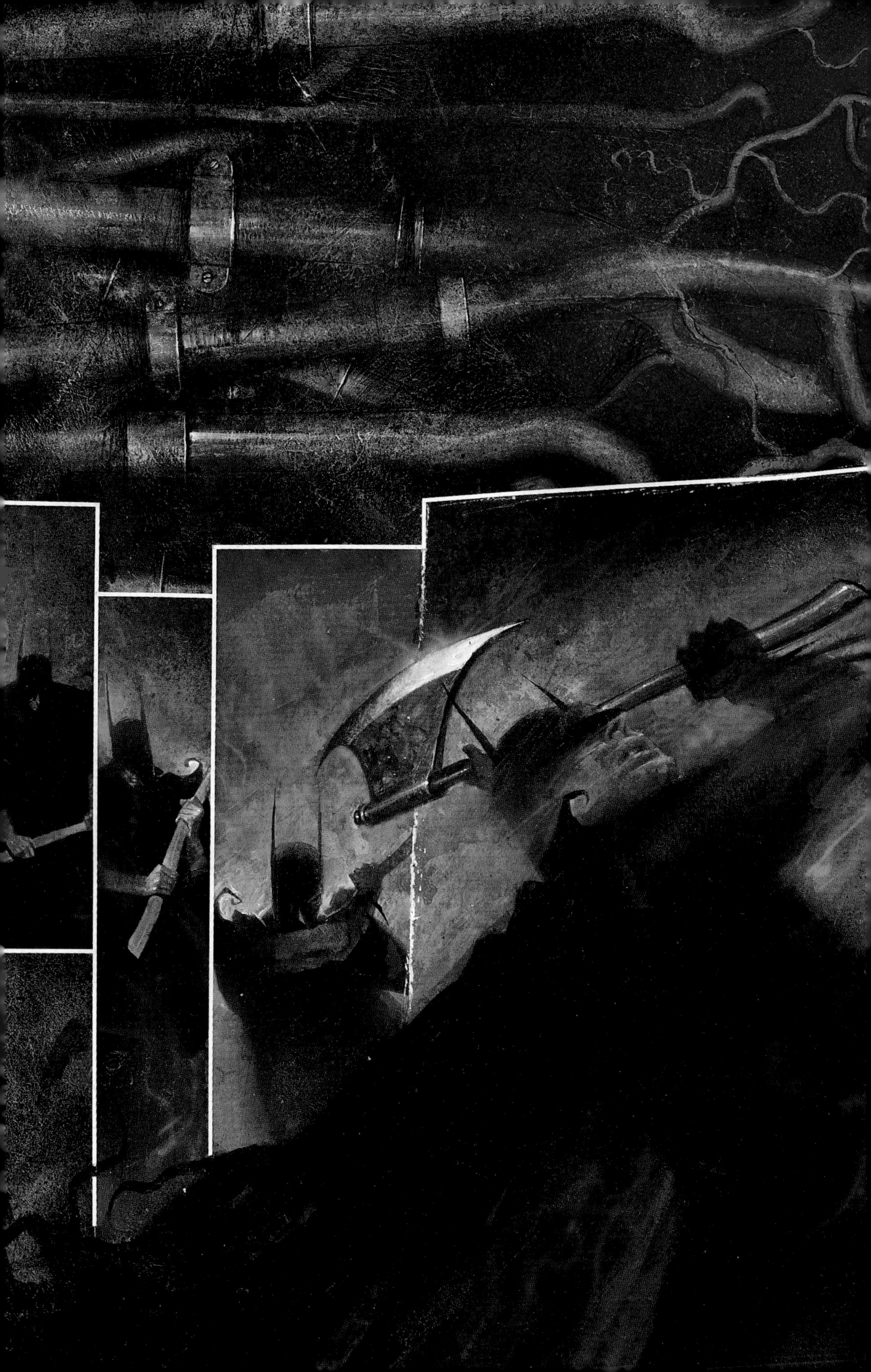

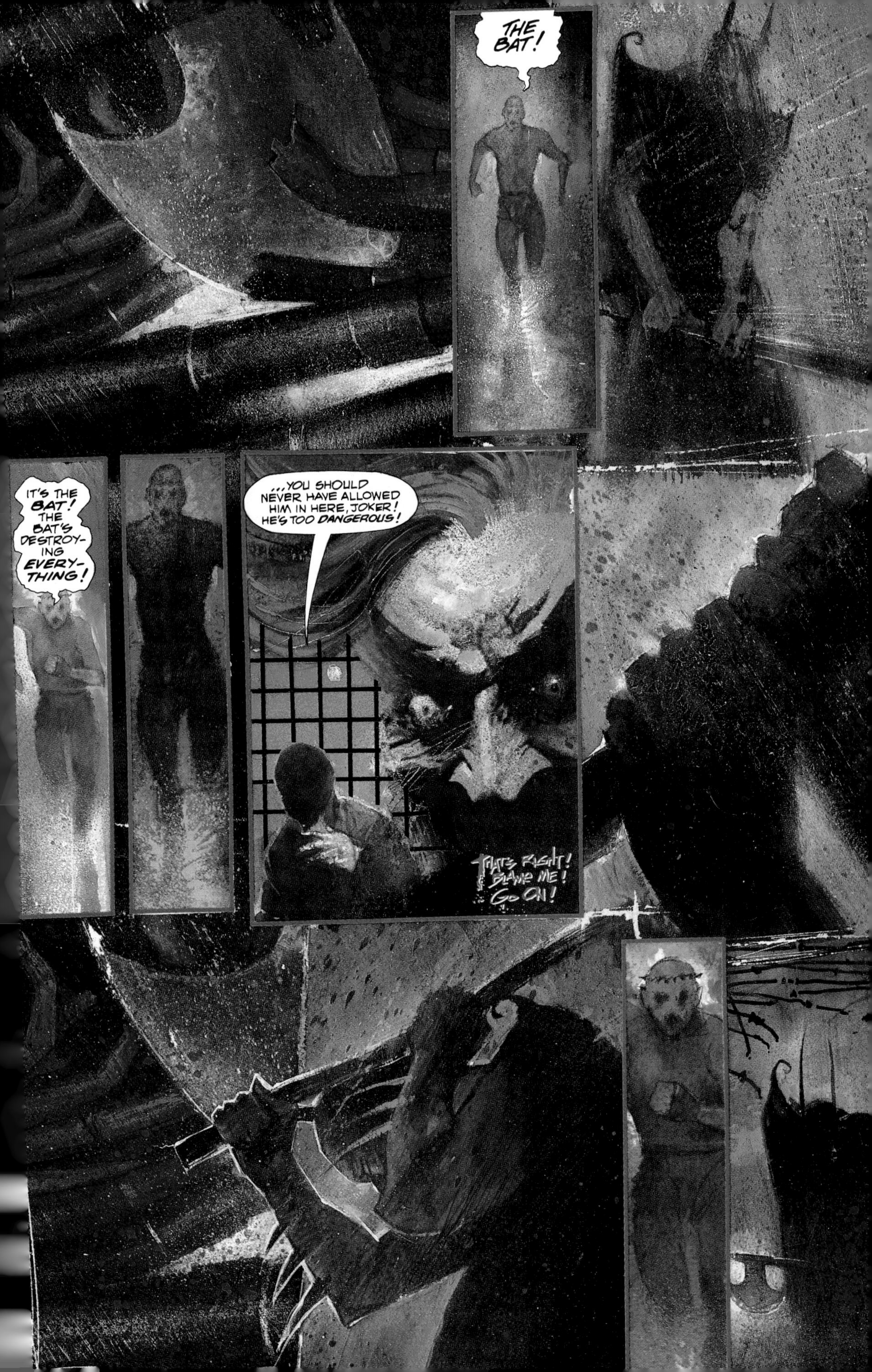
THE BAT!
IT'S THE BAT! THE BAT'S DESTROYING EVERYTHING!
...YOU SHOULD NEVER HAVE ALLOWED HIM IN HERE, JOKER! HE'S TOO DANGEROUS!
THAT'S RIGHT! BLAME ME! GO ON!

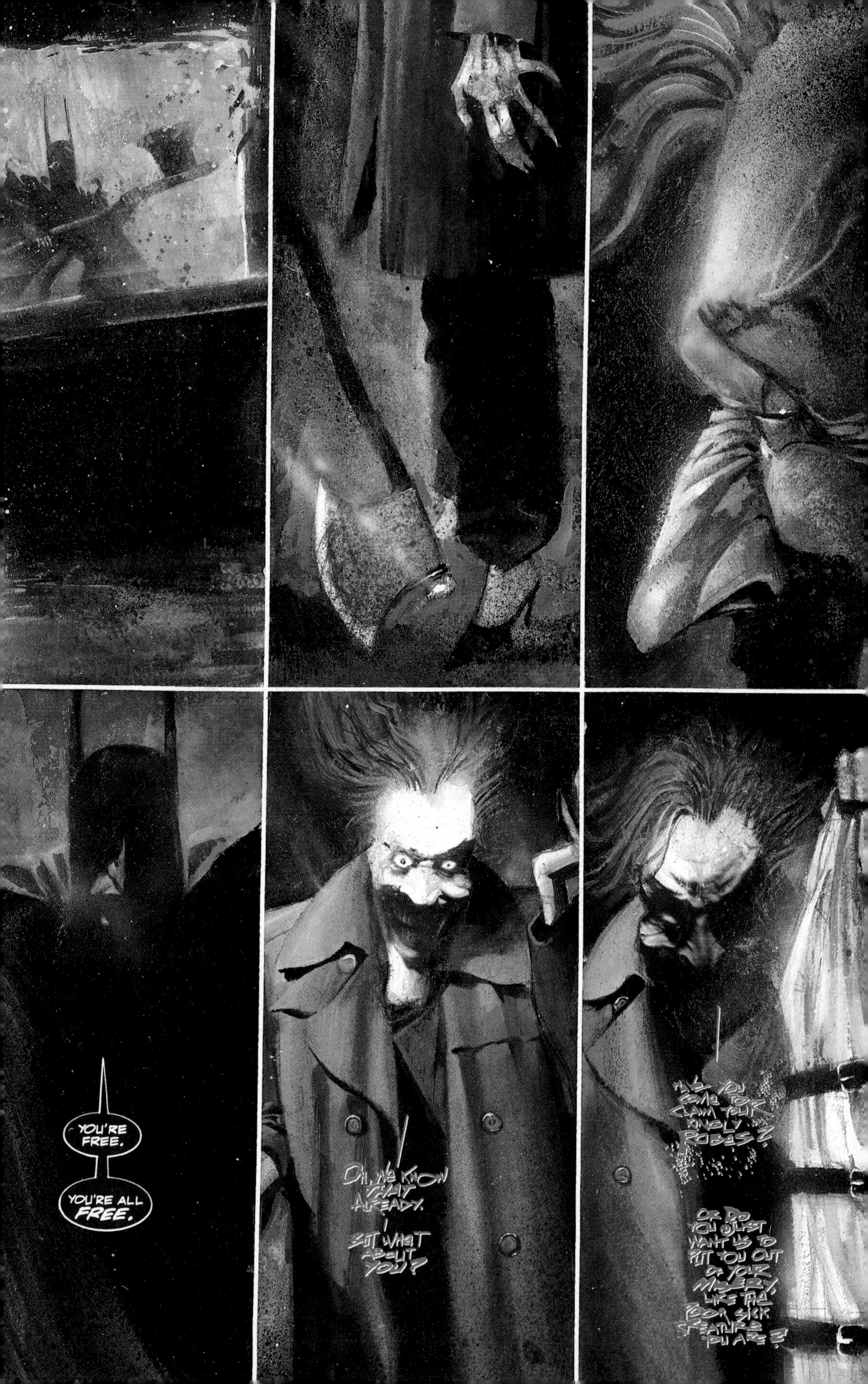
YOU'RE FREE.
YOU'RE ALL FREE.
OH, WE KNOW THAT ALREADY.
BUT WHAT ABOUT YOU?
HAVE YOU COME TO RECLAIM YOUR KINGLY ROBES?
OR DO YOU JUST WANT US TO PUT YOU OUT OF YOUR MISERY, LIKE THE POOR SICK CREATURE YOU ARE?

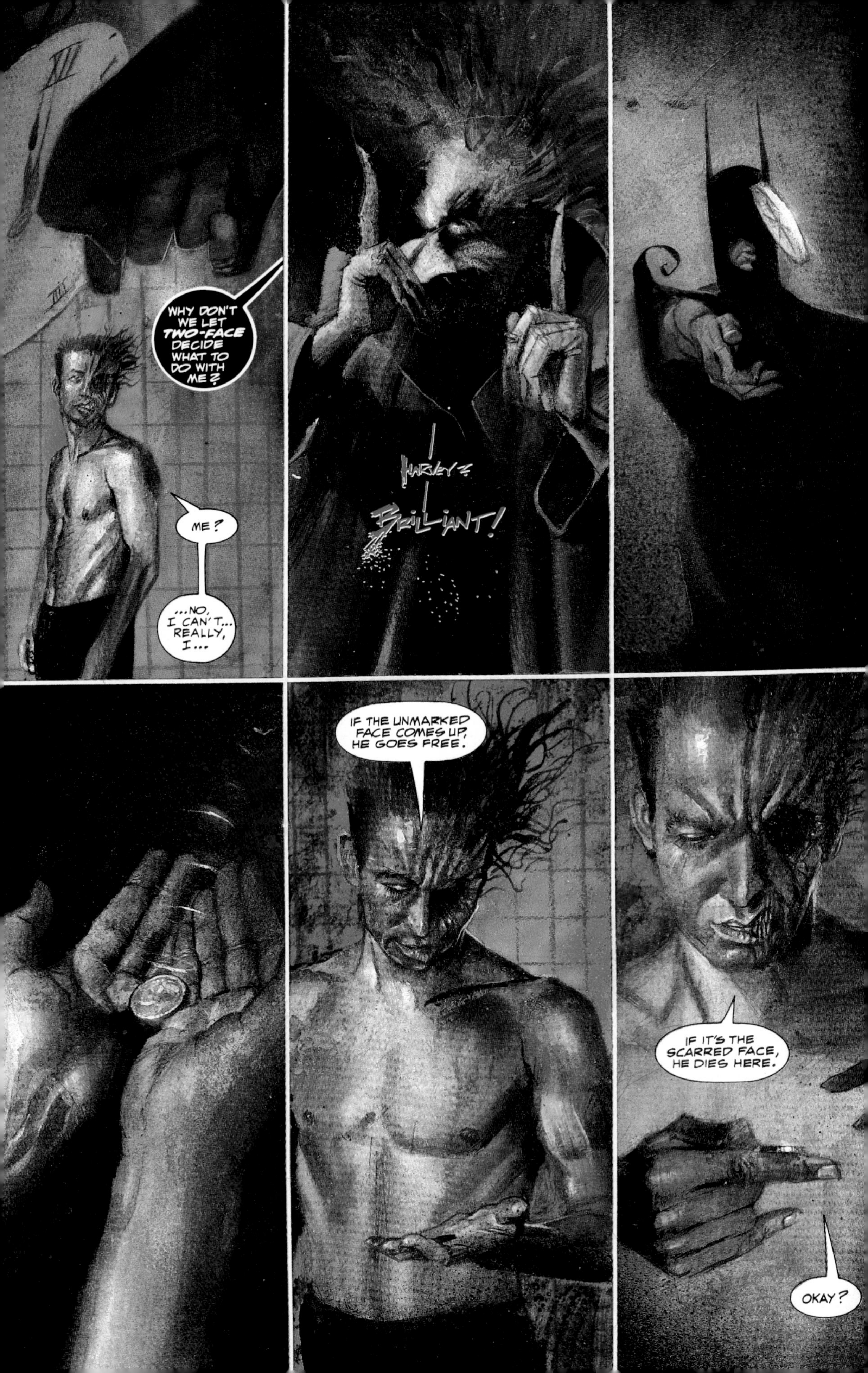
WHY DON'T WE LET **TWO-FACE** DECIDE WHAT TO DO WITH ME?
ME?
...NO, I CAN'T... REALLY, I...
HARVEY!
BRILLIANT!
IF THE UNMARKED FACE COMES UP, HE GOES FREE.
IF IT'S THE SCARRED FACE, HE DIES HERE.
OKAY?

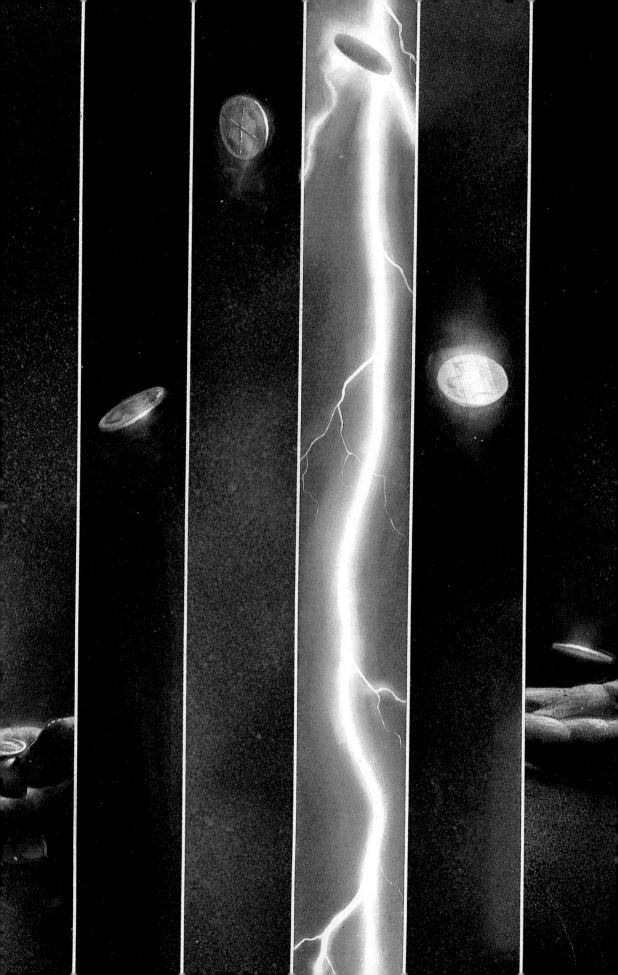

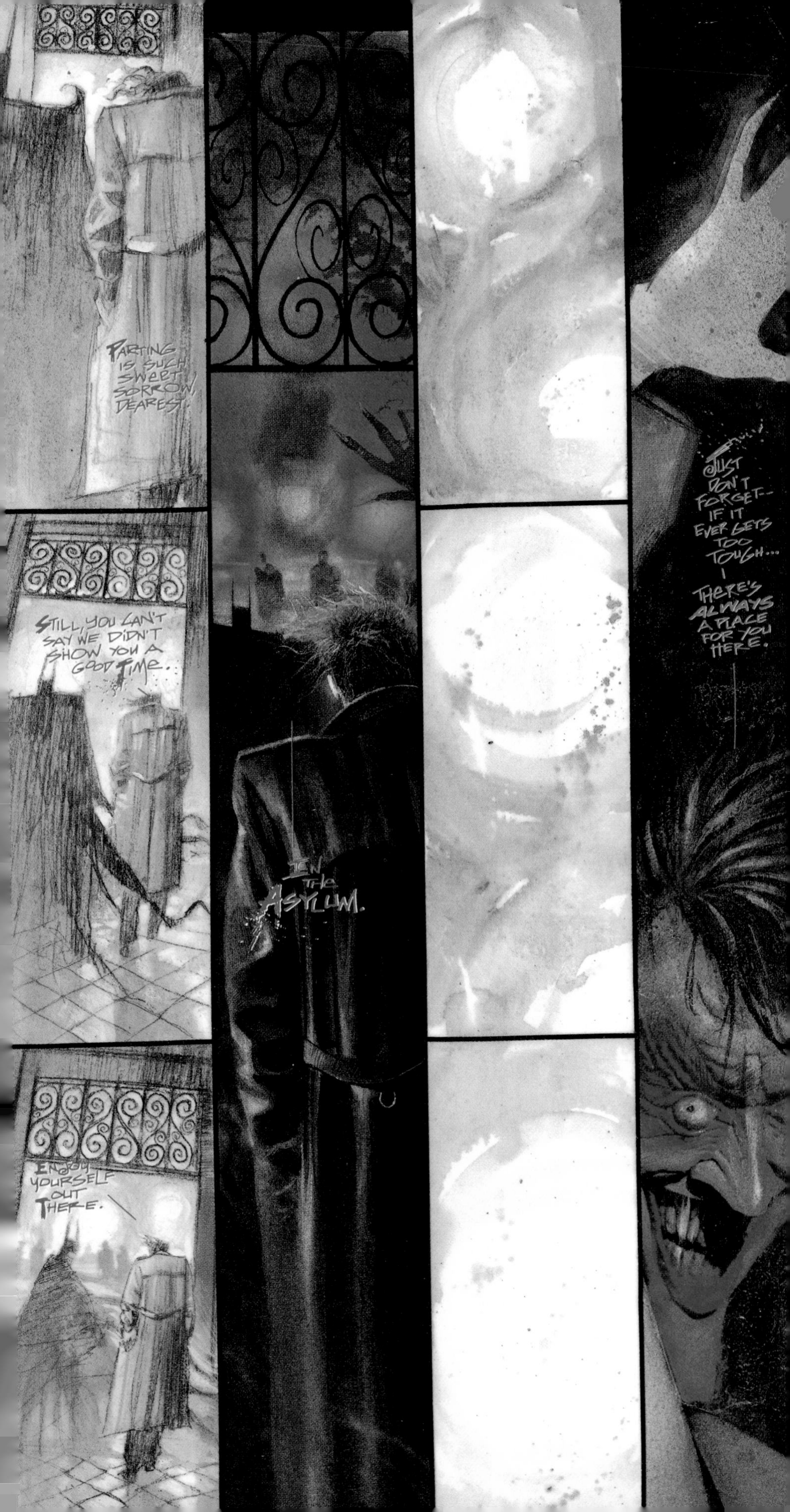
PARTING IS SUCH SWEET SORROW, DEAREST.
STILL, YOU CAN'T SAY WE DIDN'T SHOW YOU A GOOD TIME...
ENJOY YOURSELF OUT THERE.
IN THE ASYLUM.
JUST DON'T FORGET-- IF IT EVER GETS TOO TOUGH...
THERE'S ALWAYS A PLACE FOR YOU HERE.

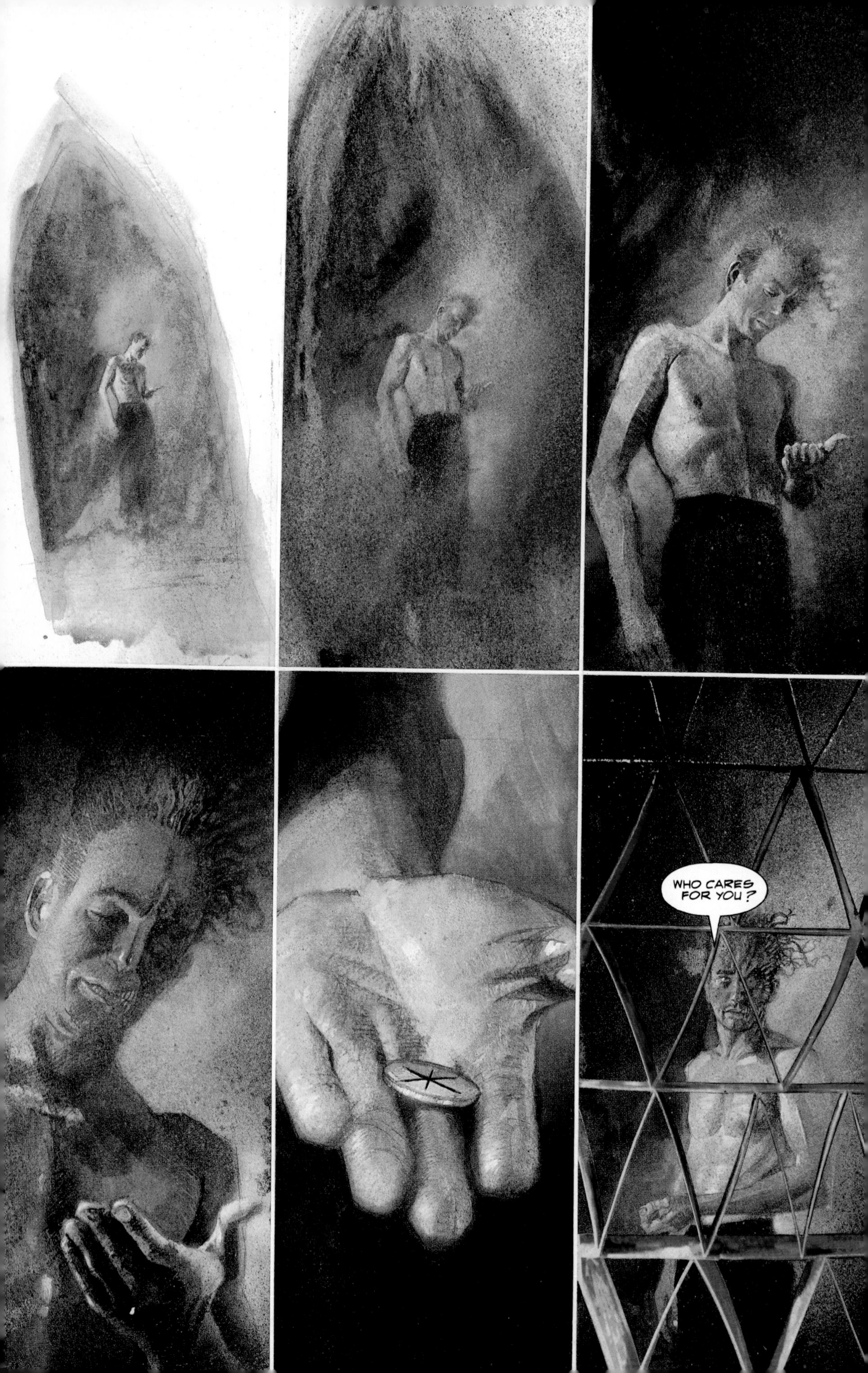
WHO CARES FOR YOU?

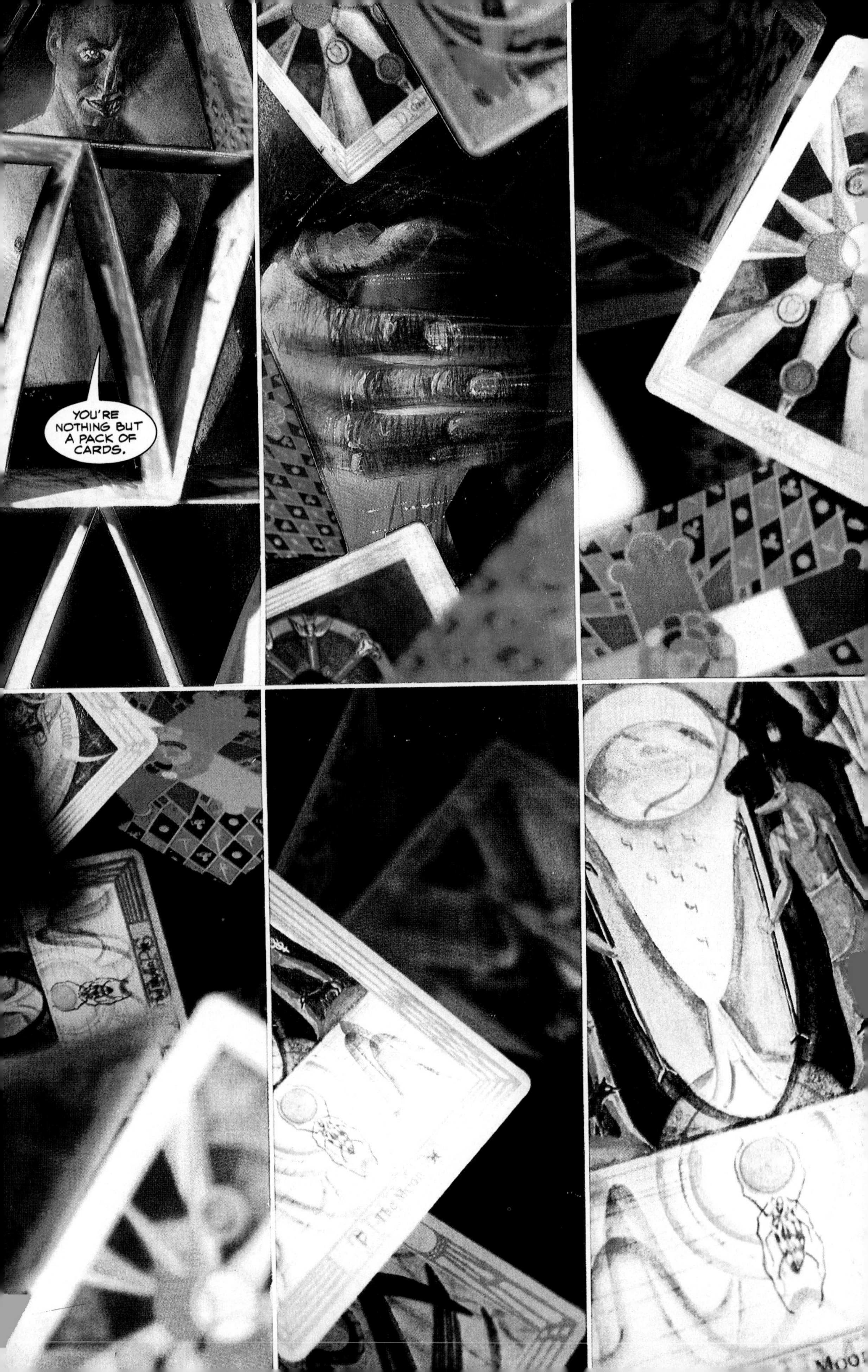
YOU'RE NOTHING BUT A PACK OF CARDS.

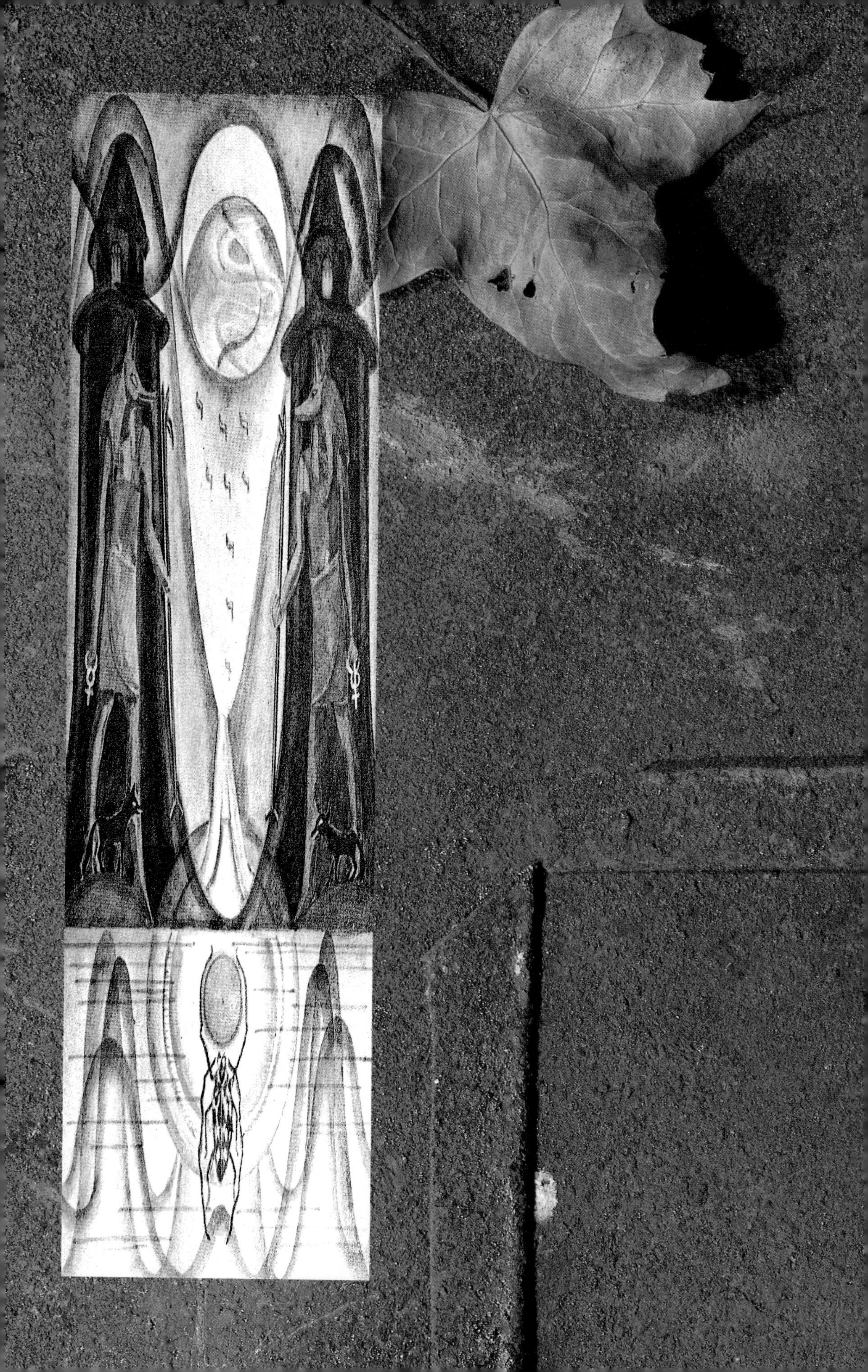

*A*ND IS NOT THAT A MOTHER'S GENTLE HAND THAT WITHDRAWS YOUR CURTAINS,

AND A MOTHER'S SWEET VOICE THAT SUMMONS YOU TO RISE?

TO RISE AND FORGET, IN THE BRIGHT SUNLIGHT,

THE UGLY DREAMS THAT FRIGHTENED YOU SO WHEN ALL WAS DARK –

LEWIS CARROLL

'Alice's Adventures in Wonderland'

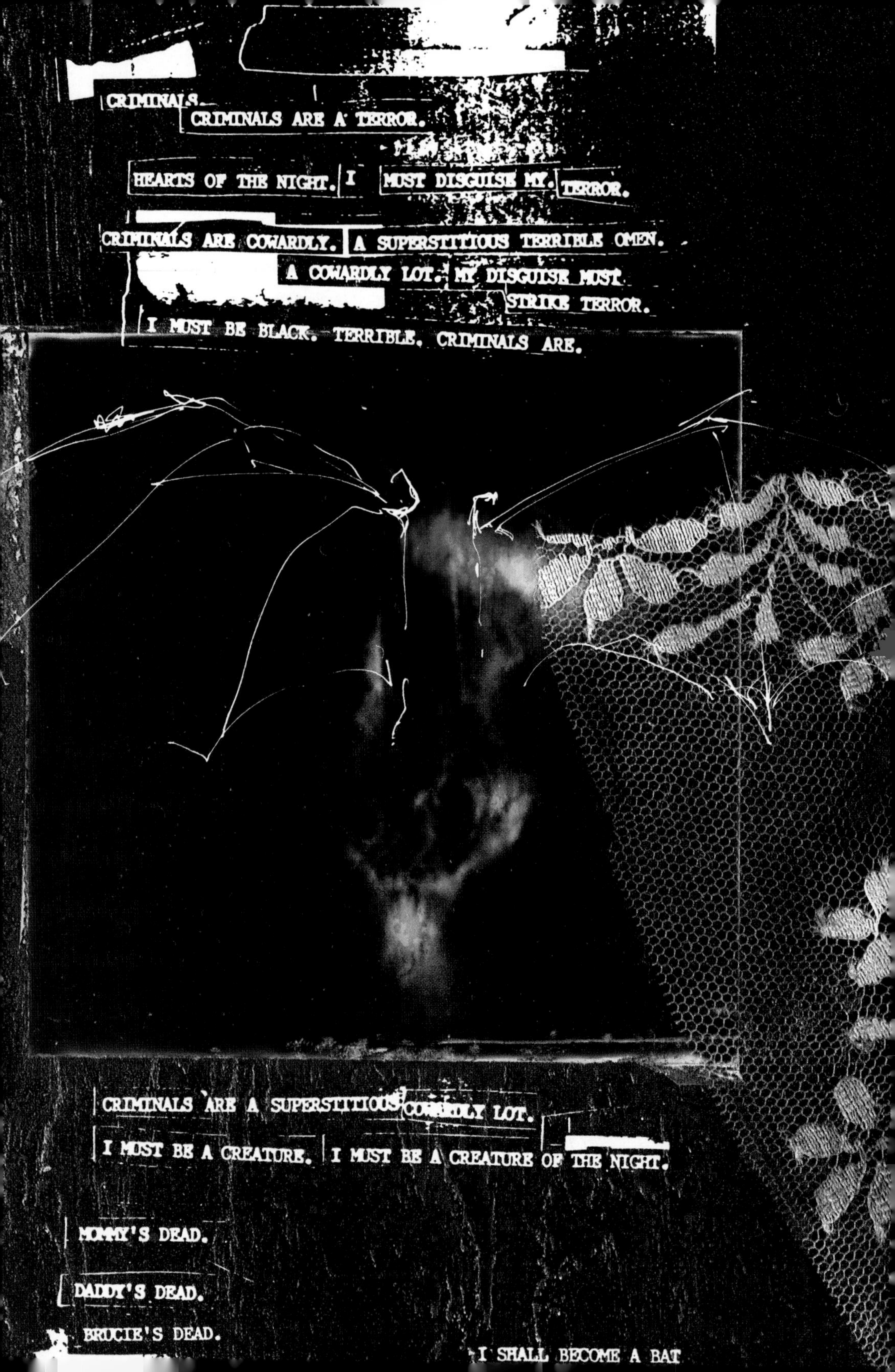
CRIMINALS.
CRIMINALS ARE A TERROR.
HEARTS OF THE NIGHT.
I
MUST DISGUISE MY.
TERROR.
CRIMINALS ARE COWARDLY.
A SUPERSTITIOUS TERRIBLE OMEN.
A COWARDLY LOT.
MY DISGUISE MUST.
STRIKE TERROR.
I MUST BE BLACK. TERRIBLE. CRIMINALS ARE.
CRIMINALS ARE A SUPERSTITIOUS
COWARDLY LOT.
I MUST BE A CREATURE.
I MUST BE A CREATURE OF THE NIGHT.
MOMMY'S DEAD.
DADDY'S DEAD.
BRUCIE'S DEAD.
I SHALL BECOME A BAT

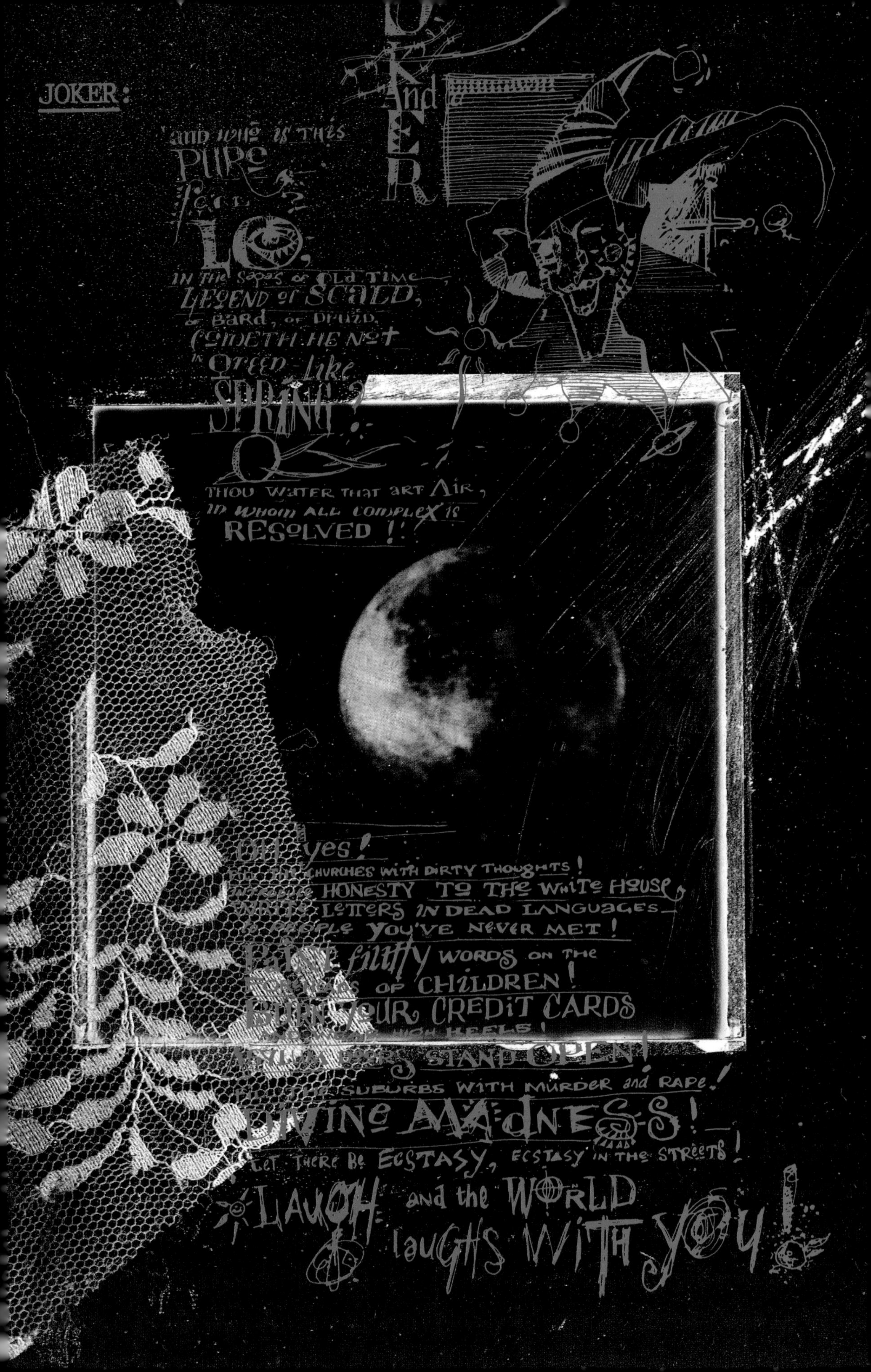
JOKER:
And who is this pure face? Lo, in the sagas of old time, legend of scald, or bard, or druid, cometh he not in green-like spring?
O thou water that art air, in whom all complex is resolved!!
Oh yes!
Fill the churches with dirty thoughts!
Introduce honesty to the White House
Write letters in dead languages to people you've never met!
Paint filthy words on the foreheads of children!
Burn your credit cards
high heels!
Asylum doors stand open!
suburbs with murder and rape!
Divine madness!
Let there be ecstasy, ecstasy in the streets!
Laugh and the world laughs with you!

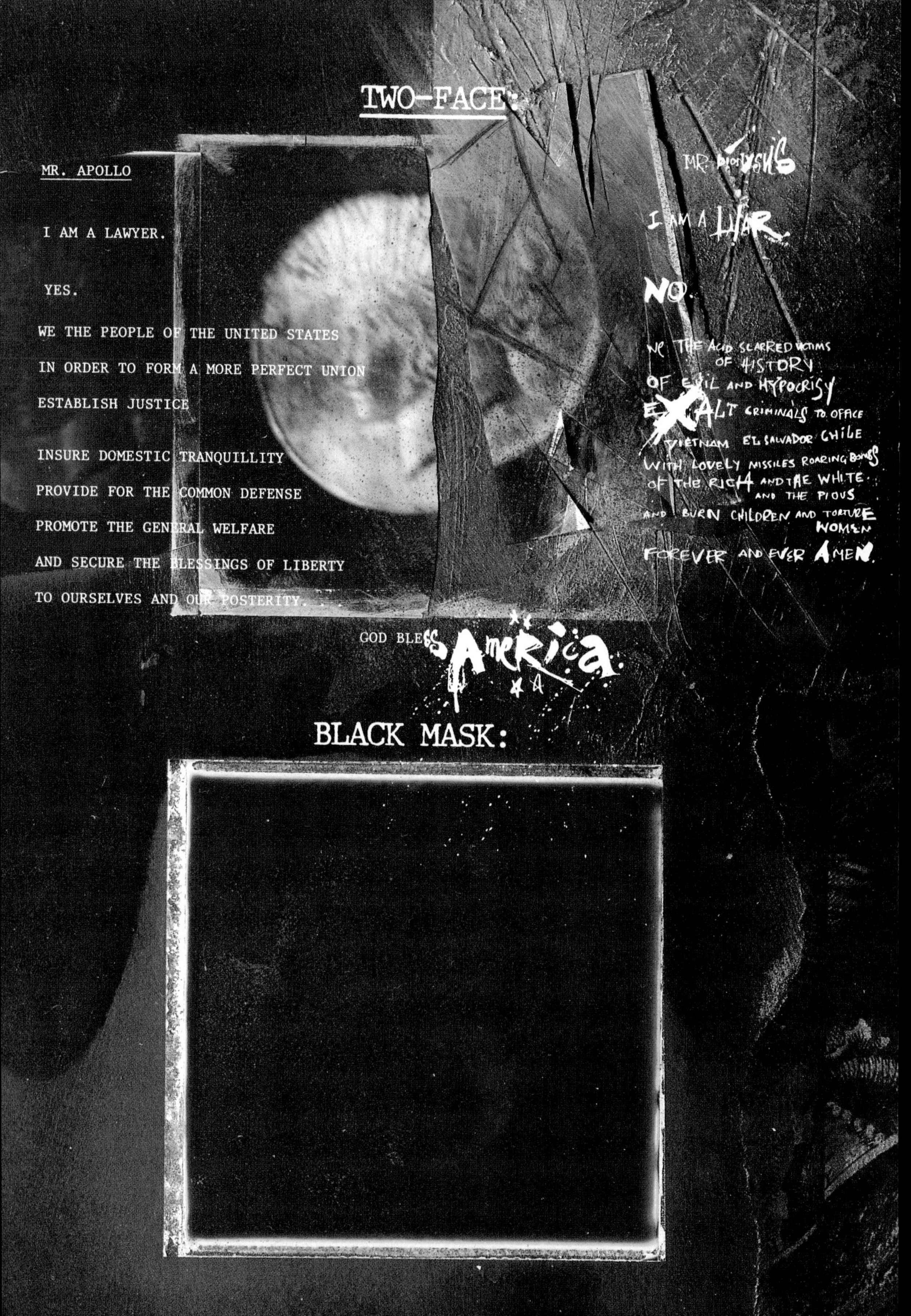
TWO-FACE:
MR. APOLLO
I AM A LAWYER.
YES.
WE THE PEOPLE OF THE UNITED STATES
IN ORDER TO FORM A MORE PERFECT UNION
ESTABLISH JUSTICE
INSURE DOMESTIC TRANQUILLITY
PROVIDE FOR THE COMMON DEFENSE
PROMOTE THE GENERAL WELFARE
AND SECURE THE BLESSINGS OF LIBERTY
TO OURSELVES AND OUR POSTERITY. . .
MR. DIONYSUS
I AM A LIAR.
NO.
WE THE ACID SCARRED VICTIMS OF HISTORY
OF EVIL AND HYPOCRISY
EXALT CRIMINALS TO OFFICE
VIETNAM EL SALVADOR CHILE
WITH LOVELY MISSILES ROARING BOMBS
OF THE RICH AND THE WHITE AND THE PIOUS
AND BURN CHILDREN AND TORTURE WOMEN
FOREVER AND EVER AMEN.
GOD BLESS America
BLACK MASK:

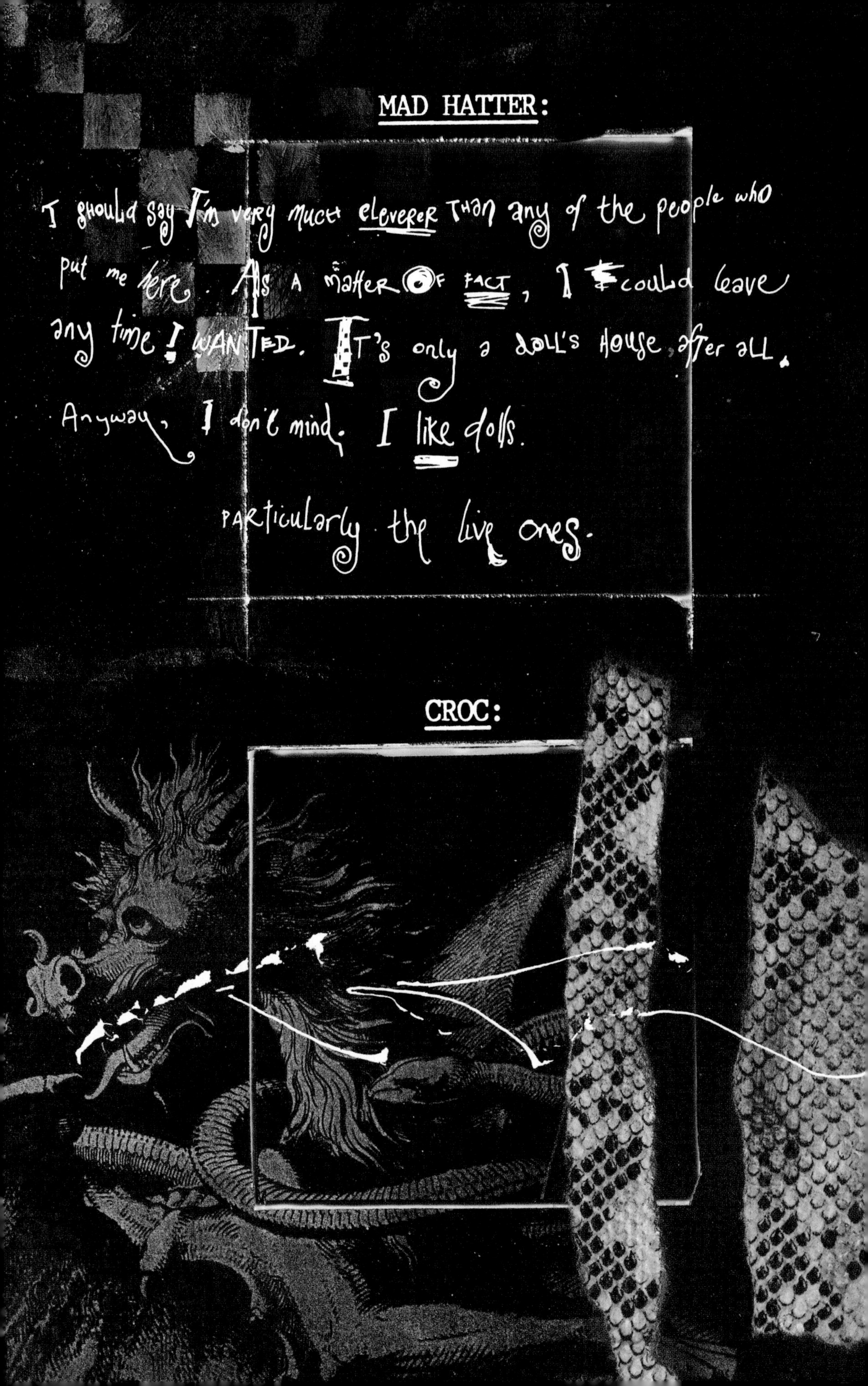
MAD HATTER:
I should say I'm very much cleverer than any of the people who put me here. As a matter of fact, I could leave any time I wanted. It's only a doll's house after all.
Anyway, I don't mind. I like dolls.
particularly the live ones.
CROC:

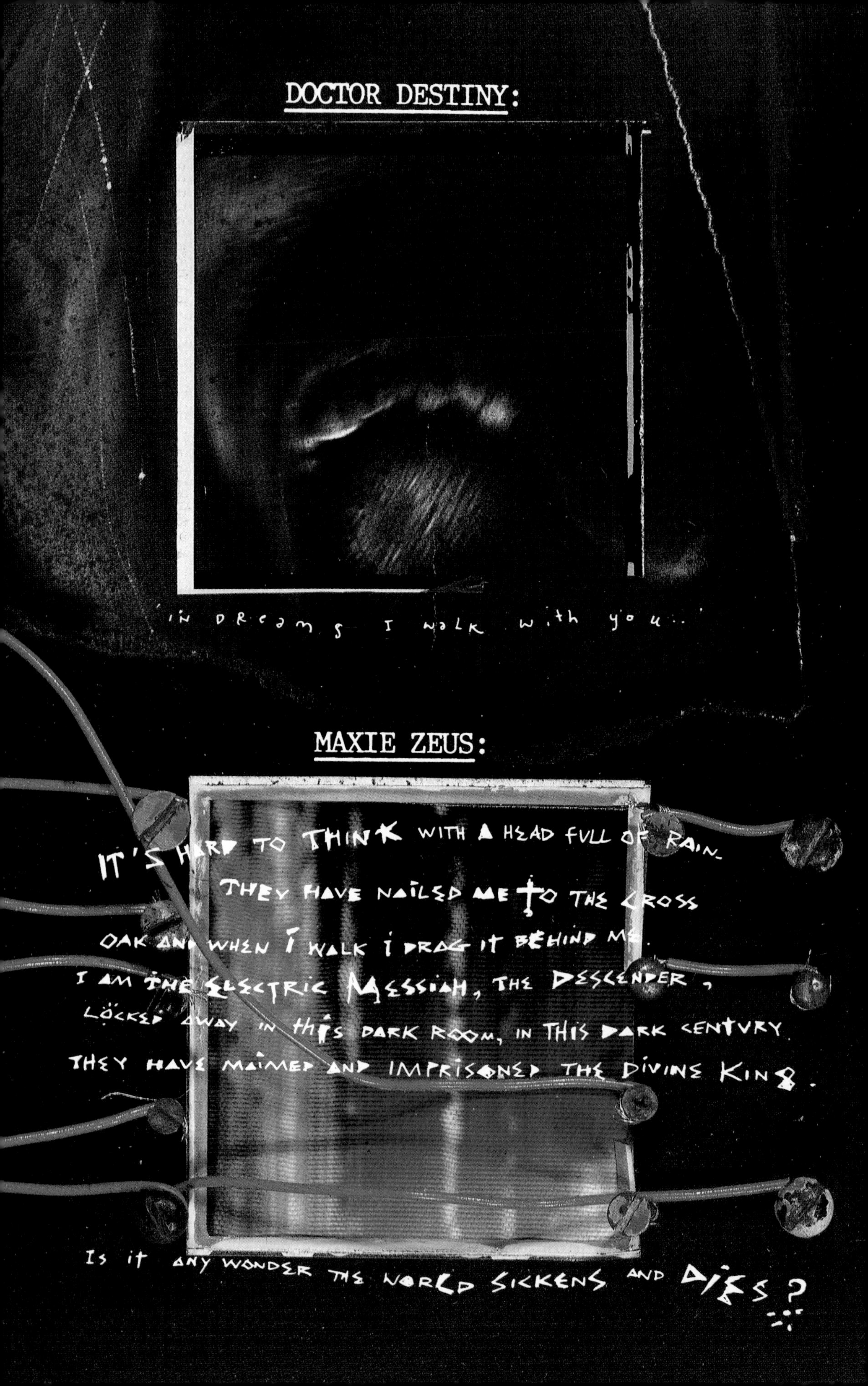
DOCTOR DESTINY:
'in dreams I walk with you..'
MAXIE ZEUS:
IT'S HARD TO THINK WITH A HEAD FULL OF RAIN.
THEY HAVE NAILED ME TO THE CROSS
OAK AND WHEN I WALK I DRAG IT BEHIND ME.
I AM THE ELECTRIC MESSIAH, THE DESCENDER,
LOCKED AWAY IN THIS DARK ROOM, IN THIS DARK CENTURY.
THEY HAVE MAIMED AND IMPRISONED THE DIVINE KING.
Is it any wonder the world sickens and dies?

CLAYFACE:

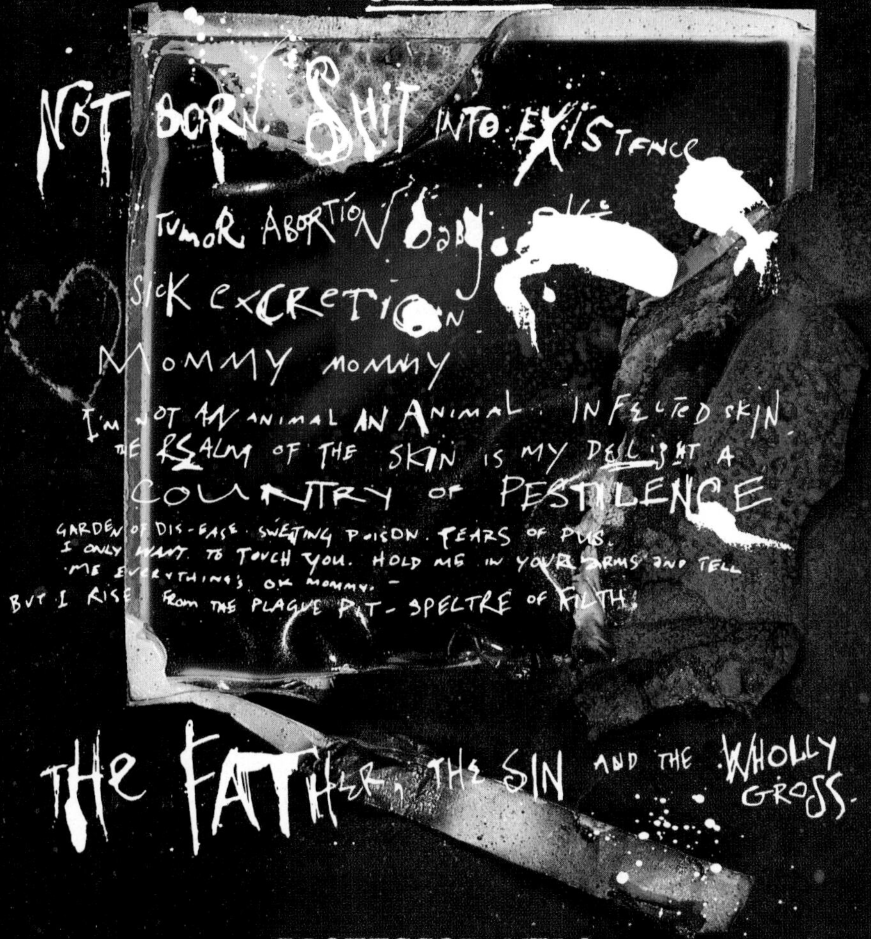
NOT BORN. SHIT INTO EXISTENCE
TUMOR ABORTION baby.
SICK EXCRETION.
MOMMY MOMMY
I'M NOT AN ANIMAL AN ANIMAL. INFECTED SKIN.
THE REALM OF THE SKIN IS MY DELIGHT A
COUNTRY OF PESTILENCE
GARDEN OF DIS-EASE. SWETING POISON. TEARS OF PUS.
I ONLY WANT TO TOUCH YOU. HOLD ME IN YOUR ARMS AND TELL
ME EVERYTHING'S OK MOMMY. –
BUT I RISE FROM THE PLAGUE PIT - SPECTRE OF FILTH.
THE FATHER, THE SIN AND THE WHOLLY GROSS.

PROFESSOR MILO:

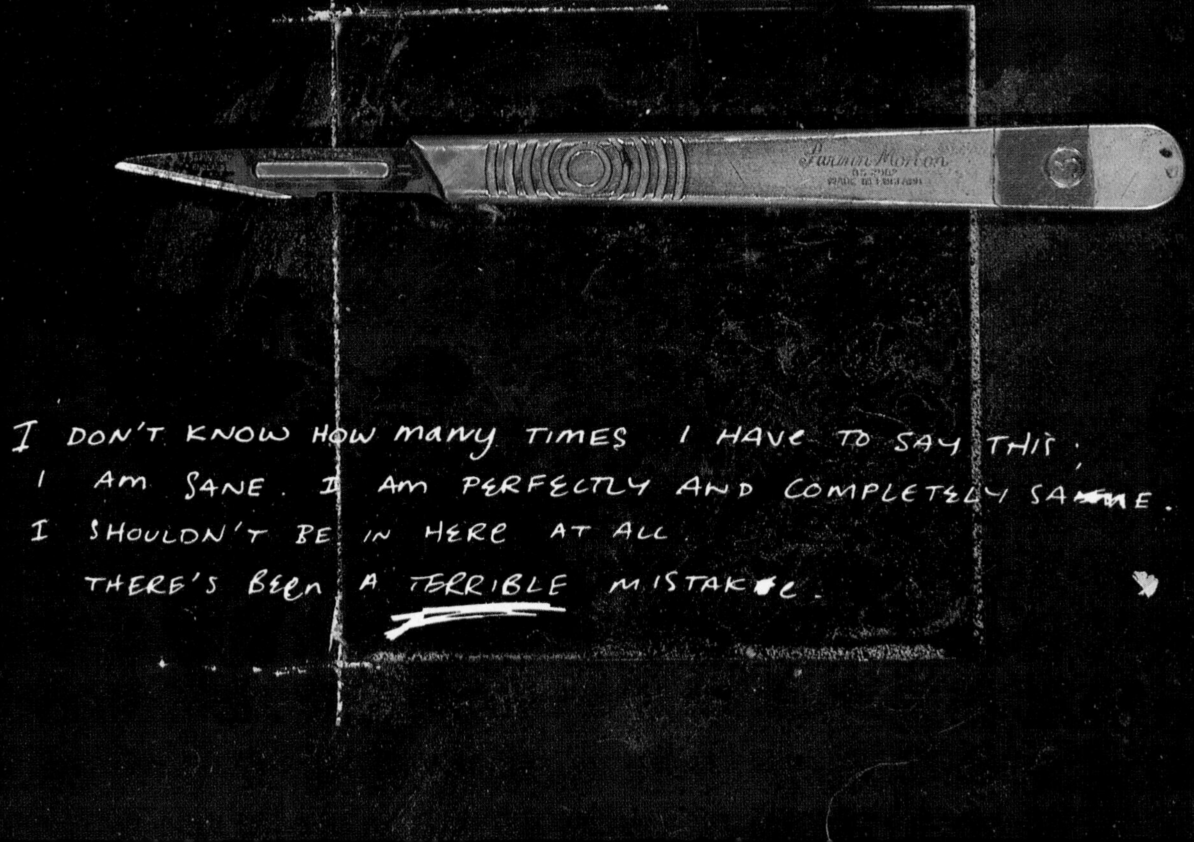
I DON'T KNOW HOW MANY TIMES I HAVE TO SAY THIS,
I AM SANE. I AM PERFECTLY AND COMPLETELY SANE.
I SHOULDN'T BE IN HERE AT ALL.
THERE'S BEEN A TERRIBLE MISTAKE.

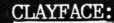

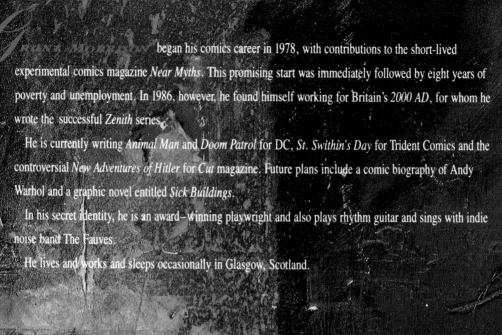

GRANT MORRISON began his comics career in 1978, with contributions to the short-lived experimental comics magazine *Near Myths*. This promising start was immediately followed by eight years of poverty and unemployment. In 1986, however, he found himself working for Britain's *2000 AD*, for whom he wrote the successful *Zenith* series.

He is currently writing *Animal Man* and *Doom Patrol* for DC, *St. Swithin's Day* for Trident Comics and the controversial *New Adventures of Hitler* for *Cut* magazine. Future plans include a comic biography of Andy Warhol and a graphic novel entitled *Sick Buildings*.

In his secret identity, he is an award–winning playwright and also plays rhythm guitar and sings with indie noise band The Fauves.

He lives and works and sleeps occasionally in Glasgow, Scotland.

Dave McKean lives and works in Surrey, England, with his partner, Clare, and a piano. He studied design, illustration and film at Berkshire College of Art and Design for four years, where he subsequently returned to teach audio visuals and film for a year and a half. Dave has illustrated two comics, both with writer Neil Gaiman. *Violent Cases* was published by Escape in 1987 and has won three Eagle and Mekon awards. *Black Orchid* was published by DC in 1988 and was nominated for an Eisner and a Harvey award.

Dave is also working with Gaiman on *Signal to Noise*, a continuing story running in *The Face* magazine; *Black Cocktail*, an illustrated novel by Jonathan Carroll; numerous book covers; and various other works.

He has written and performed music soundtracks for TV commercials and video and played at the Bracknell Jazz Festival in 1986.

Thanks to Judy Cartwright, Jim Clements, Neil Jones, Neil Gaiman, Clare and Delia Haythornthwaite, Ron Tiner, Mark Nevelow, Mary Dalton, Keith Harris, Dick Jude, Andrew and Christopher Waring, Len Wein, Rolie Green, Tony Stochmal and all at Splash of Paint Design.

GRANT MORRISON

DAVE McKEAN

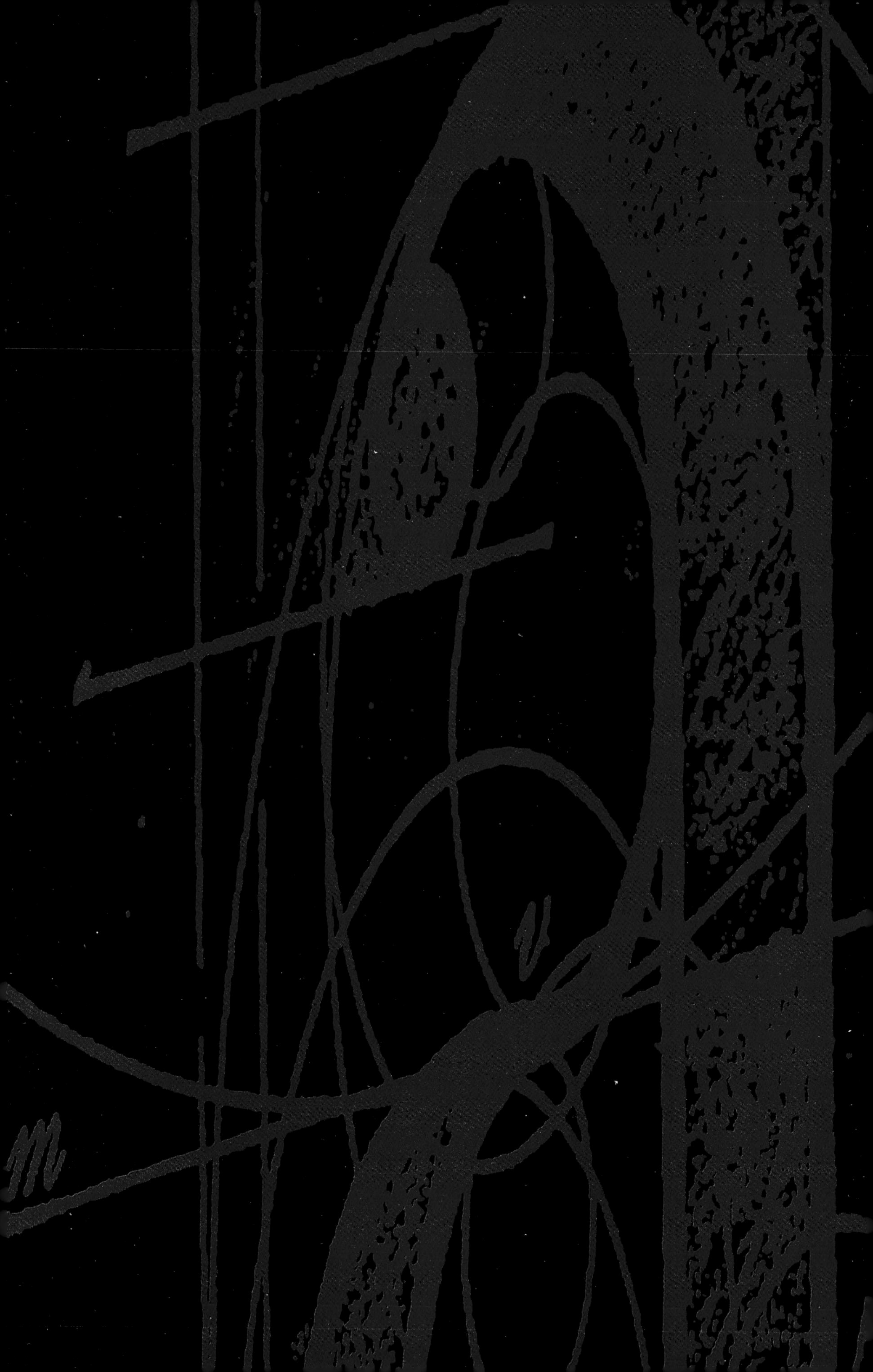

BATMAN

A SERIOUS HOUSE ON SERIOUS EARTH

Grant Morrison

ARKHAM ASYLUM: A SERIOUS HOUSE ON SERIOUS EARTH
Full script and notes by Grant Morrison

The original idea to do a book focusing on DC Comics' notorious insane asylum came out of discussions with my friend at the time, the brilliant but wayward Jim Clements (who is named in the dedications at the end). Jim spent decades of man-hours writing *Fiery, The Angels Fell*, a mindblowing, unpublished comic book sequel to *Blade Runner,* packed to the brim with deep emotion, ultra-violence, dreamlike symbolism and a relentless outpouring of philosophical ideas which made even Philip K. Dick look like an under-achiever. He also worked endlessly on a sequel to the *Hellraiser 2* movie, which fused Clive Barker's Cenobites with Lewis Carroll to quite startling and beautiful effect. He had a short story published in *2000 AD*, then disappeared into his own life. I have no idea what happened to him in the end but back in the mid-'80s, we'd spend a lot of time walking around town and talking about what we'd do with our favorite comic book characters if we ever got the chance. We both shared a love of Nicolas Roeg movies, Dennis Potter dramas, psychoanalytical theory, comic books and post-modernist thought.

And we were both fascinated by the little entry in the DC WHO'S WHO concordance. Len Wein (coincidentally the writer whose work on JUSTICE LEAGUE OF AMERICA turned me into a rabid teenage comics fan and set me on the path to writing comic book stories) had written a few short and evocative paragraphs on the history of Arkham Asylum and it was here I learned of poor Amadeus Arkham, the hospital's founder, whose wife and daughter had been murdered by Martin "Mad Dog" Hawkins. In Wein's *précis*, Arkham's madness was described as a result of the Stock Market crash of 1929. It occurred to me that having one's wife and daughter slaughtered by a man named "Mad Dog" might have been sufficient cause for a nervous breakdown, so I decided to explore and expand on the life of this throwaway character, and from this seed the story that became "A Serious House on Serious Earth," which in all honesty I wrote to impress Jim Clements.

Jim's presence haunts the text in two places — the idea of Two-Face being weaned off his decision-making coin and onto a die was Jim's, although I developed the notion by moving him onto the I-Ching. Also, in the first draft of the script, I had Batman injuring Killer Croc by wrapping his explosive utility belt around the monster's neck. Jim pointed out that I'd missed the obvious by not using the spear from the St. Michael statue as a weapon. His idea of a bearded Joker, as a grotesque visual allusion to the *vagina dentata* notion from Freudian theory, was left on the drawing board for the sake of all right-thinking folk.

The subtitle was taken from Philip Larkin's poem "Church Going." The story's themes were inspired by Lewis Carroll, quantum physics, Jung and Crowley, its visual style by surrealism, Eastern European creepiness, Cocteau, Artaud, Svankmajer, the Brothers Quay, etc. The intention was to create something that was more like a piece of music or an experimental film than a typical adventure comic book. I wanted to approach Batman from the point of view of the dreamlike, emotional and irrational hemisphere, as a response to the very literal, "realistic" "left brain" treatment of superheroes which was in vogue at the time, in the wake of THE DARK KNIGHT RETURNS, WATCHMEN and others.

The script was laid out as a monstrous hybrid between the traditional "Full Script" comic book method and a movie screenplay.

When I went down to London to meet the folks at DC for the first time during one of their annual talent scouting trips, I pitched both the idea for the ANIMAL MAN series and ARKHAM ASYLUM (which was a 48-page book pitch at the time). Both were accepted.

The script became a 64-page book which was later expanded into 120 pages for the final edition. This was due to Dave McKean requiring more pages to complete the story. It took a year to research and plan and was written in one fevered month in 1987, generally late at night and after long periods of no sleep. In those days I was straight-edge to the core and the only way I could approximate a genuinely deranged consciousness was via the use of matchsticks between the eyelids.

I found out later that the script had been passed around a group of comics professionals who allegedly shit themselves laughing at my high-falutin' pop psych panel descriptions. Who's laughing now, @$$hole? ✳

'But I don't want to go among mad people,' Alice remarked.

"Oh, you can't help that," said the Cat: "We're all mad here. I'm mad. You're mad."

'How do you know I'm mad ?' said Alice.

'You must be,' said the Cat, "or you wouldn't have come here.'

Lewis Carroll

'Alice's Adventures in Wonderland'

We open with a shot of the moon, caught between two chimneys on the roof of the Arkham House as it was in 1901. The roof is wet with rain and the reflection of a lit, semi-circular window lies directly below the face of the moon - it appears almost to be a perfect twin of the moon above. The sky is dark and stormy, full of stress. ((This image establishes the theme of our story by duplicating several of the visual elements of Tarot trump 18 - The Moon. In this card, we see the moon between two forbidding towers in a bleak nocturnal landscape. At the bottom of the card, a Scarab beetle bears the sun through a polluted lake. The Moon card basically represents the darkness through which we must pass to reach the dawn. It is the card of lunacy and illusion but its real significance runs a good deal deeper than that as Uncle Aleister Crowley will now explain:

'...Upon the hills are the black towers of nameless mystery, of horror and of fear...It needs unconquerable courage to begin to tread this path. Here is a weird, deceptive life. The fiery sense is baulked. The moon has no air. The knight upon this quest has to rely on the three lower senses: touch, taste and smell. Such light as there may be is deadlier than darkness, and the silence is wounded by the howling of wild beasts.

This is the threshold of life; this is the threshold of death. All is doubtful, all is mysterious, all is intoxicating. Not the benign solar intoxication of Dionysus, but the dreadful madness of pernicious drugs; this is a drunkenness of sense, after the mind has been abolished by the venom of this Moon.

...One is reminded of the mental echo of subconscious realization, of that supreme iniquity which mystics have constantly celebrated in their accounts of the Dark Night of the Soul. But the best men, the true men, do not consider the matter in such terms at all. Whatever horrors may afflict the soul, whatever abominations may excite the loathing of the heart, whatever terrors may assail the mind, the answer is the same at every stage: 'How splendid is the Adventure!'"

The Moon card then, represents trial and initiation - the supreme testing of the

PAGE 1: From the opening titles: *Icaronycteris index,* an early Eocene bat (Chiroptera) is the oldest complete fossil bat. Found in Wyoming, USA. ✷

soul, where we must face our deepest fears, confront them and survive or be broken. In this single image are encoded all the themes of our entire story.

Adam West, where are you now ?))

Pull right back for an establishing shot of the house. It broods in Gothic silence beneath ragged, wind-driven clouds. Leaves, stripped from branches, whirl on the wind. The full moon peeks from behind the chimneys like the face of a pale, mad child, playing hide and seek. There is a bad feeling; we do not like this place, we dare not go any closer but somehow, we are compelled.

CAP.:   FROM THE JOURNALS OF AMADEUS ARKHAM:

CAP.:   IN THE YEARS FOLLOWING MY FATHER'S DEATH, I THINK IT'S TRUE TO
            SAY THAT THE HOUSE BECAME MY WHOLE WORLD. (I'd like these journal
                                    captions to be lettered
                                    in some kind of 'hand-
                                    writing' style.)

We are inside the house, looking down a long corridor. One wall is lined with tall windows that let in moonlight and cast stylized, German Expressionist shadows. A boy walks towards us, dwarfed into insignificance by the scale of the corridor and the windows. His shadow is huge, thrown ahead of him by ornamental flambeaux on the wall. ((This is a reference to Jung's concept of the Shadow - the repressed and dangerous material that lurks in the slime of the unconscious mind. This image foreshadows the triumph of Arkham's shadow at the conclusion of the story.)) The boy is young Amadeus Arkham, 11 years old, carrying a tray of food.

CAP.:   DURING THE LONG PERIOD OF MOTHER'S ILLNESS, THE HOUSE OFTEN
            SEEMED SO VAST, SO CONFIDENTLY REAL, THAT BY COMPARISON, I
            FELT LITTLE MORE THAN A GHOST, HAUNTING ITS CORRIDORS.

CAP.:   SCARCELY AWARE THAT ANYTHING COULD EXIST BEYOND THOSE
            MELANCHOLY WALLS.

A round, convex mirror hangs in a corner where the corridor bends in a right angle. Arkham glances nervously at the mirror, which takes his face and deforms it into an elongated fright mask.

CAP.:   UNTIL THE NIGHT IN 1901, WHEN I FIRST CAUGHT A GLIMPSE OF
            THAT OTHER WORLD.

Arkham knocks on a door and pauses tentatively, as though hoping there will be no reply.

CAP.:   THE WORLD ON THE DARK SIDE.

PAGE 2: The story is woven tightly around a small number of symbolic elements, which combine and recombine throughout, as if in a dream.

The MOON, the SHADOW, the MIRROR, the TOWER and the MOTHER'S SON.

The construction of the story was influenced by the architecture of a house — the past and the tale of Amadeus Arkham forms the basement levels. Secret passages connect ideas and segments of the book. There are upper stories of unfolding symbol and metaphor. We were also referencing sacred geometry, and the plan of the Arkham House was based on Glastonbury Abbey and Chartres Cathedral. The journey through the book is like moving through the floors of the house itself. The house and the head become one.

Most of the ideas which appear here are ones I've explored and dissected obsessively again and again throughout my career. ❋

ARKHAM: MOTHER ?

He opens the door, looks in cautiously, eyes wide. His mother sits up in a four poster bed. An open jar lies on the counterpane but we cannot see anything of its contents.

ARKHAM: MOTHER ?

ARKHAM: IT'S ME.

ARKHAM: I'VE BROUGHT YOU SOMETHING TO EAT.

Arkham crosses the room. Tension builds. His mother sits up in bed, smiling in a bland and chilling way. She is not a very old woman - perhaps in her late 30's - but her hair hangs in prematurely gray wisps and her eyes are sunken. Her hands are hidden behind her back. Her cheeks bulge slightly. Two Irish Wolfhounds sit at either side of her bed - identifying her with Hecate, the goddess of witchcraft and the Moon. ((The women of Arkham's immediate family form a Classical Triad - his mother, the Hag aspect, his wife, the fertile mother, and his daughter, the virgin.))

ARKHAM: PLEASE. I THINK YOU SHOULD TRY TO EAT SOME OF THIS.

MOTHER: MMF

MOTHER   EATEN.

Arkham's mother lifts a fastidious hand up to her mouth, pushing back some of the squirming bodies that try to escape from her opening mouth. Her expression is that of a guilty child.

MOTHER: I'VE EATEN.

MOTHER: I'VE EATEN.

Tears spill from her eyes. An expression of helpless horror sketches itself across her face as a shower of beetles - some mashed, some crippled, some alive and kicking - falls from her lips onto the counterpane. Her tongue hangs out, lapping at the air. The image is grotesque.

MOTHER: I'VE EATEN.

Arkham stands shellshocked. He stares at the beetles as his mother's fingers scrabble across the counterpane after the escapees. Her other hand stuffs pulped bodies back into her mouth.

MOTHER: MRRF

MOTHER   UFF

CAP.:   THAT WAS THE MOMENT WHEN I FIRST FELT TRULY ALONE.

Still standing paralysed, with shock and horror scrawled upon his face, Arkham lets the tray of food fall from frozen fingers. Its contents - soup bowl, bread, salt and pepper shakers, a small vase with a red rose in it etc. - fall in slow motion.

CAP.:   MANY YEARS LATER, WHEN I BECAME AWARE OF THE SIGNIFICANCE OF THE
BEETLE AS A SYMBOL OF REBIRTH, I REALIZED THAT SHE WAS SIMPLY
TRYING TO PROTECT HERSELF FROM SOMETHING, IN THE ONLY WAY THAT
MADE SENSE TO HER.

Close up on Arkham's face. His lip quivers, on the edge of tears. He simply does not know what to do.

CAP.:   BUT EVEN THEN, I THINK I UNDERSTOOD THAT MOTHER HAD BEEN BORN
AGAIN, INTO THAT OTHER WORLD.

CAP.:   A WORLD OF FATHOMLESS SIGNS AND PORTENTS.

CAP.:   OF MAGIC AND TERROR.

Arkham's mother rises up in bed, eerily spectral. Terror-stricken, staring into a corner of the room, she holds up her hands in front of her face — thumbs together, fingers spread. Her hands, thus arranged, cast a huge batlike shadow behind her. The image is mysterious, inexplicable, almost religious in intensity. The dogs sit up on their haunches, adding to the ritual power of the image.

CAP.:   AND MYSTERIOUS SYMBOLS.

The skyline of Gotham City replaces the scenes of trauma in the Arkham House as we move forward eighty eight years to the present day. Art Deco towers rise up out of a fog of hot neon. The night sky is heavy with turbulent clouds. A storm is brewing. A powerful searchlight beam projects the Bat Signal onto the cloud ceiling.

Batman sweeps up the steps at the entrance to Gotham City Police headquarters. (We can see a sign somewhere, identifying the building.) Commissioner Gordon greets him at the top of the stairs.

BATMAN: SORRY I'M LATE, COMMISSIONER. PROBLEMS OUT OF TOWN.

BATMAN: WHAT'S UP.

Gordon leads Batman up a narrow flight of stairs. The Commissioner looks edgy and harassed - his tie is loosened, his collar unbuttoned and his sleeves rolled up. He's clearly had a hard day. He's turning to speak to Batman, who grimly mounts the stairs just behind him.

GORDON: THERE'S BEEN A RIOT AT ARKHAM ASYLUM. THAT'S WHAT'S UP.

GORDON: THE INMATES SEIZED CONTROL OF THE BUILDING EARLY THIS
MORNING. WE DON'T KNOW HOW IT HAPPENED.

Gordon pushes open the frosted glass door to his office. (Again, there's some identifying lettering on the glass.)

GORDON: THEY'RE HOLDING THE ASYLUM STAFF HOSTAGE, MAKING ALL KINDS OF

PAGE 4: Ma Arkham is, in fact, trying to protect herself from the Bat and the dreadful spirit of the Asylum, which can be seen as a haunting from the future, one of many in the book.

The original first draft of the script included the character of Robin as Batman's sidekick. Robin appeared in a few scenes at the beginning then remained at Police Headquarters for the bulk of the book, where he spent his time studying plans and histories of the house, in order to find a way in to help his mentor. Dave McKean, however, felt that he had already compromised his artistic integrity sufficiently by drawing Batman and refused point blank to bend over for the Boy Wonder — so after one brave but ridiculous attempt to put him in a trench coat, I wisely removed him from the script. ◉

```
                        CRAZY DEMANDS.
GORDON:                 WE'VE HAD TO SEND IN FURNITURE, STORE DUMMIES, FOOD, CLOTHING..
BATMAN:                 AND ?..
```

There are several worried-looking policemen - uniformed and plainclothes - in Gordon's office as he enters with Batman. There's a feeling of tension that is only beginning to be relieved now that Batman has come on the scene. It is obvious that everyone has been waiting for him.

```
GORDON:                 THEY SAY THERE'S ONLY ONE FINAL DEMAND, THANK GOD.
GORDON:                 THEY'VE BEEN WAITING TO TALK TO YOU PERSONALLY.
BATMAN:                 I SEE.
```

Gordon points to the phone, which sits on the table in foreground. Beside it we can clearly see a desktop calendar which thoughtfully provides us with the all-important date - APRIL 1st. (The telephone receiver is hooked up to one of those speaker systems which allows you to talk to a caller without actually picking up the phone and which also allows everyone else in the room to hear what's being said. I know there's a proper name for this apparatus but I can't remember what it is, coming, as I do, from a land where the wheel is regarded as technology run rampant. I'm sure you know the sort of thing I mean anyway. Don't you ?) Batman stiffens and seems to be hanging back, suspecting what is to come.

```
GORDON:                 IT'S THE JOKER.
```

Batman stands by the desk, looking down at the phone. His features barely change as he speaks. If we see the others behind him, they're looking on with an expectant, almost religious awe - this man has come to deliver them from evil, as he always does.

((The portrayal of Batman here and throughout is quite important - his posture reveals a man constantly on the defensive, constantly expecting attack from some quarter. His body is a fortress of flesh, bulwarked against the ravages of a merciless world. Consequently, he stands perfectly straight to the point of stiffness. We can imagine him walking with his buttocks clenched. His is the posture of an obsessive, anal personality. This Batman is a frightened, threatened boy who has made himself terrible at the cost of his own humanity. He is completely incapable of any kind of sexual relationship. He has made himself hard and domineering in order that he might never be hurt or abandoned again. Only in action does this rigidity relax, and then Batman becomes a fluid shadow.))

```
BATMAN:                 JOKER! ARE YOU THERE ? THIS IS BATMAN.
BATMAN:                 WHAT DO YOU WANT ?
PHONE:                  WELL HELLO, BIG BOY!
PHONE:                  HOW'S IT HANGING ?
```

PAGE 5: Desktop calendar shows the all-important date of April 1st, a perfect day for the Joker to have arranged his "display" at the Asylum.

Much of the body language required for this particular depiction of Batman was omitted from the art when Dave chose to render Batman more impressionistically as a hunched, ambiguous figure.

I'd also like to stress that the portrayal of Batman presented here is not definitive and is not necessarily how I would write the character otherwise. The repressed, armoured, uncertain and sexually frozen man in ARKHAM ASYLUM was intended as a critique of the '80s interpretation of Batman as violent, driven and borderline psychopathic. My own later portrayal of Batman in the JLA comic was one which emphasized the character's sanity and dignity; in the end, I figured that anyone who had gone so far and been so successful in his quest to avenge his parents' death and to help other people would have ended up pretty much straightened out. Bruce Wayne would only have become conflicted and mentally unstable if he had NOT put on his scary bat-suit and found the perfect outlet for his feelings of rage, guilt and revenge. ◉

Close in on Batman's face. His eyes narrow but his features retain their cold, expressionless quality.

BATMAN: DON'T WASTE MY TIME, JOKER. JUST TELL ME WHAT IT IS YOU WANT.

PHONE: OH, I THINK YOU CAN GUESS..

The phone and the calendar sit innocently on the desk.

PHONE: WE WANT YOU

PHONE: IN HERE. WITH US. IN THE MADHOUSE.

PHONE: WHERE YOU BELONG.

Batman draws back a little, as though from a venomous snake. For just a moment, there is the merest hint of apprehension on his face.

BATMAN: AND..AND WHAT IF I SAY NO ?

PHONE: skrit skritch (Lettered small as though very quiet.)

PHONE: WELL..

PHONE: WE HAVE SO MANY FRIENDS HERE, SWEETHEART.

Close in on the phone, cranking up the tension.

PHONE: SAY HELLO TO PEARL.

PHONE: OH BUH-BAT-BAT-BAT OHHH

Gordon and the others beginning to look uneasy. Gordon's hand is frozen in the act of lifting his pipe to his lips.

PHONE: SUCH A CRYBABY, ISN'T SHE ?

PHONE: skritch skritch (Still quiet.)

GORDON: WHAT'S THAT NOISE ? CAN YOU HEAR IT ? THAT SCRATCHING. KIND OF GRINDING.

GORDON: WHAT'S HE DOING ?

Batman in close up. His face remains icily tight.

PHONE: PEARL IS NINETEEN YEARS OLD.

PHONE: skritch skrit (Quiet.)

PHONE: SHE JUST STARTED WORK IN THE KITCHENS HERE. TO EARN SOME EXTRA MONEY.

Move in close on the phone.

PHONE: PEARL WANTS TO BE AN ARTIST, DON'T YOU PEARL, DARLING ?

PHONE: UH-HUH..OHHHH..

Batman's eyes suddenly widen aas he identifies the scratching noise.

PHONE: skrit skrit (Still quiet.)

PHONE: SHE JUST DREW ME A BEAUTIFUL HOUSE.

PHONE: SHE DREW IT WITH THIS PENCIL.

PAGE 6: This first uneasy telephone conversation with the Joker shows that he is immediately aware of Batman's sexual weakness. The language he uses throughout is overtly provocative and designed to cause this uptight Batman the most discomfort.

He has also seen through his old enemy's other insecurities and challenges the idea of Batman even being sane, in order to lead him into his trap. ✳

Final close up on the phone. Right into the speaker as the unpleasant truth is revealed.

PHONE: skrrit* (Suddenly bigger, as though becoming louder.)

PHONE: THE ONE I'VE JUST SHARPENED.

PHONE: OPEN YOUR EYES WIDE, PEARL !

PHONE: BEAUTIFUL

PHONE: BLUE

PHONE: OH

Batman yells out in hopeless horror, as though simply the sound of his voice over the phone will be sufficient to halt the atrocity.

BATMAN: JESUS NO!

PHONE: EEEEEEE (Letered bigger than normal. An ear-splitting cry of pain.)

From behind Batman as he grips the edge of the desk, shoulders bowed. His body shakes with chained anger.

PHONE: YOU HAVE HALF AN HOUR.

PHONE: AND BRING A WHITE STICK.

BATMAN: NO. (Lettered small, under the breath.)

Batman screams with murderous but quite impotent rage. (At the same time, it's impossible to tell whether his 'NO!' is directed at fate for allowing such a thing to happen to an innocent girl or whether it's his gut response to being told that he has to go into Arkham.)

BATMAN: NO! (Lettered big. A murderous but quite impotent scream of
           rage etc.)

PHONE: HAHAHAHAHAHAHA*

Gordon tentatively approaches Batman, who still stands gripping the edge of the desk. One of the other cops in the office mops his brow with a handkerchief. Batman looks like a bomb that's about to go off.

GORDON: OH JESUS, THAT POOR GIRL.

GORDON: BATMAN..I..

BATMAN: I'M GOING IN THERE.

Batman turns, monolithic, expressionless. Gordon looks frail and human by comparison. Batman's words are more command than request.

BATMAN: JIM, CAN WE TALK ?

Batman walks away. The assembled police officers watch as Gordon follows.

PAGE 7: Batman's hand is reaching down and picking up traces of salt. Drawing a circle around oneself with salt was traditionally considered a means of protecting against evil. ✸

We follow Batman and Gordon up a flight of stairs. At the top of the stairs, they emerge out on the roof of Police Headquarters.

GORDON: YOU OKAY ?

GORDON: YOU KNOW YOU DON'T <u>HAVE</u> TO GO IN THERE. LET ME ORGANIZE A <u>SWAT</u> TEAM OR SOMETHING.

BATMAN: NO. THIS IS SOMETHING I <u>DO</u> HAVE TO DO.

BATMAN: IT'S JUST..

The two men walk towards the massive searchlight that projects the Bat Signal Clouds brood over the skyline. Even up here in the open, there is a sense of feverish heat. The city is contained by it and the sky seals it in, like the lid of a pressure cooker. The lights are too bright, too hot.

GORDON: LISTEN, I CAN UNDERSTAND IT IF EVEN <u>YOU'RE</u> AFRAID.

GORDON: I MEAN, <u>ARKHAM</u> HAS A REPUTATION..

Batman turns to look back over his shoulder at Gordon. His face shows the faintest trace of black amusement.

BATMAN: AFRAID ?

BATMAN: BATMAN'S NOT AFRAID OF <u>ANYTHING</u>.

He stands on the edge of the roof, a ragged silhouette, dwarfed by the searchlight behind him. The black bat shape painted onto the glass of the searchlight dominates the picture, stronger and more real than the man it represents. The mask goes down at this moment and we catch a glimpse of the bereaved child underneath.

BATMAN: HE'S TOO <u>BIG</u> TO BE AFRAID.

BATMAN: IT'S <u>ME</u>

BATMEN: <u>I'M</u> AFRAID.

Move in on Batman. He rubs the side of his head. It is a gesture of vulnerability and self doubt.

BATMAN: I'M AFRAID THAT THE JOKER MAY BE <u>RIGHT</u> ABOUT ME.

BATMAN: SOMETIMES I..<u>QUESTION</u> THE RATIONALITY OF MY ACTIONS.

Continue to move in as Batman stares out across the city, almost talking to himself Behind him, Gordon is lighting his pipe. The glass in Gordon's spectacles is blank are white. There is something of the atmosphere of the confessional here.

BATMAN: AND I'M AFRAID THAT WHEN I WALK THROUGH THOSE ASYLUM GATES..

WHEN I WALK INTO <u>ARKHAM</u> AND THE DOORS CLOSE BEHIND ME..

Move in for the final tight close up on Batman's face. Illuminated from below by the lights of Gotham, he stares into space, seeing nothing and nowhere.

BATMAN: IT'LL BE JUST LIKE COMING HOME.

Cut to Amadeus Arkham. He's just alighted from an old-style taxi cab and is setting down a suitcase outside the Arkham House. It looms up darkly under a bright spring sky. Blossom drifts on the breeze.

CAP.:   I RETURN TO THE FAMILY HOME ON A COOL SPRING MORNING IN 1920, SHORTLY AFTER MOTHER'S FUNERAL.

CAP.:   SHE OPENED HER OWN THROAT WITH A PEARL-HANDLED RAZOR.

CAP.:   IN THE END, PERHAPS, IT WAS FOR THE BEST. I HAVE TO BELIEVE THAT.

Arkham is a silhouette standing in the doorframe as he opens the front door. The hallway is dark and objects appear as barely suggested shapes in the gloom. There is a sense of disuse. Underlying that, a feeling that Arkham has somehow stirred something and opened the door to set it free.

CAP.:   AS THE ONLY CHILD, I AM TO INHERIT THE HOUSE AND THE ACRE OF LAND UPON WHICH IT STANDS.

From overhead, we look down on Arkham as he stands in the huge hallway, gazing up, claiming the house with his eyes.

CAP.:   ALONE IN A GLOOM THAT SMELLS OF LOST CHILDHOOD, I DEDICATE MYSELF TO THE PREVENTION OF SUCH SUFFERING AS MY POOR MOTHER KNEW.

CAP.:   AND I BEGIN TO MAKE MY PLANS.

Arkham lies in bed, wide-eyed, sleepless, flanked by high windows.

CAP.:   FOR THE FIRST TIME IN TWELVE YEARS I SPEND THE NIGHT IN MY OLD ROOM.

CAP.:   I DO NOT SLEEP WELL. MY DREAMS ARE HAUNTED BY BEATING WINGS.

CAP.:   AND OUTSIDE, FAR OFF, A DOG BARKS, ON AND ON THROUGH THE WHOLE RESTLESS NIGHT.

A rainwashed, fresh spring day on the outskirts of Metropolis. We see the Metropolis Psychiatric Hospital. (And a sign somewhere to identify it.) Where Gotham is dark and claustrophobic, Metropolis appears open and spacious. People come and go. Any vehicles we see are, of course, of '20's design.

CAP.:   NEXT DAY, I RETURN TO METROPOLIS, WHERE MY FAMILY AND I HAVE BEEN LIVING FOR SOME TIME.

CAP.:   I'M WORKING AT THE STATE PSYCHIATRIC HOSPITAL AND ONE OF MY PATIENTS TODAY HAS BEEN REFERRED TO ME FROM METROPOLIS PENITENTIARY.

Close up on the face of 'Mad Dog' Martin Hawkins. He looks degenerate. His hair is cropped brutally close. There's a scar on his face. He's grinning unpleasantly and givin us a look that's full of animal cunning. His expression is that of a vicious child who's about to squish a bug just for the fun of it.

CAP.: HIS NAME IS <u>MARTIN HAWKINS</u>.

CAP.: "<u>MAD DOG</u>" HAWKINS.

Hawkins sits in a chair in Arkham's office. One hand is thrust into the pocket of his trousers. He is talking. Behind him, Arkham paces thoughtfully.

CAP.: I LISTEN AS HE TELLS ME HOW HE WAS BEATEN AND SEXUALLY ABUSED BY HIS FATHER.

CAP.: I ASK HIM WHY HE CHOSE ████████ TO DESTROY THE FACES AND SEXUAL ORGANS OF HIS VICTIMS.

Hawkins continues to stare ahead, with that sly expression.

HAWKINS: IT WAS THE VIRGIN MARY'S IDEA.

HAWKINS: <u>SHE</u> SAYS IT'S THE BEST WAY TO STOP THE DIRTY SLUTS SPREADING THEIR DISEASE.

CAP.: AND I ASK HIM WHY HE CUTS HIS ARMS WITH A RAZOR.

Arkham stands behind Hawkins who still stares straight ahead, in a manner that has become quite disconcerting.

HAWKINS: JUST TO <u>FEEL</u>.

HAWKINS: JUST TO FEEL <u>SOMETHING</u>.

Two prison officers are leading Hawkins out of Arkham's office. He is turning his head, looking back and fixing Arkham with his grinning, bug-squishing stare.

CAP.: AFTER TWO HOURS, HE IS TAKEN BACK TO THE PENITENTIARY TO AWAIT TRIAL.

CAP.: HOW MANY MORE LIKE HIM MUST THERE BE ?

Arkham walks home, head bowed, lost in thought. His reflection is distorted in the wet sidewalk.

CAP.: MEN WHOSE ONLY REAL CRIME IS MENTAL ILLNESS, TRAPPED IN THE PENAL SYSYTEM WITH NO HOPE OF TREATMENT.

CAP.: MY COURSE IS CLEAR.

Arkham at home. Happily, he is swinging his daughter Harriet, (She's blonde, about 9 years old.), up into his arms. She hugs him, smiling. His wife, Constance, also smiling, is taking Arkham's coat. It is a scene of warm, domestic bliss.

CAP.: I TELL MY DEAR CONSTANCE AND LITTLE HARRIET THAT WE WILL SHORTLY BE RETURNING TO MY FAMILY HOME IN GOTHAM CITY, THERE TO BEGIN

PAGE 10: "Mad Dog" Hawkins was posed by Mark Nevelow, who headed up DC's Piranha Press imprint in the early 1990s. Nevelow, captured here for all time as a psychotic killer, also commissioned the story "A Glass of Water," my only other collaboration to date with Dave McKean. ✸

ITS CONVERSION INTO A FACILITY FOR THE MENTALLY ILL.

Arkham in bed beside his wife. His eyes are closed but his brow is furrowed and his hand clutches at the pillow. He is clearly having a bad dream.

CAP.: THAT NIGHT I DREAM I AM A <u>CHILD</u> AGAIN.

Arkham, aged about seven, stands in a hall of mirrors. The mirrors seem to loom over the boy and surround him threateningly. In each one, his image is subject to some fresh distortion. It appears as though insane and evil and terrified and deformed doppelgangers encircle him menacingly. Between two of the mirrors is a hanging curtain that covers a dark entranceway. Above the curtain is a love heart sign and the words 'Tunnel of Love'. ((This actually happened to me when I was a kid: I got stuck in a ghastly funhouse called 'The House that Jack Built' and I was so scared of what might possibly lie behind the 'Tunnel of Love' curtain - for some reason, even at that age, the phrase 'Tunnel of Love' conjured up images of prostitution and venereal disease - that I just froze in the Hall of Mirrors until my Dad came looking for me. I was so scared that something might happen to <u>him</u> in the Tunnel of Love, that I made him take me back out the way he'd come in. Does anyone have the number of a good psychiatrist ?))

CAP.: LOST IN A <u>FUNHOUSE</u>, I FIND MYSELF IN THE HALL OF MIRRORS.

CAP.: THERE ARE STRANGERS IN THE MIRRORS AND I FREEZE, NOT DARING
TO GO ANY FURTHER.

The Tunnel of Love entrance takes on an oppressive, nightmare significance. Its soiled curtain is suggestive of some terrible world beyond - a world of unspeakable sin and carnal horror.

CAP.: NOT THROUGH THAT DOOR.

Arkham's father appears and lays his hand on the frightened boy's shoulder. (I'd thought of having his father's face indistinct - Arkham cannot recall it in precise detail and the man he remembers is almost an archetypal father-protector figure, rather than a specific, identifiable man.)

CAP.: AT LAST, MY FATHER COMES LOOKING FOR ME. I BEG HIM NOT TO TAKE
ME INTO THE TUNNEL OF LOVE, SO WE RETURN BY THE WAY WE ENTERED.

The young Arkham writhes in his bed, caught in the throes of a nightmare, kicking away the sheets.

CAP.: THAT NIGHT I DREAM THAT THE MIRROR PEOPLE HAVE <u>ESCAPED</u> FROM THE
GLASS AND COME LOOKING FOR ME.

The adult Arkham wakes suddenly from a double nightmare, eyes opening wide. He is sweating, panicked. His fingers twist in the fabric of the pillowcase.

CAP.: I WAKE, SWEATING AND ADULT, AND FOR A MOMENT.

CAP.:   JUST A MOMENT.

CAP.:   I FEEL AS THOUGH I'M BACK. WHERE I BELONG.

CAP.:   BACK IN THE OLD HOUSE.

Arkham's frightened face gives way to the small figure of Batman, standing at the open gates of the Asylum. We can see the plaque which reads 'ARKHAM ASYLUM FOR THE CRIMINALLY INSANE'. The house bulks up beneath the moon and the cloud-ridden sky. It is a bad dream house whose windows are lit with a weird, delirious light. A mystery in stone and timber, best left unsolved. Batman's shadow is thrown back. (The atmosphere of the film poster for 'The Exorcist' is what I'm thinking of here. Only better.) On the roof, high above the doorway, a statue stands - St. Michael, spear in hand subduing the Old Dragon.

Batman walks reluctantly down the gravel path, towards a white trail. (The entire house has been contained within a vast circle, drawn in salt.)

He crouches down, examines the trail and touches his gloved finger to his tongue.

JOKER: IT'S SALT. (From off panel.)

Batman looks up grimly as the light from an opening door falls across him. He also recognises the voice.

JOKER: WHY DON'T YOU SPRINKLE SOME ON ME, HONEY ? (From off panel.)

The main doors of the Asylum stand open and the Joker waits on the threshold.

Behind the Joker we can glimpse the waiting hostages.

JOKER: AREN'T I JUST GOOD ENOUGH TO EAT ?

Batman's mouth twists into a grimace of disgust at the sight of his old enemy.

BATMAN: I'M HERE, JOKER.

PAGES 12-13: The look of the Joker is very different from the original script. Karen and the powers-that-be didn't go for my take on the Joker's fashion sense.

The original first draft is quoted as: "The main doors of the Asylum are open and the Joker stands on the threshold, posed enticingly, like a calendar cutie. He is dressed as "Madonna," in a black basque, seamed tights and lace-up stiletto boots (From "Open Your Heart" video). His face is a grinning horror mask of powder and paint — his eyes are heavily made up with kohl eyeliner, mascara and false eyelashes. His lips are a screaming scarlet and his skin is whiter than bone. His hair is gelled up into green spikes. An anarchy "A" badge is pinned to one of the basque's empty cups. Pale and emaciated, he should look simply grotesque but standing there, hand on out-thrust hip, he projects an absolute confidence that confers upon him a bizarre kind of attractiveness and sexuality. It is the attraction of the perverse and the forbidden. The Joker personifies the irrational dark side of us all." "He appears as 'Madonna' in yet another allusion to our recurring ('Mother') theme. Also, and more simply, because she has become an instantly recognisable cultural icon of the type which the Joker loves to mock." ☞

BATMAN: RELEASE THE HOSTAGES.

      The hostages begin to file out past the Joker. There are doctors and nurses and orderlies and guards and kitchen staff. There are probably even a few lunatics, taking this opportunity to escape. Most of the hostages look appalled, as though they have just been given a guided tour round the suburbs of Hell. Some look completely shellshocked. One girl snuffles into a handkerchief. (This is the apparently mutilated Pearl from the telephone scene.) The Joker squeezes her shoulder with mock sincerity and concern.

JOKER: YOU HEARD HIM FOLKS! HIT THE TRAIL!

JOKER: 'BYE PEARL.

JOKER: LET'S DO IT AGAIN SOMETIME.

      Confused, Batman stares at Pearl as she goes past. She shoots him a shy glance from her lowered head. Batman is losing his cool and some of his stoked up rage.

BATMAN: BUT WHAT ABOUT HER EYES ?

BATMAN: YOU SAID.

      The Joker's eyes light up with manic glee. His grin widens into a hideous predatory leer. Hysterically, he waves his hands beside his face.

JOKER: APRIL FOOL!

JOKER: AHAHAHAHAHAHAH

      ((Dave - instead of the 'AHAHA's, you could do the Joker holding up a 'LAUGHTER' cue card.))

      The hostages watch Batman cross the threshold into the asylum. The Joker stands aside to let him past, waving back to the hostages. There is a dreadful inevitability about the whole thing - it is like watching a man walk naked into a blast furnace. (I don't know if it would be too much, but I'd thought of having two stone figures of the Egyptian god Anubis flanking the doorway and identifying the Asylum as a place of trial and judgement. This also draws a parallel between the house itself and Amadeus Arkham's mad mother. If it's done properly, and I'm sure it will be, I don't think it'll be too much.)

      The hostages exchange pessimistic glances as the door slams shut, sealing Batman inside.

      Inside. ((This is Alice-down-the-rabbit-hole territory. We are now outside logic. The recognisable Batman world of Gotham City and Commisioner Gordon and Bat Signals is behind us now. We have come to the Heart of Darkness.)) Batman walks towards us through the reception hall. He's looking up and around. Balloons and streamers decorate the hall. There is a cryptic splash of blood across the reception desk, a discarded gun. The Joker

Millions of daytime television viewers were shown this page on BBC's "Pebble Mill at One" when Dave and I appeared with Adam West (who wasn't in the studio — they had a red flashing "Hot Line" phone so that he could join in from Los Angeles) in 1989. It provoked the reaction from the presenter of "Ooh, he looks a bit creepy…". No shit, Sister… ●

minces along behind, insistently irritating.

JOKER: CHEER UP, HONEYPIE!

JOKER: LISTEN; HOW MANY BRITTLE BONE BABIES DOES IT TAKE TO..

BATMAN: SHUT UP.

The Joker places his hand on his chest in an exaggerated, theatrical gesture of mock aggrievance.

JOKER: OOOH!

JOKER: AT HOME TO MR. TETCHY, ARE WE ?

Suddenly, aggressively sexual, the Joker swings his arm down to squeeze Batman's buttocks. Batman jumps as though bitten by a poisonous snake. He is profoundly shocked. (The Joker's effeminate actions are thus seen to be quite deliberate. He knows exactly how to rattle Batman, who, as I've mentioned, has serious problems in the whole area of normal human relationships. This one act has expertly broken right through all of Batman's carefully constructed defenses. The Joker has not only invaded Batman's precious personal space but he has done so in an overt and threateningly sexual manner. He has precisely discerned how to make Batman most uncomfortable, most intimidated. As a result, Batman is temporarily losing all his dignity.)

JOKER: LOOSEN UP, TIGHT ASS!

Batman turns, pointing. His face is distorted by undiluted rage, hatred and shock.

BATMAN: TAKE YOUR FILTHY HANDS OFF ME!

While Batman stands seething, the Joker breezes past him, grinning wickedly and keeping up the assault. ((By the time this comes out, DC's bloodthirsty readers may have voted to decide the death of Robin - I don't think this invalidates the Joker's comments here. In fact, it makes them even more unpleasant.))

JOKER: WHAT'S THE MATTER ? HAVE I TOUCHED A NERVE ?

JOKER: HOW IS THE BOY WONDER ? STARTED SHAVING YET ?

BATMAN: FILTHY DEGENERATE!

The Joker leers at us as he pushes open the doors to the dining area. Batman follows him.

JOKER: FLATTERY WILL GET YOU NOWHERE.

JOKER: YOU'RE IN THE REAL WORLD NOW AND THE LUNATICS HAVE TAKEN OVER THE ASYLUM..

The Joker throws wide his arms as they enter the dining area. A ghastly party is in full swing here with flashing lights and balloons and streamers. The inmates of Arkham are gathered for a lunatic feast. (The main allusions I want here are to the Mad Hatter's Tea

PAGE 14: The Joker does Fredric Wertham. ❋

PAGE 15: The balloons are randomly placed to suggest a confused babble of voices. The dialogue used is taken from literature and film:
- "'FATHER DEAR FATHER I HAVE TO CONFESS'" — title of a song by The Fauves (Grant Morrison's band in the 1980s), written by Ronnie Bookless.
- "TAKE TAKE TAKE" — from a Television Personalities song: full line is "Take, take, take. Have another slice of lemonade cake."
- "EINSTEIN WAS WRONG! I'M THE SPEED OF LIGHT CRACKLING THROUGH SHIVERY ATOMS AND GOD THE SKY WHIRLS AND WITHERS LIKE A MELTING RAINBOW" — Grant's own words.
- "MILLIONS OF ROBINS" — from the David Lynch film *Blue Velvet*.
- "OH DADDY, MAKE HIM STOP! HE'S HURTING ME! THE DOG'S HURTING ME!" — Arkham's daughter's ghostly voice coming in through time from earlier in the book. ☞

Party in 'Alice' and also to the Last Supper. Some sort of parody of Da Vinci's painting would be nice - done in such a way that it's not made the centre of the picture. It's going on in background and we only notice it if we're familiar with the painting. The Mad Hatter can be seen pouring the tea. The Joker would have been great in the place of Christ but someone else will just have to do.) I'll offer some suggestions here, Dave, but I'd like you to improvise in these scenes - what we want are a few nice, disturbing images and a sense of the world gone mad. Something to give Francis Bacon nightmares. There is no reason here. We have reached the frayed edge of the rational world. In this first scene, just a general impression of chaos and festivity.

JOKER: <u>SO WELCOME TO THE FEAST OF FOOLS!</u>

Batman gazes around the hall, appalled.

Two inmates cuddle and kiss with demented abandon amid the tea and cakes. A security guard, dead, is slumped over the table.

. Another lunatic sobs, head in hands, uncontrollably. All this as the Mad Hatter blithely pours tea over the tablecloth and the blasphemous Last Supper is enacted.

HATTER: <u>NO ROOM! NO ROOM!</u>

BALLOON: FATHER DEAR FATHER I HAVE TO CONFESS

BALLOON: TAKE TAKE TAKE

.BALLOON   EINSTEIN WAS WRONG! I'M THE SPEED OF LIGHT CRACKING THROUGH
                    SHIVERY ATOMS AND GOD THE SKY WHIRLS AND WITHERS LIKE A MELTING
                    RAINBOW!

BALLOON   MILLIONS OF ROBINS!

(These and subsequent balloons on this page should be drawn without tails and placed overlapping each other, to suggest a confused babble of voices.)

A nurse hangs by one ankle from the ceiling. (In an attitude similar to that of the Hanged Man in the Tarot pack.) Her throat has been slit and as she turns slowly, like some grotesque decoration, her blood drips onto a tiered wedding cake. A lunatic, glancing furtively around him, smears bloody cake across his face. A security man stands dead still, with tears running from his eyes. His face is blank - all personality erased by the horrors he has witnessed.

BALLOON: NOW IT'S TIME TO JOIN THE CLUB THAT'S MADE FOR YOU AND ME

BALLOOON: OH DADDY, MAKE HIM STOP! HE'S HURTING ME! THE DOG'S HURTING ME!

BALLOON: SOME SAY GOD IS AN INSECT

BALLOON: CHARLOTTE CORDAY! CHARLOTTE CORDAY! CHARLOTTE CORDAY!

Batman's lip curls in disgust.

(handwritten in left margin:) the date - make sure this is sympathetic, not gratuitous

---

• "SOME SAY GOD IS AN INSECT..." — from the film *WUSA* (starring Anthony Perkins). A number of Anthony Perkins lines are contained within the book.

• "CHARLOTTE CORDAY! CHARLOTTE CORDAY! CHARLOTTE CORDAY!" - from the *Marat-Sade* play by Peter Weiss.

• "DIRT EVERYWHERE! CHRIST LOOK AT IT! DIRT! DIRT!" — Grant talking about his own house!

• "DEAD IN A BATH" — reference again to the Marat-Sade, referring to him as he was, in fact, dead in a bath in the play.

• "I BELIEVE GOD IS IN MAN" — also from *WUSA*, the continuation of the 'God is an insect.' line.

• "WHO KILLED BAMBI" — from *The Great Rock 'n' Roll Swindle*.

• "DICTATOR OF THE RATS" — from the *Marat Sade*.

• "BLOOD AND ORANGES?" — one of Dave's. Doesn't this phrase also turn up in Bill Sienkiewicz's *Stray Toasters?*

There was to be a tiered wedding cake beneath the "Hanged Man" which was to represent the Tower, mirroring the house of cards that is knocked down at the end. ❀

A huge shaven-headed man sits watching television. He looks subnormal, inbred. Saliva runs down his weak chin. He smiles faintly, stupidly, clutching a rag doll to his breast. (This guy is a killer called Bambi. His name doesn't get mentioned but he does turn up later.) Batman and the Joker walk past him.

BALLOON: DIRT EVERYWHERE! CHRIST LOOK AT IT! DIRT! DIRT!

BALLOON: DEAD IN A BATH.

BALLOON: WHO KILLED BAMBI ?

BALLOON: EMM EYE SEA KAY EE WYE

BALLOON: I BELIEVE GOD IS IN MAN.

Facing away from us, Bambi avidly watches television, utterly engrossed. Part of Batman's cape intrudes into the scene.

TV: ..WELL..A..A BOY'S BEST FRIEND IS HIS MOTHER..

((The TV balloon is, of course, a piece of dialogue from 'Psycho'. Bambi watches the film throughout and relevant pieces of dialogue intrude into the action. The use of 'Psycho' alludes in a deeper sense to some of the themes of our story - the dead mother, the Bad House, transvestitism and madness. Downhome stuff like that.))

Batman inadvertently walks in front of the television, obscuring Bambi's view.

Bambi glares with sullen, pressure cooker anger at the blackness of Batman's cape, which fills much of the scene.

BAMBI: TEEVEE.

BAMBI: TEEVEE. (Lettered small. Manic muttering.)

Bambi lashes out suddenly, taking Batman quite by surprise.

BAMBI: TEE

BAMBI: VEE!

The force of the blow sends Batman crashing back across the table. Food and drink scatters. Seated nearby are Arkham Administrator Charles Cavendish and psychotherapist Ruth Adams. Cavendish is dressed in a clown costume and is dripping wet. (Having recently been hosed down.) Adams has been decked out in a white wedding dress. They are both startled by Batman's sudden and unorthodox appearance. Rorschach blot test cards which have been stacked on the table are also sent flying.

BATMAN: UNNH

Batman is lying across the table, groggily. The Joker prances up and leans over him, grinning with malevolent pleasure. Charles Cavendish rises up, thunderously angry.

JOKER: I THINK HE LIKES YOU.

PAGE 16: When Dave McKean and I arrived in Los Angeles on the Coast to Coast U.S. signing tour for the book, we were pleased to learn that Anthony Perkins was a big fan of the book. As a great admirer of his 'neurotic boy outsider' acting style in films like *Psycho*, *WUSA* and *Pretty Poison*, this was rare praise.

BALLOON: …WELL…A…A BOY'S BEST FRIEND IS HIS MOTHER.

This is a line of dialogue from *Psycho*, of course, and that's Perkins' face, distorted, on TV. Bambi watches the film throughout the story with relevant pieces of dialogue intruding into the action. The use of *Psycho* alludes in a deeper sense to some of the themes of the story — the dead mother, the Bad House, transvestites and madness.

A whole scene from the original draft was omitted here and involved the character BAMBI hitting Batman. This scene also describes a clown outfit worn by Cavendish and a wedding dress worn by Adams which didn't make it to the final art. Although the clown make-up was still used on Cavendish. ❈

CAVENDISH: JOKER! I'VE HAD ENOUGH OF THIS MADNESS!

The Joker reaches out and pinches Cavendish's cheek, the way one might a baby's - a 'coochy-coo' gesture. Cavendish is purple with seething rage but thanks to his circus garb and the soaking he's received, he looks simply ludicrous.

JOKER: ENOUGH MADNESS ? ENOUGH ? AND HOW DO YOU MEASURE MADNESS ? NOT
              WITH RODS AND WHEELS AND CLOCKS SURELY ?

JOKER: YOU KNOW YOU LOOK SO PRETTY WHEN YOU'RE MAD.

The Joker pulls Cavendish towards him, pouts and flutters his eyelashes like Marilyn Monroe. Disgusted, Cavendish tries to pull away. He tugs at the Joker's fingers, attempting to free them from the fabric of his clown suit.

JOKER: KISS ME, CHARLIE! RAVISH ME!

JOKER: BUT NO TONGUES, Y'HEAR ? NOT ON OUR FIRST DATE.

CAVENDISH: I'M WARNING YOU...

The Joker pushes Cavendish heavily back into a seat and brings his face up nose to nose with Cavendish's face. The Joker suddenly looks terribly scary.

JOKER: YOU'RE IN NO POSITION TO ISSUE WARNINGS, CHARLIE. NOT WITH YOUR
              GUILTY SECRET.

JOKER: NOW SIT DOWN AND STAY DOWN BEFORE I THINK OF SOMETHING FUNNY
              TO DO WITH YOU.

Ruth Adams is helping Batman to his feet. He ignores her, looking over at the Joker.

BATMAN: WHO ARE THESE PEOPLE, JOKER ?

BATMAN: YOU TOLD ME YOU'D RELEASE ALL THE HOSTAGES.

Ruth Adams stands by Batman. She's lighting up a cigarette, looking a little apologetic. He turns his head only slightly to acknowledge her.

ADAMS: WELL..WE INSISTED ON STAYING, BATMAN.

ADAMS: I'M RUTH ADAMS. I'M A PSYCHOTHERAPIST HERE.

The Joker leans over behind Cavendish, teasing up his thinning hair. Cavendish sits with arms folded tightly across his chest, stoically, stubbornly.

JOKER: AND THIS IS DEAR OLD DOC CAVENDISH, OUR CURRENT ADMINISTRATOR.

JOKER: A MAN WHO JUST LOVES TO ADMINISTER CURRENT TO ECT PATIENTS !
              EH, CHARLIE ?

CAVENDISH: I HAVE A DUTY TO THE STATE.

CAVENDISH: I WILL NOT LEAVE THIS ASYLUM IN THE HANDS OF..OF MADMEN!

Losing interest in Cavendish, the Joker suddenly turns and looks down at the floor. Fastidiously he lifts one foot up out of the puddle in which he finds himself standing.

PAGE 17-19: As an example of a missing sequence from the original first draft script, the following unconvincing "lineup" scene was replaced, as shown in the script above.

In the first version, the Joker leads Batman past a handy lineup of the inmates. The script states:

'The Joker leads a zombie-like Batman past his enemies, who have assembled to greet him. (I saw this as one picture with the villains waiting in line. This single illustration would be divided up to accommodate the word balloons introducing each character in turn.)

JOKER   WELL DON'T JUST STAND THERE.

JOKER: THE GANG'S ALL HERE!

Professor Milo stands sullenly, arms folded. He's trying hard to pretend he's not really with the others.

JOKER: I THINK YOU KNOW PROFESSOR MILO.

MILO: THERE'S NOTHING WRONG WITH ME, YOU KNOW.

Black Mask stands motionless, like a cigar store Indian.

JOKER: BLACK MASK. ☞

JOKER: AND WHILE WE'RE DISCUSSING DUTY, IT LOOKS LIKE SOMEONE'S DONE
THEIRS ON THE FLOOR.

The Joker leans over a table set aside from the main dining table. Two-Face sits there, disconsolate and confused. There is a spread of Tarot cards on the table in front of him but he's using the remainder of the pack to build a house of cards, which is already in a fairly advanced state of construction. He rubs the side of his head as though this action will help his brain work properly. He is not at all the Two-Face we are familiar with - he seems a pitiable, feeble figure who is quite unsure of himself.

JOKER: OH JESUS, HARVEY! IS IT YOU AGAIN ?
JOKER: YOU TRYING TO RUIN MY ~~shoes?~~
TWO-FACE: I'M SORRY..I COULDN'T HELP IT..
TWO-FACE: ..IT TAKES SO LONG TO DECIDE..SO MANY OPTIONS..I'M REALLY SORRY.

The Joker turns and raises his hand, like a schoolkid trying to attract the attention of a teacher. Two-Face seems to be thinking hard.

TWO-FACE: I THINK.
JOKER: PLEASE MISS!
JOKER: TWO-FACE HAS PISSED HIMSELF AGAIN!

Batman looks over at Two-Face and as his only concession to the expression of feeling, his lip curls yet again. Adams looks annoyed. (You'll notice also, that while she insists that the inmates be called by their real names, she continues to refer to Batman as Batman.)

BATMAN: TWO-FACE ?
ADAMS: EXCUSE ME, BATMAN, BUT WE'D REALLY PREFER IT IF YOU CALL HARVEY
DENT BY HIS REAL NAME.

Two-Face picks up the Tarot trump 'The Lovers',(('A glyph of duality', according to Crowley, representing 'the continuous see-saw of contradictory ideas.')), and places it carefully onto his house of cards. He looks somehow heartbroken. Batman continues to watch him. (Of all his great villains, Two-Face is possibly the only one towards whom Batman feels really sympathetic. He is shocked to see his old enemy brought so low.) Adams draws on her cigarette.

BATMAN: WHAT HAVE YOU DONE TO HIM ?
ADAMS: DONE ?
ADAMS: HE'S BEING CURED. THIS PLACE IS A HOSPITAL, BATMAN, AND WE'RE
HERE TO TREAT PEOPLE, IN CASE YOU'D FORGOTTEN.

Adams holds up Two-Face's scarred silver dollar. She blows smoke in Batman's direction and he waves it away irritably. We get the feeling he doesn't like Adams very

Doctor Destiny sits folded up in his wheelchair. His eyes are red coals, glaring balefully from sunken sockets. (As I mentioned before, the conventional depiction of the Doctor Destiny character doesn't really make a great deal of sense — he is supposed to be a man whose body has withered horribly because he has been robbed of the ability to dream. Well, you would, wouldn't you? He is, however, usually drawn as a six foot plus muscleman with a skull for a head. What I want to go for here is a more appropriate and scary visualisation of the character. He looks like a victim of cerebral palsy or severe spasticity — his muscles have atrophied, his legs and arms are twisted by flexion contractures and his head lolls uselessly. He has some control over his arms and is thus able to operate the controls on his electric wheelchair. Otherwise, he is pushed around by whatever kindly soul is available. In this case it's Clayface.)

JOKER: DOCTOR DESTINY.
DESTINY: ...IN DREAMS..I WALK..WITH YOU..
(This is lettered small, in a wavery balloon.)
Clayface stands dutifully behind the wheelchair, clenching and unclenching his hands compulsively.
JOKER: CLAYFACE.
Maxie Zeus regards the others with a look of superiority and contempt. He is dressed in a Roman style toga.

much.

ADAMS: AS A MATTER OF FACT, WE'VE SUCCESSFULLY TACKLED HARVEY'S
           OBSESSION WITH <u>DUALITY</u>.

ADAMS: I'M SURE YOU'RE FAMILIAR WITH THIS SILVER DOLLAR - SCARRED ON
           ONE SIDE, UNMARKED ON THE OTHER. HE USED TO MAKE ALL HIS
           DECISIONS WITH THIS, AS THOUGH IT SOMEHOW REPRESENTED THE
           CONTRADICTORY HALVES OF HIS PERSONALITY.

Dr. Ruth explains. She's becoming quite animated now as she talks excitedly about her work.

ADAMS: WHAT WE DID WAS WEAN HIM OFF THE COIN AND ONTO A <u>DIE</u>.

ADAMS: THAT GAVE HIM <u>SIX</u> DECISION OPTIONS INSTEAD OF THE FORMER <u>TWO</u>.

What I'd like here is perhaps some sort of big montage that shows Two-Face and sums up Adams miracle cure - the coin, the tumbling die, the Tarot cards. Maybe even some I-Ching hexagrams. I'll leave it to you to come up with something brilliantly appropriate.

CAP.:   'HE DID SO WELL WITH THE DIE THAT WE'VE BEEN ABLE TO MOVE HIM
           ONTO A PACK OF TAROT CARDS.'

CAP.:   'THAT'S <u>SEVENTY-EIGHT</u> OPTIONS OPEN TO HIM NOW, BATMAN.'

CAP.:   'NEXT, WE PLAN TO INTRODUCE HIM TO THE I-CHING.'

CAP.:   'SOON HE'LL HAVE A COMPLETELY FUNCTIONAL JUDGEMENTAL FACILITY
           THAT DOESN'T RELY SO MUCH ON BLACK AND WHITE ABSOLUTES.'

Two-Face laboriously places the Tarot card 'The Fool' into position on his house of cards. Batman watches him, obviously unimpressed by what Adams has just told him. She takes a puff on her cigarette.

BATMAN: BUT RIGHT NOW, HE CAN'T EVEN MAKE A SIMPLE DECISION, LIKE GOING
           TO THE BATHROOM, WITHOUT CONSULTING THE CARDS ?

BATMAN: SEEMS TO ME YOU'VE EFFECTIVELY <u>DESTROYED</u> THE MAN'S PERSONALITY,
           DOCTOR.

Close in on Two-Face. There is a look of misery on the handsome side of his face as he lifts another card. It's The Tower this time and it's important that we see it clearly enough to be able to know exactly what it is.

ADAMS: SOMETIME'S WE HAVE TO PULL DOWN IN ORDER TO <u>REBUILD</u>, BATMAN.

ADAMS: PSYCHIATRY'S LIKE THAT. (From off panel.)

Still unconvinced, Batman refuses to let Adams off the hook. He looks slightly derisive.

JOKER: MAXIE ZEUS.

JOKER: LOVE THE TOGA, MAXIE?

The Mad Hatter looks up slyly, guiltily. He looks like he's been caught playing with himself in the toilets.

JOKER: THE MAD HATTER, OF COURSE.

JOKER: ARE YOU HAPPY IN PRISON, DEAR CHILD?

MAD HATTER: NO ROOM? NO ROOM?

The Joker leans over Batman's shoulder confidentially.

JOKER: ONE TOO MANY ACID TRIPS IN THE '60s I'M AFRAID.

JOKER: AND LASTLY, THE LEGENDARY LIZARD KING OF ARKHAM.

Killer Croc bulks up over Batman. Croc grins horribly with saw-edged teeth. (Instead of the traditional portrayal of Croc, I'd thought we might do him more along the lines of the Elephant Man — make him look misshapen and deformed, the victim of some unspecified disease of the skin and the joints.)

JOKER: KILLER CROC! ☞

BATMAN: YOU MUST ADMIT IT'S HARD TO IMAGINE THIS PLACE BEING
                  CONDUCIVE TO ANYONE'S MENTAL HEALTH.

She smiles a little, familiar with Batman's personality type.

ADAMS: YOU'RE GOING TO HIT ME WITH ALL THE LOCAL FOLKLORE NOW,
                  RIGHT ?

ADAMS: SECRET PASSAGES, THE GHOST OF MAD AMADEUS ARKHAM, THE WALL
                  THAT'S SUPPOSED TO BLEED. GOTHIC CRAP.

Batman refuses to let up. As he talks an Arkham inmate crawls into view on all fours, wearing a clerical dog collar.

BATMAN: WELL, YOU'LL PARDON ME FOR SAYING, BUT YOUR TECHNIQUES DON'T
                  SEEM TO HAVE HAD MUCH EFFECT ON THE JOKER.

Adams becomes more serious, looks down at the dog-man as he goes by. She takes the stub of her cigarette from her mouth, releases smoke from between her lips.

ADAMS: THE JOKER'S A SPECIAL CASE. SOME OF US FEEL HE MAY BE
                  BEYOND TREATMENT.

ADAMS: IN FACT, WE'RE NOT EVEN SURE IF HE CAN BE PROPERLY DEFINED
                  AS INSANE.

Adams grinds out her cigarette in an ashtray.

ADAMS: HE CLAIMS HE'S POSSESSED BY BARON GHEDE, THE VOODOO LOA.

ADAMS: WE'RE BEGINNING TO THINK IT MAY BE A NEUROLOGICAL DISORDERING,
                  SIMILAR TO TOURETTE'S SYNDROME.

Pull back. Adams looks down at the Rorschach test cards that lie scattered on the floor. These are proper Rorschach cards, unlike the stylised ones invented by Alan and Dave for WATCHMEN - they are raggedly symmetrical blots of different coloured ink, printed onto big cards. Batman stands belligerently straight.

ADAMS: IT'S QUITE POSSIBLE WE MAY ACTUALLY BE LOOKING AT SOME KIND OF
                  SUPER-SANITY HERE.

ADAMS: A BRILLIANT NEW MODIFICATION OF HUMAN PERCEPTION. MORE SUITED
                  TO URBAN LIFE AT THE END OF THE TWENTIETH CENTURY.

Adams crouches down and begins to gather together the scattered Rorschach cards. Batman folds his arms, showing that he's looking for a fight by adopting this defensive posture. Adams all but ignores him. She has no intention of being drawn.

BATMAN: TELL THAT TO HIS VICTIMS.

ADAMS: UNLIKE YOU AND I, THE JOKER SEEMS TO HAVE NO CONTROL OVER THE
                  SENSORY INFORMATION HE'S RECEIVING FROM THE OUTSIDE WORLD.

Croc lashes out suddenly, taking Batman quite by surprise.

CROC: SCUM!

The force of the blow sends Batman crashing back across a table. Food and drink scatters. Seated at the table are Arkham Administrator Charles Cavendish and psychotherapist Ruth Adams. Cavendish is dressed in a clown costume and is dripping wet (having been recently hosed down). Adams has been decked out in a white wedding dress. They are both startled by Batman's sudden and unorthodox appearance.

BATMAN: UNNH

The next scene in the book is started abruptly from the end of this missing scene. ❋

PAGE 20: The idea of the Joker's "super-sanity" haunted me for years and eventually developed into my theories of multiple personality complexes as the next stage in human consciousness development. ❋

ADAMS: HE CAN ONLY COPE WITH THAT CHAOTIC BARRAGE OF INPUT BY GOING
WITH THE FLOW.

Close up on Adams as she turns to fix us and Batman with a cool and measured gaze that says 'I know what I'm talking about, asshole. All you do is beat these people up.'

ADAMS: THAT'S WHY SOME DAYS HE'S A MISCHIEVOUS CLOWN, OTHERS A
PSYCHOPATHIC KILLER. HE HAS NO REAL PERSONALITY.

Adams stands up again, shuffling the big cards together neatly. The Joker's shadow falls across her though she's not aware of his approach. Batman sees him but doesn't warn her.

ADAMS: HE CREATES HIMSELF EACH DAY.

ADAMS: HE SEES HIMSELF AS THE LORD OF MISRULE AND THE WORLD AS A
THEATRE OF THE ABSURD.

Adams is startled by the sudden appearance of the Joker. He snatches a card out of her hands.

ADAMS: WE..AHH!..

JOKER: CARD GAMES, DR. RUTH ?

JOKER: YOU KNOW ME, I JUST ADORE CARD GAMES!

Batman sits down, regarding the Joker with baleful eyes. Cheerfully, the Joker studies the Rorschach card. One hand strokes his chin in an effeminately thoughtful gesture.

JOKER: WELL, I SEE TWO ANGELS SCREWING IN THE STRATOSPHERE, A
CONSTELLATION OF BLACK HOLES, A BIOLOGICAL PROCESS BEYOND
THE CONCEPTION OF MAN, A   VENTRILOQUIST ACT LOCKED IN
THE TRUNK OF A RED CHEVROLET..

JOKER: WHAT ABOUT YOU, BATMAN ?

The Joker holds up the Rorschach card, smirking.

JOKER: WHAT DO YOU SEE ?

On the turnover page for maximum shock value, we have a single image - a terrible, nightmarish bat crashing through a window. This is not just any bat, this is the Bat. It is primal, atavistic, the embodiment in one picture of the rage and terror that fuels Batman's existence. A totem creature.

Under the impact of the Bat, metal glazing rods snap like twigs and glass explodes in our faces. All power and violence and raw terror.

Batman's face is blank, betraying nothing of the vision the Rorschach test has just induced.

BATMAN: NOTHING.

BATMAN: I DON'T SEE ANYTHING.

The Joker leans over and leers in Batman's ear. Tweedle Dum and Tweedle Dee point angrily at the Joker. Wires connect the heads of the Tweed Brothers, binding them together - electronic Siamese twins. (Tweedle Dum, on our left, is the one who's doing the pointing. He shouts angrily, impassioned. Tweedle Dee is calm and rational.) Black Mask and a few others hang around avidly.

JOKER: NOT EVEN A CUTE LITTLE LONG-LEGGED BOY IN SWIMMING TRUNKS ?

TWEEDLE DUM: STOP WASTING TIME, YOU UGLY, PRANCING BASTARD!

TWEEDLE DEE: HE IS OURS TOO, YOU KNOW.

Black Mask comes forward, spectral, funereal, to make his wishes known.

BLACK MASK: I SAY WE TAKE OFF HIS MASK.

BLACK MASK: I WANT TO SEE HIS REAL FACE.

The Joker turns on him, hissing irritably. He just can't believe the lack of imagination his fellow inmates are displaying.

JOKER: OH, DON'T BE SO PREDICTABLE, FOR CHRIST'S SAKE!

JOKER: THAT IS HIS REAL FACE.

The Joker cocks his head and strokes his chin thoughtfully. He appears to be sizing Batman up as though wondering whether or not to buy him.

JOKER: AND I WANT TO GO MUCH DEEPER THAN THAT.

JOKER: I WANT HIM TO KNOW WHAT IT'S LIKE TO HAVE STICKY FINGERS PICK
                 THROUGH THE DIRTY CORNERS OF HIS MIND.

The Joker comes up behind Ruth Adams and grips her shoulders with claw-like hands. She shoots him an apprehensive, sidelong glance.

JOKER: SO LET'S START WITH A WORD ASSOCIATION TEST, SHALL WE ?

JOKER: RUTHIE ?

Adams looks down at Batman. He sits meditatively, head resting on his fists. He seems to be mentally preparing himself for the coming ordeal.

ADAMS: I DON'T REALLY WANT TO DO THIS..

BATMAN: GO AHEAD, DR. ADAMS. I'M NOT AFRAID.

BATMAN: IT'S JUST WORDS.

Lit from overhead, Batman and Adams face each other across the table. The Joker stands between them, like a referee. Adams is lighting up a cigarette.

PAGE 22: This throwaway version of the Tweedle Dum and Tweedle Dee characters casts them as living embodiments of so-called "split brain" theory – Tweedle Dum, on the left side, represents dominant right hemispheric or "intuitive" brain functions, while Dee on the right embodies dominant "left hemisphere" or "rational" functions. ✸

JOKER: THAT'S THE SPIRIT, BATMAN!

Move in towards the Joker, grinning with evil delight.

JOKER: STICKS AND STONES.

Close up on the insane features of the Joker.

JOKER: I LIKE A MAN WHO CAN TAKE THE PRESSURE!

Amadeus Arkham, fairly close up, squinting against the sun as he looks up at something off panel. There is a trace of awe in his expression - a dream is taking shape before his eyes and he is not unaware of the fact. In his hands, he is holding a plan of the Arkham house. (We can see that the house is built upon a Vescica Piscis, if we study the ground plan carefully. Two huge intersecting circles bind the geometry of the building.)

CAP.:   ''MICHAEL AND HIS ANGELS FOUGHT AGAINST THE DRAGON; AND THE
      DRAGON FOUGHT AND HIS ANGELS.'

Pull back from Arkham, rising into the air. We can see part of a shadow, cast from above, that suddenly falls over Arkham.

CAP.:   ''AND THE GREAT DRAGON WAS CAST OUT, THAT OLD SERPENT, CALLED
      THE DEVIL, AND SATAN, WHICH DECEIVETH THE WHOLE WORLD.'

Pull back up. Below us, Arkham stands in a winged shadow. (That is, by no coincidence, reminiscent of the Bat shadow that plays an important part in his life.) In foreground, we are aware of the edge of the roof of the house and part of what appears to be a statue.

CAP.:   JUST AS THE ARCHANGEL SUBDUED THE OLD DRAGON, SO SHALL I
      BEND THIS HOUSE TO MY WILL.

CAP.:   I WILL BRING LIGHT TO THOSE DISMAL CORRIDORS OF MY CHILDHOOD, I
      WILL OPEN UP THE LOCKED DOORS AND FILL THE EMPTY ROOMS.

Finally pull back and up once more. Big pic. We're looking down on workmen as the make the final adjustments and set a large statue in place. It is the statue of St. Michael that we saw earlier. Perhaps about nine feet tall - a powerful and regal rendering of the archangel subduing the Dragon, Satan. In his hands, he wields a metal spear. The statue seems charged with a supernatural intensity. It is an awesome thing. A workman regards it with a kind of superstitious nervousness as he helps to set it in place. The statue is reminiscent of Epstein's famous work except that in this case, Satan is in more reptilian, less human aspect. The sun shines down from off panel throwing the shadow of the house and the statue onto Arkham below.

CAP.:   AND SET ABOVE IT ALL AN IMAGE OF THE TRIUMPH OF <u>REASON</u> OVER
THE IRRATIONAL.

Arkham is in the nursery, sitting by his daughter's bed. The book on the bedside table tells us that he's just been reading to her. (The book is 'Alice's Adventures in Wonderland') Harriet has fallen asleep and Arkham gently folds the bedcover over her shoulders. A nightlight burns.

Arkham crouches down to gather up some drawings which Harriet has left on the floor beside her coloured pencils. We see the big dolls house that is to play its own grim part a few pages down the line.

CAP.:   HARRIET IS PLAGUED BY <u>NIGHTMARES</u>.

Arkham studies the drawings. They are childish renditions of monsters - a two-headed man and a man with a dog's head. We have to see the drawings clearly. (I'd originally intended to spell it out to the readers by saying 'A Two-Headed man in the nursery and a rabid dog' but it'll be more fun for them to just look at the drawings and suddenly realise the supernatural connection.)

CAP.:   I BLAME THE <u>LEWIS CARROLL</u>, BUT SHE WILL INSIST ON READING AND
REREADING THE BOOKS.

CAP.:   PERHAPS THINGS WILL SETTLE WHEN THE WORK ON THE HOUSE IS
FINISHED.

Overhead view. As Arkham leaves the nursery and quietly closes the door, he catches sight of something lying on the floor - a small pasteboard rectangle.

CAP.:   PERHAPS.

Arkham's hand reaches down to pick up what is revealed to be a playing card. It is the familiar Joker playing card which appeared in the first ever Joker story in 1940. The face on the card is ghastly and debauched, the image of dark unreason.

Arkham looks at the card, troubled without knowing exactly why. This thing shouldn't be here. It is an alien intrusion and he's not entirely convinced by his own explanation for its appearance.

CAP.:   ONE OF THE WORKMEN MUST HAVE DROPPED IT.

Batman and Adams face each other across the table. Adams takes her cigarette from her mouth. Batman sits stiffly, head slightly bowed, hands clasped on the table.

ADAMS: MOTHER.

Move in on Batman. Cigarette smoke rises lazily. Batman has brought his fists up to

---

PAGES 24-25: The word association test with Batman. His answers betray his damaged psychology and hark back to his known insecurities, particularly the death of his parents. This was probably inspired by the much more complex word association scene which appears in Dennis Potter's *The Singing Detective.*

MOTHER — PEARL
HANDLE — REVOLVER
GUN — FATHER
FATHER — DEATH
END — STOP
There are other PEARL/MOTHER references in the book. Can you spot them all? ❁

his chin. He looks straight at Adams, trying desperately not to show any emotion. He thinks he has evaded her her but he is, in fact, skating on very thin ice indeed.

BATMAN: AH.

BATMAN: <u>PEARL.</u>

Move around so that we're looking at Adams over Batman's shoulder. The cigarette burns in her unmoving hand. She tries to give him an escape hatch. He misses it and walks over a precipice.

ADAMS: HANDLE.

BATMAN: REVOLVER.

Move in on Adams' face. She wears an intrigued expression. She knows Batman is in deep trouble now but her professional curiousity cannot resist pushing him this time.

ADAMS: GUN.

Close in on Batman's face, concentrating on the eyes. He is intense, almost lost in memory. He cannot stop himself.

BATMAN: FATHER.

Close in on Adams face. Her eyes widen at this surprising reply.

ADAMS: FATHER ?

Right in on Batman - concentrate on one terrifying eye. He is still playing the game, still unable to stem the tide of memory.

BATMAN: DEATH.

Tight close up on Adams. She looks almost frightened. She knows she must finish this before it goes too far.

ADAMS: END.

Pull back from Batman's face. His expression crumbles. He looks for a moment like a lost child.

BATMAN: STOP.

Pull right back. Batman isolated under the spotlight, head bowed, resting on his fists. His shoulders slump, defeated.

BATMAN: STOP. (Lettered small. A barely spoken word.)

Adams takes a long nervous drag on her cigarette and shoots Batman a pitying, apologetic glance.

The Joker explodes into hysterical, malicious laughter.

JOKER: <u>AHAHAHAHAHAHAHA</u>

Maybe some sort of montage scene here with something to suggest Arkham, Europe and Jung, all in one fairly big image. This is the sort of thing you do very well, so I'll leave you to it.

CAP.:   IN THE FALL OF 1920, I AM INVITED TO EUROPE.

CAP.:   I FINALLY MEET PROFESSOR JUNG IN SWITZERLAND.

Arkham meets Aleister Crowley at what appears to be an upmarket dinner party of the period. (You'll have to check how Jung and Crowley looked in 1920. Both men were born in 1875 and would thus be in their mid-40's at the time of Arkham's visit.)

CAP.:   AND IN ENGLAND, I AM INTRODUCED TO THE SO-CALLED 'WICKEDEST
               MAN ON EARTH' - ALEISTER CROWLEY.

A table with tarot cards laid out on it. A hand, (Crowley's.), is laid on the table. The cards here are not those from Crowley's own Tarot pack. (In 1920, he hadn't yet begun his own version.) They are instead the traditional Marseilles pack - the ones based on Mediaeval woodcuts. Most prominent among them is The Fool. (Recalling the earlier image of Arkham's hand with the Joker card. Other ominous auguries are present in the shape of the Nine of Swords, the Hanged Man and The Moon. We see part of a chessboard beside the cards and, sitting on the board, a black knight and a black rook.

CAP.:   I FIND HIM CHARMING AND HIGHLY EDUCATED. WE DISCUSS THE
               SYMBOLISM OF THE EGYPTIAN-TAROT AND HE BEATS ME AT CHESS.

CAP.:   TWICE.

Arkham stands alone on the deck of a ship, bound for home. He is smoking, watching the full moon rise up over the horizon and turn the sea silver. He wears a long coat and a hat, protection against the cold.

CAP.:   I RUN OUT OF FRENCH CIGARETTES IN THE MID-ATLANTIC.

It is Christmas and we're looking through at the Arkham house under a glowing mysterious sky. The clouds are heavy with the promise of more snow. St. Michael is frozen on the roof, spear in hand, somehow ominous.

Move in on a cheerfully lit window. Its sill is edged with snow, like in a postcard. The scene is benign enough but this slow movement in towards the window should give us the impression of something unseen creeping up on the Arkham family.

Looking through the window now. The room beyond glows with a magical combination of firelight and tinsel. We can see Arkham crouching down by a fishtank. Constance bends over behind him, with a hand laid lightly on his shoulder. There are balloons and decorations and crumpled wrapping paper. Constance is four months pregnant. (This is really to identify her more closely with her role in the Classical Triad.)

CAP.:   I ARRIVE HOME IN TIME FOR CHRISTMAS AND FIND THE CONVERSION OF
                  THE HOUSE TO BE WELL UNDER WAY.

CAP.:   CONSTANCE SURPRISES ME WITH A WONDERFUL ADDITION TO MY AQUARIUM.

Arkham peers into the weirdly lit submarine world of the aquarium. Clown fish dart among the anemones. (The Clown Fish is brightly coloured, about two inches long and always lives close to anemones. You should be able to find a picture of one in a wildlife encyclopaedia.)

CAP.:   JAPANESE CLOWN FISH ARE A FASCINATING SPECIES.

CAP.:   WHEN A DOMINANT FEMALE DIES, ONE OF THE MALES IN HER ENTOURAGE
                  WILL ACTUALLY CHANGE SEX AND ASSUME HER FORMER ROLE.

Constance smiles warmly behind him but Arkham looks strangely troubled. The fish swim backwards and forwards, none the wiser.

CAP.:   FOR SOME REASON, I AM REMINDED OF THE FRENCH NAME FOR THE
                  VICTIM OF AN APRIL FOOL PRANK.

CAP.:   POISSON D'AVRIL. APRIL FISH.

CAP.:   I EXPERIENCE AN INEXPLICABLE FRISSON OF DÉJÀ VU.

Both Arkham and Constance turn from the aquarium. She looks surprised. He looks mildly irritated at this intrusion.

CAP.:   AND THEN THE TELEPHONE RINGS.

ARKHAM: I'LL GET IT.

Arkham, still with that look of irritability, picks up the phone. It is a '20's style phone so perhaps you could check out telephone design of the period.

CAP.:   IT TRANSPIRES THAT MARTIN HAWKINS HAS ESCAPED FROM THE
                  PENITENTIARY AND THE POLICE WOULD LIKE MY CONSIDERED OPINION AS
                  TO HIS STATE OF MIND.

CAP.:   I TELL THEM HE MAY BE HIGHLY DANGEROUS AND I LEAVE THEM TO IT.

Arkham cradles the receiver and turns his head, smiling slightly. Constance aproaches him, hand raised tentatively, her face questioning.

CAP.:   IT'S NOT MY PROBLEM.

CAP.:   NOT TONIGHT.

CONSTANCE: IS SOMETHING WRONG ?

Arkham takes hold of her shoulders, smiles affectionately.

ARKHAM: NO. IT'S NOTHING.

ARKHAM: NOTHING AT ALL.

They both turn to look at Harriet. Wearing a child's dressing gown and slippers, she

---

PAGE 27: Clown Fish are represented for the purpose of illustrating the circus clown/Joker imagery. Their ability to change sex being another reference to the shamanic transvestism theme which appears throughout.

The Fish is also representative of Christ (think of the classic Christian Fish symbol which appears on bumper stickers across America, also known as *Vescica Pisces*). ⬤

sits by the Christmas tree, opening her presents. She is unwrapping a Swiss cuckoo clock. A fire blazes in the hearth. Baubles wink on the tree.

CAP.:   HARRIET IS ENCHANTED BY THE CUCKOO CLOCK I HAVE BROUGHT HERE FROM SWITZERLAND.

CAP.:   I PRAY THAT IT MIGHT TAKE HER MIND FROM THE BAD DREAMS.

Harriet, delighted, holds the beautifully made clock in her hands. Arkham and Constance - she with her arms around his waist, he with his hands on her shoulders - watch her, sharing in her happiness.

HARRIET: OH DADDY, IT'S WONDERFUL!

CAP,:   THEN I REMIND MYSELF THAT ALL INTELLIGENT CHILDREN SUFFER BAD DREAMS.

Close up on Harriet as she turns, smiling. Her face is radiant, full of hope and youth and happiness. It is the last time we shall see her alive. The hands of the clock are seen to stand at half past nine.

CAP.:   AND SHE IS SO VERY INTELLIGENT.

CAP.:   AND PERFECTLY BEAUTIFUL.

CAP.:   I ALMOST WISH THAT SHE NEED NEVER GROW UP.

Close up on the clock in the Asylum dining area. It stands at half past nine.

JOKER: IT'S GETTING LATE. (From off panel, bottom.)

Pull back from the clock for a view of the dining area. Batman stands with his cape wrapped about him. (An unconscious gesture of self-protection.) He looks as grim as ever, trying to pretend that none of this is having any effect on him whatsoever. The Joker has sidled up to him,   . The other villains hang around like a pack of hyenas waiting for their prey to get tired. Adams and Cavendish can be seen somewhere. Adams looks worried but Cavendish's face bears traces of the same subtly greedy expression as the rest of Batman's enemies.

JOKER: TIME TO BEGIN THE EVENING'S ENTERTAINMENT, I THINK.

JOKER: IF YOU'RE FEELING UP TO IT.

BATMAN: UP TO WHAT ?

Close in on the Joker leaning his head over Batman's shoulder. His expression is one of diabolical mirth.

JOKER: A NICE LITTLE GAME OF HIDE AND SEEK.

JOKER: YOU HAVE ONE HOUR, SWEETHEART AND THERE'S NO WAY OUT OF THE BUILDING.

JOKER.:   ONE HOUR BEFORE ALL YOUR FRIENDS COME LOOKING FOR YOU.

The Joker walks around Batman, continuing to taunt him, to psyche him out. The Joker is acting blase.

JOKER: THERE'S THE SCARECROW AND CLAYFACE AND DOCTOR DESTINY, OF
                    COURSE.

JOKER: HE SEEMS SO FRAIL IN THAT WHEELCHAIR BUT ALL HE HAS TO DO
                    IS LOOK AT YOU AND YOU STOP BEING REAL.

JOKER: HE DOES SO WANT TO LOOK AT YOU, DARLING.

The Joker stops in front of Batman, grins in his face and flips his hand in a
dismissive gesture. Batman is confused, disoriented and a little worried but he's trying
to maintain his iron facade.

JOKER: OH, AND DON'T LET'S FORGET CROC. HE CAME UP OUT OF THAT DAMP,
                    DARK CELLAR THIS MORNING, DRAGGING HIS CHAINS BEHIND HIM.

JOKER: THEY ALL WANT TO SEE YOU, SO WHY DON'T YOU JUST RUN ALONG
                    NOW ?

BATMAN: I DON'T TAKE ORDERS FROM YOU.

The Joker's hand reaches down to take a pistol from the table. It probably belonged
to one of the security men.

JOKER: WELL...

The Joker picks up the gun, looks at it speculatively as he begins to tell a joke.

JOKER: THIS GUY GOES INTO THE HOSPITAL, OKAY ?..HIS WIFE'S JUST HAD
                    A BABY AND HE CAN'T WAIT TO SEE THEM BOTH.

JOKER: SO HE MEETS THE DOCTOR AND HE SAYS, 'OH, DOC, I'VE BEEN SO
                    WORRIED. HOW ARE THEY ?'

Batman watches as the Joker crosses the room towards the security guard we saw
earlier - the one who's just standing there, in shock, with tears running from his eyes.
The Joker waves his hand theatrically, telling the joke more to himself than to his
captive audience. He commands centre stage. All eyes are upon this terrifyingly
unpredictable man.

JOKER: AND THE DOCTOR SMILES AND SAYS, "THEY'RE FINE. JUST FINE.
                    YOUR WIFE'S BEEN DELIVERED OF A HEALTHY BABY BOY AND THEY'RE
                    BOTH IN TIP-TOP FORM."

JOKER: "YOU'RE ONE LUCKY GUY."

The Joker comes round behind the immobilised guard. Oblivious, the guard continues
to stare ahead, continues to weep silently. The Joker looks over his shoulder
mischievously, wide-eyed with mock surprise.

JOKER: SO THE GUY RUSHES INTO THE MATERNITY WARD WITH HIS FLOWERS.

JOKER: BUT IT'S <u>EMPTY</u>.

JOKER: HIS WIFE'S BED IS <u>EMPTY</u>.

      The Joker steps back, gun in hand, looking at the guard as if expecting a reaction to the upcoming punchline.

JOKER: 'DOC ?' HE SAYS AND TURNS AROUND AND THE DOCTOR AND ALL THE
                NURSES WAVE THEIR ARMS AND SCREAM IN HIS FACE

      The Joker screeches hysterically, utterly insane and terrifying. He waves his free hand wildly in the air and fires the pistol straight at us.

JOKER: <u>APRIL FOOL! YOUR WIFE'S DEAD AND THE BABY'S A SPASTIC</u>!!

      The security man lies sprawled across the table. Smoke rises from his head and blood begins to spread across the table. The Joker looks at the dead man with gleeful joy.

JOKER: GET IT ?

      The Joker claps a hand to his face, terribly camp, and raises his eyes heavenward. The gun smokes in his other hand.

JOKER: OH, WHAT A SENSELESS WASTE OF HUMAN LIFE!

      Sudden tight close up on the Joker's face as he turns to look back at Batman. Strands of hair flop across his dead white features. Sweat beads on his brow. He looks like a shark - merciless and profoundly frightening.

JOKER: NOW, BATMAN.

      The Joker holds the gun to Ruth Adams' head now, still staring in Batman's direction. She gives it a sideways glance. Her body stiffens, trying not to betray her fear.

JOKER: RUN.

      Batman, in close up, looks back over his shoulder. The glance is lethal - a look of pure distilled hatred. An 'I'm coming back for you, you bastard!' glance.

      Batman runs out of the dining area while the madmen whoop and cheer him on his way.

JOKER: THE GAME ENDS AT <u>MIDNIGHT</u>!

JOKER: RUN!

JOKER: <u>RUN</u>!

      Batman runs towards us through the menacing oppressive corridors of Arkham. He runs blindly as though fleeing from some invisible terror.

      Suddenly we are outside a cinema. We can see the posters for Disney's 'Bambi'. (You may remember the traumatic scene when Bambi's mother is shot.) A very young Bruce Wayne is sobbing inconsolably as his mother angrily propels him out onto the sidewalk.

PAGE 30-31: The Joker's cruel jest is one of only two jokes I can remember. The other one is about a donkey's severed knob and two nuns in a convent garden.

    Young Bruce Wayne's emotional outburst during *Bambi* at the cinema suggests some creepy foreshadowing of his own mother's death. ◉

MOTHER: HOW DARE YOU EMBARRASS ME THAT WAY, BRUCE!

MOTHER: IT'S ONLY A MOVIE, FOR GOD'S SAKE!

MOTHER: IT'S NOT REAL.

In Arkham, Batman, still running, comes closer. His face twists with the pain of recollection. The word association test has obviously stirred up the silt.

The young Bruce continues to weep. His mother bends over him, wagging her finger.

MOTHER: BRUCE, I'M WARNING YOU !

MOTHER: IF YOU DON'T STOP CRYING AND ACT LIKE A GROWN-UP, I'M LEAVING
                        YOU RIGHT HERE.

Batman falters, leans against the wall, clutching his head. Above him is the convex distorting mirror we saw earlier.

CAP.:   'UNDERSTAND ?'

Bruce Wayne, an older child now, on that fateful night when his world was blown apart. He cavorts along the street, miming a swordfight. His parents walk together behind him, smiling indulgently. All seems right with the world.

CAP.:   'I'M LEAVING YOU RIGHT HERE.'

Almost involuntarily, as though it will somehow stop the memory from reaching its awful and inevitable conclusion, Batman snaps his fist up to smash the convex mirror.

The gunman, Joe Chill, steps from the shadows, shoots Thomas Wayne, Bruce's father. Bruce and his mother shrink back, shocked, horrified. She's trying to protect the boy.

CAP.:   'LEAVING YOU.'

Batman takes a shard of mirror glass and presses the point to his palm. He grimaces in anticipation of the pain.

CAP.:   'RIGHT HERE.'

His mother screams hopelessly as Chill presses his gun to her throat. Her pearls, tangled around Chill's hand, are tearing loose.

CAP.:   'RIGHT'

CAP.:   'HERE.'

Batman pushes the glass into his palm. His face creases with the flare of pain. ((This act deepens some of the ritual symbolism of the story. The recurring Fish motif – which relates to Pisces, the astrological attribution of the Moon card - also relates to Christ, who in turn can be linked to the Egyptian God Osiris, whose life and descent into the underworld parallels with the story of Amadeus Arkham. We also see later that the Asylum is built upon a Vescica Piscis - this symbol ⟨◐⟩ forms the ground plan of much religious architecture and is used in the construction of most of the major buildings of antiquity, like Stonehenge and Avebury in England. It is a development of the Greek symbol for Christ 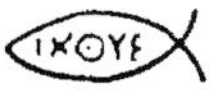 . We also have the Clown Fish in our story, of course. Interestingly enough, while doing some research into folklore, I came across a book, published in the 16th century by quack doctor Andrew Borde, called 'Merrie Tales of the Mad Men of Gotham'. The English village of Gotham in Nottinghamshire was famous for the antics of its fools and the three stories mentioned all contained some reference to images in our Arkham story. One one occasion, for instance, the Gotham villagers, upon seeing the reflection of the moon in a pool attempted to fish it out. In another story, they surround a bush with stakes in an attempt to trap a cuckoo. The third story tells of how an eel was eating all the fish in their pond. The villagers take the eel and throw it into another pond, leaving it to drown. Synchronicity is alive and well!

As a final interesting aside on the subject of fish, the Vescica Piscis symbol is a very basic representation of the holographic process in which intersecting circular wave patterns produce three dimensional images. Physicist David Bohm believes the hologram to be an analogy for his vision of a vast interconnecting universe, in which every part is in some sense a reflection of every other part. In a few pages time, the Mad Hatter will endeavour to outline Bohm's theories as applied to child molestation.

In the same way, everything in this story reflects and comments upon everything else.

What was I talking about anyway ?

Yeah, so Batman is here inflicting upon himself one of Christ's wounds and it's all got something to do with fish, okay ?

Maybe I've been doing this for too long.))

BATMAN: UH!

BATMAN: JESUS!

In magnified, slow motion close up, a drop of blood spatters on the ground. It's impossible to tell whether we're in the past here or the present. Nor does it really matter.

BATMAN: MOMMY ? (From off panel.)

Back in the dining area, the revels continue. The villains are growing agitated, eager to begin the chase. They gather to appeal to the Joker. Bambi continues to watch TV, smiling and drooling. Almost unnoticed, Cavendish is getting up and laying his hand on Ruth Adams' shoulder. She turns. It looks like he's planning an escape bid. (this little bit of business with Cavendish and Adams needn't be brought attention to. It happens in the background.)

TV: MOTHER! OH GOD, MOTHER!

PAGE 32: This simple scene was intended to show Batman pricking his palm with glass to shock himself out of Joker-induced trauma. In Dave's hands the scene wound up as an unforgettable, apocalyptic bloodletting which would surely have rendered Batman's hand entirely useless for the rest of the book, and possibly the remainder of his useless life.

Neil Gaiman posed for this sequence, using his trademark sunglasses in lieu of a vicious glass shard. No expense was spared to bring you this startling scene…

TV: BLOOD! BLOOD!

BLACK MASK: I SAY WE GO AFTER HIM NOW!

JOKER: LISTEN, WE PROMISED HIM AN HOUR!

    Professor Milo, disgusted, is walking over to where Two-Face stands staring out of the window. We see the handsome profile of Harvey Dent lit by the pallid ghost-light of the full moon. Cavendish is steering Adams across the hall in background. The Joker waves his arms irritably.

JOKER: HE'S ONLY BEEN GONE TEN MINUTES! (Lettered small, as though the
                                                                               voice has faded down.)

MILO: THIS IS RIDICULOUS!

MILO: WHAT D'YOU THINK, DENT ?

TWO-FACE: THE MOON IS SO BEAUTIFUL.

    Milo stands behind Two-Face, who continues to gaze up raptly. Two-Face is crying. Milo simply looks bad-tempered. (The thing about Milo is that he's supposed to have been exposed to a 'madness gas' of his own devising. According to 'Who's Who', 'the effects of the madness gas have not been neutralized and Professor Milo remains in custody at Arkham Asylum.' What we're implying here is that the gas has worn off but the poor bastard can't convince anyone that he's back to normal.)

MILO: WHAT ?

TWO-FACE: IT'S A BIG SILVER DOLLAR, FLIPPED BY GOD.

TWO-FACE: AND IT LANDED SCARRED SIDE UP, SEE ?

    We see only the acid-scarred left hand side of Dent's face as he continues to stare at the moon, continues to cry and delivers his bleak punchline.

TWO-FACE: SO HE MADE THE WORLD.

    Milo throws up his arms in despair, walking away from Two-Face, who continues to stare. The house of cards is on a table near him.

MILO: JESUS CHRIST! CAN'T I GET A DECENT CONVERSATION IN THIS PLACE ?

MILO: YOU'RE ALL INSANE!

    Milo sits down grumpily. The Joker leans on a table, making up his mind while the assembled inmates watch. The Mad Hatter whines like an impatient child.

MAD HATTER: JO-KER!

MAD HATTER: WE'RE BORED!

JOKER: OH, ALL RIGHT THEN!

    The Joker turns, in close up, to look straight at us. He grins with malicious insanity. Behind him, on the wall, we see the clock approaching a quarter to ten.

JOKER: LET'S JUST PRETEND IT'S BEEN AN HOUR.

Cut to the Arkham House, 1921. (I see the first part of this scene as one picture of the hall, the stairs and the landing - divided into four to show Arkham ascending the stairs.)

At the bottom of the stairs Arkham stands in the open doorway onto the hall. (Perhaps the hall might show some of evidence of the reconstruction work going on in the building.) Arkham pauses, examining the open front door.

CAP.: SPRING IS A DECEITFUL SEASON AND APRIL 1st, 1921 IS COLD.

CAP.: MERCILESSLY COLD.

Arkham stands at the foot of the stairs, calls up expectantly.

ARKHAM: CONNIE ?

ARKHAM: DID YOU KNOW THE FRONT DOOR WAS WIDE OPEN ?

Arkham climbs the stairs apprehensively.

He walks towards the open door of the nursery. His steps are hesitant. He has begun to suspect that something is wrong.

ARKHAM: CONNIE ?

He pushes the nursery door fully open and freezes on the threshold.

ARKHAM: ARE YOU IN

CAP.: I SEE MY WIFE FIRST, MY DEAR CONSTANCE.

Arkham stands in the doorway. His bag slips from his fingers as he surveys the appalling carnage in the nursery. Blood is splashed everywhere. On the wall behind the door, daubed in blood are the words 'MAD DOG'. Toy animals have been slashed, . A black rocking horse is smashed. Constance, naked, hangs over the foot of the bed. Mercifully, we cannot see her face, only her back, which is spattered with blood. The big dolls house obscures most of Harriet's body - she is lying on her back on the floor. She too is torn and bloody. Having said all that, I don't want to show too much here - suggestion is much more unpleasant than close up mutilations. If there's some way to suggest the hideous vertiginous horror that Arkham experiences at this sight, that would be ideal. The cuckoo clock can be seen hanging innocently on the wall somewhere.

Dave - Again - suggestive, not graphic

CAP.,: HER BODY IS IN PIECES.

CAP.: HARRIET LIES NEARBY, VIOLATED.

Arkham looks down. His face is wiped of expression, drained.

CAP.: ALMOST IDLY, I WONDER WHERE HER HEAD IS.

CAP.: AND THEN I LOOK AT THE DOLLS HOUSE.

The dolls house draws our attention. It too has been splashed by streaks of blood.

CAP.:   AND THE DOLLS HOUSE

     Close in on the dolls house windows. Harriet's staring eyes look out at us nightmarishly. Her head has been stuffed into the house. Her mouth, glimpsed through another window, hangs open limply. Her face and hair are bloody. ((The dolls house is, of course, symbolic of the Arkham house itself and the head connects with the Mad Hatter's speech later on. Arkham has gazed into the Abyss and as Nietzche - and Alan Moore - have pointed out, 'The Abyss gazes also.')) To a certain extent, this single image is the pivot around which the entire story revolves   . It is not only horrific but mysterious and, like many of the other images in the story, charged with a mythic, numinous potency.

CAP.:   LOOKS

CAP.:   AT

CAP.:   ME.

     Arkham's eyes bulge with horror and he clamps one hand over his mouth. His sanity i. stretched to breaking point.

ARKHAM: MMF!

     And suddenly, cheerfully oblivious of the tragedy, the cuckoo pops out of its clock to announce ten.

CLOCK: CU-KOO!

CLOCK: CU-KOO!

     Close right in on Arkham's eye. Something fuses inside. His eye is big and round, the pupil shrinks to a dot. A single tear slides onto his cheek.

CLOCK: CU-KOO!

     We're looking down on Arkham. He is kneeling on the floor, wearing a white wedding dress of old-fashioned design. It is spattered with blood. On the floor beside him is a carving knife. One hand touches his mouth, red with blood. The perspective seems forced and unnatural - it all seems to collide in towards Arkham.

CAP.:   SLOWLY, METHODICALLY, I PUT ON MY MOTHER'S WEDDING DRESS, and I KNEEL
                    DOWN IN THAT NURSERY ABATTOIR,

CAP.:   IT ALL SEEMS PERFECTLY RATIONAL; DID NOT TRIBAL SHAMANS DRESS
                    IN WOMEN'S CLOTHING TO MAKE CONTACT WITH THE SPIRIT WORLD ?

CAP.:   PERFECTLY, PERFECTLY RATIONAL.

PAGE 35: This was originally a shamanic cannibal sequence, of which only vague hints, suggestions and shadowy threats remain. ❈

Still in the wedding dress, Arkham kneels and vomits into the porcelain lavatory bowl in his bathroom. His shoulders heave, wracked with sobs.

CAP.: LATER, IN THE LAVATORY, CHOKING AND SOBBING, I BRING UP BILE.

CAP.: IS THIS WHAT IT ALL COMES DOWN TO - ALL OUR DREAMS AND HOPES
       AND ASPIRATIONS ?

Reflected in the mirror above the sink, we see the top of Arkham's head as he pulls himself up laboriously.

CAP.: NOTHING BUT VOMIT ?

CAP.: OH GOD, I'M AFRAID.

CAP.: I'M SO AFRAID.

Arkham stares at his own reflected face. He seems hardly to recognise himself. There is a kind of pathetic despair there. His lips and chin are wet with blood and bile and saliva. His hair sticks up.

CAP.: I THINK I MAY BE ILL.

Cut to a close up on Clayface's hand. His glove has been removed to expose his melted deformed flesh. His skin glows with an unhealthy spectral luminescence. He trails his fingers slowly, slowly along the wall of a corridor. The paint on the wall bubbles and runs under his withering touch. ((As with the other villains, Clayface is being given a slightly different portrayl than usual. He is seen here as an avatar of filth and corruption, the personification of pestilence and infection, whose impure touch carries instant contagion. Alert readers will perceive him as AIDS on two legs and realise that he represents the fear of what lies beyond the curtain in the Tunnel of Love. If we take all the encounters with villains as corresponding to various psycholgical states, then this one is Batman's fear of sexuality as something intrinsically unclean.))

CLAYFACE: SICK.

CLAYFACE: SICK.

CLAYFACE: SICK.

Pull back from Clayface as he advances down the corridor, leaving a trail of blistered, dripping paint.

CLAYFACE: MY SKIN IS SICK, BAT-MAN.

CLAYFACE: IT'S ROTTEN AND SEEPING.

Pull back again. We can now see Batman backed up against the wall of an alcove. Shrinking back, trying not to be seen. Clayface continues down the corridor with eerie deliberation.

PAGE 36: The original line was:

"LATER, IN THE LAVATORY, CHOKING AND SOBBING, I BRING UP THE HALF DIGESTED REMAINS OF MY FAMILY"

The cannibal scene was intended to show Arkham reverting to hard-wired primordial behaviour patterns as his psyche disintegrates. Early tribal societies often consumed parts of their dead as a way of retaining something of the spiritual essence of the departed. ⬤

CLAYFACE: ONLY YOU CAN HELP ME.

CLAYFACE: BAT-MAN.

Batman shrinks back as much as he can as Clayface comes closer and seems to be walking right past.

CLAYFACE: I JUST WANT TO <u>SHARE</u> MY DISEASE.

Close up on Clayface as he turns and his eyes light up. He sees Batman. His face is a seeping mess of bubbling, running flesh, filled with a terrible, mad ecstasy. He licks ruined lips.

CLAYFACE: OHH.

Batman is backed up in the alcove, with nowhere to go. He looks really panicked, sick with utter disgust and the possibility that this filthy creature might touch him. Clayface reaches out a luminous hand, eager and twitching.

BATMAN: DON'T TOUCH ME.

Batman flinches, draws his head back suddenly to avoid the corrupt touch. His face is filled with utter and absolute loathing and fear. The hand connects with the wall behind his head, causing the wood surface to bubble and rot to running pulp.

BATMAN: DON'T.

The hand strokes past him again, this time grazing his arm. At this slight touch, Batman's skin comes up in blisters which burst and release pus.

In sheer desperation now, Batman ducks low under another grab.

He lashes out with his foot. The blow connects with Clayface's gut, sending him flying back.

BATMAN: <u>DON'T TOUCH ME!</u>

As Clayface falls back, winded, Batman moves into a poised crouch. His boot smokes after its contact with Clayface's skin.

Dazed, holding his stomach, Clayface leans back heavily against the wall. His legs are straight, making a triangle with the wall and the floor. Batman rushes towards him with predatory swiftness. He must put this lethal creature out of action as quickly as possible. Clayface sees what's coming.

CLAYFACE: NO..WAIT!..

CLAYFACE: I DIDN'T <u>MEAN</u> IT..I..

Expertly, with surgical economy, Batman kicks down hard.

Clayface goes down, crawls painfully towards us,
desperately trying to escape from Batman. Batman comes after him, unstoppable and
terrifying.

CLAYFACE: OH JESUS CHRIST MY LEGS!

CLAYFACE: OH MY

Batman delivers a hefty kick at Clayface.

Clayface goes limp as Batman runs off down the corridor in a swirl of cruel and
ragged shadows. ((The importance of these scenes is that they show us a Batman we are not
accustomed to seeing - the Batman his enemies experience and fear. We begin to see him now
shorn of humanity as he surrenders to the spirit of the Arkham house and to the demon that
drives him. He becomes a primal force that knows no more mercy than a hurricane. This is
the Batman distilled to his essence - a vengeful, violent, nightmare figure. He does not
regain his humanity until the story's end.))

Doctor Destiny's electric wheelchair buzzes towards us down another gloomy,
Kafkaesque corridor. His gnarled hand shakes over the control buttons. He is approaching
Clayface's cell and the door stands open. Imagine Destiny's voice - sibilant, high and
whispering in the dark.

DESTINY: CLAYFACE ?

DESTOINY: CLAYFACE, WHERE ARE YOU ?

Destiny stops at the open door. Inside, in the murky shadows, we can discern the
shapes of dozens of store dummies, posed in lingerie - Clayface's harem. Across the wall
behind Destiny and unseen by him, Batman's shadow is cast, coming closer.

DESTINY: DON'T ANSWER THEN, YOU DIRTY ROTTING BASTARD! I DON'T NEED YOU!

DESTINY: I CAN EASILY FIND SOMEONE ELSE TO

Destiny turns his head, suddenly alarmed as Batman's foot kicks the back of his
chair.

DESTINY: PUSH

DESTINY: ME.

DESTINY: NO!

Out of control, Destiny's wheelchair speeds down the corridor towards a flight of
stairs. He screams in hopeless panic.

DESTINY: NO!

    And is tipped out of the chair, tumbling head over heels down the stairs.

    Then he and the wheelchair lie at the bottom of the stairs.

    The wheelchair's wheel spins idiotically. Batman is a grim silhouette at the top of the stairs, looking down.

    Cut to the feet of the Scarecrow as he shambles along a corridor. A pitchfork hangs down, its tines dragging across the floor, striking tiny sparks.

    Close up. Batman's eyes widen with alarm as he looks over his shoulder.

    Now we get a good look at the Scarecrow as he continues on his way, lifting up his pitchfork. Scarecrows are frightening at the best of times but this one is actually on the move and looks even worse. Everything bad and scary about scarecrows is embodied in this one figure that moves with a disjointed, spastic gait, lurching and rolling as it goes. The Scarecrow is passing a cell door which we can see is slightly ajar.

    Move in on the door as the Scarecrow shambles past.

    His face lit by a sliver of light, Batman looks out through the crack of the door, obviously watching the Scarecrow go past.

    Now he looks down, as though becoming aware of something down by his feet. The room he's in is unlit.

    His fingers run across the floor as though reading braille. There seem to be indentations in the surface of the floor.

    Batman's hand flicks on the light switch , illuminating the cell.

    In the new light, Batman looks down at the floor. His eyes widen with surprise.

    We look down on Batman. He seems small, set against the mind-staggering and surreal sight of a floor that is entirely covered with words, scratched into its very surface. Millions of words, a book cut in stone. The concept is staggering.

BATMAN: MY GOD. (Lettered small in a big balloon.)

    Batman is emerging from the cell into the corridor when he catches sight of a shadow, thrown on the wall ahead. The shadow is being cast from another corridor which runs off at right angles to the one Batman's in.

    Batman, taking a final glance at the shadow as it grows larger, is ducking back into the cell he's just left.

Round the corner and into the corridor comes Black Mask - an eerie figure carrying a candelabra. Batman is nowhere to be seen.

On the other side of the door, Batman stands warily, stiffly upright, taking in his new environment. The cell that was behind the door is no longer there. He is in a short corridor with a door at either end. The doors are mirrors, reflecting each other endlessly to create the illusion of an unending hallway.

Batman walks slowly towards his infinitely repeated reflection.

He pushes open the mirror door and finds himself in a room of swirling smoke and coloured light.

MAD HATTER: TWINKLE, TWINKLE, LITTLE BAT! (From off panel.)

Imagine now that you can hear Jefferson Airplane's 'White Rabbit' begin to play here and continue throughout this scene. We're in a big room that's littered with all sorts of curious stuff. (A tip of the hat here to the Batman tradition of giant props.) The floor is marked out with black and white chess squares and we can see huge chess figures - ivory white and dark red - standing or lying fallen around the room. There is an Eastern ambience in the huge tasselled cushions scattered about the floor and in the big, ornate, hookah pipe we can see. The most important chess piece to see here is the black rook which represents the Dark Tower or Chapel Perilous. ((As mentioned before, Arkham itself is the Dark Tower - the place of trial and initiation, wherein waits all that we fear.)) There is also a giant teapot and a huge mirror with a baroque frame. Throw in anything else you feel might add to the atmosphere. A liquid slide projector fills the room with psychedelic swirls and whorls of marbled colour. Sweet, cloying drifts of smoke fill the room. It looks most of all like a 1967 nightclub - a hallucinogenic paradise. The main element in the picture is, however, a huge mushroom, (An Amanita naturally. Red with white spots.), upon which the Mad Hatter sits, cross-legged, hokah pipe in hand. Batman looks small as he approaches the mushroom. This whole three page sequence has a trippy, illogical quality to it.

MAD HATTER: HOW I WONDER WHAT YOU'RE AT!

Close up on the Mad Hatter as he looks up with heavy, druggy eyes. (I want to go for a really unpleasant visual portrayal of the Mad Hatter here - ignore all previous visualisations. The red haired character with the hat obsession doesn't really interest me a great deal, so I'd like to get back to the roots of the character. Using all the 'Alice stuff makes for a much more interesting and sinister portrayal. He looks more like a Victorian pervert here - the kind of man who'd follow children into public toilets and offer them sweets. His hair is sparse, straggly and greasy, hanging down under his

PAGE 40: Some of the ideas on these pages are developed in greater depth and to greater effect in my Lewis Carroll play "Red King Rising." ❁

battered top hat. His clothes - based on the traditional Mad Hatter outfit - are soiled and stained with God know what. His two front teeth are prominent, like the teeth of a rabbit. The way I see him, he's been an eccentric San Francisco alchemist in the '60's - kind of Owsley figure, with a talent for brewing up new mind-blowing concoctions every day. Basically, an acid casualty paedophile who's become a brilliantly pathological criminal.)

HATTER: I'M SO GLAD YOU COULD MAKE IT.

HATTER: I HAVE SO MANY THINGS TO TELL YOU.

   Batman stands, looking grim but quite at a loss. Violence, yeah, but this is something he just doesn't know how to react to. Coloured light plays across him. Right beside him is one of the chess pieces - a big, dark red knight. It is badly cracked. (Do I hear symbolism, anyone ?)

HATTER: YOU MUST BE FEELING QUITE FRAGILE BY NOW, I EXPECT.

HATTER: THIS HOUSE, IT..DOES THINGS TO THE MIND.

   (This whole page consists of a close up monologue delivered by the Hatter. We stay with his face and hands, concentrating on every gesture and change of expression.)

   Eyes closed, the Hatter takes a deep drag on his hookah pipe. His brows knit together, almost as though he's in pain.

HATTER: FFP

   He exhales blissfully. His fingers stroke his face as though smoothing ointment into the skin.

HATTER: NOW WHERE WAS I ?

HATTER: WHERE AM I ?

HATTER: WHERE WILL I BE ?

   He spreads his fingers and looks up, suddenly bright, as though visited by inspiration.

HATTER: AH YES. THE APPARENT DISORDER OF THE UNIVERSE IS SIMPLY A
          HIGHER ORDER, AN IMPLICATE ORDER BEYOND OUR COMPREHENSION.

   He picks up a child's doll, a little girl doll. The doll is dressed in vaguely Alice in Wonderland fashion. It is also headless. The Hatter smiles with lascivious delight as he pulls back the doll's dress to reveal the plastic legs.

HATTER: THAT'S WHY CHILDREN..INTEREST ME.

HATTER: THEY'RE ALL MAD, YOU SEE. BUT IN EACH OF THEM IS AN IMPLICATE
          ADULT. ORDER OUT OF CHAOS.

HATTER: OR IS IT THE OTHER WAY AROUND ?

The Hatter fondles the doll lovingly,

HATTER: TO KNOW THEM IS TO KNOW <u>MYSELF</u>.

HATTER: LITTLE GIRLS, ESPECIALLY.

He clasps the doll to the side of his face, rubbing it against his skin. His eyes are squeezed shut in anguish. Tears begin to flow.

HATTER: LITTLE <u>BLONDE</u> GIRLS.

HATTER: LITTLE SHAMELESS BITCHES!

HATTER: OH GOD.

His hands drop out of sight. Eyes still closed, the Hatter continues to cry.

HATTER: GOD HELP US ALL.

Suddenly he opens his eyes and looks up with fearful wonder.

HATTER: SOMETIMES..SOMETIMES I THINK THE ASYLUM IS A <u>HEAD</u>.

The Hatter taps his head, grins madly, with tears running from his bulging eyes.

HATTER: WE'RE INSIDE A HUGE HEAD THAT DREAMS US ALL INTO BEING.

Batman delivers his by-now-famous Clint Eastwood lip curl. Behind him, we can see the Red King chess piece. ((Alluding to the Red King in 'Through the Looking Glass' who is said to dream the world into being.))

HATTER: --- . PERHAPS IT'S YOUR HEAD, BATMAN. (From off panel.)

As Batman walks towards him, the Hatter's image begins to fade out, to be replaced by Batman's reflection. (The Hatter is simply an image in a hologram plate.)

HATTER: ARKHAM IS A <u>LOOKING GLASS</u>.

The Mad Hatter is gone and Batman simply confronts his own reflection.

HATTER: AND <u>WE</u> ARE <u>YOU</u>. (A tail-less, directionless balloon here.)

Batman reaches out to touch his own reflected hand. 'White Rabbit' reaches a crescendo, the lights swirl.

He pushes open a door. His face shows surprise and confusion.

The music cuts dead, the lights are gone and Batman stands perplexed, back in the corridor where he started, with the door closed behind him.

It's 1921 and we take an establishing shot of the newly-opened Arkham Asylum. It looks busy and efficient, somehow less menacing in the crisp, fresh light of a winter's day.

CAP.:   IN SPITE OF EVERYTHING, THE ELIZABETH ARKHAM ASYLUM FOR THE
         CRIMINALLY INSANE OPENS ITS DOORS OFFICIALLY, ON SCHEDULE, IN
         NOVEMBER 1921.

PAGE 42: The Mad Hatter obligingly explains the book for anyone who hasn't figured it out yet... ◉

Arkham faces 'Mad Dog' Hawkins across a desk. Hawkins sits up straight in his chair, smiling. Arkham draws on a cigarette, trying not to show his nervousness. Smoky light slants through the window blinds.

CAP.:   ONE OF MY FIRST PATIENTS IS MARTIN HAWKINS.

CAP.:   'MAD DOG'.

CAP.:   HE DELIGHTS IN RECOUNTING TO ME EVERY DETAIL OF THE ATROCITIES
HE INFLICTED UPON CONSTANCE AND HARRIET.

Hawkins leans across the table, grinning wetly. His face is ghastly, demonic, gleeful.

CAP.:   HE GIGGLES AND DROOLS AND TELLS ME THEY BEGGED HIM TO ABUSE
THEM. HE CALLS MY DAUGHTER A WHORE.

CAP.:   AND I LISTEN.

Six months later, Hawkins lies on the electroconvulsive therapy couch. (I'm not entirely sure how these looked in the '20's - probably like a Frankenstein apparatus. Perhaps you could check up on the visual.) Hawkins looks relaxed and trusting. Arkham injects him with a muscle relaxant.

CAP.:   I TREAT HIM FOR SIX MONTHS. I AM PRAISED FOR MY COURAGE AND
COMPASSION.

CAP.:   AND ON APRIL 1st, 1922 - ONE YEAR TO THE DAY - I STRAP HIM INTO
THE ELECTROSHOCK COUCH.

Arkham's face is lit by the harsh, metallic glare of raw electricity. There is a lok of terrible satisfaction on his face. Hawkins' hand clutches convusively, spasming into a claw.

CAP.:   AND I BURN THE FILTHY BASTARD.

Two orderlies run into the ECT room, faltering as they catch sight of Hawkins' body smouldering on the couch. Arkham looks down at the body, stony-faced, unrepentant.

CAP.:   IT IS TREATED AS AN ACCIDENT. THESE THINGS HAPPEN.

CAP.:   THERE IS OZONE AND THE SMELL OF BURNED SKIN IN MY NOSTRILS.

CAP.:   BUT I FEEL NOTHING.

Arkham is halfway down a long corridor, lined with cell doors, walking towards us. The lighting is muted and gloomy, the perspective somehow threatening and unsettling. The walls seem wracked by stresses, haunted by ambiguous forms, Rorschach stains and cracks that seem set to burst and suppurate. Very subtle.

CAP.:   I TAKE TO PATROLLING THE CORRIDORS BETWEEN THE HOURS OF THREE
AND FOUR IN THE MORNING.

CAP.:   I VISIT THE SECRET ROOM OFTEN, IN ORDER THAT I MIGHT KEEP MY
                    JOURNAL UP TO DATE.

      Arkham walks closer. A cigarette burns in one hand. The other is thrust into his jacket pocket. He looks at first like a man on an evening stroll but the essence of the place is so disturbing that we are forced to dwell upon the abnormality of such utter normality in this context.

CAP.:   ROUTINE IS IMPORTANT, I THINK. A GOOD ROUTINE DIVERTS THE MIND
                    FROM MORBID IMAGININGS.

      Arkham lifts the cigarette to his lips, inhales. His eyes dart nervously from side to side.

CAP.:   SOMETIMES I AM SURE I HEAR HYSTERICAL LAUGHTER FROM A CELL I
                    KNOW TO BE EMPTY.

      Arkham methodically covers the surface of the mirror in his study with heavy duty tape.

CAP.:   I TAPE OVER THE MIRROR IN MY STUDY.

CAP.:   THE LAUGHTER CEASES.

      Again, Arkham begins to walk through the twisting, endless corridors of the Asylum. Pale moonlight shines through the tall windows. The whole impression is of ceaseless, sleepless walking, on and on, like a spirit condemned to retrace its own steps forever. And somehow, too, the Asylum seems bigger, divorced from objective reality. It becomes an avatar of itself, the archetypal Asylum of endless depressing corridors and narrow stairways.

CAP.:   AND I RETURN TO MY RITUAL PERAMBULATIONS.

CAP.:   MY MOVEMENTS THROUGH THE HOUSE HAVE BECOME AS FORMALIZED AS
                    BALLET AND I FEEL THAT I HAVE BECOME AN ESSENTIAL PART OF SOME
                    INCOMPREHENSIBLE BIOLOGICAL PROCESS.

      Arkham walks away from us down the long, dreamlike corridor.

CAP.:   THE HOUSE IS AN ORGANISM, HUNGRY FOR MADNESS.

CAP.:   IT IS THE MAZE THAT DREAMS.

CAP.:   AND I AM LOST.

      Point of view shot as we move towards an open door. Again, there's that feeling that this is a dream which we're unable to control. We don't want to have to approach this room but we are forced towards it. Two cheap plaster columns flank the door, taken from a big store window display. Scrawled above the door, in bold and childish letters are the Greek words ΓΝΩΘΙ ΣΕΛΥΤΟΝ — 'Discover Thyself'. (Which is of course what this whole book is about, as far as Batman's concerned.) The door opens onto the Electroconvulsive Therapy room, which is lit by an eerie, electric blue light. We can't quite make out what's happening in there but it doesn't look nice. There seems to be someone strapped to what we can see of the couch.

We move closer, unseen by the occupants of the room. It seems that we are invisble attendants on this mysterious and unsettling scene. The figure on the couch jerks violently. The figure is that of a partially naked man, a security guard. His hat and clothes lie nearby. We can see Maxie Zeus, kneeling on the floor, reaching up to operate the equipment that produces the shock.

Suddenly Maxie turns to look at us and we realise to our horror that we're not invisible after all. We are participants in this ghastly dream. Maxie's eyes are wide and marbled, he grins broadly and insanely – the very image of a down market Olympian. He is dressed in a toga and his face has been badly made up with theatrical paint and powder. Two circles with dots in the centre have been drawn on the chest of the toga – a crude rendering of breasts. More flies than are normal are buzzing around the room. The guard relaxes on the couch and fixes us with a deranged, slack grin. He's enjoying this.

((As an aside, if you've seen the film of Peter Barnes' wonderful play 'The Ruling Class' – Peter O'Toole played the lead in the film – you may remember a character who called himself the AC/DC Messiah. The play is basically a bitter satire on the English aristocracy and tells the story of the mad Earl of Gurney, who belives himself to be Christ. Halfway through the play, the young Earl's relatives and his doctor attempt a drastic cure – a raving maniac from the local asylum is brought along to challenge the Earl to a battle of will. This loony is a wild Scottish Presbyterian who believes himself to be the incarnation of the Old Testament God of bloody retribution. He sticks his fingers into a live light socket, calling himself the AC/DC Messiah and then begins a bizarre duel with Jack, the Earl of Gurney, who by this time is hanging up on a cross in the living room, bleating about turning the other cheek and loving thy neighbour. This conflict between the God of Love and the God of Vengeance ends in a nightmarish defeat for Jack – who then assumes the persona of Jack the Ripper for the horrifying second half of the film. Anyway that's partly what inspired this portrayal of Zeus and if you haven't seen 'The Ruling Class' it's a must.))

ZEUS: AH.

ZEUS: A PILGRIM.

Batman stands in the doorway, where we were. He looks at Maxie. Maxie, still kneeling draws himself up a little. The room is lit by an abrasive electric radiance, which seems to come from no particular source. Flies buzz around.

ZEUS: COME INTO MY PRESENCE, PILGRIM.

ZEUS: GAZE UPON THE LORD THY GOD.

GUARD: more

GUARD: please

GUARD: do it again (Lettered small, a weak, slurring voice.)

Maxie leans over and pulls a lidded oak barrel towards himself. ((The oak tree was sacred to Zeus because it tended to attract lightning.)) He keeps his mad eyes on Batman. The flies seem to cluster more around the barrel.

ZEUS: ZEUS ARRHENOTHELUS. PART MAN, PART WOMAN. ELECTRICITY ENFLAMES
MY BRAIN. VOLTAGE. CURRENT.

ZEUS: THE FIRE OF HEAVEN.

ZEUS: LOOK HERE.

Zeus pulls the lid off the top of the barrel and the flies congregate over it, buzzing inside. Zeus looks pleased with himself, smug and self-important.

ZEUS: I'VE SAVED IT ALL. THERE'S POWER IN IT, YOU SEE.

ZEUS: ELECTRICITY.

Zeus hugs the barrel lovingly. He holds his face over the open top and closes his eyes blissfully, smelling the perfume within. More flies. Batman stands in the doorway, just watching.

ZEUS: AHH.

ZEUS: GIFT OF MY BODY. DIVINE. FERTILE. IT SHALL TRANSFORM THE DRY LANDS
OF AFRICA INTO THE PERFUMED ORCHARDS OF PARADISE AND MEN WILL
WORSHIP ME ANEW.

Close in suddenly on Zeus as he bows his head and stares directly, menacingly, out at us. There are flecks of saliva on his beard. His eyes are bloodshot, bruised looking.

ZEUS: FOR I AM ZEUS. LORD OF ECT. GOD OF ELECTRIC RETRIBUTION.

He plunges both hands deep into the barrel. A ritual act which he clearly takes very seriously indeed. Disturbed flies rise in an angry cloud.

ZEUS: I GIVE, SO THAT THOU SHOULDST GIVE.

ZEUS: HERE. MY GIFT TO YOU.

Zeus turns to look at us again. He has something in his hands but we never see it. He's beginning to look a little dangerous.

ZEUS: DO YOU WANT POWER ?

ZEUS: I CAN GIVE YOU POWER.

Batman turns on his heels and walks towards us away from the ECT room. Zeus rises, following him. He stumbles as though drunk. Flies circle around him. Something darkens his hands and forearms. He reaches out after Batman with one grubby hand.

ZEUS: EAT. DRINK.

ZEUS: THIS IS MY BODY. THIS IS MY BLOOD.

Batman's boots come towards us. He's simply walking away from the room. It's just been another bizarre encounter that hasn't needed force to resolve it. Maxie hangs out of the door, pleading. He seems somehow unable to actually leave the room. ((The pun on the two meanings of 'AC/DC' here is quite deliberate.))

ZEUS: THE AC/DC ALTAR AWAITS! LET ME KNOW YOU IN THE FORM OF A
       SHOWER OF SPARKS!

ZEUS: WAIT! (A last despairing cry.)

Three amanita mushrooms lie on a piece of newspaper on a table. A still life.

Arkham's hands enter the scene. He holds one of the mushrooms down on the table and is cutting the speckled cap into sections with a scalpel. Another two whole mushrooms sit nearby.

CAP.: SHOCKED BY MY 'ILL HEALTH', SOME FRIENDS TAKE ME TO THE OPERA –
       WAGNER'S PARSIFAL.

Flashforward. In his darkened study, Arkham writes by the light of a lamp. His free hand rubs his temple. A long aquarium glows behind him. There's no newspaper or mushroom here.

CAP.: DON'T THEY UNDERSTAND ?

CAP.: CAN'T THEY SEE I'M BREAKING IN A THOUSAND PLACES ?

Arkham lifts the mushroom section to his lips. He looks a little nervous.

CAP.: TIME

CAP.: TIME BECOMES

CAP.: STRANGE.

Flashforward. Move in on Arkham. He clutches his head now, closes his eyes. Behind him, the aquarium fills the entire background. Among the clown fish, the anemones and the ferns is an ornamental ruined castle. It is dark, symbolising yet again the Dark Tower, Chapel Perilous and the Arkham House itself. ((Parsifal, or Perceval, is also important here. He is the Piscean hero who faced trial in the Dark Tower of Klingsor. Also, his father was killed and his mother died afterwards of a broken heart – in as manner not unlike that of Arkham's own parents.))

CAP.: FORTY MINUTES HAVE PASSED NOW SINCE I INGESTED THREE PORTIONS

PAGE 47: In the earliest version of Batman's origin story Bruce Wayne's mother dies of a heart attack after her husband is shot dead. This is clearly the more "archetypal" sequence of events and later versions, in which Mrs Wayne is also shot, gain in brutality but lose the deep connection to myth .

Masonic ideas of the "Widow's Son," Christ, the Celtic figure of Mabon vab Modron and other esoteric mysteries are all alluded to here. ❈

OF THE AMANITA MUSHROOM.

CAP.:   SO FAR, NO EFFECT.

Flashback. Arkham washes down the mushrooms with a glass of water. His face is screwed up slightly - a reaction to the bitter taste.

We're looking out through the aquarium glass. Fish swim in foreground. Two in particular move slowly towards one another. Beyond, in the study, Arkham is turning in his chair to look back at the aquarium.

CAP.:   ABRUPTLY, I BECOME CONVINCED THAT THE HOUSE IS ALIVE AND IS
                  TRYING TO COMMUNICATE WITH ME.

CAP.:   A PRESSURE AT THE BACK OF MY HEAD MAKES ME TURN.

((The Hebrew name for the Moon card is Qoph, which means the back of the head. This is also where the 'dragon' sits in the form of the older, reptilian portions of our brains.))

Arkham kneels by the aquarium and places his palms reverently on the glass. His rapt face is illuminated by the glow of the tank. The two clown fish continue to swim towards one another.

CAP.:   IN THEIR TINY, CONTAINED UNIVERSE, TWO VAST AND SHIMMERING CLOWN
                  FISH GLIDE TOWARDS ONE ANOTHER.

The two fish pass each other, one over the other and are caught in the sign of Pisces. Arkham stares at them through the glass. His face fills with awe and wonder and the perfect understanding of the mushroom head. The ornamental castle rises up out of the ferns, charged with mystery.

CAP.:   AND MAKE THE SIGN OF PISCES!

CAP.:   PISCES! THE ASTROLOGICAL ATTRIBUTION OF THE MOON CARD IN THE
                  TAROT PACK!

CAP.:   THE SYMBOL OF TRIAL AND INTITIATION. DEATH AND REBIRTH.

Batman turns a corner and suddenly notices a trail of blood spots which lead directly into the wall and then stop, cut cleanly by the skirting at the bottom of the wall.

CAP.:   I HAVE BEEN SHOWN THE PATH.

Close in on Batman as he crouches down to examine the bloodspots. He runs his fingers along the skirting, searching for some opening as the only explanation for the way the blood spots disappear. Behind him, approaching through the dark, we glimpse a huge wet bulk, a pair of glittering eyes.

CAP.:   I MUST FOLLOW WHERE IT LEADS.

PAGE 48: *Amanita Muscaria* is a highly dangerous and immensely potent psychoactive agent most famous for the radical distortions in scale which are typical of hallucinations on the mushroom. See "Alice's Adventures in Wonderland." ✱

CAP.:   LIKE PARSIFAL, I MUST <u>CONFRONT</u> THE UNREASON THAT THREATENS ME.

Close up of Batman. He's becoming aware of something bearing down on him. He casts a backward glance.

CAP.:   I MUST GO ALONE INTO THE <u>DARK TOWER</u>, WITHOUT A BACKWARD GLANCE.

Batman whirls round to face the massive bulk of **Killer Croc**, who falls upon him, vast, implacable – our evolutionary past rising up to threaten us with destruction. Croc looks misshapen and deformed, dragging broken chains. As a strange, almost poignant touch, he wears a small and pretty locket around his all but nonexistent neck.

CAP.:   AND FACE THE <u>DRAGON</u> WITHIN.

Croc hits Batman, sends him thudding painfully into a wall.

CAP.:   I HAVE ONLY ONE FEAR.

Again, Croc mercilessly pounds Batman. This time the blow takes him in the back and his face contorts with pain. There is a sense of elemental conflict here – these are fundamental forces at war. Mindless strength against cunning shadow.

CAP.:   WHAT IF I AM NOT STRONG ENOUGH TO DEFEAT IT ?

CAP.:   WHAT THEN ?

Batman drops to his knees. Croc seizes him.

CAP.:   THE DRUG TAKES HOLD OF ME. I FEEL SMALL AND AFRAID.

CAP.:   PERHAPS I'VE DONE THE WRONG THING.

Croc lifts Batman up over his head and stands poised to hurl him through a tall window.

CAP.:   SOMEWHERE, NOT FAR AWAY, THE DRAGON HAULS ITS TERRIBLE WEIGHT
                        THROUGH THE CORRIDORS OF THE ASYLUM.

CAP.:   I AM BORNE UP ON A WAVE OF PERFECT <u>TERROR</u>.

Batman comes crashing through the window in a detonation of glass. Handy gargoyles are ranked below the Asylum guttering.

CAP.:   AND THEN THE WORLD SUDDENLY SHATTERS AND FLIES INTO RAZOR-EDGED
                        FRAGMENTS.

Batman's arm flails wildly and he catches hold of a jackal-like gargoyle. (Anubis.) Glass rains down to the ground far below but Batman hangs on grimly, his arm wracked.

CAP.:   THERE IS NOTHING TO HOLD ONTO.

CAP.:   NO ANCHOR.

Nevertheless, he manages to haul himself up, almost inhuman in the way he seems to scale the wall.

CAP.:   PANIC-STRICKEN, I FLEE.

CAP.:   I RUN BLINDLY THROUGH THE MADHOUSE.

Batman drags himself up onto the roof of Arkham. More gargoyles brood on the roof ledge. Batman looks towards the object we can see in foreground - it is the lower part of the statue of St. Michael and Satan.

CAP.:   AND I CANNOT EVEN PRAY.

Close up on Batman's reaction to what he's seeing. His face shows a mixture of awe and inspiration - like the face of a saint, visited by the holy spirit.

CAP.:   FOR I HAVE NO GOD.

Powerful image now of the statue, set against the stressed and churning sky. It is a religious, fearful moment, full of that same mythical intensity I keep talking about. There is an unearthly light source that adds spiritual drama and grandeur to the scene. Just looking at it should make us want to fall to our knees and hide our faces from the terrible holy actuality of it.

In a decisive moment, Batman's hand closes around the metal spear in the statue's grip. The spear is old and dulled, eaten by rust.

Croc slouches terrifyingly towards us down the corridor. Ahead of him, moonlight slants down from the skylight.

CAP.:   DOORS OPEN AND CLOSE, APPLAUDING MY FLIGHT. KEYHOLES BEGIN TO
                    MENSTRUATE. A CHOIR OF SEXUALLY MAIMED CHILDREN SINGS MY NAME
                    OVER AND OVER AGAIN.

Croc looms over us. Above him we see the unmistakable shape of Batman, silhouetted in the skylight window, looking down.

CAP.:   'ARKHAM.'

CAP.:   'ARKHAM.'

CAP.:   'ARKHAM.'

Croc turns as Batman crashes down through the skylight in a hail of glass. Batman carries the big metal spear in two hands. ·

CAP.:   I'M FALLING.

Batman hangs onto Croc's back, grimly determined, like the Old Man of the Sea, using the spear like a garrotte almost, to block Croc's windpipe and pull back his huge head. Enraged, Croc twists and roars.

Then he hurls Batman off his back and into the wall. Batman lands heavily, losing his grip on the spear.

Croc bulks over him, moving in for the kill. Desperately, keeping his eye on the oncoming bulk, Batman moves into a crouch and reaches out for the spear.

CAP.:   OH MOTHER, WHAT TREE IS THIS ?

As Croc falls upon him, Batman swings up the spear. Croc's terrible momentum is impaling him on the point. Batman grimaces, trying to support the huge weight that descends upon him.

CAP.:   WHAT WOUNDS ARE THESE ?

Forced backwards through his grip, the blunt end of the spear is pushed into Batman's side. Batman screams, agonized.

CAP.:   I AM ATTIS ON THE PINE.

CAP.:   CHRIST ON THE CEDAR.

CAP.:   ODIN ON THE WORLD-ASH.

The spear emerges through the muscle of Batman's side and strikes sparks from the wall behind. Batman is in an extremity of pain.

CAP.:   'HUNG ON THE WINDY TREE FOR NINE WHOLE NIGHTS
                    WOUNDED WITH THE SPEAR.'

Vibrating with tension, teeth gritted, Batman tries to force the spear back, to push Croc away from him. This whole page takes place in a fraction of a second.

CAP.:   DEDICATED TO ODIN'...

Croc takes hold of the spear and pulls Batman around. Batman can do nothing but follow. The two antagonists turn in grotesque synchronisation, linked like Siamese twins.

CAP.:   MYSELF TO MYSELF.'

CAP.:   I MUST SEE MY REFLECTION, TO PROVE I STILL EXIST.

Batman makes a final effort to pull the spear away. He looks in terrible pain, tortured.

CAP.:   OUTSIDE, I HEAR THE DRAGON COMING CLOSER, CLOSER.

CAP.:   DESPERATELY, I PEEL THE TAPE FROM THE MIRROR, BREAKING MY
                    FINGERS, STRIP BY STRIP.

Instead of coming free, the spear, weakened by rust, abruptly snaps. Croc stumbles back towards a tall window. Batman is similiarly hurled back by centifugal force.

CAP.:   UNTIL I STAND REVEALED IN THE GLASS.

CAP.:   AND I STARE INTO OLD FAMILIAR EYES.

Croc is framed in the shattering window as it explodes beneath his weight. His arms are thrown wide, in an attitude of crucifixion. The broken spear juts from his side and

PAGE 51: Killer Croc stands in for the Old Dragon of Revelations. The Dragon can be seen to represent primal chaos, the R complex lizard brain. The spear, the weapon of rational intellect, is used to conquer the brute appetites of nature and man. St. Michael thus bound the dragon in Hell, just as Croc is bound in the cellars of Arkham.

In Qabalistic numerology, Christ = Satan = Messiah, which is why Croc appears here in crucifixion pose, taking the place of Christ on this blasphemous cross. In this scene, Batman reunites Christ and Serpent, then confronts and overcomes his own attachment to his Mother in a perverse nightmare of lizards, lace and bridal embroidery.

Much of this subtextual material was lost on the casual reader but that didn't seem to stop us from shifting mega-amounts of copies. I do believe that people respond emotionally to deep mythical patterns whether or not they actually recognise or "understand" them as such, but the fact that our book launched at the time of the outrageously successful *Batman* film by Tim Burton probably helped more than anything else. ❀

the shattering glass creates a jagged halo around his vast, deformed head. He becomes the image of the Serpent/Christ, (And also evokes Moby Dick, with the harpoon in his side.), a mediaeval allegory which Jung interpreted as being symbolic of 'an overcoming of the unconscious and, at the same time, of the attitude of the son who unconsciously hangs on his mother.' Perfect for our purposes.

CAP.: MOTHER!

Broken glass falls, spinning in perfect slow motion.

Glass falls. Croc's body blurs past, falling fast.

Glass shatters on the ground where there are a few drops of blood.

CAP.: I MUST HAVE FAINTED THEN, FOR IT MORNING WHEN NEXT I OPEN MY EYES.

CAP.: NO LONGER ABLE TO TELL WHERE THE DRAGON ENDED.

Batman staggers towards us, tugging the broken spear shaft from his bleeding side. He leans heavily against the wall, badly hurt. He is limping and his teeth are set in a stoic grimace. Torn and bloody and quite terrifying. His forward motion seems awful, impelled, and we almost wish this ghastly apparition would stop and not continue to advance towards us.

CAP.: AND I BEGIN.

Batman's booted feet approach us. On the floor in front of them, the blood spots vanish into the wall.

CAP.: YET AM I NOT THE HERO, THE MAN OF DESTINY ? HAVE I NOT CONFRONTED THE GREAT DRAGON ?

CAP.: WHERE THEN IS MY GRAIL ? MY TREASURE HORDE ?

In a single moment of unstoppable violence, Batman kicks down through the fake wall, smashing it into splinters. This is a pivotal image of revelation by destructive means. ((Arkham attained his revelation by passive, contemplative means. Batman's life is dominated by violence.))

CAP.: MY FINAL REWARD ?

Framed in the shattered 'door' he has made for himself, Batman's bloody face is lit by the stale light in the room he has uncovered. His eyes widen.

CAVENDISH: GOOD EVENING, BATMAN. (From off panel.)

Batman stands in the smashed entrance he has created. He has broken into Elizabeth Arkham's bedroom, which has been preserved exactly as it was in 1920, with the four poster bed and the old furniture. (If we did do the flashback scenes in sepia tones, it occurred

PAGE 52: "Bats" in the attic, you might say…

to me that we might use the same idea in this scene — the room is coloured in sepia while Batman, Cavendish and Adams are rendered as normal. Just a thought.) Cavendish sits on a chair by the bed, holding an open pearl-handled razor to Adams throat. She's sitting on the bed where old Ma Arkham sat. Adams looks terribly frightened. She really doesn't want to die. (Inexplicably, she's now in the clown suit and Cavendish wears the wedding dress.) The bedside oil lamp is lit, lending the room an eerie, shadowy glamour. Old blood stains the bedclothes and pillowcase.

BATMAN:	DR. CAVENDISH.
ADAMS:	DON'T COME NEAR HIM, BATMAN!
ADAMS:	HE..CUT ME..
ADAMS:	JUST KEEP BACK.

Batman grimaces slightly. He's worked it all out now.

BATMAN:	YOU FREED THE INMATES. YOU ALLOWED THIS TO HAPPEN.
BATMAN:	WHY, CAVENDISH ?

Still holding the razor to Adams' throat, Cavendish points with his free hand. There's already a nasty cut on Adam's face. She continues to look terrified. Cavendish looks hot and bothered but filled with a kind of feverish excitement.

CAVENDISH:	NOW LISTEN, I ONLY DID WHAT HAD TO BE DONE.
CAVENDISH:	YOU READ THE BOOK ON THE TABLE BESIDE YOU AND YOU'LL SEE.

Batman slowly picks up a bound leather book from the table beside him, keeping an eye on Cavendish.

CAVENDISH:	GO ON. IT'S AMADEUS ARKHAM'S JOURNAL.
CAVENDISH:	GO ON. READ IT. I'VE MARKED THE PLACE FOR YOU.

Batman opens the Journal about a quarter of the way through. The place is indeed marked by a silk ribbon bookmark. He looks down at the pages. He reads.

CAVENDISH:	READ IT. YOU'LL SEE. (From off panel.)
CAP.:	AND SUDDENLY THE LONGED FOR REVELATION COMES IN THE FORM OF A MEMORY MY MIND HAD SUPPRESSED.

In 1920, the Arkham house crouches under the weight of a terrible storm. Lightning cracks across the turbulent, boiling sky. A raging wind tears at the budding trees. Rain rides the wind, gusting down with blind ferocity. In the midst of this elemental conflict sits the house. The semi-circular window is lit up.

CAP.:	IT IS 1920. TREES THRASH IN THE DARK UNDER A RESTLESS SKY. RAIN RATTLES THE WINDOWS.
CAP.:	WHY ?

PAGE 53: Like Clown Fish, Cavendish and Adams have reversed sex roles here in this bizarre little secret room. ❋

In his mother's room, Arkham sits by her bed. He reaches out tentatively to comfort her as she thrashes and covers her eyes and turns her head away. (He keeps one hand in his pocket throughout this sequence.) The room is lit mysteriously, (Again.), by the oil lamp at the bedside table. Mother is older now, in her 50's and even more wild and crazy-looking than before. The dogs are still there, even though logic dictates that they should have died of old age before now.

CAP.:   WHY HAVE I COME HERE ?

MOTHER: IT'S HERE!

MOTHER: IT'S HERE!

ARKHAM: MOTHER, PLEASE, THERE'S NOTHING.

His mother suddenly sits bolt upright in bed, staring with terrified eyes into the centre of the room. Arkham follows her gaze, plainly losing control and becoming terribly frightened.

CAP.:   AND WHY AM I SO AFRAID ?

MOTHER: EVERY NIGHT!

MOTHER: EVERY NIGHT!

CAP.:   BENEATH THE BED, GREAT WINGS BEGIN TO BEAT.

She points madly into the middle of the room. Arkham's eyes narrow and he turns his head away slightly as though trying not to avert his gaze. The light grows feverishly brighter.

CAP.:   I AM NOT MAD.

MOTHER: SEE ? THERE ?

MOTHER: IT'S COME FOR ME!

CAP.:   I AM NOT MAD.

She screams suddenly and pulls up the bedclothes as if to protect herself. Arkham leans back heavily in his seat, eyes becoming round, mouth falling open. The heavy curtains blow up wildly as if stirred by a raging wind. Papers and other loose objects fly up. Arkham's hair is whipped up by the phantom wind. A vast jagged shadow falls across the wall.

CAP.:   BUT GOD HELP ME, I SEE IT.

CAP.:   I SEE THE THING THAT HAS HAUNTED AND TORMENTED MY POOR MOTHER
                         THESE LONG YEARS.

CAP.:   I SEE IT.

The room all but disappears, casting the bed and Arkham beside it into a dimensionless space that is dominated by the unmistakable shadow of a nightmarish bat. The Bat is an elemental, awesomely frightening shadow of primal terror. Make this one as

---

PAGE 54: Batman's rage and confusion echoes back through time to haunt the past and send poor Mrs. Arkham right around the bend into mythic reality. ✳

powerful and scary as you possibly can.

CAP.:   AND IT IS A <u>BAT</u>.

CAP.:   THE "BLIND DEATH" OF FOLK TRADITION.

CAP.:   A <u>BAT</u>!

Arkham's mother shrieks, throws back her head in terrible despair, begging to be released from this torture.

CAP.:   OH, MY POOR MOTHER.

MOTHER: DON'T LET IT TAKE ME!

MOTHER: PLEASE DON'T LET IT!

As if in a dream, Arkham opens up the pearl-handled razor. He stares not at it but at his mother and tears start in his eyes. The curtains blow behind him. Loose papers swirl in a wind from nowhere. The room is in chaos. A scalloped shadow falls across Arkham's face, like that of a bat's wing.

ARKHAM: IT WON'T TAKE YOU, I PROMISE.

ARKHAM: DON'T BE AFRAID, MOTHER.

Arkham's hand rises up, holding the open blade. A frozen moment.

ARKHAM: I LOVE YOU.

There is an almost abstract splattering of blood.

Pull back. Arkham's mother lies dead in her bloodsoaked bed. Arkham holds her hand. He is bent over the bed, shoulders heaving with sobs. The curtains are still, nothing has been blown over or disturbed. But for the blood, the scene is almost normal.

CAP.:   I UNDERSTAND NOW WHAT MY MEMORY TRIED TO KEEP FROM ME.

Arkham, dressed as a bride, walks towards us down a corridor. Two hounds trot at his either side. There is something disturbing about the image. The rational world has become lost to myth and ritual.

CAP.:   MADNESS IS BORN IN THE BLOOD. IT IS MY BIRTHRIGHT.

CAP.:   MY INHERITANCE.

CAP.:   MY <u>DESTINY</u>.

Arkham comes closer. His hair sticks up in spikes and his face is lit by the perfect radiant confidence of the insane. Perspectives seem distorted and the shadow shape of the Bat can be discerned in the very fabric of the wall.

CAP.:   I SHALL <u>CONTAIN</u> THE PRESENCES THAT ROAM THESE ROOMS AND NARROW
                   STAIRWAYS.

CAP.:   I SHALL SURROUND THEM WITH BARS AND WALLS AND ELECTRIFIED

FENCES AND PRAY THEY NEVER BREAK FREE.

CAP.:   I AM THE DRAGON'S BRIDE, THE SON OF THE WIDOW.

Cavendish, eyes bright, points at Batman. He is like a teacher patiently explaining the obvious to a foolish child. There is a kind of delight in revelation. He can't wait for Batman's response to this shattering news.

CAP.:   LEATHER WINGS ENFOLD ME.

CAVENDISH: YOU SEE NOW ?

CAVENDISH: YOU UNDERSTAND ?

Batman grips the closed journal in his hands, holding onto it like a lifebelt. His eyes widen.

CAVENDISH: YOU WHO'VE KEPT THIS PLACE SUPPLIED WITH POOR MAD SOULS FOR
                     YEARS. YOU WHO'VE FED THIS HUNGRY HOUSE.

CAVENDISH: DO YOU SEE ? (From off panel.)

Close in on Batman. He is faltering, vulnerable.

CAVENDISH: YOU ARE THE BAT! (From off panel.)

BATMAN: NO.

BATMAN: I..I'M JUST A MAN (Small letters. Weak.)

Eyes staring and mad, Cavendish fans his fingers in front of his face. They cast a bat shadow back across his features.

CAVENDISH: I'M NOT FOOLED BY THAT CHEAP DISGUISE. I KNOW WHAT YOU ARE!

CAVENDISH: ARKHAM TRIED TO KILL HIS STOCKBROKER IN 1929. THAT'S WHAT THEY
                     FINALLY LOCKED HIM AWAY FOR, DID YOU KNOW THAT?

Cavendish lifts his hands up beside his face, raising his eyes dreamily heavenward.

CAVENDISH: IT DIDN'T STOP HIM. HE'D READ "THE GOLDEN BOUGH", HE'D STUDIED
                     SHAMANISTIC PRACTICES AND HE KNEW THAT ONLY RITUAL, ONLY
                     MAGIC COULD CONTAIN THE BAT.

CAVENDISH: SO DO YOU KNOW WHAT HE DID ?

Cavendish's fingers scratch at the air.

CAVENDISH: HE SCRATCHED A BINDING SPELL INTO THE FLOOR OF HIS CELL.

CAVENDISH: HE USED HIS FINGERNAILS. CAN YOU IMAGINE THAT ?

CAVENDISH: HIS FINGERNAILS.

Close up on drawings and notes tacked to a wall. We see a plan of the Arkham House contained in the Vescica Piscis. Tacked onto that, Arkham's own drawing of the interlocked circles with the words 'VESICICA PISCIS' written carefully underneath and on the same piece of paper the Greek Fish symbol for Christ. Also a diagram showing the phases of the moon, from new, through full to old. Also something with this symbol and some scribbled notes. 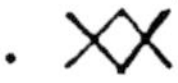 ((This is the Voodoo symbol for 'Androgynous Totality'.)) A mediaeval alchemical illustration of the Rebis - the Man/Woman fusion. A page of crabbed handwriting. Just loads of pieces of paper tacked onto the plan of the house, which is itself pinned to the wall.

CAP.: "IT TOOK YEARS."

ARKHAM: ..O SAY CAN YOU SEE ? (From off panel, bottom. Small and muttery.)

Pull back from the stuff on the wall. Arkham confined to a cell, obviously mad. His hair is white now and he is in his early 50's, busily working on a project that will consume the rest of his life. Leaning on his elbows, he is laboriously scratching into the floor with his fingernails. A cigarette hangs from the corner of his mouth as he sings to himself. There is a sense of measured urgency in his work. Several paragraphs are already etched into the floor.

ARKHAM: BY THE DAWN'S EARLY LIGHT..(Small and muttery still.)

Twenty years have passed, wars have come and wars have gone, the Beatles are newly famous, Kennedy spends his last months in the White House and Arkham is still working. His hair is pure white, cropped down to the skull. There is white, coarse stubble on his aged features. A new sense of desperate elation has entered his work - he knows the end is near, both for him and for his great spell. The race is now on to see which will reach its end first. He painfully coughs up a gout of blood. His fingers too, are bloody with scratching. Early morning light enters through the barred windows of his cell. There is something bright and optimistic in the air, despite Arkham's pain.

CAP.: I SEE NOW THE VIRTUE IN MADNESS, FOR THIS COUNTRY KNOWS NO LAW NOR ANY BOUNDARY

CAP.: I PITY THE POOR SHADES CONFINED TO THE EUCLIDEAN PRISON THAT IS SANITY

Arkham suddenly goes limp. His face hits the floor.

CAP.: ALL THINGS ARE POSSIBLE HERE AND I AM WHAT MADNESS HAS MADE ME

CAP.: WHOLE

CAP.: AND COMPLETE

Arkham rolls over onto his back. Blood runs from his mouth, his fingers are red ruins but he is smiling. His face is illuminated. The floor beneath him is covered with line after line after line after line of scratched writing. Our minds reel at the thought.

CAP.: AND FREE AT LAST.

ARKHAM: FINISHED. (Very small, a bubbling whisper of triumph.)

PAGE 57: According to Len Wein's original WHO'S WHO entry, Arkham died singing "The Battle Hymn of the Republic," but for some reason I got confused and had him belting out "The Star Spangled Banner" instead. Let's face it, the guy was a nut, he might as well have been singing "Hello Dolly!."

We're looking down on Arkham, from high up on the ceiling. He lies in the attitude of the Hanged Man of the Tarot. ((This is the card of Osiris and Christ, Odin and Attis The card of sacrifice that brings light out of darkness.))

ARKHAM: IT'S FINISHED. (Again, small and weak.)

Move very slowly down towards Arkham again. An attendant and a doctor are bursting into the cell, followed by a nun. (They've been doing their rounds of the patients. Everything that happens below us seems diminished by our perspective. We are outside human affairs and they seem small and unimportant, set against the mythic truth of Arkham's great sacrifice.

DOCTOR: GET SOMEONE UP HERE! QUICKLY!

NUN: OH, HIS HANDS!

NUN: WHO IS THIS MAN, DOCTOR ?

Move in on Arkham. The nun and the doctor seem simply decoration. They are no longer important. Arkham's face draws all our attention. He begins to smile. His words take on an extra significance as he identifies himself with the house.

CAP.: I'M ARKHAM.

CAP.: I'M HOME.

CAP.: WHERE I BELONG.

Close right in on Arkham's face. He is dead. Blood runs from between his lips but cannot erase his smile. This final smile is subtle but transforming. ((Another film reference here - at the end of Lindsay Anderson's 'O Lucky Man', after three hours of tribulation, Malcolm McDowell is asked to smile by the director himself. McDowell, having seen all the darkness of the human spirit, says 'What is there to smile about ?' Anderson whacks him with a script and repeats himself, 'Smile.'

And in one of the great moments of cinema, the camera closes on McDowell's face and holds there for what seems like forever. The smile begins in his eyes, his face illuminates and just as the smile reaches his lips, the camera cuts away. It's probably quite impossible to achieve that degree of subtlety in a drawing but that's what to aim for. A Mona Lisa smile.))

CAP.: "HE GAVE EVERYTHING. EVERYTHING."

((Before we move on, a note about the appearance of the nun. This is really just a little joke for people who take the trouble to check up on the Tarot. The Hebrew word 'Nun' means 'fish' and is the name of the Death card in the Tarot pack. How the fish connects with the Moon and with Death is something that would take the rest of the day to explain. You'll just have to take it from me.))

PAGE 58: *O Lucky Man!* my favourite film ever.

Close up on Cavendish, looking more and more deranged with every passing moment. He seems pleased with himself even though it's plain to those of us who aren't completely round the bend that his logic seems a little skewed. Sweat stands out on his brow.

CAVENDISH: BUT IT STILL WASN'T ENOUGH.

CAVENDISH: TWO YEARS AGO, I FOUND THIS HIDDEN ROOM. READ THE JOURNAL THEN TOO.

CAVENDISH: I JUST COULDN'T STOP THINKING ABOUT WHAT ARKHAM HAD SAID AND I REALIZED IT WAS MY DESTINY TO FINISH WHAT HE STARTED.

Cavendish rises, holding up the open razor, making quite plain his intent. Ruth Adams grabs his arm, trying to stop him.

CAVENDISH: I SET A TRAP FOR THE BAT, YOU SEE. I SURROUNDED THE ASYLUM WITH A CIRCLE OF SALT SO IT COULDN'T ESCAPE AGAIN.

CAVENDISH: AND NOW..WELL..

ADAMS: DOCTOR CAVENDISH! CHARLES!..

Cavendish knocks Adams back viciously and advances on Batman. Batman, injured and in no mood for a fight, holds up his hand as though to ward Cavendish off.

CAVENDISH: SHUT UP YOU IGNORANT COW!

BATMAN: CAVENDISH, YOU'RE SICK.

BATMAN: YOU NEED HELP.

The razor glitters in Cavendish's hand. He's taking Batman's last remark somewhat badly.

CAVENDISH: I'M SICK ? HAVE YOU LOOKED IN A MIRROR LATELY ?

CAVENDISH: HAVE YOU ?

Cavendish suddenly lunges forward, swinging the razor up over his head. Weakly, Batman throws up his arms to protect his face.

BATMAN: CAVENDISH!

BATMAN: NO!

Berserk, Cavendish descends upon Batman, slashing wildly with the razor. Batman's arm bursts open in a gout of blood. This whole scene is a whirl of frenzied motion. Batman cries out with the sudden shock of pain.

BATMAN: JESUS!

Batman punches the razor out of Cavendish's hand. With his other hand, Cavendish seizes Batman's throat.

BATMAN: UNNH

CAVENDISH: MOMMY'S

PAGE 59: The deranged Cavendish has clearly worked an act of bad magic — in a misguided effort to exorcise the spirit of Arkham he has instead invoked the demonic Death Bat in its form as Batman. As we've seen all polarities go into reverse on All Fools Day, including those of magical intent. ❋

CAVENDISH: BOY!

  The razor hits the bedside table.

CAVENDISH: MOMMY'S BOY!

  Close up on Ruth Adams as she watches the conflict. She wants to do something but her rattled mind won't seem to co-operate. (She's no longer sitting on the bed by the way.)

ADAMS: NO. (Lettered fairly small.)

  Cavendish, possessed of a madman's strength, forces Batman back onto the bed, still trying to throttle him. Batman shouts desperately to Adams.

CAVENDISH: MOMMY'S BOY!

CAVENDISH: MOMMY'S BOY!

  As though mesmerised, she picks up the razor from the bedside table. She does not even look at it. Her wide, frightened eyes are fixed on the combatants on the bed.

BATMAN: HELP ME! (From off panel.)

  Cavendish sits on Batman's chest, sinking his fingers into his throat. He does not see Adams moving up behind him. Her shadow falls across his back.

BATMAN: FOR GOD'S SAKE!

BATMAN: DO SOMETHING!

  Adams grips Cavendish's hair, (What there is of it.), and pulls his head back. The razor is in her other hand. An insane rage contorts her features. For his part, Cavendish screams and his eyes bulge wildly. There is a sense of inevitability, of destiny. Nothing can possibly stop what is to happen next.

ADAMS: NO!

CAVENDISH: MOMMY!

  Tight close up on Adams' maddened features. Gouts of blood splatter up across her face.

ADAMS: NO!

  Adams holds up the bloody razor. She gives it a sidelong, horrified glance, unable to believe what she has done. She looks at the razor as though it were responsible for the deed and not her. Her face is spattered with blood. Her clown costume bears an enormous splash of red.

ADAMS: OH GOD.

ADAMS: OH MY GOD.

  The razor falls from her nerveless fingers and strikes the blood-bespattered floor. Cavendish lies dead on the bed, clad in the wedding dress. His throat is slit almost

---

PAGE 60: Batman, at his most ineffectual, is here wrestling the very embodied heart of his own insanity. Under normal circumstances, of course, a superb martial arts master such as Batman would have no trouble defending himself against a skinny, lunatic doctor, but here we are watching the very essence of Batman crumble in the face of its own potential abnormality. In this sense, he is fighting himself while calling on another aspect of himself for help in the struggle. ✷

from ear to ear. One hand lies limply across the wound, as though he was trying somehow to close the gash before he died. Blood continues to pump sluggishly onto the pillow and the bedclothes, dyeing them dark red.

Adams stands as though turned to stone, spellbound. Batman approaches her grimly. Blood runs down his gashed arm but he has taken all this carnage in his stride. He shows no emotion and no concern.

ADAMS: OH GOD.

ADAMS: HIS THROAT.

BATMAN: HE GOT WHAT HE DESERVED.

BATMAN: COME ON.

Adams cannot take her eyes from the bed. Batman grips her arm and pulls her towards the opening in the wall that leads onto the secret passageway.

ADAMS: I DIDN'T MEAN TO..

ADAMS: I REALLY DIDN'T..

In the mysterious darkness of the secret passage, Batman looks around inquiringly. Adams covers her face with her hands, breathing deeply, trying to find some way through to a state of normality. It's quite clear that Batman doesn't give a damn for her feelings. His mind is on other things. ((As far as this interpretation goes, Batman doesn't like women — women are weak, women leave you when you need them most, women can't be trusted, women will always let you down. That's the way Batman thinks. I remember an interesting scene in a mid-'70's Batman - he's seen at the end of the story adding a photograph, (of Talia or Catwoman or somebody.), to a line of similar photographs of all the great 'loves' of his life. As he does this, he moans to Robin about losing all the women he cares about and how he's cursed to love only women on the wrong side of the law or something similarly dreary. I couldn't help imagining Batman in love with a row of glossy photographs that never woke up looking like shit or complained about whose turn it was to wash the dishes...He could happily fantasise over these photographs without them ever contradicting him, betraying him or telling him to stop acting like an asshole. Despite all the Talia stories and the Silver St. Cloud stuff, my own feeling is that, given the traumatic events of his youth and the way he currently lives his life, Batman would be quite incapable of sustaining any kind of relationship with a woman.))

BATMAN: I TAKE IT THIS PASSAGE IS THE WAY OUT ?

ADAMS: YES..YES, IT MUST BE..

Batman and Adams are small figures in the pitch blackness of the passageway. Adams points off down the passage.

PAGE 61: Again, this appraisal of Batman's sexuality applies only to the "damaged" version of the character presented within these pages. I prefer to think of him now as Neal Adams drew him — the hairy-chested globetrotting love god of the '70s stories. ❋

ADAMS: I..I THINK IT'S THIS WAY.

ADAMS: THIS WAY OUT.

BATMAN: I KNOW.

BATMAN: DO YOU STILL HAVE TWO-FACE'S COIN ?

Move in on Batman and Adams. He holds out his hand for the coin. ((Really, it's pretty unlikely that she would still be carrying it but it's important to show that another kind of logic is at work here. Almost a dream logic.))

ADAMS: YES..I..

ADAMS: OH CHRIST, I JUST KILLED SOMEONE.

BATMAN: JUST GIVE ME THE COIN.

Adams meekly hands it over. She's so badly shaken that she's simply going wherever she's pushed and doing what she's told. Batman seems not to care about the distress she's in.

ADAMS: YOU'RE GOING BACK IN, AREN'T YOU ? YOU'RE GOING TO UNDO ALL MY
                WORK..

ADAMS: WHAT ARE YOU ?

Batman turns away from her, preoccupied. She looks lost and vulnerable. The world she knew has collapsed into chaos and she stands alone and mapless in strange territory.

BATMAN: ---- STRONGER THAN THEM. STRONGER THAN THIS PLACE.

BATMAN: I HAVE TO SHOW THEM. —

ADAMS: THAT'S INSANE.

Batman holds up the scarred dollar and regards it with cold, empty eyes.

BATMAN: EXACTLY.

BATMAN: ARKHAM WAS RIGHT; SOMETIMES IT'S ONLY MADNESS THAT MAKES US
                WHAT WE ARE.

Batman sweeps his cape up around him and melts into the darkness.

BATMAN: OR DESTINY PERHAPS.

Adams is a white, isolated figure in the darkness. Batman's cape, a tattered shado disappearing off the panel.

Everything suddenly begins to happen very fast. A series of rapid cuts. We open with Batman's hand closing round an axe handle.

One of the inmates of Arkham runs towards us down a corridor, utterly terrified It's nobody famous, just a wild-eyed effeminate youth with straggly hair and a white smock. He looks like a debauched extra from Jarman's 'Carravaggio'. He has a laurel wreathe on his head and he's dropping a bottle of wine as he runs. There are wine stains too of

PAGE 62: The "weak," confused Batman of the earlier parts of the book vanishes here to be replaced by a more familiar character. From a Jungian POV, his anima has vanquished his shadow. He has merged with his own myth — the Death Bat — and become part man, part numinous legend. ❋

his smock. (Allusions here to Bacchus, the presiding deity of the Greek version of the Saturnalia.)

Batman stalks forward with the axe, filled with a black and dreadful purpose. The shadow of a tall, barred window falls upon him.

The mad youth runs away from us. His wreath lies in foreground as he flees down the sombre corridors.

Cut to the dining area. Black Mask is railing angrily at the Joker, who assumes an exaggerated air of deep personal injury. (At this point the party is winding down. The inmates have fallen asleep or are walking round in circles or staring at the wall.)

BLACK MASK: ..YOU SHOULD NEVER HAVE ALLOWED HIM IN HERE, JOKER! HE'S TOO
               DANGEROUS!

JOKER: THAT'S RIGHT! BLAME ME! GO ON!

The mad youth bursts into the dining area, screeching hysterically, gasping for breath. His eyes bulge. The others turn to look at him.

YOUTH: THE BAT!

YOUTH: IT'S THE BAT! THE BAT'S DESTROYING EVERYTHING!

Cut to Batman. Powered by a cold fury, he brings the axe down into the window. Glass explodes.

Close in on him as he hacks a door off its hinges.

Close in again as he wields the axe. Chips of wood and stone fly up. Almost abstract images of destruction. ((Here, Batman is physically demonstrating his new-found dominance over the spirit of the Arkham House. If you decide to make the place more organic then this scene may work even better. What we're evoking here is another series of Christ images - by conquering the unconscious in the shape of Croc, Batman has embraced the unconscious. As in the case of Arkham, Dragon and Man are now one whole being. This is why we identified Croc so strongly with Batman. The images here are designed to recall Christ's clearing the temple and even more importantly, the Harrowing of Hell. This event has no scriptural basis but formed a powerful part of the ritual imagery of mediaeval Christianity. In the story of Hell's Harrowing, Christ descends into Hell, has a confrontation with the Devil and his minions and then, at the climactic moment, tears down the Gates of Hell and sets free the tormented souls within.))

We end with a door crashing down.

We're on the Joker's feet as the axe is hurled down in front of them, like a challenge.

Batman stands in the doorway. The assembled inmates back off behind the Joker. The

Joker looks up from the axe at his feet, at Batman.

BATMAN: YOU'RE FREE.

     Close up on Batman - bloody, majestic, the hero emerged from the Underworld. His words here refer to a spiritual rather than a physical truth. He has broken the house.

BATMAN: YOU'RE ALL <u>FREE</u>.

     The inmates look at each other, lost, frightened. They don't <u>want</u> to be free. Only the Joker continues to look at Batman, intrigued.

     The Mad Hatter appears and hands the Joker a straitjacket. The Hatter looks fearfully in Batman's direction. The Joker, too, never takes his eyes off Batman. There is something almost like admiration in his expression but he still has to push the evening to its conclusion.

JOKER: OH, WE KNOW <u>THAT</u> ALREADY.

JOKER: BUT WHAT ABOUT <u>YOU</u> ?

     The Joker holds up the straitjacket.

JOKER: HAVE YOU COME TO CLAIM YOUR KINGLY ROBES ?

JOKER: OR DO YOU JUST WANT US TO PUT YOU OUT OF YOUR <u>MISERY</u>, LIKE THE
                 POOR SICK CREATURE YOU ARE ?

     Batman stands, imperturbable. He's back in command now, having passed through the refiner's fire. The silver dollar glints in his right hand.

BATMAN: WHY DON'T WE LET <u>TWO-FACE</u> DECIDE WHAT TO DO WITH ME ?

     The Joker claps a hand to his face and shrieks with demented delight. He obviously wishes he'd thought of this. Two-Face looks like a schoolboy who's just been asked a question he can't answer. He's been put on the spot and he can't think straight. He's a pitiful, broken figure. A whipped dog of a man.

JOKER: HARVEY ?

JOKER: <u>BRILLIANT</u> !

TWO-FACE: ME ?

TWO-FACE: ..NO, I CAN'T..REALLY, I..

     Batman, ignoring Two-Face's feeble resistance, flips him the coin.

BATMAN: HERE.

     Two-Face catches it in his cupped hands. His whole posture changes. He straightens up, loses all the slackness of indecision, becomes himself again, made whole by the holy coin.

PAGE 64: Batman transforms from sacrificial lamb to Redeemer here. More Christian mystery biz.

Two-Face stands below the clock. It is seconds from midnight. He holds the coin in his hand, looks down upon it.

TWO-FACE: IF THE UNMARKED FACE COMES UP, HE GOES FREE.

Move in on Two-Face as he gravely prepares to flip the coin.

TWO-FACE: IF IT'S THE SCARRED FACE, HE DIES HERE.

TWO-FACE: OKAY ?

Close in on Two-Face's hand. His thumb springs up. The silver dollar rises in slow motion.

The hands of the clock are frozen at a second to twelve.

The coin rises with a slow, spinning grace. Behind it is the dark window of the dining area.

The coin reaches the apex of its spin. The window is lit by a crack of lightning as the storm finally breaks. Light flares off the silver dollar, caught in this breathless moment, on the very hinge of destiny.

The coin turns slowly, still at the height of its spin, revealing the scarred face. The moment passes and the coin falls through space.

Falls into the outstretched hand of Two-Face. We cannot see how it has landed.

Pull back. Two-Face stands motionless, looking down into his palm.

He looks up, fixes us with a gaze of flawless intensity.

Move in for a close up as Two-Face impassively pronounces judgement.

TWO-FACE: HE GOES FREE.

At last we are released into the open air. Rain batters down. The front doors of Arkham swing open and Batman steps out. Police cars and an ambulance wait in the pouring rain, lights flashing. Ruth Adams is being led to the ambulance. Armed cops move in towards the Asylum. Gordon stands with an umbrella. It all looks wet and busy. The real world after a nightmare.

As Batman leaves, the Joker poses in the doorway, bidding him farewell. Batman turns only slightly in response.

JOKER: PARTING IS SUCH SWEET SORROW, DEAREST.

JOKER: STILL, YOU CAN'T SAY WE DIDN'T SHOW YOU A GOOD TIME.

Batman does not look back. He walks out into the rain. The Joker blows him a kiss.

JOKER: ENJOY YOURSELF OUT THERE.

JOKER: IN THE ASYLUM.

The armed cops move in, eyeing the Joker with disgust. He simply gazes out after Batman.

PAGE 65: Harvey Dent transcends his role here and steps out of the game, ending it with an act of defiant compassion.

The Joker's role as Trickster/Guide through the underworld is no more apparent than here, where he seems happy to let Batman go. The Joker's work is done, he has broken and remade his old enemy. In the reversal reality of the Feast of Fools, it's the arch-villain who does the most good, while the hero is ineffective and lost until the conclusion. This seemed a much richer, more satisfying and more adult way to consider the Batman/Joker dynamic. ✳

JOKER: JUST DON'T FORGET — IF IT EVER GETS TOO TOUGH..

JOKER: THERE'S <u>ALWAYS</u> A PLACE FOR YOU HERE.

As the policemen enter the reception hall, threatening the Joker and the others with their weapons, we begin to move down across the hall towards the corridor that leads down into the dining area. The tiny, motionless figure of Two-Face can be seen, drawing ever nearer as we advance slowly down the corridor.

We pass through the corridor into the dining area. All is calm and still, like the aftermath of a riotous party. Two-Face does not move.

We move in closer and still he stands. On the table behind him is the house of cards, undisturbed.

Two-Face looks down at his outstretched palm. It has not moved since the coin fell and he pronounced Batman's fate.

Lying in his palm we see the silver dollar, scarred face clearly uppermost.

Two-Face smiles a smile intended only for himself, slipping the coin into his breast ket. At the end, he has transcended destiny and made himself free, if only for this one time in his life.

He turns to regard the house made of Tarot cards — the symbol of the Arkham house and the endless depths of interpretation it contains. His face is impassive as he quotes from the end of 'Alice'.

TWO-FACE: WHO CARES FOR YOU ?

And sweeps his arm up through the fragile construction. The house of cards explodes into its component parts.

TWO-FACE: YOU'RE NOTHING BUT A PACK OF CARDS.

The cards tumble through space in languid slow motion, falling towards us — the Fool, the Lovers, the Hanged Man, Art and The Moon. This final card spins through blackness, closer and closer, larger and larger.

Until it fills our whole space and we close with a visual echo of our beginning.

PAGE 66: Batman has faced his own personal Abyss, integrated his psychological demons and emerged stronger and more sane from the other side of the looking glass.

The dream ends here. We can almost imagine a final, unseen page in which Bruce Wayne wakes up in his bed at 3pm, bruised, blinking and shaking his head...but feeling somehow cleansed and invigorated by this bizarre insight into his own drives.

Having been through this reversal of all his normal valencies, the '80s Batman, purified and purged of negative elements, is returned to Gotham City to become the super-confident, zen warrior of my subsequent JLA stories. ✸

"And is not that a Mother's gentle hand that withdraws your curtains,
and a Mother's sweet voice that summons you to rise ?
To rise and forget, in the bright sunlight,
the ugly dreams that frightened you so when all was dark - "

Lewis Carroll
"Alice's Adventures in Wonderland"

The book ends as it began with this Lewis Carroll quote, which like the opening epigrammatic exchange seemed to perfectly sum up the themes of the book. ✱

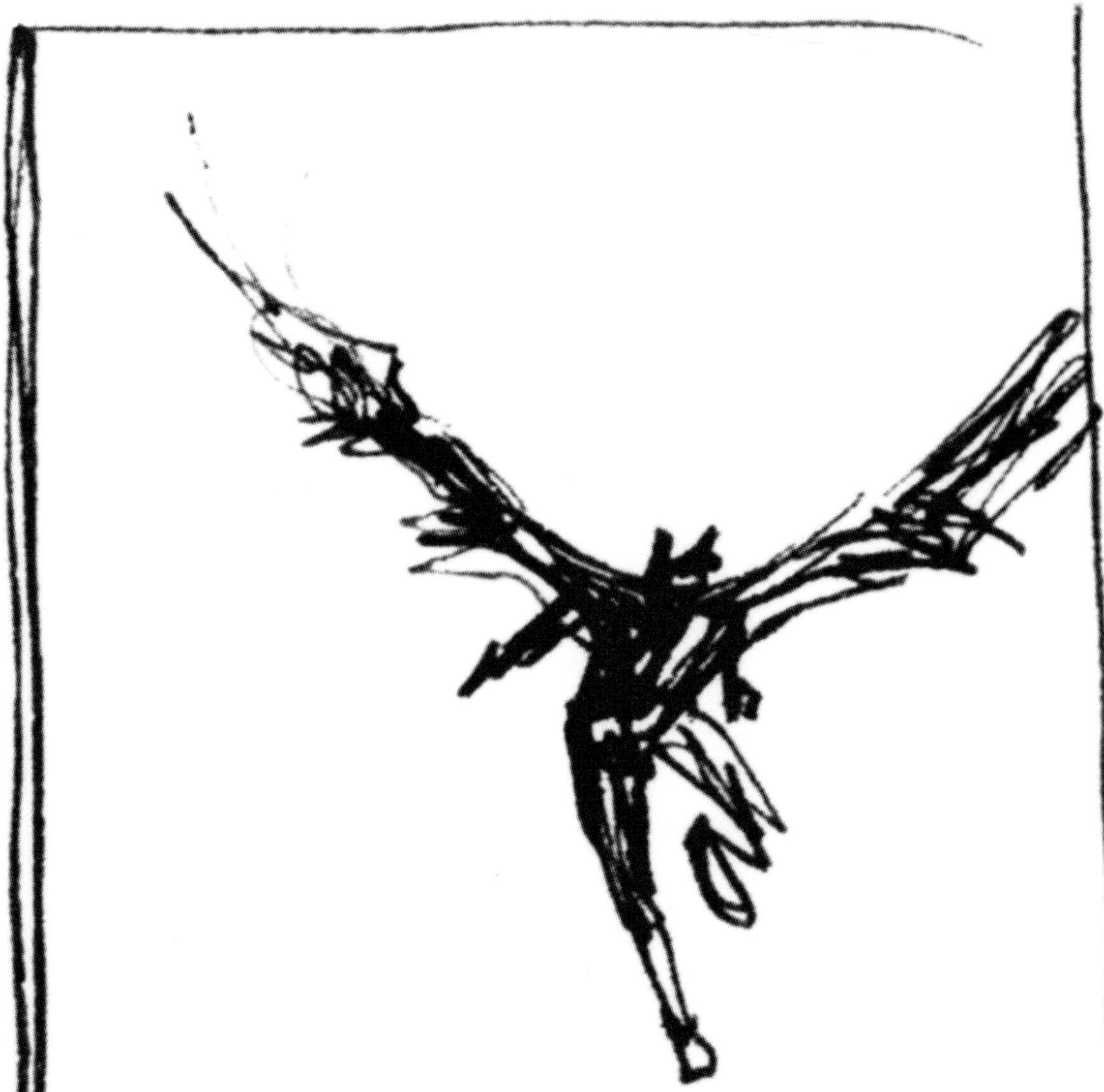

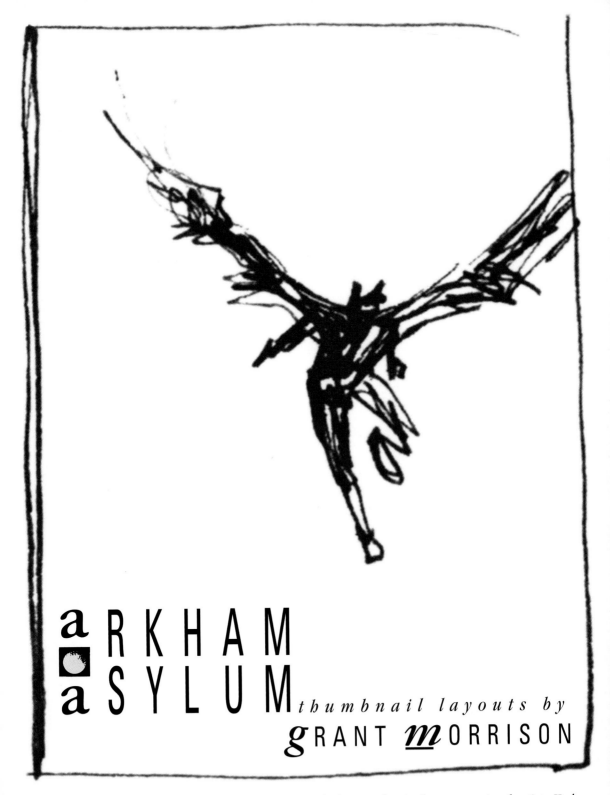

ARKHAM ASYLUM

thumbnail layouts by

GRANT MORRISON

ARKHAM ASYLUM author Grant Morrison is not only a gifted writer, but is also an occasional artist. He has created many of the concept and character designs for numerous titles he's worked on, from DOOM PATROL to THE INVISIBLES to THE FILTH and more. Many times he also creates full thumbnail layouts for these projects.

ARKHAM was originally slated to be a 64-page Prestige Format one-shot, and Morrison sketched out the thumbnails for the entire book. The following pages contain the layouts (which Morrison supplied to painter Dave McKean) for pages 13-64 of ARKHAM during this early stage of its development. Shortly after, the project then nearly doubled in size and scope. McKean used the layouts as a guide, but opened them up to accommodate the now larger story.

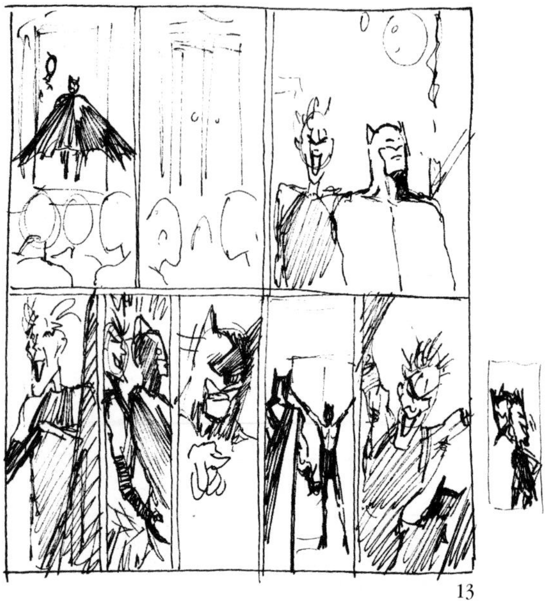

13

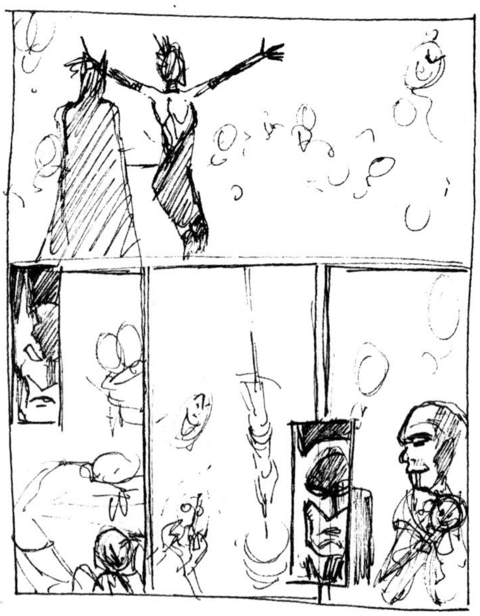

14

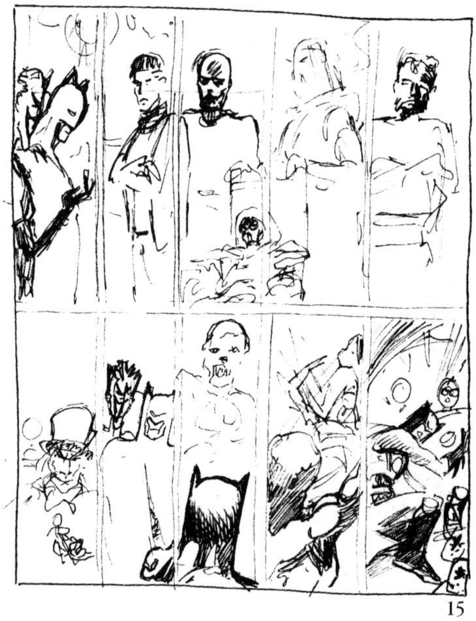

15

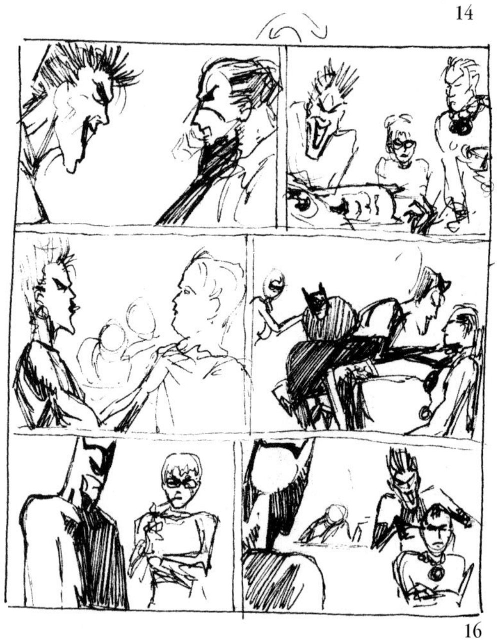

16

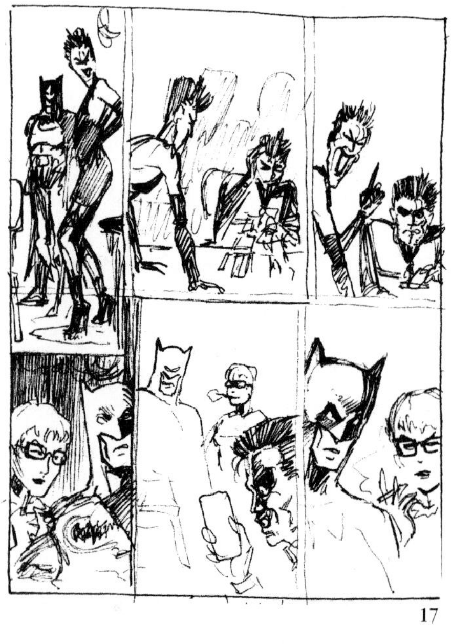

17

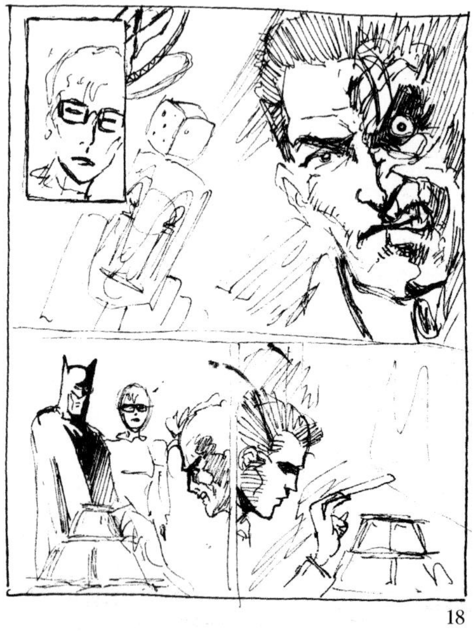

18

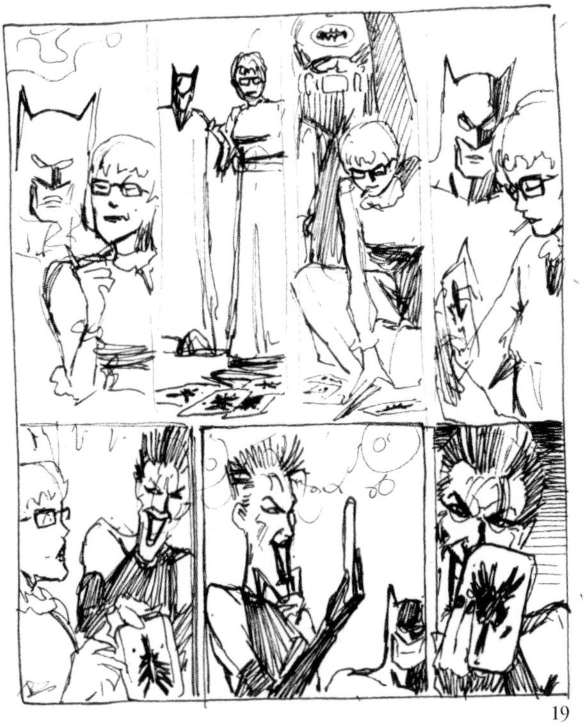

19

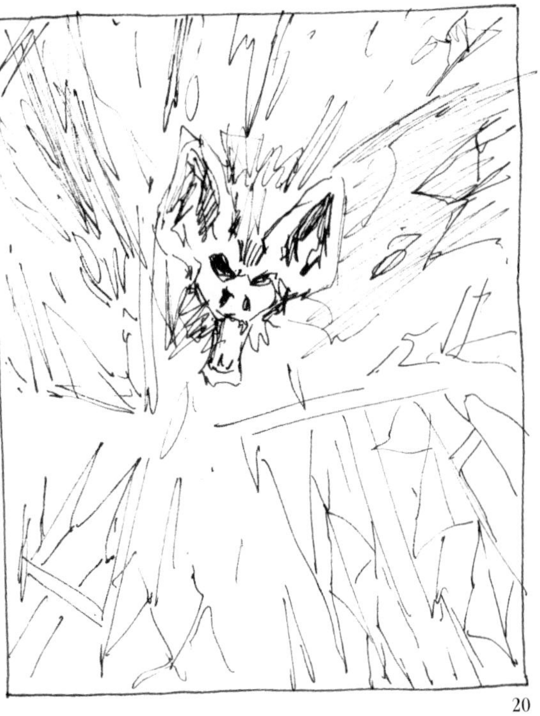

20

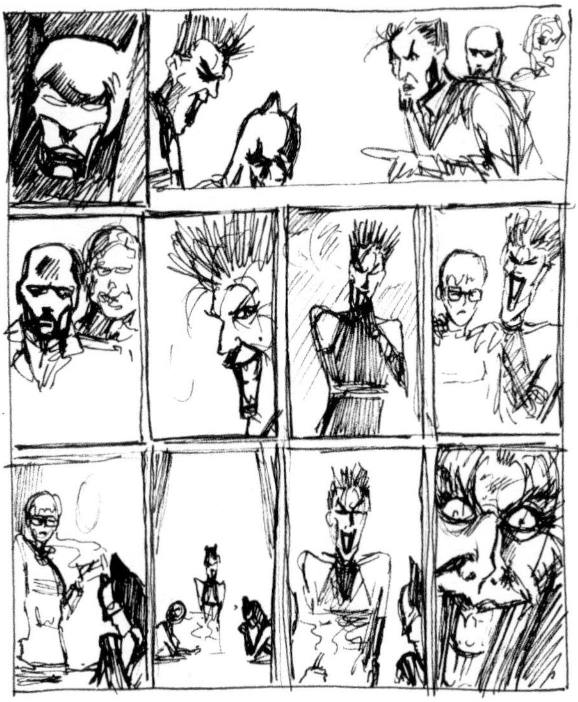

21

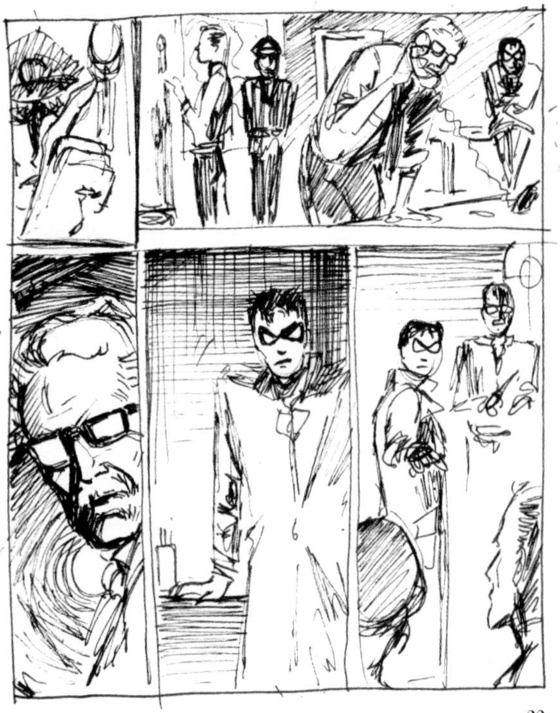

22

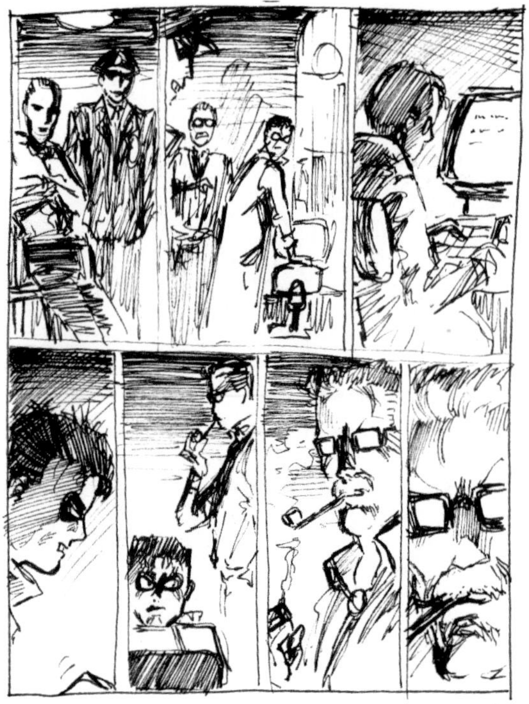

23

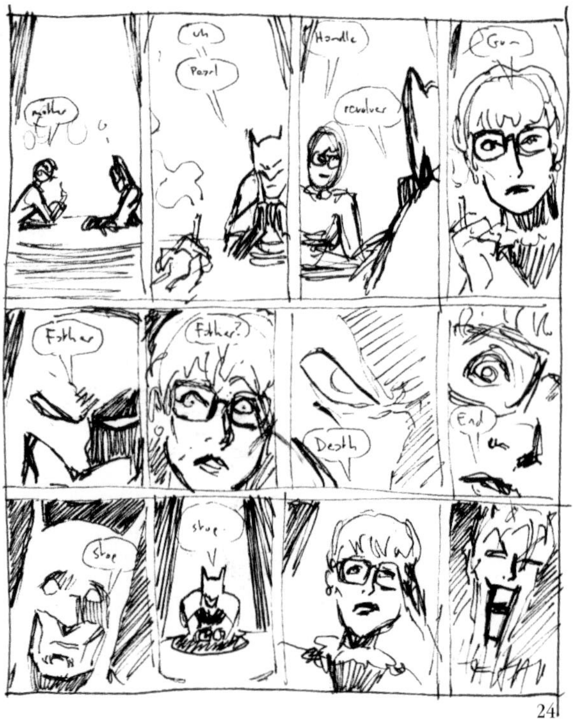
mother
uh
Pearl
Handle
revolver
Gun
Father
Father?
Death
End
shoe
shoe

24

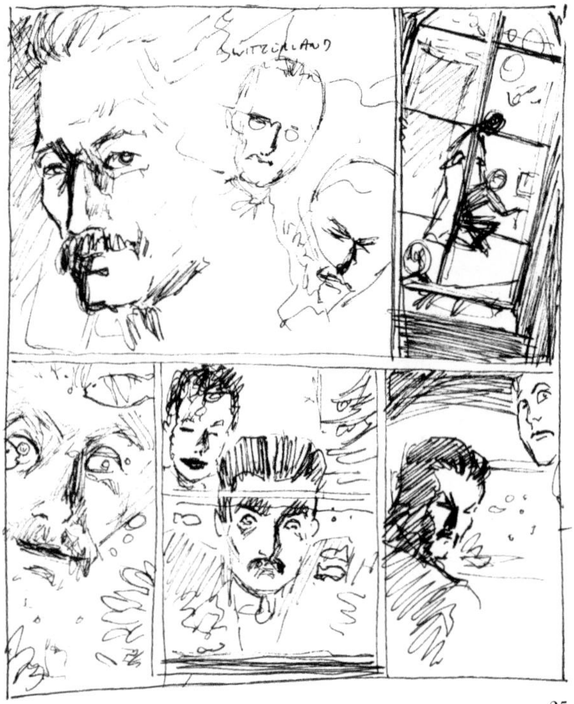
SWITZERLAND

25

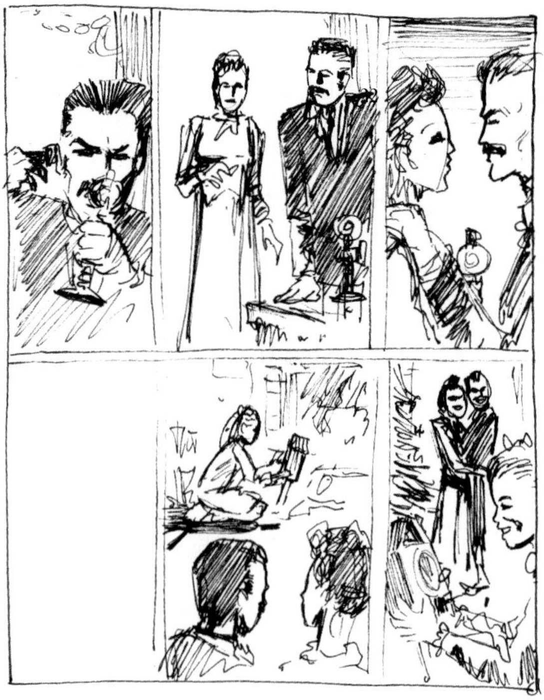

26

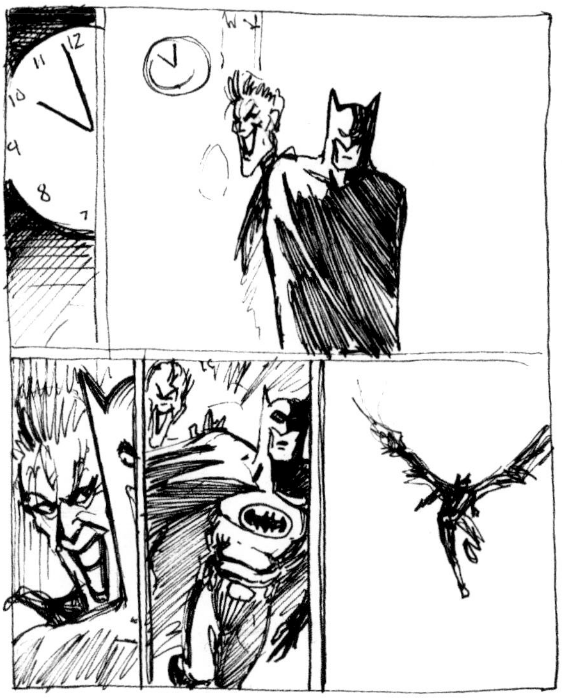

27

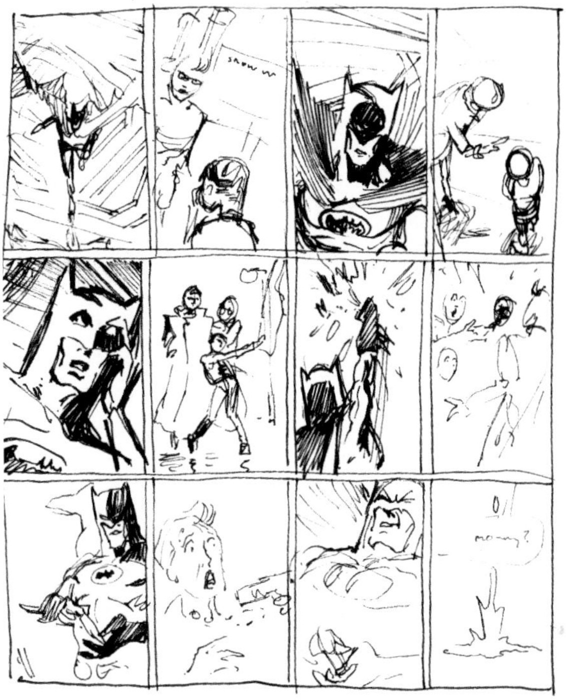

28

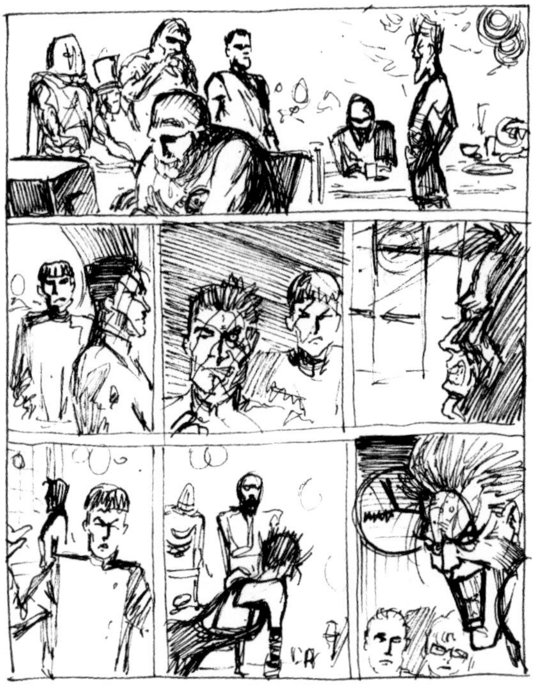

29

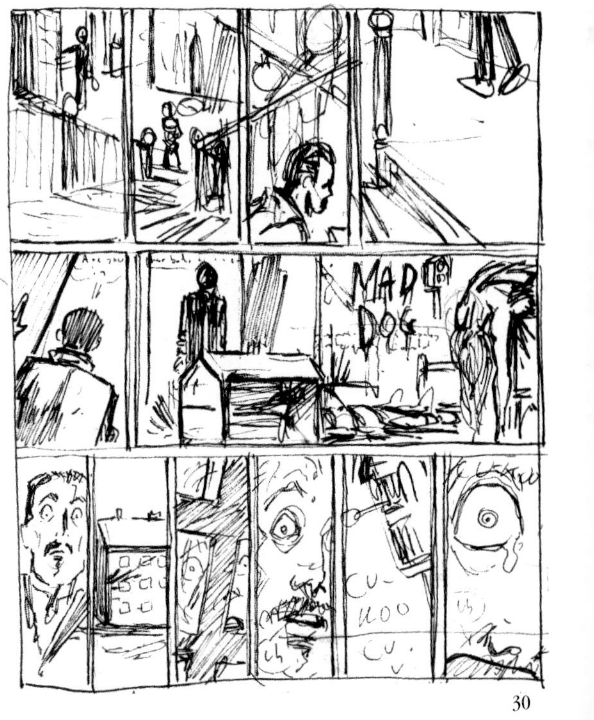
MAD DOG

30

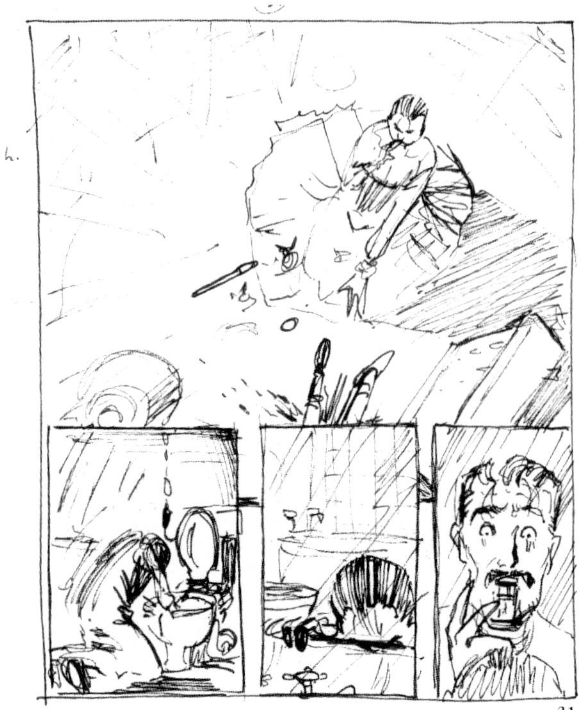

31

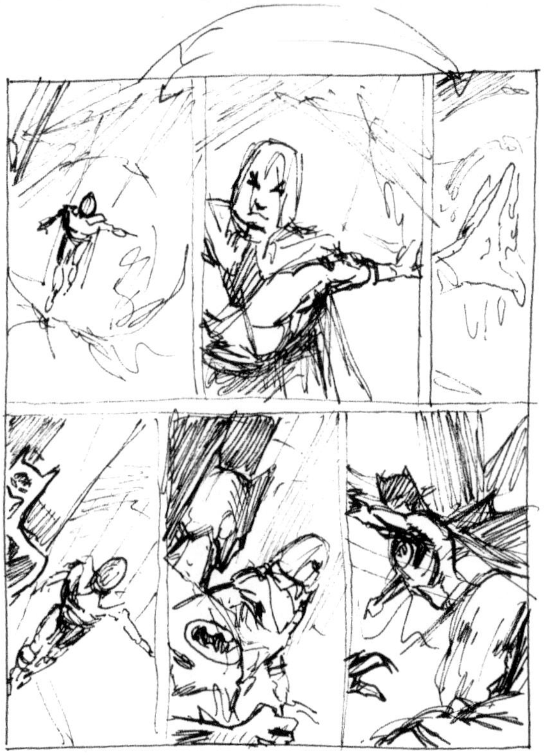

32

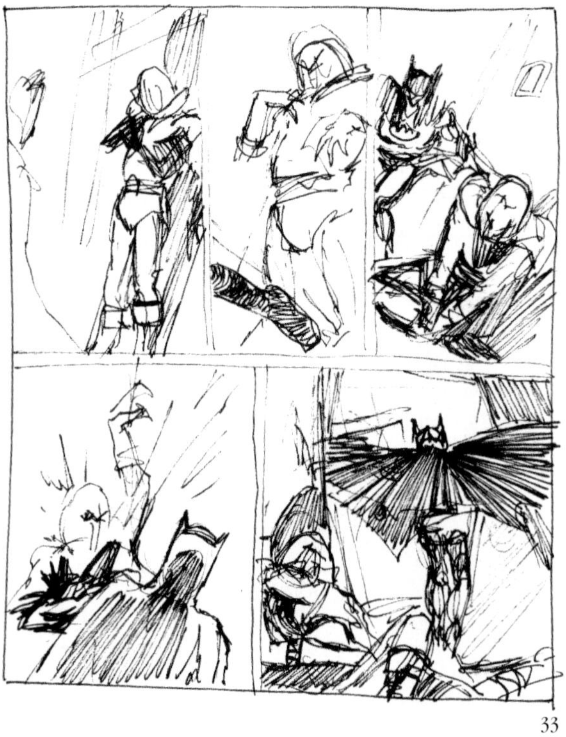

33

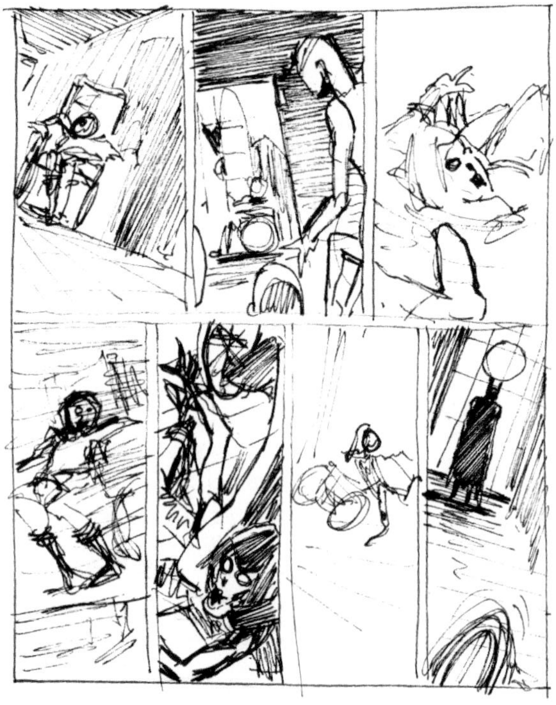

34

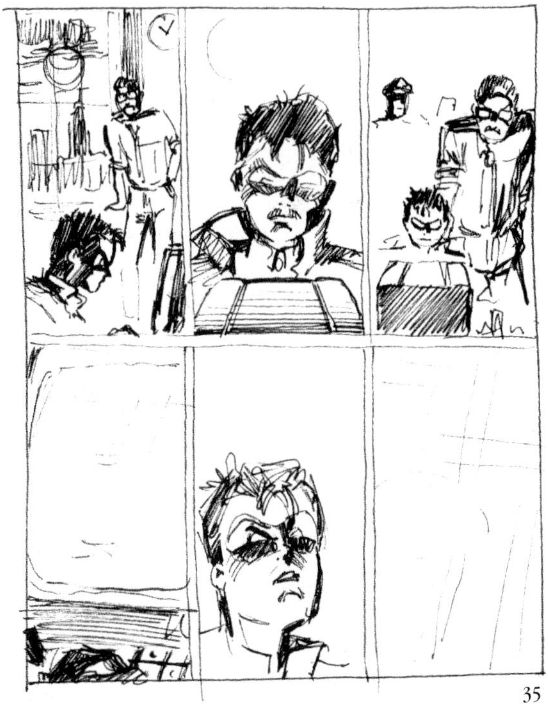

35

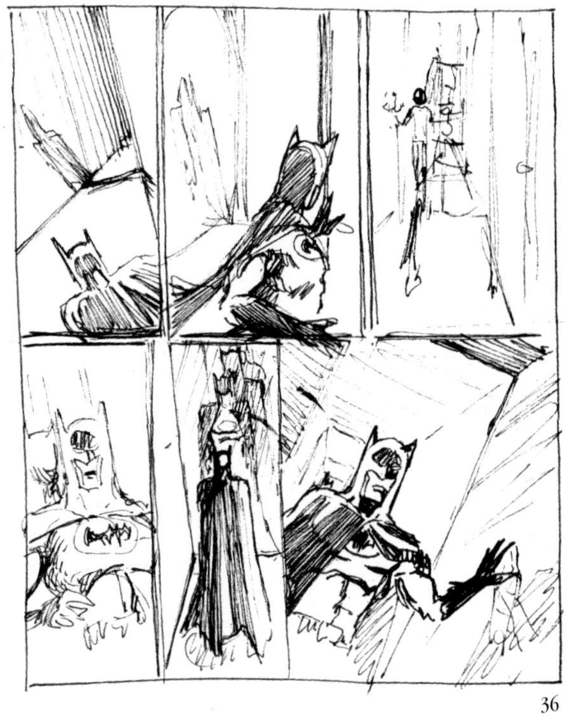

36

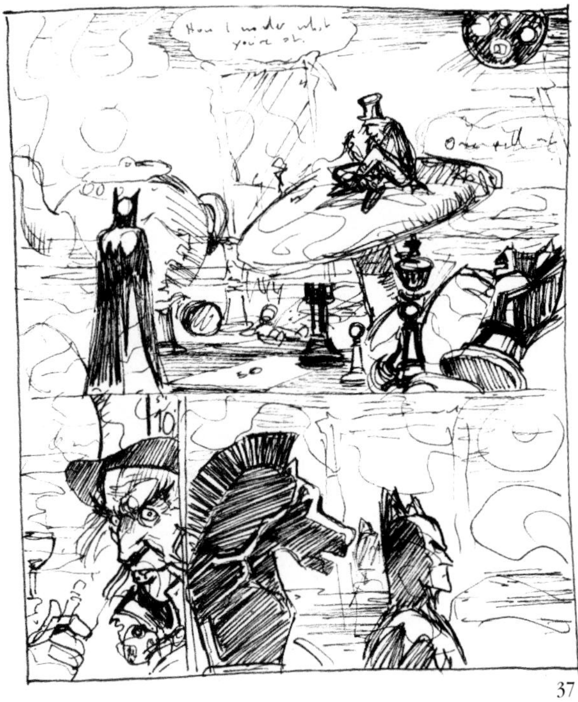

37

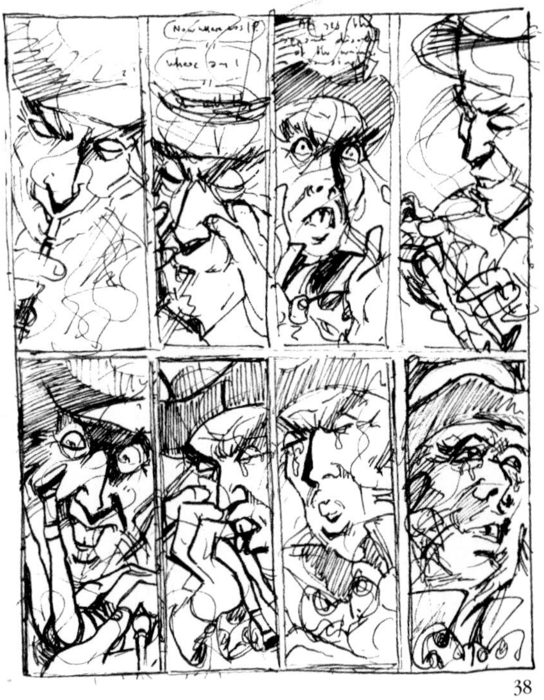
where am I

38

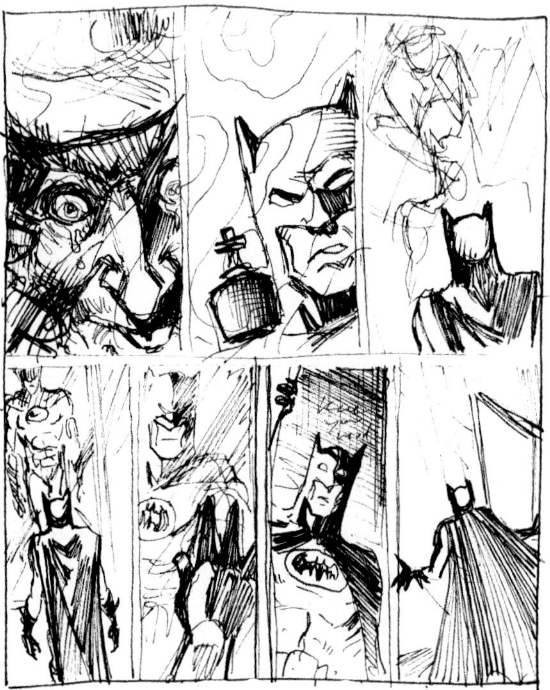

39

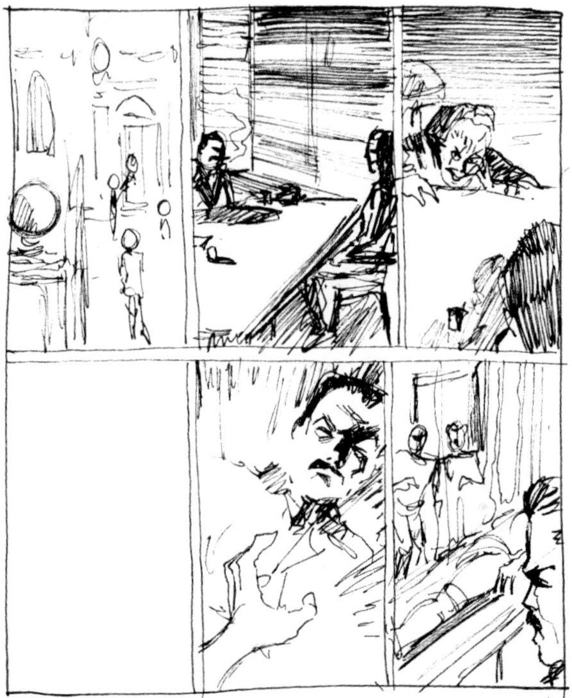

40

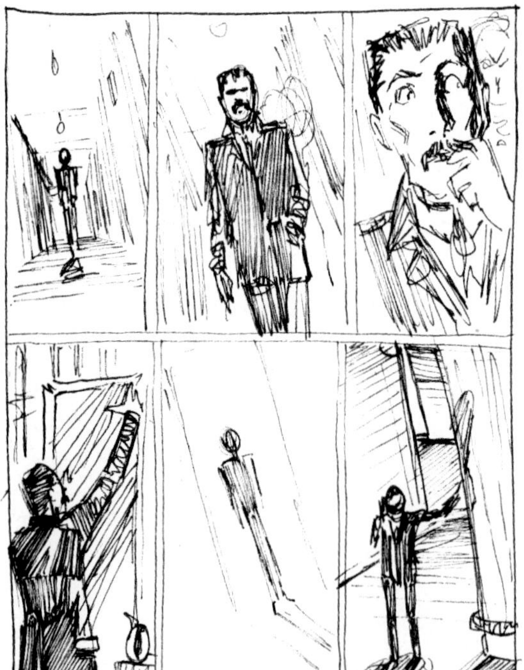

41

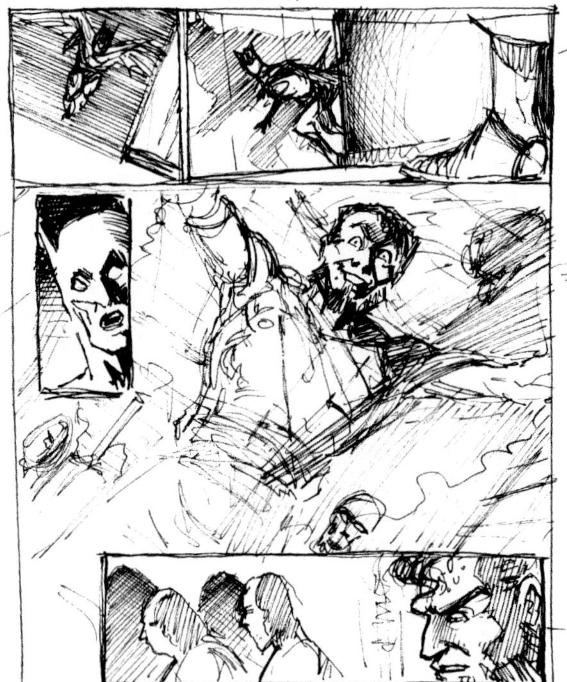

42

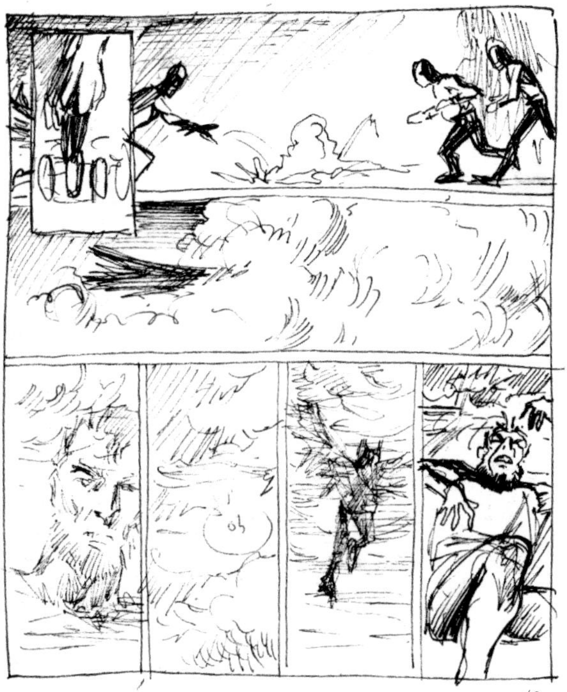

43

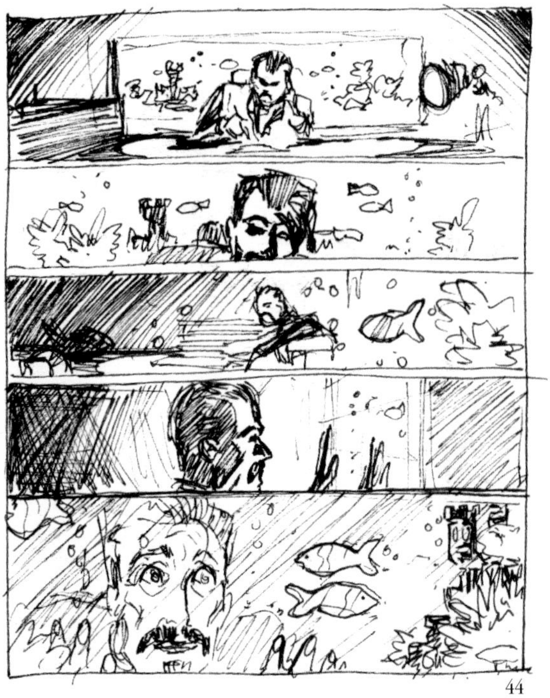

44

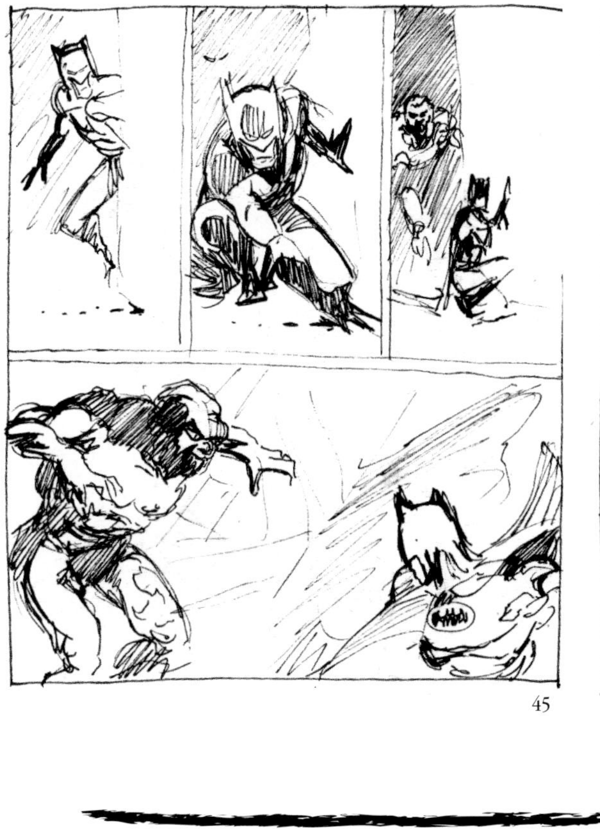

45

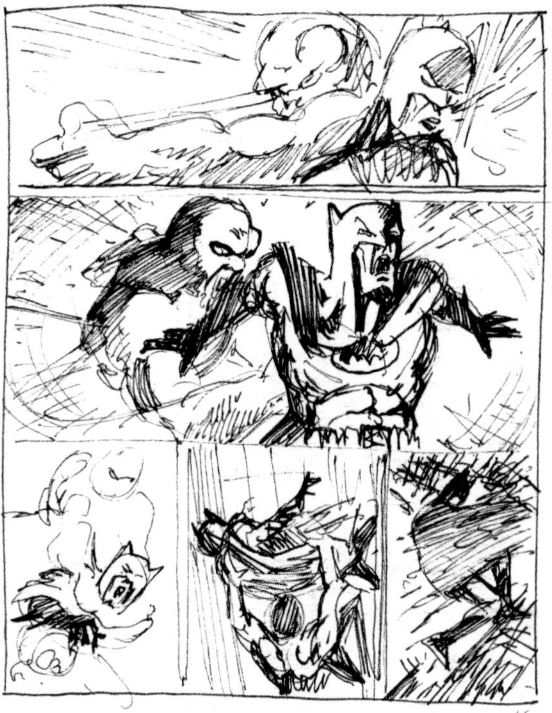

46

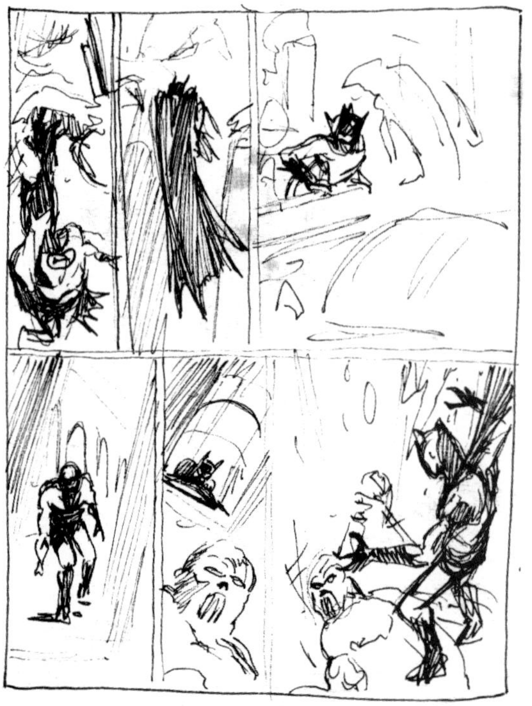

47

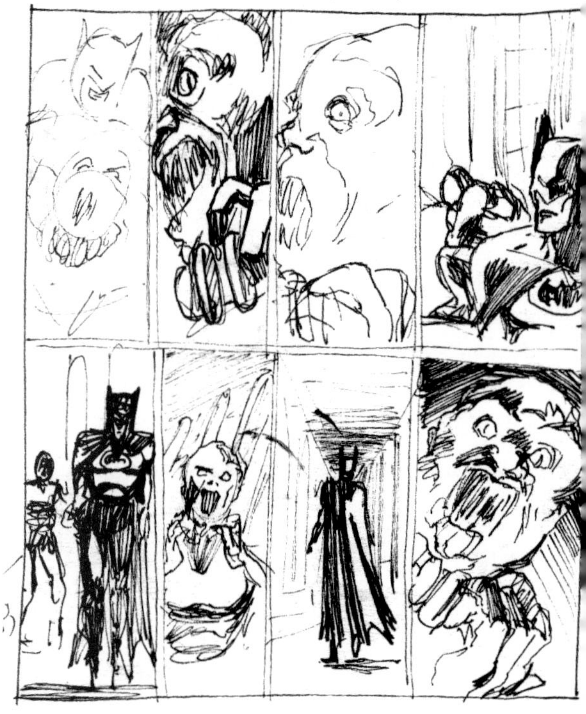

48

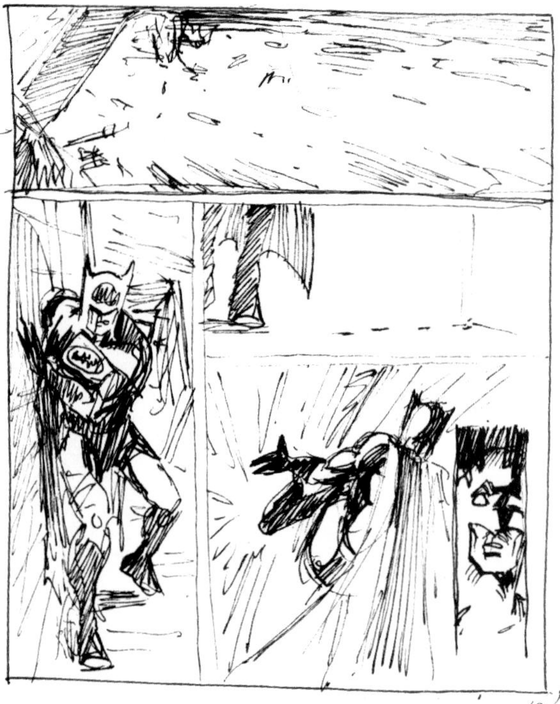

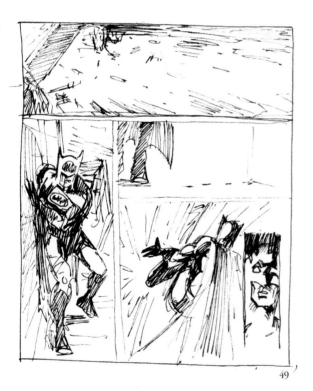

49

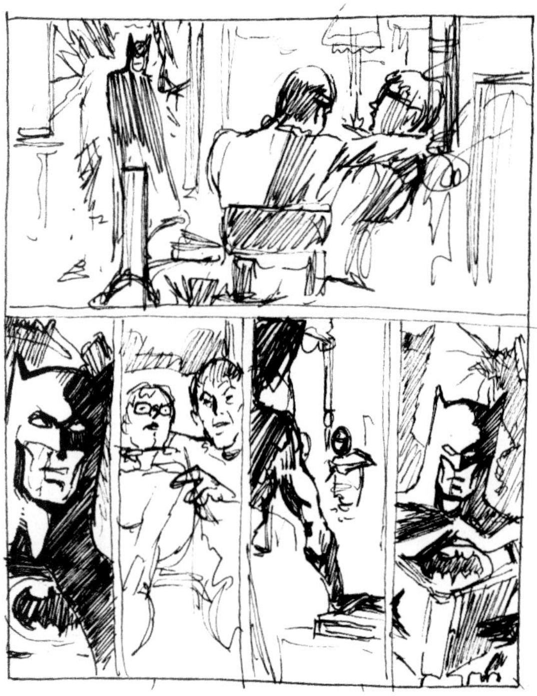

50

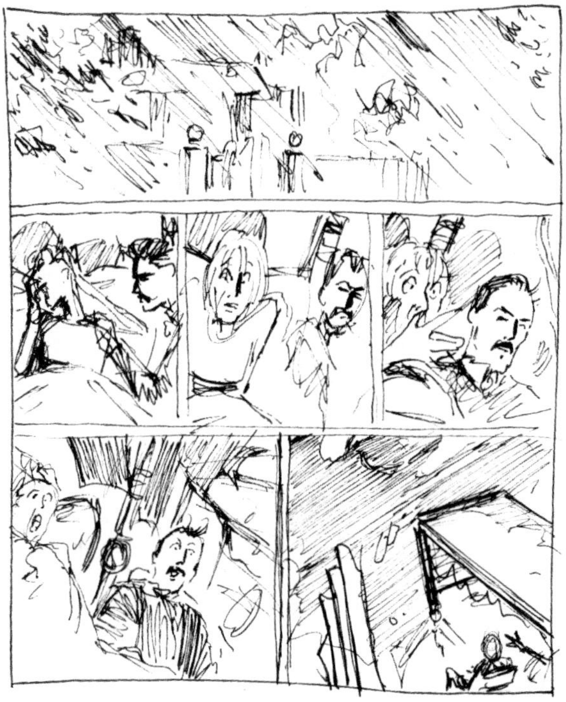

51

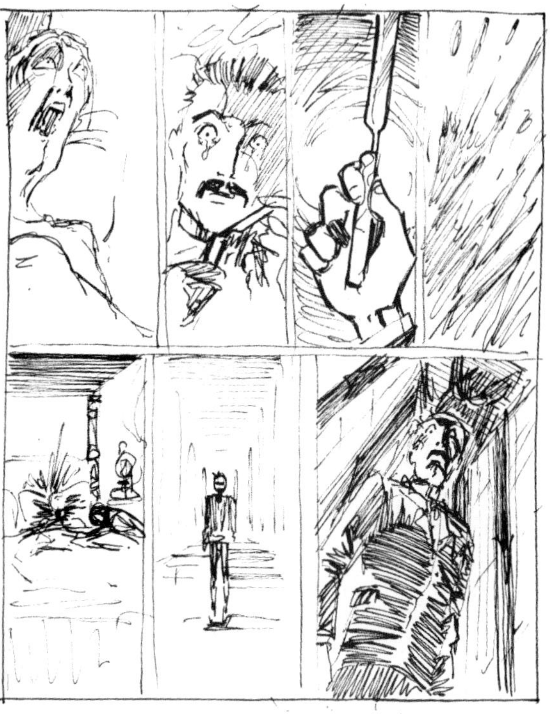

51

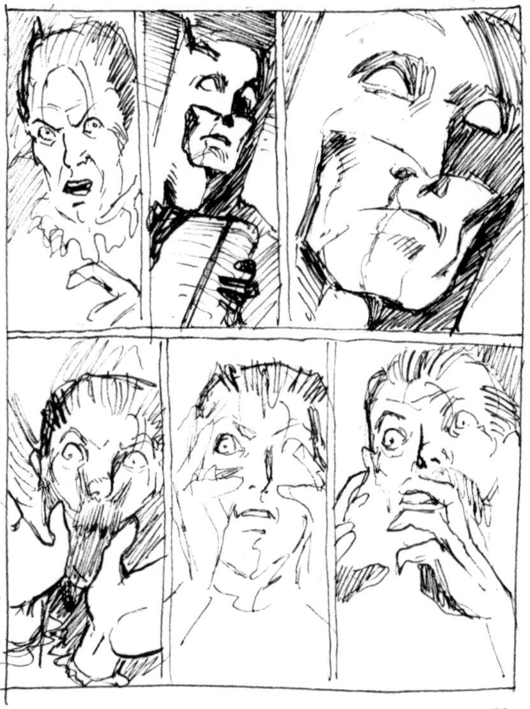

52

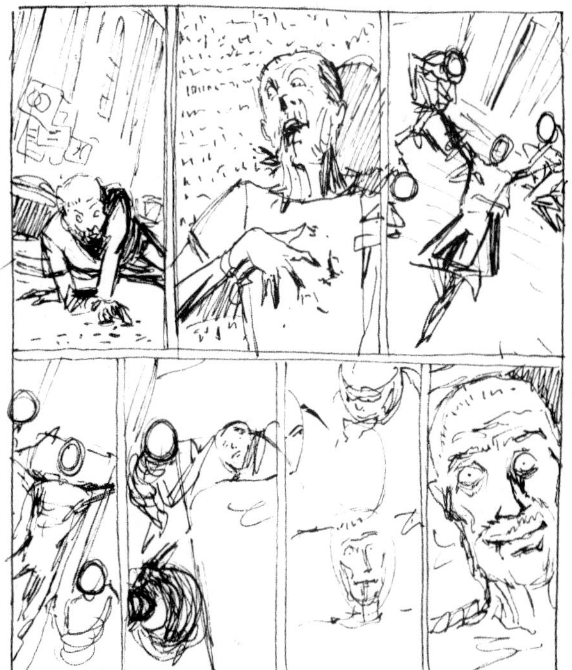

53

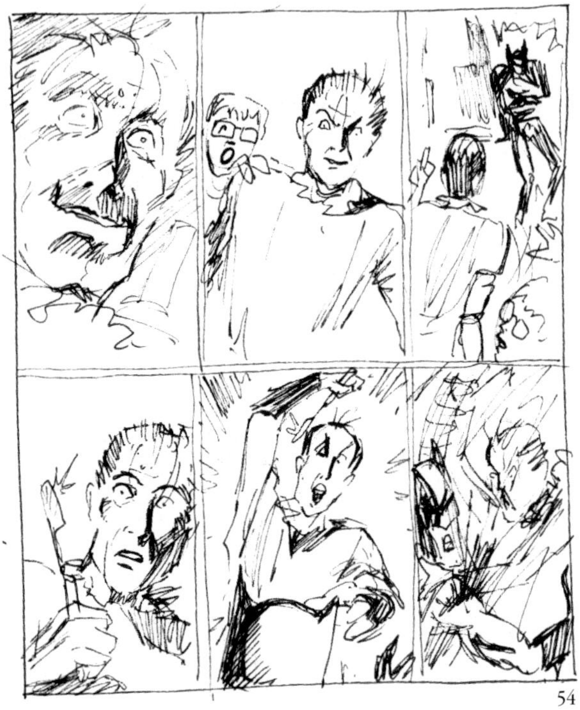
54

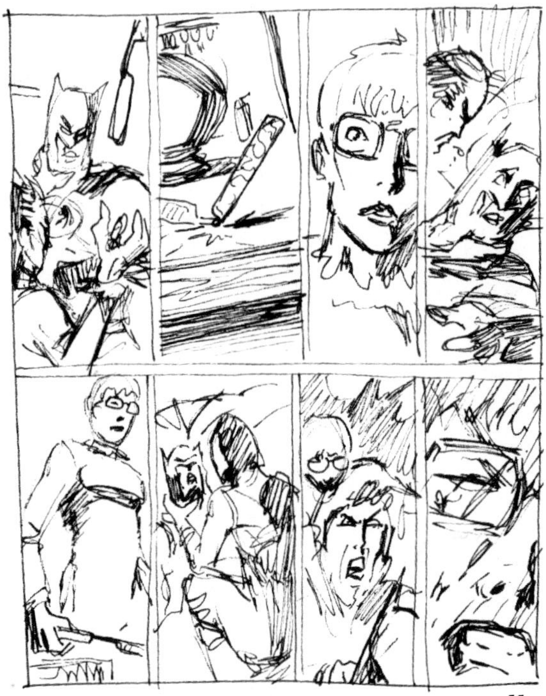
55

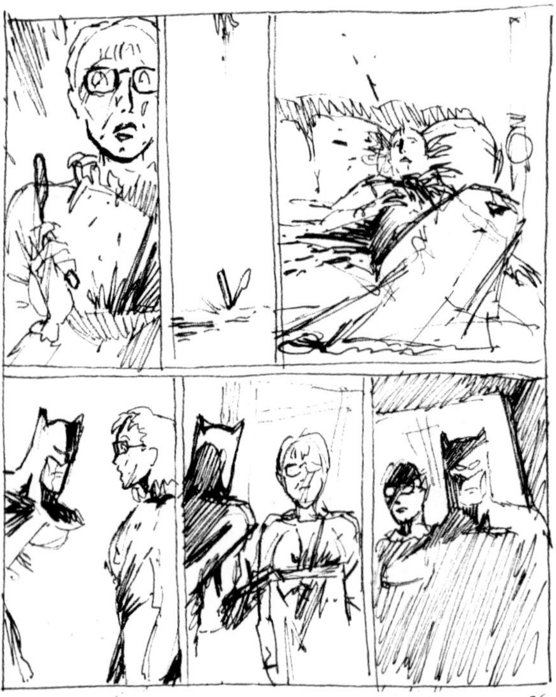
56

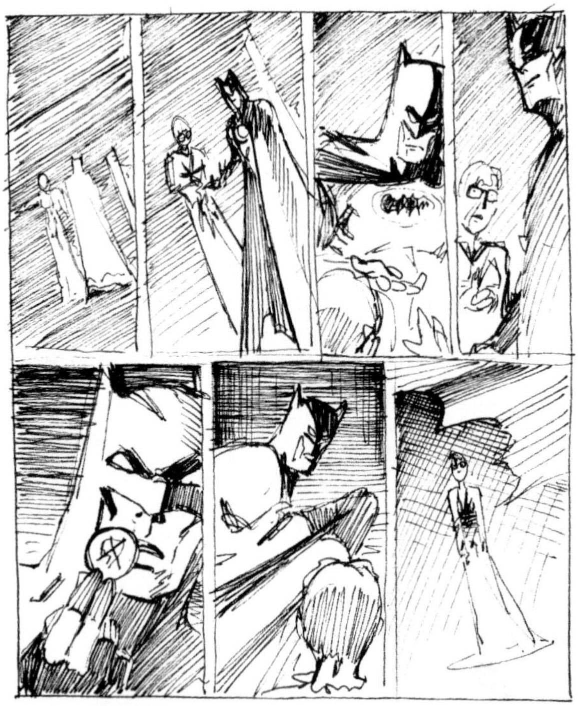
57

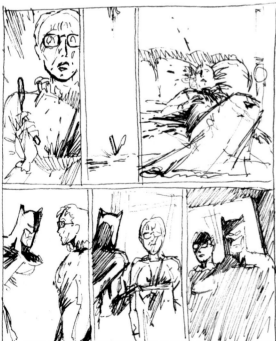

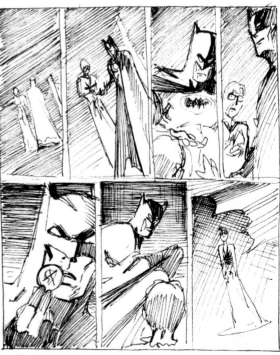

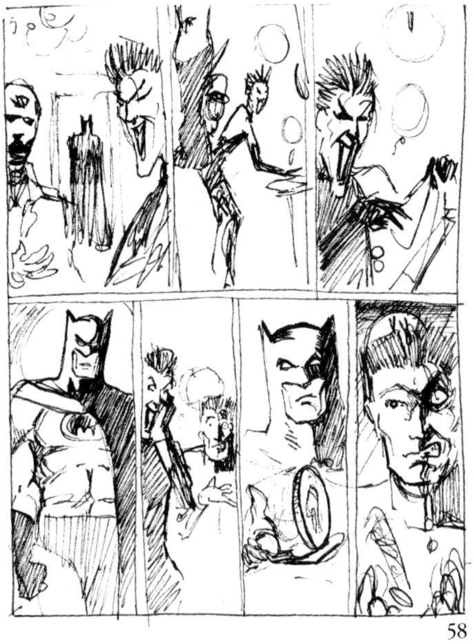

58

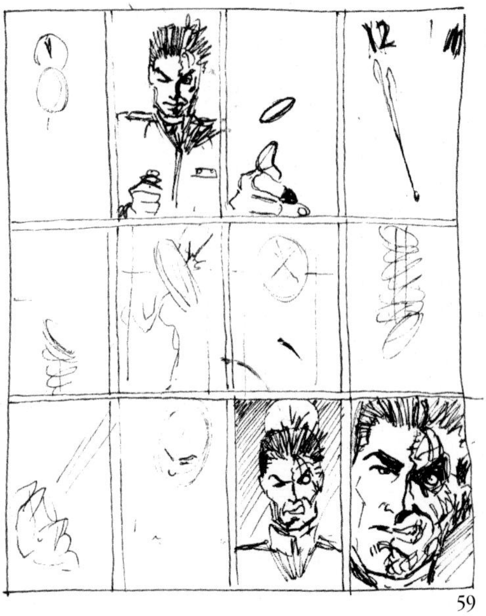

59

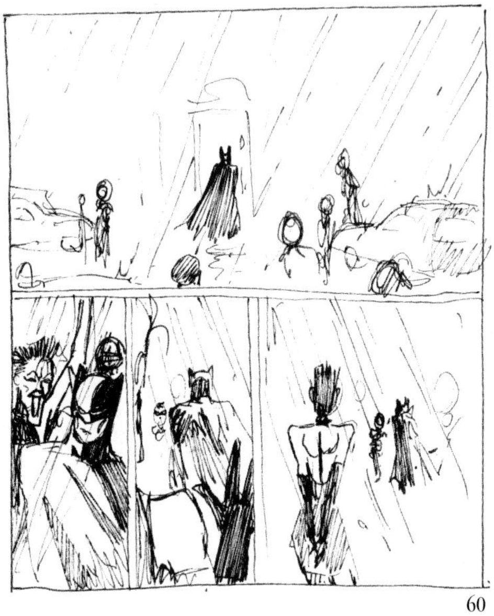

60

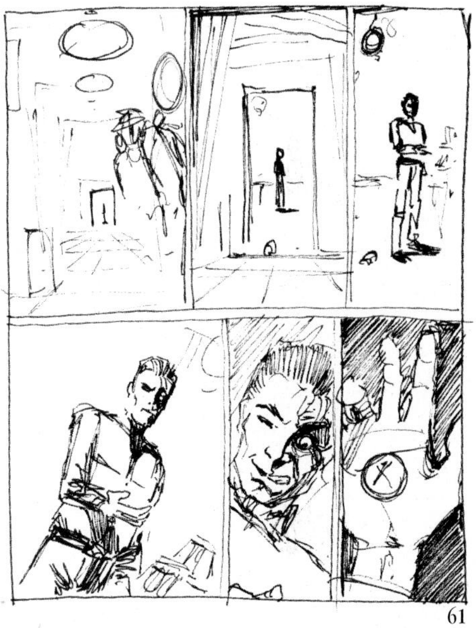

61

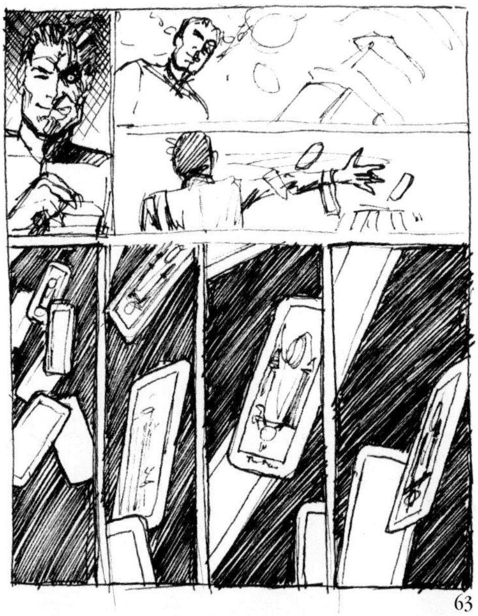

63

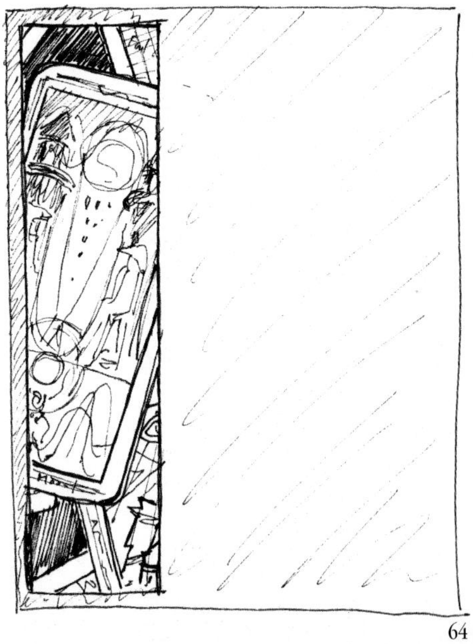

64

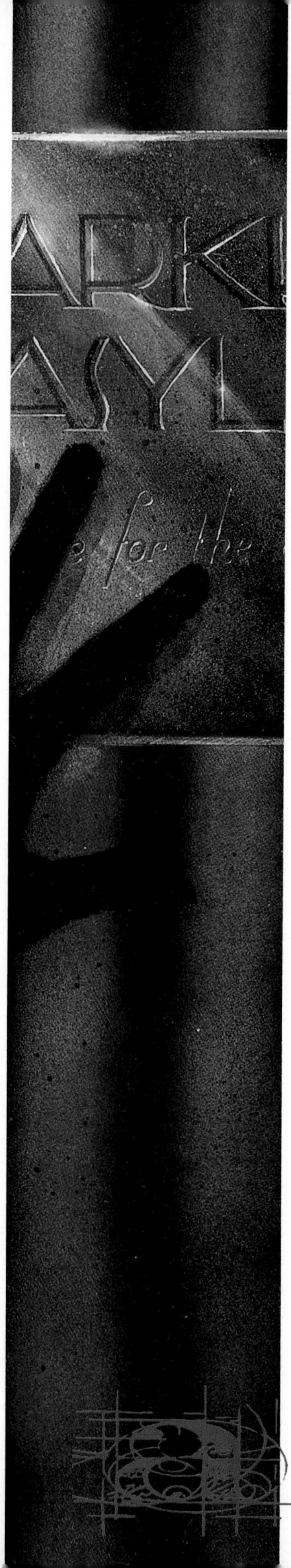

by karen berger

AFTERWORD

CHANGING THE FACE OF COMICS

Or was it facing the changes in comics?

It was 1986, and it was an incredible time in our field. The industry was electrified by two revolutionary works, Frank Miller's THE DARK KNIGHT RETURNS and WATCHMEN by Alan Moore and Dave Gibbons. Both projects were smart, provocative and powerful in different ways, and they both took comics an evolutionary step further. We had finally entered the modern age. Anything seemed possible.

I had recently been charged by Jenette Kahn to become DC's liaison with the British freelance writers and artists. It was on my second trip to London to meet with established creators and recruit new talent that I first met Grant Morrison and Dave McKean, though it was in separate pitch meetings. Grant, a relatively new writer in British comics, flew down from Scotland, and with his almost indecipherable Glaswegian accent pitched a number of intriguing ideas — one of them was revitalizing Animal Man, the other was a psychological thriller featuring Batman at his most vulnerable mental state — trapped in a madhouse with his criminally insane enemies. A few hours earlier, Dave had been sitting silently by Neil Gaiman's side, as Neil pitched BLACK ORCHID and inquired about doing a new SANDMAN series. Then Dave opened his portfolio and showed me his work on *Violent Cases,* and I was totally blown away by his fresh approach to comics art and storytelling. Dave was fresh out of art school, and his influences weren't comics oriented, but a mix of contemporary illustration and design, which was something entirely different from what any of us was used to seeing in traditional comics.

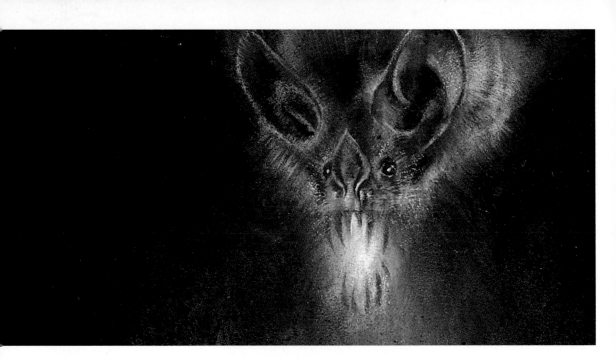

Soon after, Grant developed his initial treatment for ARKHAM ASYLUM as a 48-page story, yet it had transformed into a much richer and complex work than originally pitched. For now it was really two tales: one a disturbing and revealing picture of Batman faced not only by his deadliest foes, but by his own personal horrors and demons. The other story, arguably the more poignant one, was told in the form of the diary of Amadeus Arkham, the founder of the asylum that bears his name, whose descent into madness over the years is chronicled in his own hand. Grant's ideas and imagery had become larger and more nuanced than he had allowed himself the space for. He was on to something truly special, so we asked him to expand the story so his vision could be better and completely realized. And we knew that there was only one artist who could fully bring this story into view. And then some.

Grant's script was not broken down like a traditional page-by-page comic script, but more like a shooting script for a film. This allowed Dave freedom to not only bring his own interpretation to the story, but to also gauge the pacing and the eventual length of the book which had now grown from 64 pages to a 128-page experience, which also integrated many spectacular design pages. As you just read, Grant's script is an incredible story unto itself, with its own underlying themes and symbolism, imbued with the intensity and passion of a young writer. Grant also provided Dave with thumbnail sketches of the scenes, some of which Dave integrated into the final and some of which he changed.

Dave's approach was anything but ordinary. His inventive storytelling technique aside, it was his expert mix of media — painting, photography, sculpture, assemblage of odd objects — that created such a resonant and powerful look to this haunting and horrific tale. Hard to believe this was done in the pre-computer age, of which Dave soon became one of the first artists to fully and quickly embrace.

This was not an easy book to assemble and produce. Special note must be made of Gaspar Saladino for his extraordinary lettering, and for creating a look for this book that matched the ambitious art of Dave, no easy task. As the talents wanted to challenge what a comic could be in every way possible, new production, separation and printing obstacles had to be tested and overcome. Twelve sets of color proofs were required and long nights of press checks in the cold nights of Montreal endured.

In the beginning of winter in December 1989, ARKHAM ASYLUM: A SERIOUS HOUSE ON SERIOUS EARTH was released, followed by a huge and successful signing tour across America. The book shattered all sales records, with sales that are unthinkable by today's standards. With domestic and foreign sales of the hardcover and softcover to date, it has sold close to a half million copies, remaining the best-selling original graphic novel in the entire comics industry. Grant and Dave went on to become two of the most acclaimed and influential figures in comics, and have also expanded their horizons into other creative fields.

So, here we are fifteen years later celebrating a special point in time in comics history. Whether by changing the face of comics or facing the changes in comics, I think you'll agree that this innovative and daring book can lay claim to a bit of both.

Karen Berger
VP-EXECUTIVE EDITOR, VERTIGO

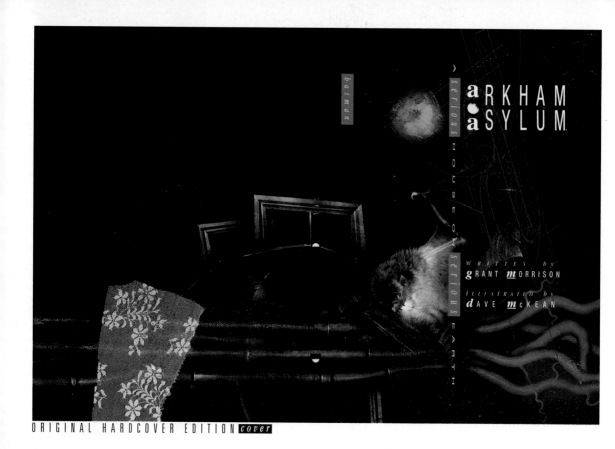

batman

a **a**RKHAM
aSYLUM.

a serious house on serious earth

WRITTEN by
gRANT **m**ORRISON

ILLUSTRATED by
dAVE **m**cKEAN

ORIGINAL HARDCOVER EDITION cover

ORIGINAL SOFTCOVER EDITION cover

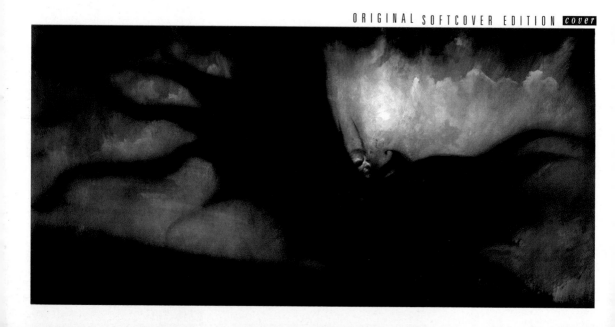